About the Author

Karen Troshynski-Thomas's overlapping careers as gardener, writer/editor, and mother of one-year-old Jack Henry have been nurtured into Taproot Writers Collective, a home-based business in Berkley, Michigan. Karen's gardening experience began with tomato plants grown at her college apartment. (They were pitched from a terrace during a neighbor's party.) Undaunted, she earned her Master Gardening certificate through the Michigan State University Extension Service in Oakland County, Michigan.

THE
HANDY
GARDEN
ANSWER
BOOK™

THE HANDY GARDEN ANSWER BOOK™

Karen Troshynski-Thomas
Master Gardener

Willard Library

VISIBLE INK PRESS

DETROIT • SAN FRANCISCO • LONDON • BOSTON • WOODBRIDGE, CT

The Handy Garden Answer Book™

COPYRIGHT © 1999 BY VISIBLE INK PRESS

Published by Visible Ink Press™
a division of The Gale Group
27500 Drake Road
Farmington Hills, MI 48331-3535

Visible Ink Press is a trademark of The Gale Group.

Most Visible Ink Press™ books are available at special quantity discounts when purchased in bulk by corporations, organizations, or groups. Customized printings, special imprints, messages, and excerpts can be produced to meet your needs. For more information, contact Special Markets Manager, Visible Ink Press, 27500 Drake Road, Farmington Hills, MI 48331-3535, or call 1-800-776-6265.

Art Directors: Michelle DiMercurio and Cindy Baldwin
Typesetting: Graphix Group

Library of Congress Cataloging-in-Publication Data

Troshynski-Thomas, Karen, 1966–
    The handy garden answer book / Karen Troshynski-Thomas.
        p.   cm.
    Includes index.
    ISBN 1-57859-088-4 (softcover)
    1. Gardening—Miscellanea. I. Title.
SB453.T76 1999
635—dc21   99-11480
                                                                CIP

Contents

PLANT AND SOIL SCIENCE ... 1

SEEDING, PROPAGATION, AND PLANTING ... 31

CARE AND FEEDING ... 61

PERENNIALS ... 211

ANNUALS AND BIENNIALS ... 247

VEGETABLES AND FRUITS ... 275

TREES AND SHRUBS ... 307

LAWNS, GROUNDCOVERS, AND ORNAMENTAL GRASSES ... 337

HERBS ... 365

Introduction

Welcome to the world of gardening. Whether you're a new gardener or an old hand, I hope to provide you with a few tips to help you get your garden growing. I know I learned a great deal in putting this book together.

I have been gardening for more than ten years (a drop in the bucket for many "dirt gardeners"). Like many gardeners, I started with annuals and a few vegetables, graduated to too many perennials, and have branched out, so to speak, into trees and shrubs. My interest in gardening grew after signing up for a Master Gardener certification course through the Michigan State University Extension Service of Oakland County. If you'd like more information on the Master Gardener program, contact your county's Extension Service.

Although the glossy new publications springing up everywhere would have you believe gardening is the latest and greatest hobby, it has actually been America's favorite pastime for quite a while. These same publications profess that there is a right and wrong way to garden. While botany is a science, gardening is an art. Every gardener has her or his own particular ways of doing things. I've tried to offer the more common methods of tackling gardening tasks, but there are certainly others. So get out there and experiment—it's half the fun of gardening!

I do admit to a basic bias toward gardening organically. The act of gardening is always an invasive one, as it imposes one's will on plants and soil. With native plant and animal species rapidly disappearing, however, I feel it is important for modern gardeners to tread as lightly as possible on the earth. So you won't find information on ad-hoc tomato-dusting and rose-spraying in this book. What you will find is information on good gardening practices that put nutrients back into the soil, maximize watering efficiency, and promote healthy plants that will be well equipped to fend off insects and disease.

In the interest of clarification, all common names of flowers, plants, woody ornamentals, and herbs are followed by their botanical names. Vegetables, fruits, and lawn grasses and weeds, however, are listed by their common name or the common name followed by the cultivar, in order to make these less cumbersome for the reader. This is a generally accepted treatment for these types of plants. I used the following sources to double-check the names: *The American Horticultural Society A–Z Encyclopedia of Plants; Wyman's Gardening Encyclopedia* (1986 edition); and *Timber Press Dictionary of Plant Names.*

As I write this, the morning sun is shining on our vegetable garden and perennial border. Despite an early, warm spring, we got a late start this year. It looks like everything has caught up rapidly in our raised beds, including the weeds. My son is singing his happy, good-morning tune that signals he's ready to go out to the garden. So am I. And with this book, I hope you will be too.

Acknowledgments

Writing a book, even about something you enjoy, is difficult at best. A newborn son makes things even more complicated. This effort would not have been possible without the support of my partner in gardening and life, Tim Thomas. Thanks for everything, darling. Thank you, too, Jack Henry Thomas—your love of the outdoors and inquisitive nature have shed new light on your mom's used-to-be favorite pastime.

Thanks also to both our families (Jim, Rena, Kathie, Brian, Bob, Tina, Don, Angelica, John, and Grandma M.), who provided much-needed and appreciated support in many ways throughout these busy months. Thanks especially to my mom, Kathie, and my father-in-law, Jim, for their gardening inspiration. Mom's beautiful flower beds reveal her artist's eye while Jim's mostly-organic, homegrown vegetables are an amazing sight.

Thanks to Laurie Hillstrom for her compost expertise.

I can't overemphasize the value of the terrific information to be found through your local Extension Service. I really enjoyed the Master Gardener certificate course offered through the Michigan State University Extension Service of Oakland County and strongly suggest you check out the Master Gardening program in your own area.

The folks at Visible Ink Press and the Gale Group were most crucial in getting this book to you. Thank you first to Terri Schell for suggesting a *Handy Garden* book and me to do it! Julia Furtaw championed the idea, Gina Misiroglu copyedited the manuscript, Marco Di Vita of the Graphix Group typeset the book, Devra Sladics and Christa Brelin ushered the project to publication, Bob Huffman of Field Mark Publications and Steven Nikkila of Perennial Favorites were responsible for the striking photography, and Cindy Baldwin (a fellow MG candidate) and Michelle DiMercurio developed the lovely cover and page design.

Finally, thanks to you, the reader, for selecting this gardening book in the midst of dozens of them. I hope these questions and answers will help you in your own backyard endeavors and provide you with enough confidence to keep you experimenting. Happy gardening!

Photo Credits

Parts of a flower illustration courtesy of Fred Fretz.

USDA Plant Hardiness Zone Map courtesy of the United States Department of Agriculture.

All others courtesy of Robert J. Huffman/Field Mark Publications or Steven Nikkila/Perennial Favorites.

THE
HANDY
GARDEN
ANSWER
BOOK™

PLANT AND SOIL SCIENCE

PLANT SCIENCE

How are **plants classified**?

Plants are classified by different categories of similarity. The method of classification gives two names to each plant (binomial nomenclature). Plants that share similar flowering and fruiting habits belong to the same *family*. This information can be helpful to the home gardener since plants in the same family are often susceptible to similar diseases. For example, roses and pear trees belong to the Rosaceae family.

On a plant tag, you will often see three words, or names, such as *Echinacea purpurea* 'White Swan'. The first two words are in Latin and the last term is in English. The first name (*Echinacea*) and the classification after family is genus. Plants in the same genus share similar flowers, roots, stems, buds, and leaves. The genus is always capitalized and underlined or in italics. The second name (*purpurea*) is a plant's species. This refers to a primary descriptive characteristic of a plant such as its coloring (in this case, purple). The species name is italicized and in lowercase. The third name ('White Swan') is called a plant's cultivar or variety. The cultivar can refer to a wide variety of characteristics the plant may have, from hardiness to flower color. Whatever the characteristic, it is retained in the plant after it is reproduced.

I know the **common names** of the plants in my garden. Why should I care about the plant's scientific name?

While common names can be charming, they tend to be imprecise. This is because different plants can be referred to by the same common name. For example, *Brugmansia sanguinea*, *Bilbergia nutans*, *Narcissus triandrus*, and *Soleirolia soleirolii* are all some-

1

times known as angel's-tears. Since *Brugmansia sanguinea* spp. is also often called angel's trumpet, *Bilbergia nutans* is generally referred to as queen's tears, and *Soleirolia soleirolli* is usually called baby's tears, it is easy to see how one could get muddled in the common names. In other cases, a plant's common name may be misleading: the toad-lily is not a member of the lily (*Lilium*) genus. Finally, common names may vary from region to region; for example, *Caltha palustris* may be known as cowslip, meadow bright, marsh marigold, or May-blob in different areas of the country.

What do those **scientific names** mean, anyway?

While space prevents detailing the meaning of thousands of botanical names (find a good botanical dictionary), there are some Linnaean basics. The genus (first name, capitalized) is always a noun and has gender like those in French and Spanish. The names themselves can be taken from a myriad of places. The genus may refer to something the plant resembles or a growth characteristic. Or it could honor a person (real or mythological).

The species is always an adjective and agrees with the gender of the genus. Species names usually indicate some of the plant's characteristics. They may reveal color (*albus,* or white), size (*minimus,* or small), the habit of growth (*lanatus,* or woolly), where the plant originally came from (*japonicus,* or from Japan) or the environment they enjoy (*pratensis,* or in a meadow). Or the species name may honor the discoverer of the plant, such as *Tradescantia* (spiderwort) after John Tradescant (see related question in Gardens, Gardeners, and Gardening chapter). So, while deciphering a plant's Latin name can be tricky, it is the key to unlocking some important information about a plant.

On the tag of a native plant I purchased it said something about being of **garden origin.** What does that mean?

The term garden origin is applied to a plant that has been bred by artificial means, rather than occurring naturally in the wild. Your plant cannot be native if it carries this term on its tag.

What are the advantages and disadvantages of **hybrid seed**?

Hybrid seed is the result of the cross-fertilization of certain plant species or varieties in order to produce plants that grow more vigorously, produce more fruits of a uniform quality, and have greater disease resistance. They tend to be more expensive than open-pollinated seed.

Why are there more
hybrid vegetables than trees and shrubs?

This has to do with the difference in their life cycles. With annual plants such as vegetables, you have the opportunity to breed and improve the plant every year. Trees and shrubs, however, have much longer life cycles, so plant breeders must wait longer to determine if their hybrid has been successful.

What is an F_1 hybrid?

An F_1 (F_1 stands for first filial) hybrid is the first generation offspring from two distinct, purebred plants. These plants are vigorous in growth and uniform in appearance. Offspring from two F_1 hybrids (known as F_2 hybrids, fittingly enough), do not "breed true." That is, they vary in appearance and tend to be weaker plants.

What is the difference between a **self-pollinated plant** and a **cross-pollinated one**?

The entire process of pollination happens within the flower of a self-pollinated plant, while a cross-pollinated plant requires the presence of another flower (possibly on the same plant), another plant, the wind, or an insect or animal. Self-pollinated or homozygous plants include peas and tomatoes. Cross-pollinated or heterozygous plants include the cabbage and squash families. If a cross-pollinator is grown with plants outside of its variety, a majority of the offspring in the next generation of plants will have different characteristics from its parents.

What is an **open-pollinated** plant?

An open-pollinated plant is one that has been left to pollinate on its own, through random or natural means. This also implies that an open-pollinated plant will breed true or that it will reproduce itself with the same characteristics as the parent plant. A self-pollinated plant will breed true if left to open pollinate but a cross-pollinated one will not maintain its identity unless the parent plants can be controlled in some way.

What is a **cultivar**?

A cultivar or variety is a group of plants that have the same characteristics (such as color, height, and flavor) that they retain even when reproduced.

What is the main advantage of **genetic diversity** in plants?

Through genetic diversity, plant species have the ability to adjust themselves to their surroundings in order to survive. This ability to overcome insects, disease, and a changing climate is usually a desirable characteristic for any population.

How does the development of **cultivars affect genetic diversity**?

The point of breeding a cultivar is to develop a plant that breeds true—so that it will *not* adapt to its surroundings or change its characteristics. Many cultivars are bred asexually—through cuttings or other forms of vegetative propagation—which is the surest way to replicate the traits of the parent plant. Although some cultivars may be propagated by seed, genetic variation is almost completely eliminated in order to gain a dependable cultivar.

While this breeding process can yield plants that are dependable in the garden, it can also have negative consequences. Some cultivars are unable to survive without human intervention or have proven unpredictable in the wild. Invasive species, for example, may interbreed with native species, causing their eventual decline.

What is a **sport**?

A sport is a genetic mutation that results in the development of flowers or shoots that are different than those of the parent plant. The mutation is frequently a change in flower color, although other types of changes occur. If the mutation is cloned or increased through asexual means, it may be named a cultivar. Finally, the change is not necessarily permanent—many spontaneous sports revert to the parent plant's characteristics.

What do **grass, cattails, corn, iris, and bamboo** have in common?

All of these plants are monocots; that is, they belong to the monocotyledons group of flowering plants. The leaves of a monocot have veins that run parallel. Because of this, monocots are generally small-stemmed since their leaves will not support anything larger. As seedlings, monocots grow just one seed leaf.

What do **beans, marigolds, and maple trees** have in common?

All of these plants are dicots (part of the dicotyledons group of flowering plants). As seedlings, dicots generate two seed leaves. Later, rather than running parallel, their leaf venation forms branches, enabling the leaves themselves to be larger and to provide more support for a large-stemmed plant. Some herbicides selectively affect either monocots or dicots, which is why a broadleaf herbicide can kill dandelions but not grass.

What is an **epiphyte**?

An epiphyte is a plant that grows on another plant without obtaining food from it. In shady areas of the rain forest, seeds of sun-loving plants are carried by the birds and wind to tree branches, placing them closer to the sun. They use rainwater and minerals from the organic matter trapped around the tree's bark. Ferns, orchids, and most bromeliads are epiphytes in their native environments. But you can find epiphytes closer to home: Chances are a multistemmed tree in your neighborhood has a tiny pine or oak seedling moored in its base.

What kind of plant is **moss**?

Despite their plantish appearance, mosses are not related to the largest portion of the plant kingdom—vascular plants. Instead, they are nonvascular plants, which means they lack the conductive tissue most plants have to circulate water and nutrients. Mosses and ferns (although ferns are vascular) are members of the pteridophytes—a group of plants without flowers that reproduce by spores, as opposed to seeds. The spores root themselves and create a kind of seed from which the next generation of pteridophytes grows.

Bamboos (*Bambusa* spp.) are mostly tropical grasses with hard-walled stems and ringed joints. (Robert J. Huffman/Field Mark Publications)

PLANT PARTS

What is the difference between **plants and animals**?

Although there are many, the basic difference between plants and animals lies in their cells. Plant cells have a rigid cell wall that provides support to the plant. Animal cells do not have these since they receive support from their skeleton.

How does a plant receive **food and water**?

Vascular tissues known as the xylem and the phloem move food (the result of photosynthesis) and water throughout a plant. Xylem tubes carry water and some minerals upward, mainly from the root system to the rest of the plant. The phloem tubes take food released through photosynthesis to other parts of the plant.

What is the impact of **too much or too little water** on a plant?

Too much or too little water can sever the oxygen supply to a plant. In saturated soil, air pockets in the soil are eliminated and the roots essentially drown. In dry soil, the topmost plant roots can die, forcing remaining roots deeper into the soil in search of water and oxygen. Since oxygen is crucial for plant respiration, this can kill a plant. To assist plant roots in receiving the proper amount of oxygen, you should be sure your soil is properly aerated (there is enough space between soil particles) and well drained.

What are the main functions of **plant roots**?

Roots provide a secure mooring for the plant by branching out, and they make sure that the plant receives water and nutrients by absorbing these from the soil. Roots also provide storage for the plant—housing carbohydrates to be used later.

What is a **taproot**?

A taproot is a deep-growing large root that has fine, small roots branching off it. Carrots and parsnips are taproots. Plants with taproots are difficult to transplant or uproot since the root system runs deep. The beloved dandelion (*Taraxacum officinale*) is a prime example of this.

What are some **alternative root systems** grown by plants?

English ivy (*Hedera helix*) grows aerial roots at various places on its stem. These adhere to surfaces and penetrate cracks in order to provide firm support to the plant. Periwinkle (both *Vinca major* and *Vinca minor*) grows roots from nodes on its stem. New plants can be produced by cutting sections of the stem that have these roots. Some rainforest trees such as banyans (*Ficus benghalensis*) grow additional roots above the ground in order to provide extra support when the tree is mature.

The dandelion's (*Taraxacum officinale*) long taproot tends to snap when pulled, which is why it is one of the most persistent lawn weeds. (Robert J. Huffman/Field Mark Publications)

What do **a rhizome, a bulb, a corm, a tuber, a stolon, and a runner** all have in common?

All are specialized types of stems that can be used to propagate a plant, but each reproduces differently. The rhizome, the tuber, the bulb, and the corm are belowground stems. A rhizome grows horizontally and can be divided into pieces in order to generate new rhizomes. Tubers have eyes (think of a potato) or nodes where shoots develop; they remain stationary and multiply. Bulbs multiply by generating bulblets from the

Leaves of Boston ivy (*Parthenocissus tricuspidata*). Despite its common name, this ivy is imported from Asia. It is also called Japanese ivy. Boston ivy and Virginia creeper (*Parthenocissus quinquefolia*) are part of the grape family (*Vitaceceae*) and climb using modified roots equipped with adhesive pads that cling to walls and other surfaces. (Robert J. Huffman/ Field Mark Publications)

"mother bulb." Corms are similar to bulbs and generate cormels. However, unlike bulbs, the main mother cormel doesn't survive this. Stolons and runners are above-ground stems that can be divided into sections containing nodes. These new cuttings can then be rooted to produce new plants.

What are the functions of a **plant's leaves**?

The flat surface of most leaves helps them to efficiently absorb sunlight to be used in photosynthesis. Stomata, or microscopic pores in the leaves, also function in plant respiration. During heavy rainstorms, leaves can help to drain water off the plant, protecting the rest of the plant from damage. Leaves can also be used in plant reproduction.

How does a plant's different **leaf shape and thickness** help it to withstand a particular environment?

Plants that grow in shady areas tend to have larger leaves so that they have a bigger surface area for absorbing light. The needles of conifers help them to withstand particularly windy conditions. A plant that receives a great deal of sunlight will have smaller leaves with thicker cuticles (a waxy layer that covers a plant's epidermis or skin) in order to retain moisture in the plant. The leaves of cactus have transformed themselves to thorns, with photosynthesis occurring in the plant's stem.

What are some different **arrangements of plant leaves**?

When a plant's leaves are opposite it means they are arranged in pairs along the plant's stem and are in the same plane. When a plant's leaves are alternate, single leaves are arranged on alternate sides of the stem. A whorled arrangement means the plant's leaves are in groups of three or more around the stem. A rosette is formed when leaves radiate from a single point on the plant's stem or base.

What determines **leaf color** in a plant?

Leaf color is an expression of the levels of pigments in a plant. The most obvious one is chlorophyll—the greener the leaf, the greater the level of chlorophyll. Red and burgundy leaves have more anthocyanin, a wine red pigment. Carotene (the same pigment found in carrots) causes leaves to be orange, and the xanthrophyll pigment causes leaves to be yellow or neutral in color. Different levels of these pigments provide the environment with a rainbow of color, such as limy yellow, a buttery yellow, or gold.

What impact do leaf characteristics such as color and texture have on a plant's survival?

Leaf characteristics such as color and texture can help a plant thrive in its environment. In areas that are constantly sunny, many plants tend to have gray leaves. This is because, in such conditions, plant leaves do not require a high chlorophyll content (which would make them green). Their gray color also helps the plant to reflect light and reduce the plant's surface temperature. Plants in warm, dry climates tend to be fuzzy or hairy, which helps reduce water loss. In the rainforest, plant leaves may have waxy, shiny surfaces to encourage water to roll off the plant during heavy rainstorms.

Why do tree **leaves turn color** in the fall?

The autumn color change of leaves is a plant's response to seasonal changes of decreased sunlight and cooler temperatures. Once a plant begins to shut down for the winter, it focuses its energy on storing food, rather than producing it. This can happen gradually or overnight, depending on the natural rhythms of the plant. Some plants are affected by weather changes, but others change color consistently year after year.

What are the **optimum conditions for fall color change**?

This is somewhat dependent on the plant. Some plants change color consistently from year to year. However, in a natural setting, the combination of dry, sunny days and crisp nights seem to elicit the best color from trees and shrubs.

What causes **variegated foliage** on trees and shrubs?

Some variegations of plant foliage are mutations indicating the plant has a virus or possibly a genetic abnormality. If these conditions persist over a long period of time, they can become part of the genetic makeup of the plant, making the variegation a permanent (as much as can be possible) characteristic.

What **impact** does variegated foliage have on a plant's functions?

If the variegation is indicative of a virus or genetic abnormality, this may cause the plant to decline or eventually die. Because the green of a leaf is an indication of the amount of chlorophyll present, the more variegated a leaf, the less chlorophyll it contains. A heavily variegated tree, then, is less able to absorb sunlight.

What is an **inflorescence**?

An inflorescence is a flower cluster or arrangement of flowers on a single axis. They include catkins, clusters, corymbs, cymes, flowerheads, panicles, racemes, spadi, spikes, and umbels. Some examples of inflorescences are the catkins on a willow (*Salix* spp.), the racemes of a lily-of-the-valley (*Convallaria majalis*), and the umbel of Queen Anne's lace (*Anthriscus sylvestris*).

What Is a **viviparous** plant?

A viviparous plant is one that forms plantlets on its leaves, stems, or inflorescences. They tend to be succulents, such as *Kalanchoe tubiflora* and *K. daigremontiana* (sometimes known as Mexican hat plant). But they also include *Tolmiea menziesii* (piggyback plant).

Tree growth rings not only reflect the age of a tree, but the climate during growth seasons. Thick rings indicate good growing conditions; thin rings indicate drought or other adverse growing conditions. (Robert J. Huffman/ Field Mark Publications)

Is a **pine cone** considered the fruit of a pine tree?

No, a pine cone is not a true fruit. While a pine cone contains the seeds of the pine (underneath its woody scales), a pine cone is not considered a true fruit since it is not formed by the ovaries of a flowering plant.

What can you tell about a plant from the **growth rings** of its stem?

By examining the stem's growth rings, you can learn about what happened to the plant in a particular year. Each ring signifies one growing year in a plant's life. The width of the ring is related to the amount of growth the plant experienced that year—the wider the ring, the better the growing season. Irregularities in a growth ring might signify damage or injury to the plant.

What are the major **parts of a flower**?

The major parts of a flower include the pistil, the stamen, the ovary, the sepal, and the petal. See the illustration on the following page.

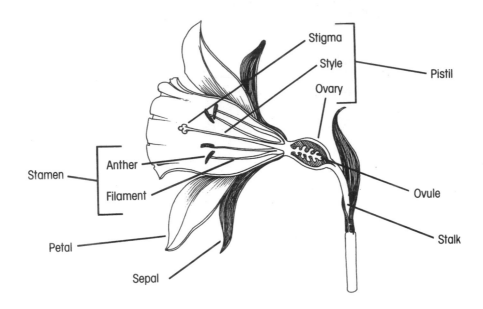

Parts of a flower. (Frank Fretz)

Why do **flowers fade**?

When a flower is fertilized by an insect, the wind, or itself, its color begins to fade and its petals fall. Fertilization marks the beginning of the next phase for the plant—using its energy to form a seed, instead of flowering. Plant geneticists who are attempting to extend the bloom of a particular variety, then, concentrate their efforts on making a plant sterile.

What is a **runner**?

A runner is a growth sprouted by the plant in order to reproduce itself. It refers to either a trailing stem or an underground shoot from which new plants emerge. Above ground, a trailing stem roots at its nodes, creating new plants with their own root systems. Underground horizontal-growing shoots sprout upright shoots, also creating new plants, at regular intervals along its length.

PLANT FUNCTIONS

What is the difference between **photosynthesis and respiration**?

Photosynthesis is the process by which plants produce their own food. After absorbing carbon dioxide from the air, light from the sun, and water from the soil, a plant converts these to sugar, storing energy for later and releasing oxygen in the process. In respiration, a plant uses the food produced by photosynthesis in order to grow. The process releases carbon dioxide and water and does not require sunlight to occur. Both photosynthesis and respiration are required for plant growth.

What is **pollination**?

Pollination is the transfer of pollen to the stigma of a plant flower where it fertilizes the flower's egg. This produces seed, which is comprised of a genetic model of its parent plant, along with a food supply.

What is **photoperiodism**?

Photoperiodism refers to a plant's dependence on day length in order to flower. Day length (that is, the number of hours in the day when it is light) regulates vegetative growth, flower budding and developing, and the beginning of plant dormancy. Plants are divided into three categories: short-day, long-day, and day neutral. Short-day plants require a day length of less than 12 hours to bloom, while long-day plants need a day length of more than 12 hours to bloom. Day-neutral plants, as their name indicates, will bloom regardless of the length of the day. However, plants are actually more concerned with the length of the night than the day, which is why short-day plants can be tricked into responding when they are kept in the dark with short interruptions of light. The plant responds as if it has been through successive days with short nights.

What is the process of **transpiration**?

Transpiration is the evaporation of water from the stems and leaves of a plant. This occurs mainly through the stomata, or microscopic pores found in the leaves. In warmer or windy weather, the rate of transpiration increases. In drier weather, the rate of transpiration drops. A plant only uses about 10 percent of the water it takes in to maintain the shape of the plant, cool the plant, move minerals from the soil, and transport sugars throughout the plant; the rest transpires.

> ## Why does the Christmas cactus need to be placed in a dark, cool area for a period of time to force its bloom?
>
> Plants have different requirements for light and temperature. Light duration, or the photoperiod, is the amount of time a plant is exposed to light or dark. All plants are either short-day, long-day, or day-neutral. The Christmas cactus (*Zygocactus truncatus*) is a short-day plant, which means it forms buds only when the day length is less than 12 hours. The Christmas cactus also has a "chilling requirement," meaning it requires low temperatures in order to bloom.

What is the concept of **apical dominance** and how does it affect pruning?

A terminal or apical bud (a bud on the growing tip of a stem) causes a hormone, auxin, to be produced in a plant. Auxin prevents the growth of buds below the terminal bud. When the terminal bud is pruned away, the hormone is no longer present and the lateral buds begin to grow. This concept is significant in pruning trees and shrubs. Hedges and shrubs that have not been pruned in some time begin to look tall and thin because the presence of terminal buds on the limbs and auxin in the plant prevents growth below the terminal bud. If you remove the terminal bud from a limb, the lateral buds below it will begin to grow, causing the shrub or hedge to become fuller and solid looking.

What is a **self-fruitful plant**?

A self-fruitful or self-pollinated plant is one whose flowers are able to pollinate themselves since they have both stamens and pistils. Most plants are self-fruitful. Some plants have flowers that are incomplete (having either stamens or pistils), with the male and female flowers being found on either the same plant (monoecious) or different plants (dioecious—see below).

Why do you need to have a **"boy" holly bush** and a **"girl" holly bush** in order to have berries?

Most holly (*Ilex* spp.) is dioecious. In order to self-pollinate, a plant needs both male (stamen) and female (pistil) flower structures. Holly plants have either all staminate flowers or all pistillate flowers. In order to produce berries, a pistillate holly needs to have a staminate holly nearby for pollination. The holly bush that produces berries is the female/pistillate holly.

The spotted geranium (*Geranium maculatum*) can grow from one to two feet in wooded areas and shady roadsides. (Robert J. Huffman/Field Mark Publications)

Why do flowers have **fragrance**?

Flower scents aid in plant reproduction. The fragrance entices bees, flies, and other insects to investigate the plant. In landing on the flower, their bodies brush against the anther, collecting pollen. The insects move from flower to flower, unknowingly picking up and dropping pollen as they go.

PLANT HARDINESS

What is **plant hardiness**?

A plant's hardiness is its ability to survive the climate of the area it is planted in. While many northern gardeners consider this to be a plant's ability to survive the winter, the term also takes into consideration a plant's heat tolerance.

How can I find out what my **hardiness zone** is?

You can determine your hardiness zone by referring to the United States Department of Agriculture (USDA) hardiness-zone map, which breaks down the United States into 11 zones based on a range of the area's average annual low temperatures. Most states contain more than one hardiness zone, so be sure to pinpoint your location on the map. Plants are then categorized by zone, based on their ability to withstand that region's annual low temperature.

I purchased a plant whose tag said it would **survive in zones** 3 to 5, but when I checked an encyclopedia, the same plant was listed as surviving in zones 2 to 5. Why is there such a discrepancy?

It is quite possible that the nursery and the encyclopedia were referencing two different hardiness-zone maps. There are actually three different hardiness-zone maps: the USDA map as noted in the previous question, the Arnold Arboretum map, and the Rutgers University map. The USDA map lists 11 zones, the Arnold Arboretum map lists 9 zones, and the Rutgers map breaks the country into 23 different zones. Some argue that the Rutgers map is the most accurate because it takes into consideration other weather factors, such as wind, sunshine, and humidity. However, the USDA map is the one most commonly used by nurseries and seedsmen.

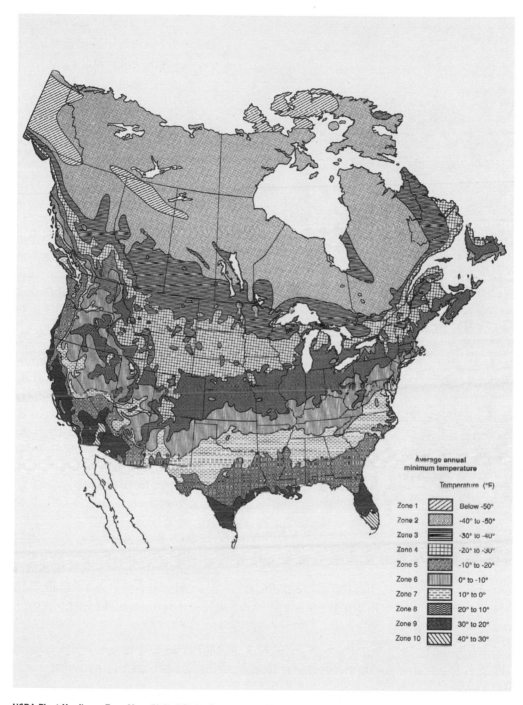

Average annual
minimum temperature

Temperature (°F)

Zone 1		Below -50°
Zone 2		-40° to -50°
Zone 3		-30° to -40°
Zone 4		-20° to -30°
Zone 5		-10° to -20°
Zone 6		0° to -10°
Zone 7		10° to 0°
Zone 8		20° to 10°
Zone 9		30° to 20°
Zone 10		40° to 30°

USDA Plant Hardiness-Zone Map. (United States Department of Agriculture)

Wrapping sensitive plants like rhododendrons in plastic sheeting or other protective material is advisable in cold climates. (Robert J. Huffman/Field Mark Publications)

I'm interested in growing some plants that are borderline hardy for my region. What can I do to improve their **chances of survival**?

While USDA hardiness zones are important indicators of a plant's ability to survive in your landscape, every area has its own microclimate—even sections of your backyard! Large bodies of water, protection from the wind, an adequate amount of moisture, and a porous soil can all help to increase a plant's hardiness. You can "baby" your plants by seeking out warmer portions of your yard to plant them in. Identify these microclimates by watching for early growth and bloom of plants as compared to other areas of your yard. You can also mulch these plants well, ensuring protection from wind and preserving moisture in the winter. While you may choose to invoke more drastic measures such as burlap shelters for "iffy" plants, remember it is always best to select the proper plant for your site. Providing a plant with the soil, light, and warmth it requires is the best way to ensure its survival.

What is the correlation between **elevation and the length of the growing season**?

For each thousand feet of elevation, the growing season is shortened by a week or so at both the beginning and end of the season. This leaves mountainous areas of Colorado in hardiness zone 3, while its high plains are in zone 5.

> ## How is it that parts of Scotland are warm enough to sustain palm trees?
>
> Scotland and the rest of western Europe are warmed by the Atlantic and the Gulf Stream. The source of cold air in Europe is the landmass of Eastern Europe, Russia, Norway, and Sweden. While in the United States the weather is warmer on average the further south you travel, in Europe the weather is warmer the further west you travel.

I live in a **cold region**. How should I site my garden to improve plant hardiness?

In the north, a garden that slopes to the south will receive more direct sunlight. By planting your garden on a southern slope, the resulting microclimate will be warmer earlier in the spring, and stay warmer in the fall. By planting on a southeastern slope, you can also shelter your plants from wind, which mainly comes from the northwest. In the south, however, you will want to plant your garden on a northern slope to decrease the influence of the sun during the summer months.

How does a **coastal climate** affect a plant's hardiness?

In inland states, most precipitation occurs in the summer and seasons are usually distinct. Warm weather in the spring encourages new growth in plants followed by a hot summer in which the growth is able to mature and survive the cold winter. In coastal areas, precipitation occurs throughout the year and the weather is moderated by the large body of water. Temperatures can fluctuate, which means new plant growth might be unable to mature before being hit with freezing temperatures.

I live in zone 2. Why can't I grow a plant that is **hardy to zone 3**?

You can if you find a warmer, sheltered spot in your yard. If your plant is exposed to temperatures that are below its normal level of tolerance, it may not die immediately. However, repeated exposure to these conditions will damage and stress the plant, killing it or weakening it to the point that other threats such as pests and disease finish it off.

What is the **Plant Heat-Zone Map**?

The American Horticultural Society Plant Heat-Zone Map was recently developed by the American Horticultural Society to help gardeners determine plant selection based on the average number of "heat days" (above 86 degrees Fahrenheit) per year in an area. Once the temperature is above 86 degrees Fahrenheit, plants begin to suffer physiological damage from the heat. The map divides the United States into 12 zones, based on daily high temperatures from the years 1974 to 1995, with zone 1 having no heat days and zone 12 having 210 or more heat days. The data was obtained from the archives of the National Climatic Data Center and the National Weather Service. An important caveat to the heat-zone rating is that it assumes that enough water is supplied to a plant at all times. Inadequate watering, even for a short time, can distort the accuracy of the zone coding. Eventually, all plants will receive a heat-zone designation, similar to a hardiness-zone designation.

What are some **effects of heat damage** on a plant?

An obvious effect of heat damage on a plant is leaf droop. In more severe cases, flower buds wither and chlorophyll production may slow or stop, causing leaves to appear brown or white. In the worst-case scenario, roots may stop growing and the plant eventually dies.

SOIL SCIENCE

What is in **dirt**?

The first thing to remember as a prospective gardener is that *dirt* is something you scour from your bathtub, but *soil* is what you plant in! Soil is made up of minerals and the remains of previously living organisms as well as pores that are filled with water and air.

What does **soil** do for plants?

Soil provides a medium for plants to grow in. It provides support to keep the plant stationary. It also provides the water, air, and nutrients a plant needs to carry out its processes. Finally, although plants can still be affected, soil serves to absorb the impact of contaminants.

What is the ideal **soil composition** for plants?

A soil made up of 45 percent minerals, 25 percent water, 25 percent air, and 5 percent organic matter would be ideal for plants. In the real world, however, soil is constantly

> ## What are some methods of increasing the amount of organic matter in soil?
>
> Cover crops, sheet composting, and digging in organic matter such as compost, manure, leaf mold, and peat moss are some ways of increasing the amount of organic matter in the soil. If you are currently growing plants in the soil, you should be careful about adding organic matter that has not yet begun to decompose, such as grass clippings. In the process of decomposition, these materials use nitrogen and so make less available for the plants themselves.

changing and does not remain at this ratio for long. In addition, every plant requires a slightly different soil, so this ideal is just a composite of those different needs.

What if my soil has **more than 5 percent organic matter**?

Since organic matter is constantly decomposing and being used by plants, an organic matter content of over 5 percent does not harm plants. Indeed, if the organic matter in your soil is higher than 5 percent, this can provide an extra "cushion" for periods when the soil is being used heavily (such as vegetable gardening in the summer, or periods of heavy growth in the garden). Current research shows that while having more than 10 percent organic matter in the soil does not harm plants, it does not provide any additional benefits.

How often do I need to **add organic matter** to the soil?

This depends on how many times you plant in the bed during the growing season. Ideally, you should add organic matter every time you plant. For an intensively planted vegetable garden, this might mean adding organic matter several times during the growing season. For a perennial bed, plenty of organic matter should be dug into the bed when it is first dug. At the beginning of the growing season, you can side-dress plants with compost and other organic matter. When you divide and separate plants, especially on a large scale, this is another opportunity to add organic matter to the soil.

How do I determine if I **need to add topsoil** to my garden?

The main reason to add topsoil to a garden is if it is not already present. In areas of new construction, it is a common practice for developers to remove the topsoil before building begins. This topsoil is then sold. After building is completed, the remaining

Which plant has blooms that can indicate the pH level of the soil they are grown in?

Hydrangea macrophylla produces flowers that may be either pink or blue, depending on the pH level of the soil they are growing in. If your hydrangea has pink flowers, your soil's pH is most likely above 7.0. If your hydrangea has blue flowers, your soil's pH is probably below 6.5. If your soil is somewhat neutral, your hydrangea may show both pink and blue flowers. Keep in mind, however, that pH levels can vary from place to place in your yard.

subsoil is regraded and topsoil must be added for any planting to take place. Even if your soil has not been stripped of its topsoil but is mainly clay or sand, you can improve it by adding either topsoil or organic matter.

How do I **select topsoil**?

It is important to get a representative sample of the topsoil you're purchasing prior to delivery. From the sample, you should be able to determine the soil's texture (clay, sand, or loam), the soil's structure (how the soil particles hold together), the percentage of organic matter present, the presence of weed seeds if possible, and the soil's pH (although this can be changed). A soil test can help you determine the soil's composition. The color of the soil can help determine whether there is sufficient organic matter in the soil. As a rule of thumb: Light-colored soils tend to have less organic matter in them while darker-colored soils tend to be rich in humus.

What is **soil pH**?

Soil pH measures the acidity or alkalinity of a soil and assigns it a number on a scale from 1.0 to 14.0 with 7.0 being neutral. An acid or "sour" soil has a pH below 7.0, with 1.0 being the most acidic soil. An alkaline or "sweet" soil has a pH range above 7.0, with 14.0 being the sweetest soil. The pH of most soils is between 4.5 and 8.0, while most plants grow best at a pH between 6.0 and 7.0.

How does **wood ash** affect the pH of the soil?

Wood ash increases the pH of the soil, making it more alkaline. It should be used with care, however, since its fine texture means ash is absorbed into the soil quickly.

Wood ashes contain 1 to 10 percent potash and 1.5 percent phosphorus—valuable nutrients for plants. (Robert J. Huffman/Field Mark Publications)

How does **peat moss** affect the pH of the soil?

Peat moss decreases the pH of the soil, making it more acidic. However, if your soil is very alkaline, it would require an impractical (that is to say, expensive) amount of peat moss to make an immediate difference in the soil pH.

What is **soil texture** and how does it affect plant growth?

Soil texture refers to the amount of sand, silt, and clay particles that make up the mineral portion of the soil. The most coarsely textured soil is sand. Since sand particles are large, they allow water and nutrients to move through the spaces between them rapidly while retaining oxygen. Also known as light soils, sandy soils warm up quickly and are easy for plant roots to penetrate but can dry out and lose nutrients too quickly. Clay particles are very small and, as a result, stay closer together, thereby holding water and nutrients much more tightly and leaving less air between particles. While clay or heavy soils can be slower to warm up, they tend to be more fertile. Different plants have different needs, but most tend to appreciate the benefits of both clay and sandy soil. A soil that is balanced between the different types of mineral particles is called a loam and is the goal of most gardeners.

What is the **saturation point** of soil?

Soil reaches its saturation point when its large pores are unable to absorb any more water and do not contain any air. This occurs following a soaking rain, before the water is able to drain out.

My nosy neighbor says my soil doesn't have enough **tilth**. What can I do to improve it?

What your neighbor is referring to is your soil structure. Soil binds together in clumps. Without clumps, water and nutrients run right through soil, passing by plant roots in the process. But if the clumps are too large or form horizontal plates, the soil retains water and prevents air from reaching plant roots. A soil that is slightly clumpy, called "friable" soil, or soil that has "crumb" or feels "mellow" is the ideal consistency. In most cases, adding organic matter such as peat or compost improves soil structure.

The weather turned warm early this year so I raced out with my new rototiller and spent hours **turning clods into beautiful loam**. But now it's midsummer and my soil is dry and crusty looking. Why?

In your zest to use your new gardening tool, you overworked the soil and broke desirable clumps into individual soil particles. When rain hit the soil, it formed a crust at

A rototiller can be used to prepare the ground for planting, to cultivate weeds, and to add mulch to the soil. (Steven Nikkila/Perennial Favorites)

the surface that prevented water and air from reaching the soil underneath. You can remedy your soil state by adding organic matter to the soil, gently working it into that top soil layer. Next year, go easy on the tilling.

How can I avoid **compacted soil**?

Soil is most commonly compacted by walking on it, since this closes up the pores between soil particles. You can avoid compacting your soil in flower beds and borders by creating paths or inserting stepping stones at intervals. In your vegetable garden, you may choose to plant your vegetables closer together, leaving paths around the beds, or create wide spaces between your rows for weeding, watering, and feeding in order to minimize the amount of foot traffic around your prized plants.

What are the **major elements** plants need and how do they affect plant growth?

Nitrogen, phosphorus, potassium, magnesium, calcium, and sulfur (known as macronutrients since plants need them in large quantities) are the most important elements to plants. Nitrogen is important for good leaf and stem growth and also keeps plants green. Since it is highly water soluble, it tends to leach from the soil quickly—not the best thing for groundwater. Plants that don't have enough nitrogen look pale and spindly. However, an overabundance of nitrogen can cause plants to grow too rapidly, making the stems and leaves soft and susceptible to problems such as disease and insects. Too much nitrogen can also cause plants to focus on growing new leaves when they should be setting fruit or growing new roots.

Phosphorus helps a plant's root system develop and encourages the setting of fruit and seeds. It is not as water soluble as nitrogen and so does not leach out of the soil as easily. Plants that don't have enough phosphorus can become stunted in their growth, have fewer flowers, and have discolored leaves. Potassium keeps plants vigorous, with strong stems and a better resistance to disease and insect problems. Plants that don't have enough potassium can also become stunted in their growth and show chlorosis or yellowing of their leaves. Potassium is also highly water soluble. Not enough magnesium in the soil can cause some chlorosis or cupping in the older leaves of a plant and reduces the number of seeds the plant produces. A shortage of calcium in the soil can cause weak stems and adversely impact budding and fruiting. An overabundance of either calcium or magnesium interferes with a plant's ability to use the other element as well. A shortage of sulfur, while rare, can cause yellowing in the entire plant.

What is done in a **soil test**?

In order to properly test your soil, you need to take 10 to 15 small samples of soil—about a cup's worth each—from all over the garden or bed you'd like tested. If a portion of the bed or garden has been fertilized differently from the rest of the garden or is located next to a street (where it might receive salt), leave it out of the testing. Then, mix these samples together and provide your local Cooperative Extension Service or other testing service with a half-cup sample, noting the past (if known) and planned use for the bed. You will receive back an analysis of your soil that generally includes soil pH, macronutrient quantities, and fertilizer recommendations. You can also purchase do-it-yourself soil test kits. If you can afford it (soil tests range widely in price starting at around 10 dollars per sample), at least test your soil's pH annually.

What is **humus**?

Humus is the slowly degrading organic matter that is left after the initial decomposition of organic matter takes place. It is high in nitrogen and is able to absorb water and nutrients.

How does **humus improve the soil** for plants?

Humus improves soil for plants in two ways: It improves the soil's water-holding capacity and it improves soil structure. In sandy soils, humus helps plant growth by holding water and nutrients that would otherwise drain too quickly. While clay soil is

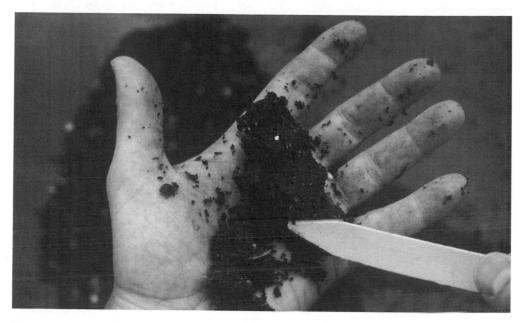

Tilth refers to the physical condition of the soil. Soil with good tilth is loose, well-aerated, and easy to break, crumble, or crush. (Robert J. Huffman/Field Mark Publications)

thought of as having an excellent (perhaps too excellent) water-holding capacity, it actually retains only 15 to 20 percent of its weight. Humus can retain up to 90 percent of its weight in water. Humus also binds small soil particles (such as those found in clay) together, which improves soil drainage.

What is the **difference between humus and organic matter**?

The terms humus and organic matter are often used interchangeably, but the difference is really in the degree of decomposition. Humus is organic matter that is highly decomposed, giving it a fine texture and making it relatively free of any trace of the original plant material. Organic matter, on the other hand, usually refers to plant material that is still in the early phases of decomposition and so may contain larger pieces of decomposing materials.

Why is **organic matter** necessary to plant health?

Organic matter improves the tilth and structure of a soil which in turn improves its water-holding capacity. This means plants can get the water they need, when they need it. Organic matter also helps "fix" nitrogen in the soil, making it available to plants for photosynthesis. It also helps make other nutrients in the soil available to plants.

27

How do chemical fertilizers work?

Chemical fertilizers are inorganic materials that are either partially or entirely synthetic and are added to the soil to provide plants with the elements they need for growth. Unlike organic materials that slowly release their nutrients to plants, these materials are available immediately for plant uptake. With the advent of soil testing and advances in the development of chemical fertilizers, the fertilizers can be applied at exact rates. Unfortunately, many farmers apply excess amounts either through error or conscious choice. Since the chemicals are available immediately, any fertilizer not used by the plant can run off or leach into the soil.

FERTILIZERS

What is **fertilizer**?

Organic gardeners believe fertilizer is essentially any substance that is added to soil for the purpose of improving its fertility. Chemical gardeners feel that fertilizers are only those substances that have measurable quantities of at least one of the major plant nutrients.

What is the impact of too much **manure** on the environment?

Nitrogen from fresh manure used as topdressing can vaporize into the air as ammonia. Excess nitrogen from the manure can also leach into and pollute groundwater, making it unsafe to ingest.

What are some characteristics of **water-soluble fertilizers**?

Water soluble fertilizers are available very quickly to the plant. Unfortunately, they are also available to everything else nearby because they leach quickly as well. As a result, these types of fertilizers can burn a plant if they are overapplied or not watered well at the time of application. They can lower the pH of a soil, they work well in cool weather, and these fertilizers tend to be inexpensive. For all of these reasons, they tend to be the most misused fertilizers by home gardeners, causing problems ranging from plant or turf burn to groundwater pollution.

What do those numbers on a bag of fertilizer stand for?

Those numbers, like 4-6-8 or 15-15-15, refer to the percentages by weight of macronutrients found in the fertilizer. The first number stands for nitrogen (N_2), the second for phosphorus (expressed as phosphate or P_2O_5), and the third for potassium (expressed as potash or K_2O). In order to determine the actual amount of each element in the fertilizer, multiply the percentage by the fertilizer's total weight in pounds. For example, in a 50-pound bag of 15-20-15, there are 7.5 pounds of nitrogen, 10 pounds of phosphorus, and 7.5 pounds of potassium. The remaining pounds are filler. By law, both organic and inorganic fertilizers must be labeled in this manner.

What are some characteristics of **slow-release fertilizers**?

Slow-release fertilizers take longer to be available to the plant but provide a more constant source of nitrogen. They tend to leach into the soil and burn plants less frequently than water-soluble fertilizers. However, they are more expensive and don't always work well in cool weather.

Why are **slow-release fertilizers** better for the environment?

Since the nitrogen in slow-release fertilizers is released over a long period of time, plants use most of what is released and there is less left over to leach into the soil and groundwater.

What is a **rock powder**?

A rock powder is a naturally occurring dust derived from rocks used to add plant nutrients such as phosphorus and trace elements to the soil. Greensand, granite dust, phosphate rock, and basalt dust are all examples of rock powders. Rock powders don't contain nitrogen, however, so they are generally applied with organic matter such as fresh manure.

SEEDING, PROPAGATION, AND PLANTING

SEED SELECTION

My ten-year-old son wants to try his hand at **starting plants from seed**. Are there any that are easier to start with than others?

Choose plants with larger seeds such as beans or peas—they are easier for smaller hands to plant. Plants that grow quickly such as lettuce, carrots, and radishes provide almost instant gratification (important for short attention spans). Finally, if you're starting the plants indoors, be sure to stay away from plants that don't transplant easily (see below).

I've never grown plants from seed before. Are there any that are difficult to **transplant**?

Be sure to check seed packets that advise outdoor sowing before you purchase them. Plants that are best sown directly in the ground include beans, corn, cucumbers, melons, pumpkins, California poppy (*Eschscholtzia californica*), cockscomb (*Celosia cristata*), balloon flower (*Platycodon grandiflorum*), moss rose (*Portulaca grandiflora*), dill (*Anethum graveolens*), chervil (*Anthriscus ceretolium*), and coriander (*Coriandrum sativum*).

What are some plants that **self-seed easily**?

Beefstake plant (*Perilla frutescens* 'Atropurpurea'), larkspur (*Consolida ajacis*), love-in-a-mist (*Nigella damascena*), Iceland poppy (*Papaver nudicaule*), opium poppy (*Papaver somniferum*), flowering tobacco (*Nicotiana alata*), verbena (*Verbena x.*

Love-in-a-mist (*Nigella* spp.) has blue or white flowers and very fine foliage. Its seeds, when broken from their pod, germinate easily. (Steven Nikkila/Perennial Favorites)

hybrida and cultivars), mountain spinach (*Atriplex hortensis*), Johnny jump-up (*Viola tricolor*), columbine (*Aquilegia*), hollyhock (*Alcea rosea*), perennial forget-me-not (*Brunnera macrophylla*), spiderflower (*Cleome*), sweet four-o'clock (*Mirabilis longiflora*), chive (*Allium schoenoprasum*), and biennial foxglove (*Digitalis purpurea*) are just some of the plants that self-seed easily. Many are biennials that set seed in order to survive. Warm-weather plants like tomatoes and marigolds (*Tagetes* spp.) will even self-seed in cold climates if the conditions are right.

What is an **heirloom seed**?

An heirloom variety is one that has been around for more than 100 years, before modern seed production and food distribution systems. They were gathered by regional seed growers who collected them from individual gardeners. These backyard gardeners selected them due to qualities such as disease or pest resistance, taste, and appearance—qualities that continue to make them popular today.

What is **stock seed**?

The term *stock seed* refers to seed that is grown specifically for the purpose of preserving a plant variety. This seed is in limited supply. The grower selects plants for their health and defining characteristics, such as color or resistance to disease, and then

> ## If I don't use up all of the seeds in a packet, can I plant them next year?
>
> **Y**ou can save seed from year to year if you store your leftovers properly. Seed viability can be reduced by heat and moisture. After opening the seed packet and planting the number of seeds you need this year, keep the remaining seeds in an airtight jar such as a recycled baby food jar. Place the jar in a cool, dry place. Next year, before planting all the remaining seeds, try sprouting a few (see page 38) to determine the viability rate of the remaining seeds.

destroys the remainder of the plants before they can produce seed. Seed from the superior plants is collected and becomes stock seed for the next planting.

Which **seeds need light to sprout**?

It is a little-known fact that, while seedlings require light to grow, most seeds don't need light to germinate. They actually just need moisture and warmth. Seeds that do require light in order to sprout include celery (*Apium graveolense dulce*), lettuce (*Lactuca sativa*), garden cress, mustard (*Brassica juncea*), and dandelion (*Taraxacum officinale*).

How do I **save seed** from plants I want to grow again?

If you're interested in saving seed from plants in your own garden, it is best to plan ahead of time and know specifically what kinds of plants you have. Don't try to save seed from hybrid plants; they won't be true to their parents. Remember that biennial plants won't set seed until the second year, so these plants must be kept going through the winter (indoors or in a protected area) until the following year. For all seeds, allow only those plants that display desirable characteristics (hardiness, disease resistance, color, etc.) to set seed.

Allow the seed to dry on the plant if possible. If the seed is within the fruit, the fruit should remain on the plant until it is overripe. Then pick the plant or fruit, remove the seeds, and soak the seeds overnight in water to remove any pulp. Dry all seed (even that which has dried on the plant) thoroughly on screens or in between sheets of paper so that it will not rot. Store in glass jars in a dark, dry, cool area. Organizations such as the Seed Savers' Exchange in Decorah, Iowa, are great sources of further information on the seed-saving process.

33

You need to harvest the seed pods when they have turned brown, dry, and brittle, but before they break apart and spill their precious cargo. Seeds from plants such as tomatoes and cucumbers can be saved by allowing the fruit to get overripe on the plant (but before it rots!). Remove the seeds from the fruit and wash them well in clean water, soaking if needed to remove any remaining fruit. Let the seeds dry for a week or so on newspaper, then place them in airtight jars and store them in a cool, dry location for next year.

What is a **seed tape**?

In order to assist with proper spacing of seeds, some seed companies implant their seeds onto biodegradable tapes. When planting, cut the tape into the length needed for your plot and plant it according to its proper depth in the ground. Don't forget to provide proper spacing between rows. Seed tapes are useful for small seeds such as carrots that are difficult to plant singly, as they enable a gardener to forgo thinning in most cases.

You can create your own seed tape by using paper towels cut in long sections and a "glue" mixture of cornstarch and water to adhere the seeds to the tape.

I saw my neighbor rolling out a carpet in an ugly area of her yard, and a month later it was a **beautiful bed of flowers**. What happened?

The flower carpet or sod you describe is one of the newest inventions to appear on the gardening scene. Designed to take the work out of planting, they work best for folks who'd like to see flowers quickly. There are a couple of different types of flower mats. One type features a felt pad that has been infused with seeds and fertilizer. Another is similar to grass sod, comprised of small, densely planted flowers with well-developed roots. To use either, select a location and remove all plants (including grass) from the area, then roughen up the soil underneath using a tined rake. Roll out the sod and water thoroughly. Water regularly to ensure that the plants take root in the new bed.

STARTING PLANTS FROM SEED

Why should I bother **growing plants from seed** when I can just purchase them at my nursery?

After spending oodles of time nursing little seedlings through February and having half of them die from lack of water when I forgot about them in March, I can understand why many folks prefer to just purchase plants. However, growing plants from seed has two advantages. Starting plants from seed is much cheaper than buying them full grown. An average packet contains 100 seeds and might cost as little as three dollars (for more exotic seeds). Even if only half of them survive, you will have 50 plants for three dollars. You can't beat that anywhere. The second advantage is that you have a greater selection of plants to choose from if you grow from seeds. Seed catalogs tend to have the best selection, but even your local garden center will stock, say, four different green bean cultivars in seed packets but only one kind of bean plant. And, of course, by growing your own plants from seed, you will experience the deep satisfaction of planting a small seed, nurturing it along, and having it grow into a healthy plant. At least, that's what you hope for.

Are there any advantages to **starting plants indoors**, rather than outdoors?

In areas with short summers, plants that need long growing seasons, such as tomatoes and peppers, can't be grown from seed unless they are started indoors. Even plants that can be started outdoors are often started indoors. This allows a gardener control over the environment for tender seedlings. While many plants germinate outdoors under ideal conditions, you can often get a better germination rate indoors. Outdoors, too much rain can rot seeds. Too little rain can mean the seeds won't have enough moisture to sprout. Insects like cutworms love nothing more than a tender young seedling or plant coming up out of the soil. While starting seeds indoors does require some work, you are very likely to be rewarded with healthy young transplants.

Do I need special grow lights to start seeds?

Some gardeners like to use basic, cheap shop-light fixtures sold at hardware stores. While you're there, pick up a length of chain and something to secure the fixture to the ceiling or shelf above your seed-starting area. You don't need to purchase expensive lightbulbs for growing—look for a cool-white bulb. For each light fixture, purchase one regular bulb and one cool-white bulb. Attach the shop lights using the chain, making sure the chain is long enough to bring the lights within three to four inches of the seed container. As the seedlings grow, reduce the length of the chain to raise the light source, keeping it four to six inches away from the leaves (any closer and they will scorch). Keep the lights on a good 15 to 16 hours a day. You can either purchase a light timer for this, or just remember to turn them on in the morning and off before you go to bed.

What does the term **direct seeding** mean?

Direct seeding means to plant seeds directly into the ground, rather than planting them in containers (inside or outside) until they are large enough to transplant into the ground. Some plants grow so quickly that it isn't worth the effort to transplant them. Corn, melons, beans, and greens are examples of this. Other plants don't like to be transplanted, so they are best direct seeded.

What **supplies** do you need to start plants from seed?

In order to start plants from seed, you need a growing medium (usually soil), containers to grow seedlings in, a watering can and bottle, labels to mark your newly sewn seeds, and, needless to say, the seeds themselves. You can recycle plastic flats from nurseries but be sure to sterilize them in a diluted bleach solution (roughly 10 percent bleach) to avoid contamination. You can also use butter tubs or the bottoms of milk cartons or purchase peat pots or new flats to start your seeds.

Seeds actually require warmth to germinate rather than light. While the heat from a grow light or sunny window can be enough for some, others require a heat source underneath the seeding container to germinate. By being placed on a refrigerator or a seed-starting heating pad (available from catalogs and some garden centers), seeds like tomatoes and peppers can successfully germinate. Keep the seeds moist by planting them in a moist mix and covering the container with plastic wrap. Once the seeds have sprouted, they need light and oxygen to grow and flourish so be sure to check your seeds daily. At the first signs of life, remove the wrap and place them in a location where they will receive between eight and 10 hours of light per day. Water them carefully using a spray mister in order not to knock the fragile seedlings over or wash away the soil. Use a highly diluted fertilizer (such as watered-down fish emulsion) every other time you water.

Help! My poor **seedlings need watering all the time** and I'm just not able to keep up with them. Any suggestions?

Fast-growing seedlings do require a great deal of water. While many books and seed catalogs recommend using a mister to avoid injuring the seedlings, some gardeners prefer to water their seedlings from the bottom. To do this, place the seedling containers in a waterproof tray and water the tray, allowing the water to "wick up" into the seedling containers. This should still be monitored regularly to avoid oversoaking the seedlings or allowing them to dry out, but if you forget a day or two, your seedlings will probably be fine.

I kept my **seeds well watered but none of them germinated**. I just purchased them this year. What happened?

You may have overwatered your tender seeds. While moisture and warmth are required for a seed to germinate, oxygen is also necessary. If seeds sit in water for too long or if the soil they sit in is waterlogged, they will rot.

What **kind of soil** should I use to start plants from seed?

You want to start with a good soil mix. It should be light enough so that the seeds can push through the soil (and also be reached by water, heat, and fertilizers) but not so porous as to fall apart once the roots start growing. It's important that the mix is sterile to avoid spreading disease to your new seedlings. You can either mix your own or purchase a mix. Mix your own by using equal parts peat or fine compost, soil, and vermiculite or perlite (for aeration and drainage). If you buy your mix, be sure it's meant for seedlings. Avoid bags marked potting soil—these usually don't include vermiculite or perlite and are too heavy for seed starting.

I'd like to use garden soil for seed starting. How do I **pasteurize garden soil**?

Pasteurization of garden soil is crucial to eliminate microorganisms that can cause disease. Place the soil in a roasting pan with the soil at a depth of three to four inches. Wet the soil thoroughly. Place a meat thermometer in the center of the soil and bake it in the oven at a low heat (less than 300 degrees Fahrenheit) until the thermometer

37

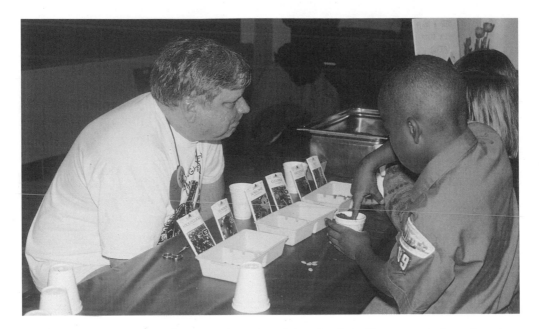

Garden expos are excellent places to introduce young people to the joys of gardening. Here, a youngster learns the proper technique to plant seeds. (Robert J. Huffman/Field Mark Publications)

reads 180 degrees Fahrenheit. Higher temperatures can kill beneficial organisms and damage the structure of the soil and the organic matter in it.

I have some seeds I bought a few years ago that I never got around to planting. Are they **still good**?

To test the viability of older seeds, you should presprout them. Place 10 seeds on a wet paper towel, spacing them apart so that they don't touch each other. Roll up the towel and place it in a plastic bag, loosely tied to be sure air can enter the bag. Set the bag in a warm place such as in the kitchen or on top of the refrigerator. Check the seeds in a few days. By multiplying the number of sprouted seeds by 10 you get a rate of germination. While anything less than 50 percent is considered poor, you could still plant the seeds by sowing them more thickly than recommended.

What is a **furrow**?

A furrow is a trench in the soil where seeds will be planted. A furrow also refers to a field or an area of plowed land. A furrow can be created by something as large as a plow or as small as a gardener's finger.

Should **seeds planted indoors** be planted at the same depth as **seeds planted outdoors**?

No. Seeds planted indoors can be planted half as deep as those outside.

Which **vegetables and herbs should be started indoors**, as opposed to being seeded directly into the ground?

Hot-weather vegetables such as tomatoes, eggplants, and peppers require warm conditions to start. While they can be seeded outdoors in warmer areas, starting them indoors will protect the germinating seeds from the elements. Basil also requires warm conditions to germinate, but since it grows fairly quickly, you can start it outdoors, even in areas with short summers. Other vegetables and herbs such as onions and leeks (started from seed, not sets), cabbage, broccoli, brussels sprouts, parsley,

There are many types of greenhouses, such as those attached to houses, window greenhouses used to grow herbs, terrariums, and freestanding greenhouses, which capture light from all directions. (Robert J. Huffman/ Field Mark Publications)

English lavender (*Lavandula angustifolia*), and rosemary (*Rosmarinus officinalis*) also do best when started indoors since they tend to be slightly finicky germinators. Starting them indoors means you can provide them with optimum conditions for germination.

Can I successfully **start seeds in my sunny kitchen window**?

It depends. Is your window leaky? Most seeds require warmth more than sun to germinate. Seeds such as tomatoes and peppers require a warmer soil to germinate than others. You may be better off starting these plants under lights close to the soil, moving the lights up as the plants grow. Better yet, start them on a warming pad made for seed starting or even on top of your refrigerator. Check them carefully every few days. Once they've sprouted, they need light to grow.

Why do **seeds remain dormant**?

Seeds remain dormant for a number of reasons, depending on the plant. Some seeds have hard seed coats that must be broken or injured in order to absorb water and germinate. The seeds of some plants in very warm climates have a kind of inhibitor in the seed coat that prevents the seed from germinating until certain weather conditions occur. Other plants require periods of dormancy in which they dry out or are exposed to moist and cold conditions in order to germinate.

I've waited until late in the winter to get my seeds started. It's already three weeks before my frost-free date. Can I still start **tomato and pepper plants** from seed?

Yes, you can. Although seed companies usually recommend starting tomato and pepper plants eight to 10 weeks prior to a region's frost-free date, it's actually better to start seeds too late rather than too early. Go ahead and start them inside. Once they're as wide as they are tall, begin to harden them off in preparation for outside planting. In the artificial environment of your house or greenhouse, it is difficult to keep plants watered and fed properly without getting leggy or undernourished. Seedlings that are a little small when set out usually catch up to their earlier-planted cousins.

What is **stratification**?

Stratification or "moist chilling" is the practice of exposing seeds to cold temperatures for a certain period of time in order for them to break their dormancy and germinate. Plants that are native to temperate regions of the world have seeds that require a moist, cold period before they sprout. Stratification duplicates this natural process. The amount of exposure varies from plant to plant.

What are some **plants that require stratification** in order to germinate?

Many perennials need to be "moist chilled" in order to germinate, including bleeding heart (*Dicentra* spp.), cardinal flower (*Lobelia cardinalis*), columbine (*Aquilegia* spp.), globeflower (*Trollius* spp.), monkshood (*Aconitum* spp.), penstemon (*Penstemon* spp.), and garden phlox (*Phlox paniculata*). There are a number of woody ornamentals that also germinate with stratification, including cedar of Lebanon (*Cedrus libani*),

> ## I've just bought a packet of morning glory seeds and can't wait to see them climbing up my mailbox. The directions on the packet tell me that I need to scarify my seeds. What does that mean?
>
> Seeds like morning glory (*Ipomoea purpurea*), sweet pea (*Lathyrus odoratus*), and baptisia (*Baptisia* spp.) that have a hard outer covering need to be scarified or scratched in order to absorb water for germination. Methods of scarification include scratching the coating with a knife or rubbing them with sandpaper. If you have more than a few seeds to scarify, line a container such as a coffee can or a jar with sandpaper. Place the seeds inside the container and shake them until the coating wears down.

shadblow (*Amelanchier* spp.), horse chestnut (*Aesculus* spp.), birch (*Betula* spp.), spruce (*Picea* spp.), lilac (*Syringa* spp.), rose (*Rosa* spp.), and bittersweet (*Celastrus*).

What does it mean for a plant to be **double dormant**?

Plants that are double dormant require a unique sort of stratification in order to germinate. These seeds must receive a warm, moist period followed by a cold period, affecting both the seed coat as well as the seed embryo in order for them to break their dormancy. Plants that germinate after a period of double dormancy include some barberries (*Berberis* spp.) and junipers (*Juniperus*), dogwood (*Cornus* spp.), arborvitae (*Thuja* spp.), lilac (*Syringa* spp.), tree peony (*Paeonia emodi*), some lilies (*Lilium* spp.), and viburnum (*Viburnum* spp.). In nature, double-dormant seeds can sometimes take up to two years to germinate.

What are some **methods for stratifying seeds**?

Stratification requires a cold environment and a coarse soil mix to allow air and moisture to reach the seeds. One method is to stratify seeds in your refrigerator. Place the seeds, along with some slightly moist sphagnum moss or sand, into a self-closing plastic bag. Store the bag in the refrigerator at around 40 degrees Fahrenheit for about six weeks. When the seeds begin to germinate, gently remove them from the bag and place them in flats in a sunny or bright location, keeping them moist while they continue to grow. Thin and transplant as needed. When the plants are large enough, they should be hardened off gradually and moved outdoors.

You can also stratify seeds outdoors. In the late fall or winter, plant the seeds in sterile containers filled with a well-moistened mixture of peat and sand. Top off the containers with additional sand to keep the potting mixture from being washed out by

41

the rain. Place the containers in a sheltered location outdoors, out of full sun. Ideally, the area should remain around 40 degrees Fahrenheit consistently, but varying temperatures will just lengthen the time needed for stratification. If you do not have a cold frame, be sure to bury the base of the pots to keep them upright and use netting or screen over the container tops to discourage critters. Check the pots periodically for moisture and water as needed.

Once the seeds have germinated (beginning in the early spring), move them to a sunny location. Thin and transplant to larger containers as needed. By the following fall, most plants will be large enough to move into the garden. Continue to water and fertilize carefully until they are well established.

CARING FOR SEEDLINGS

How do I know when to **transplant my seedlings**?

Seedlings should generally be transplanted at two different times. If the seeds were started in flats, they should be transplanted to a larger container after they have grown their first set of true leaves (leaves that look like tiny leaves rather than small stubs). They shouldn't need to be transplanted again until they're ready to be planted out, unless the weather turns cold despite the arrival of the frost-free date or if they're outgrowing their containers.

What is a **cotyledon**?

A cotyledon, or seed leaf, is the first leaf (or set of leaves) to unfold once a seed germinates. These leaves are actually in the dormant seed and can contain stored nutrients, depending on the plant. Usually rounded and cupping upward, they look different from the second or "true" set of leaves on a seedling.

How do I **transplant my seedlings**?

Fill your new containers (peat pots, larger plastic cells, or clay pots) with wet soil mix. Dampen the mix by combining water and soil mix in a separate container until the soil is thoroughly wet without being soggy. Gently dig out a seedling or group of seedlings from its original home. Try using a plastic spoon for larger transplants and its other end for smaller ones. Carefully hold the seedling by one of its leaves, being careful not to crush it or the stem. Using the handle end of the spoon, create a small hole in the damp soil mix and place the seedling inside. Gently move the soil back around the seedling and return it to its sunny window or grow light.

> ## What are the implications of transplanting a seedling too soon or too late?
>
> It is important to transplant a seedling at the proper time because it will affect the growth of the plant. If a seedling is planted outdoors too soon, the soil may not be warm enough. This will cause the seedling's growth to be checked, which can permanently affect the health of the plant. If you wait too long to transplant your seedlings, they can outgrow their containers. This can also cause a plant to become stunted or stop growing completely.

How should I **water and fertilize** my seedlings?

Use a weakened solution of fish emulsion and water in a spray bottle and spray the plants every few days. If this does not keep the soil wet enough, water from the bottom by placing water in the plant tray and allowing it to wick up to the plant.

How do I know If I'm **fertilizing or watering my seedlings properly?**

Seedlings that are receiving the proper amount of water and fertilizer will be a healthy green color, somewhat stocky, and very robust looking. If the seedling is any color other than green or if it changes color, it is probably being underfertilized. If its leaves curl under, it is probably being overfed. Plants that become leggy may be too far from their light source or overfed.

Help! I **forgot about my seedlings for a few days** and they're gasping for water. Will they all die of thirst?

No—as long as you water them immediately. While allowing your plants to become burnt to a crisp will kill them, most seedlings will recover from an occasional wilt. It is actually better for you to err on the dry side, rather than the wet side. This way, those tender seedlings won't succumb to the damping off fungus or rot in their containers.

What does a plant that has become **leggy** look like?

The term "leggy" is used to describe plants that have large gaps on their stems between their leaves or sets of leaves. They tend to be rather spindly looking as well. Legginess is usually a sign that a plant is not receiving enough sunlight. In some cases, a leggy plant may be overfed.

43

My seedlings all seem to be growing toward the light. Is this a problem?

This is a natural reaction of plants to maximize the amount of sunlight used in photosynthesis. The urge to reach toward the light is called phototropism. If you have ever seen a field of sunflowers, you will notice that they turn their faces toward the sun. As far as your seedlings are concerned, you'd like them to be sturdy and straight for transplanting out into the garden. Therefore, turn the pots every few days to keep them somewhat straight. If you've planted many seeds in a large container, instead use aluminum foil or inexpensive mirrors to reflect some of the light back in the opposite direction.

What is **damping off**?

Damping off is a soil-borne disease that attacks young seedlings, causing their stems to shrivel and collapse at soil level. Low temperature, low light, and too much water can create ideal conditions for the fungus that causes damping off, so be sure that you're providing your seedlings with enough light and warmth and watering them appropriately. To discourage the fungus, you must be sure the pots or flats you plant in are sterile. To do this yourself, you should scrub previously used containers using dish soap and water, followed by a soak in a chlorine bleach/water solution (using a 1:10 ratio) and a final rinse to remove the bleach.

What is **hardening off**?

This is the process of acclimating your newly grown seedlings (or newly purchased plants) from the climate in your house or greenhouse to the outdoors. Temperature, wind, and sunlight can all affect your fragile seedlings or plants. With seedlings, start by bringing them outside into a sheltered, somewhat shaded spot for a few hours each day, gradually increasing their exposure to the elements over a period of a week or two. If the weather takes a drastic turn for the worse, you might consider holding off for a few days or take extra precautions to be sure you don't freeze, burn, or wind-scorch your plants.

My **transplants became bleach white and died** after I began hardening them off. What did I do wrong?

You had the right idea in hardening off your transplants, but you didn't choose the right location. Tender young transplants not only need to be protected from the wind

Hardening off plants in a cold frame built against a greenhouse at Henry Ford Estate, Fair Lane, in Dearborn, Michigan. (Robert J. Huffman/Field Mark Publications)

and cold, they also need to be protected from the sun. Indoor lighting, even for plants placed in sunny windows, isn't nearly as intense as sunlight. This is because windows filter out most ultraviolet light. The next time you harden off transplants, be sure to find a location that is sheltered from wind, cold, and direct sunlight.

OTHER METHODS OF PROPAGATION

What is the difference between **sexual and asexual propagation** in plants?

Sexual propagation of plants uses seeds to reproduce plants while asexual propagation of plants uses actual parts of plants, such as a leaf or stem, to propagate. Grafting, cutting, and layering are all forms of asexual propagation.

What is **vegetative propagation**?

Vegetative propagation is asexual propagation, or a plant's ability to reproduce itself from its own plant tissue. Gardeners frequently manipulate this ability to yield additional plants. Some examples of this are rooting strawberry runners, the division of rhizomes of iris and offsets of bulbs that have multiplied, and the division of expanding clumps of many perennials. Vegetative propagation can be considered a desirable form of propagation, producing a plant's clone instead of a hybrid.

What is **grafting**?

Grafting is a form of plant propagation in which a bud, shoot, or scion of a plant is inserted in a groove or cut in the stem or stock of another plant. The plant then continues to grow. This is a common method for propagating rose bushes and fruit trees.

What is **cutting**?

Cutting is the most common form of plant propagation, in which a leaf or a part of a stem or a root is cut from a plant in order to create a new plant. Most plants can be successfully propagated in this manner. When a cutting is formed from a stem and placed in either water or a highly porous rooting medium, new roots form at the stem node (a section on the stem where a bud or leaf forms). Herbaceous plants root quite easily while woody plants sometimes need assistance in the form of a rooting hormone. Other plants such as the African violet (*Saintpaulia* spp.) are propagated through leaf cuttings. Raspberries (*Rubus idaeus*) and some perennials are propagated through root cuttings.

A greenhouse worker at Henry Ford Estate, Fair Lane, in Dearborn, Michigan, divides a plant. (Robert J. Huffman/Field Mark Publications)

When and how do I **divide a plant**?

Dividing a plant separates it into several smaller plants. Bulbs, suckering shrubs, ornamental grasses, and perennials that form clumps are some of the plants that you can divide. The best time to divide a plant is when it is dormant, although division can occur at any time with a healthy parent plant. Also, in order not to disturb bloom, plants that bloom in the spring and summer should be divided in the fall, and fall-blooming plants should be divided in the spring.

To divide a plant, gently loosen it from the soil using a spade. Lift it from the soil and examine the roots to see where smaller plants have formed. Separate these from the parent using a sharp spade or knife. Each new plant should have its own root system. If the center of the parent plant is extremely woody, remove it and cut the healthy ring that is left into individual pieces. Plant all new plants as soon as possible, making sure to water them deeply and provide mulch to protect the tender roots.

What is **layering**?

Propagation by layering is a method of inducing a section of a plant's stem to sprout new roots. It can be done by merely bending a branch to the ground and burying a part of its stem with soil. After the stem roots, it is cut away to form a new plant. With air layering, plants that are difficult to bend or propagate in other ways may be reproduced. The stem of the plant is wounded, then "bandaged" with moist sphagnum moss or a similar medium. The wound will eventually root, revealing the roots through the moss, and the new plant can be removed from its parent.

SELECTING PLANTS

What is meant by the phrase **full sun?**

Plants that thrive in full sun require at least six hours of sunlight a day. Areas without any surrounding trees or structures meet this requirement. Sun-lovers like vegetables and herbs are plants that need full sun.

What is meant by the phrase **partial sun?**

Plants that grow in partial sun still need at least three to four hours of sun per day for the best flowering, but will tolerate some shade during the day. Plants that grow in dappled shade will also grow in partial sun.

Pansies (*Viola wittrockiana*) and cultivars are extremely hardy, withstanding temperatures down to 15 degrees Fahrenheit. (Robert J. Huffman/Field Mark Publications)

What is meant by the phrase **full or dense shade**?

Full or dense shade is the kind of shade found near a building or underneath evergreens. Little to no light enters these areas of the garden, so you need to consider your plantings carefully. Some plants that do well in full shade have broad leaves that allow them to collect and use any sunlight that does manage to stray in, such as reflected sunlight.

What is meant by **dappled shade**?

Dappled shade is found under the canopy of deciduous trees. While plants under these trees don't receive much direct light, some light manages to peep in around the foliage. Plants that bloom before the trees leaf out, such as spring bulbs, tend to thrive here.

What is meant by **partial shade**?

A partially shaded area of the yard receives some direct sun during the day, making it possible for some normally sun-loving plants to find a place here. This type of shade can be found at the edge of a woods.

How can I tell the **healthy plants** from the sickly ones at the farmer's market or my local nursery?

When selecting plants, you should avoid ones with wilted or yellowed leaves. These can indicate that the plant hasn't been watered frequently enough, that it is diseased, or worse. While it might improve once it's in your garden, it's usually best to make another selection. Look for plants that are short and bushy and green, without buds. You want to have the plant do most of its growing once it's in your garden, otherwise it may falter early. Check the root ball by giving a gentle tug at the base of the stem and examining the bottom of the pot. If the plant feels loose when you tug on it, it may be damaged or have rotted roots. The roots should appear white and firm and should not be growing out of the bottom of the pot—this indicates its been growing in the pot too long. Check the leaves and stem of the plants; if they appear damaged or plagued by bugs or disease (spots, odd curling, mushiness), don't buy them! Finally, while you can buy a plant in bloom (especially if you're not confident that its color matches the tag), try to avoid it. Again, you want to have your plant do its growing in your garden.

Where is the **best place to purchase** plants?

Although this is really a matter of opinion, I would try to avoid any place that sets out its plants in between the hammers, the shoe polish, and the cereal. While you can always find a good deal, and sometimes even a healthy plant, these places don't have

A farmer's market, like Eastern Market in Detroit, Michigan, can be a great place to buy plants, flowers, fruits, and vegetables. (Robert J. Huffman/Field Mark Publications)

knowledgeable staff to help you decide if that wonderful blooming azalea is one that will survive the cold in your state or if it is meant to brighten your dining room for a few weeks. Farmer's markets can be a good source for plants, although not all the vendors grow the plants they're selling. Try to find one that does. Local nurseries that do their own propagation can be an excellent source of new cultivars, and they probably have plants that are best suited to your climate. But while they're more reliable and certainly knowledgeable, they can be more expensive. Your best bet is to purchase your expensive items such as trees and shrubs from a local nursery (since these purchases are a true investment), perennials at the same nursery or a farmer's market, and an occasional whimsical purchase at the five and dime.

Are there any **benefits to mail ordering plants**?

Again, this is a matter of opinion. If you plan on purchasing a plant that can easily be found at your local nursery (or, heaven forbid, the supermarket) such as a "Stella de Oro" daylily (*Hemerocallis* 'Stella de Oro'), there isn't much point in ordering one from a catalog. However, if you are interested in purchasing those "Stella de Oros" in bulk, a mail-order nursery might be able to provide a discount on these, or at least have enough stock to provide you with the 100 you need. Also, you can usually choose from a wider variety of plants through mail order than at your local nursery. Specialized mail-order nurseries, such as one that sells just hostas, literally have hundreds of plants to choose from. If you are looking for a specific cultivar or one of the newest, a reputable mail-order nursery can be your best bet.

How can I determine **which mail-order nursery to order from**?

The three most important factors in ordering from a mail-order nursery are, in order of importance: 1. The nursery is located in your hardiness zone, or close to it. Plants grown at nurseries in areas outside your zone may not be suitable for your garden. 2. The nursery has a liberal refund or exchange policy. Ordering by mail can be hard on plants and despite the grower's best efforts, some plants will die. A reputable nursery will send you replacements free of charge with no hassles. The nursery should also guarantee their plants for a year, since roses and other plants that are commonly purchased by mail may be shipped in a dormant state. You won't know if they've survived the trip and the planting for a while. 3. The nursery has the plants you want. Sometimes it is worth trying out a new or rare plant, or one that is borderline for your hardiness zone.

I've never liked the perennial plant known as **hens-n-chicks,** but my new house has a bed filled with them. What should I do?

Many areas have perennial exchanges or plant sales sponsored by local garden clubs. This may provide you with the opportunity to trade them for something else you'd

Hens-n-chicks (*Sempervivum tectorum*) are a ground-hugger that produce offsets at a rapid pace. They can be dug up and replanted elsewhere. (Steven Nikkila/Perennial Favorites)

really like. The usual procedure is to dig up your offering and divide it into pots or flats and identify the plants clearly with a tag. If the plant is diseased or insect ridden, just get rid of it. Other gardeners don't want or need this. As long as the plants are in good shape, you might try offering them to neighbors and friends as well. Backyard perennial giveaways are a time honored tradition. Finally, if you can't find a home for these happily spreading succulents, you can compost them.

What does the phrase **"right plant, right place"** mean?

"Right plant, right place" means selecting a plant that will thrive in the conditions of the site you will be planting it in, with little intervention other than water and food. The key word here is *thrive!* While this may sound simple, most gardeners are guilty of falling in love with a plant that doesn't quite suit his or her yard. While in some cases the plant will rally or adjust, many times the plant will just fail to thrive and fall prey to insects or disease. The best practice is to determine your site conditions (sun, wind, moisture level, pH level, and soil texture) and choose from plants that thrive in those conditions.

PREPARING THE SOIL AND PLANTING

The directions on my seed packet tell me that the peas I've purchased can be planted "as soon as the soil can be worked." How can I tell when the soil is ready to be worked?

The soil is ready for planting if no water comes out when you pick up a handful of soil and squeeze it. When you loosen your grip, the soil should still be moist enough to hold together. If you poke at the clod of soil, it should break apart into smaller clods. If you have clay soil and work the ground too early, your soil will harden and remain compacted the rest of the season. If you have sandy soil and plant when it is too dry, the soil won't be moist enough to germinate direct-seeded plants or hold newly planted seedlings.

How does the soil temperature affect the growth of plants?

If soil is too cold, most seeds will not germinate. Cold soil also impedes a plant's ability to absorb phosphorus, which is crucial for plant growth. A transplant set out in cold soil can be stopped or set back in its growth just when it should be growing rapidly. The freezing and thawing of soil can help improve the texture of clay soil by breaking it down further, which makes it easier for plants to absorb water and nutrients and expand their root systems. In sandy soil, however, the same freezing and thawing can uproot plants.

When is the best time of year to prepare a new bed?

Fall is the best time of year to prepare a new bed. While inspiration may strike in the spring, there are too many other things to do at that busy time of year. A carefully considered bed in the fall can also "dig itself" by using the no-dig method described on the next page.

How should sod be removed in an area where a new bed will be planted?

Removing sod is hard work. Decide on the shape of the bed and outline it using a garden hose, spray paint, or, if it is geometric in shape, a line and stakes. Working on your knees can help save your back. Use either a sod cutter (found in good garden tool catalogs) or a sharp spade to slice into the sod not deeper than six inches or so, following the shape of the bed. Then cut a new line 10 to 12 inches inside the bed line and cut the resulting rectangle into manageable pieces. Use the cutter or spade to slice the roots of the turf, attempting to keep as much of the soil in the bed as possible. Then lift the sod rectangle up and out of the bed and into a wheelbarrow. Continue to work your way

> ## I want a new bed in an area where sod is growing.
> ## Is there a "no-dig" method for starting a new bed?
>
> **D**ecide on the location of your new bed and make plans to prepare it in the fall. Mark out the edges of the new bed using a garden hose, spray paint, or a line and stakes. Cover the interior of the bed with a thick layer (three to five inches) of newspapers. Cover the newspaper layer with enough compost (you can add topsoil as well) to keep it from blowing around. Soak the area thoroughly. By the following spring, the newspapers (and sod) should have broken down nicely. Turn the soil over and give it a week or so to warm up. This also allows the seeds of any weeds left in the soil to sprout. Remove these weeds and begin planting!

through the bed in this manner. By starting at the top and inside of the proposed bed and working backward, you can avoid stepping on and compacting the soil underneath. The removed sod can be stacked root-side up in an unused (and preferably unseen) corner of your yard where it will eventually break down into compost.

How do I properly **prepare clay soil** for planting?

Clay soil should be dug in the fall, when the soil is moist but not wet (after a light rain or several days after a heavy downpour). This makes it easier to work with as dry clay soil is as hard as concrete! Turn the clods over, but don't bother to pulverize it. Let the winter do your work for you. In the spring, work organic matter into the soil.

How can I **improve the drainage in my sandy soil** for planting?

Work in as much organic matter as you can manage. Sandy soil loses water very quickly through both evaporation and the nature of the soil. Organic matter helps to improve soil structure and reduces the rate of evaporation. Your best bet is to grow a cover crop, whenever and wherever the bed is bare. Once the crop is ready to be turned over, lightly dig the crop into the top few inches of the soil and let it rest for a few weeks.

The **frost-free date** in my area is still two weeks away, but it's been really warm for a week now. Can I just go ahead and stick my plants in now?

You've got to ask yourself one question: Do you feel lucky? The frost-free date is determined by using an average of the dates of last freezes over previous years. Sometimes

Garden row covers protect plants from cold, drying winds, offer a greenhouse effect, and help warm the soil. (Robert J. Huffman/Field Mark Publications)

the last freeze arrives earlier, sometimes later. But the possibility for cool nights still exists. Even if there isn't a freeze, nighttime temperatures really need to be well established above the 50 degree Fahrenheit mark in order for warm-season crops like tomatoes to thrive. It's also important to remember that while air temperature is one thing, soil temperature is another. Many plants don't grow until the soil has warmed up sufficiently. It's probably best to wait until after the frost-free date to plant.

How can I **protect my vegetable garden** from frost?

In order to minimize the impact frost has on your garden, it is important to site your garden on high ground. Frost and cold air settle into low portions of the landscape (also known as frost pockets). If you are setting your plants out prior to the frost-free date, be sure to use season extenders such as row covers or cloches to protect your plants from frost. You can also use plastic sheeting or newspaper as protection.

After three days, it just stopped raining and the garden is wonderfully wet. Isn't this the best time to add a flat of **impatiens** to my flower bed?

Actually, no. A prime time to spread disease is when the garden is wet. Besides, soggy soil is more difficult and heavy to work with. It's best to wait a day or so to let things dry out before adding impatiens (*Impatiens wallerana*) or any other flowers to your garden.

The **frost-free date** has passed and my garden is dry. Should I just dig a hole and stick my plants in?

Although different plants have different needs in terms of spacing and planting depth, all plants need to be pampered at this time. Once they've been hardened off, plant your plants according to their needs and water thoroughly. Water them every few days until their roots have taken. If they're planted in an area with lots of sun or wind, monitor carefully for leaf scorch and provide a little shelter in the form of row covers, cloches, or other devices if they show any signs of this. Mulch well to retain water around the root system. A kind word or two couldn't hurt either.

A gardener plants some bulbs in his backyard plot. (Robert J. Huffman/Field Mark Publications)

Do I need to remove my home-grown transplants from their **peat pots** before planting them in the garden?

No. This is one of the advantages of peat pots—you don't need to remove the entire peat pot before planting out. However, you do need to tear down the edge of the pot to the soil line. This prevents the rim of the pot from acting like a wick and drying out the pot when it is buried in the ground.

What is **moon planting**?

Some gardeners believe that planting by the position of the moon in the sky aids the growth and health of their plants. This belief has existed for many centuries—alluded

My packet of carrot seeds tells me they need to be thinned after growing a few inches. What does that mean?

Seed that is tiny or has a low rate of germination is usually planted more thickly than needed to make sure enough seedlings come up. Once they're up, seedlings that are too close together or are weaker than other plants need to be removed. To avoid damaging other seedlings in the process, use a small pair of scissors to snip the unwanted seedlings at ground level.

to in both Greek and Roman writings—and continues to be held by many farmers today. While many scientists give little weight to this theory, many modern farmers continue to plant based on the position of the moon by using *The Farmer's Almanac*. In moon planting, plants that bear fruit or edible portions above ground should be planted during a waxing moon. Plants whose roots or tubers are eaten should be planted in the waning moon. In addition, different signs of the zodiac influence planting. For example, any plantings made during Cancer's time should be fruitful since Cancer is a fertile sign.

How deep should I **plant my seedlings**?

A basic rule of thumb is to set seedlings into the soil at the same height as they were growing in their pot. Tomatoes, however, should be placed on their sides and planted in a trench so that the stems will grow roots, providing the weighty fruits with additional support.

What is meant by the term **double digging**?

Double digging is a strenuous method of preparing the soil by digging down about one foot, setting the soil aside, working in organic soil amendments to the sublayer as well as the topsoil, and then replacing the topsoil. While it is considered by some gardeners as a badge of honor, you must be careful to keep the topsoil and subsoil separate and ensure the topsoil remains on top. Otherwise, you may end up with rockier, heavier soil than you had planned.

What does it mean to **broadcast seed**?

Broadcasting seed means scattering the seed from your hand using a kind of sweeping motion over the ground. After broadcasting, you need to rake the soil gently and water using a fine mist or a watering can.

I started my **tomato plants** from seed but I didn't transplant them to larger pots right away so the plants got **too leggy**. Can I still save them?

You can save leggy tomato plants by using a deep-transplanting technique. Dig a small trench, angling one side of it. Strip the plant of its lower leaves and lay it in the trench on the angled side. New roots will grow along the buried stem of the plant. Other plants that take well to this treatment include lettuce and cabbage.

CARE AND FEEDING

WATERING

When is the **best time of day to water** my garden?

The best time to water is in the morning, before the sun is full in the sky. Watering in midday can cause leaf scorch from the sun burning the leaves. Mostly it's just plain inefficient, as the water evaporates quickly before doing its job. Late evening is the worst time to water, as it leaves the foliage damp at night when molds and fungi are most active. However, remember that even watering at the wrong time of day is better than not watering at all.

How can I tell when my **container plant needs watering**?

One somewhat undependable indicator is the plant's leaves. A wilted plant might need water. On the other hand, a slight wilting of plants in the middle of a hot day is a plant's natural reaction to the weather. To be on the safe side, water your plants first thing in the morning. If a plant is wilted then, it most definitely needs watering. A better indicator is to stick your finger into the pot, about one to two inches down. If it feels dry, go ahead and water the plant. You can also purchase moisture-indicator strips. These are placed into the potting mixture and change color when watering is needed. A more expensive option is a moisture meter, which has a probe that's inserted into the potting mixture and indicates when watering is needed.

How can a **tin can** help me to water properly?

Watering rates for plants are frequently expressed in terms of inches of water. For example, both trees and lawns require an inch of water per week and more during hot

61

The term wet feet refers to plants whose roots are immersed in water most of the time. Plants that like their feet wet, such as ferns, river birches (*Betula nigra*), willows (*Salix*), goat's beard (*Aruncus dioicus*), monkshood (*Aconitum* spp.), yellow flag (*Iris pseudacorus*), sweet flag (*Acorus calamus*), blueberries (*Vaccinium*), spice bush (*Lindera benzoin*), witch hazel (*Hamamelis*), sweet woodruff (*Galium odoratum*), and summersweet (*Clethra alnifolia*), can be planted in moist areas. However, since plant roots require oxygen in order to go through the process of respiration, most plants prefer to be in drier conditions.

weather. But how can you determine how long it will take your sprinkler to generate an inch of water? Place empty tuna or soup cans throughout your yard. Keep an eye on the clock and the cans to see how long it takes an inch of water to accumulate in the cans. Whether you're watering flowers, vegetables, or lawn, you can use this information to ensure your garden is receiving enough water, without wasting it.

Which kind of soil requires the **most frequent watering**?

While water soaks into sandy soil very quickly, it also drains quickly. If you have sandy soil, you will need to water frequently. Clay, on the other hand, takes forever to absorb water. However, once this happens, it is very slow to drain away. So while you may water plants in clay soil less frequently, if you have a soaking rain, your plants can fall prey to wet feet.

I live in an area where drought and water shortages are common. What are some methods of **water conservation** in the garden?

A major source of heavy water usage is the all-American traditional lawn. By reducing the size of your lawn and switching to a more drought-resistant grass or groundcover, you can drastically reduce the amount of water you use. Selecting drought-resistant native plants and mulching all plantings ensures that the plants you have stay healthy and good-looking. Using a drip irrigation system to water your garden will maximize the impact of the watering you do. You can also conserve water by watering deeply and less frequently and spacing plants closer together in your vegetable garden.

An example of a typical watering can. (Robert J. Huffman/Field Mark Publications)

What are the advantages of a **drip irrigation system**?

Drip irrigation uses low water pressure to move water through pipes to precise points in your garden. It delivers water where the plants need it—directly to their root zone. Water isn't wasted in runoff or evaporation. Less water at the surface also means drier soil with less likelihood of weeds taking root. Soil doesn't erode as quickly and plants stay free of diseases caused by soil and water splashing onto their leaves. Nutrients stay put, rather than leaching out of the soil. Plants also appreciate the regular attention—they aren't stressed by over- or underwatering. Finally, for busy gardeners, drip irrigation systems save time and effort spent moving hoses and monitoring water uptake. While they are expensive to purchase and install, drip irrigation reduces water and energy costs over the long run.

What is a **soaker hose**?

A soaker or weeper hose is a hose made from old tires, canvas, or plastic that oozes or weeps water through tiny holes or pores along its length. Like a drip irrigation system, it conserves water because it is aimed directly at a plant's root zone. However, these hoses don't have the precision of a drip irrigation system and so are best reserved for long beds of plants.

What is a **sprinkler hose**?

A sprinkler hose is a flat hose with little holes spaced along its length. It works differently from a soaker hose because it actually sprinkles water out, rather than weeps. It works well for watering flower beds or narrow stretches of lawn where a regular sprinkler would waste water. Unfortunately, since the water droplets are smaller than those in a sprinkler, the water tends to evaporate more quickly. It also has an annoying tendency to kink or flip when used in any length other than a straight line.

What are the advantages of using a **water wand**?

A water wand is the latest tool in the gadgety world of watering devices. It doesn't pack the punch of the traditional pistol-style hand-held sprinkler. And that's the point: The water wand disperses the water in a gentle manner, enabling the gardener to aim a soft rain at the plant's root system. This keeps leaves dry and splash-back to a minimum.

Can I use my **sprinkler to water** my vegetable garden?

You can, but it's really not recommended. Plants absorb most of their water through their roots. Water from sprinklers mostly hits the foliage, which can encourage disease and mold, along with being inefficient. A better, though labor-intensive, method

Are there any kinds of plants that don't need frequent watering?

There are a number of plants—from lamb's ear (*Stachys byzantina*) to cactus—that will tolerate some drought. Drought-tolerant plants tend to have one or more of the following characteristics that enable them to survive with less water. Plants with smaller leaves tend to require less water than those with larger leaves. Plants with gray or fuzzy foliage tend to retain water better than others. Low-growing or mat-forming plants are not affected by drying winds. Herbs and other scented plants produce an aromatic oil that prevents them from drying out.

is to water plants individually using a cup and a pail. Soaker hoses and drip irrigation systems are other options. Sprinklers work best for lawns. If you must sprinkle your vegetables, try to do so in the morning, before the sun is full in the sky, in order to maximize the effect of the water. Avoid evening sprinkling, which leaves foliage wet and ripe for disaster.

Do I still need to water my plants when there is a **heavy dew** on the ground in the morning?

Yes, you still need to water on mornings when there is a heavy dew on the ground. Morning dew is actually the end product of a plant's transpiration (see related question in Plant and Soil Science chapter). While dew may seem to perk up plants, it is just a plant's way of giving back water to the atmosphere. Plants need additional water to continue the cycle.

FERTILIZING

What does it mean when a plant has been **burned by fertilizer**?

Salts found in fertilizer can cause a lawn or favorite plant to look burned. This is caused by the application of too much fertilizer or by using the fertilizer in a manner inconsistent with the packaging (not watering it in). The salts in the fertilizer are so concentrated they actually extract the water from the plant's cells, causing the plant to dry out. The result looks as if the plant has been burned.

What are some organic sources of nitrogen?

Some organic sources of nitrogen include compost, manure, dried blood, cottonseed meal, cocoa bean or peanut shells, and bonemeal. These can be applied as a top-dressing or used in the planting hole for those plants that are heavy feeders, depleting the nitrogen levels within the soil. However, the nitrogen content of soil is a tricky thing. It can vary on a daily basis, depending on plant uptake of the available nitrogen. A better approach is to add organic matter such as compost, dried weeds, grass clippings, and other plant material directly to the soil, which will add nitrogen to the soil as well as improve its humus content.

When should **plants be fertilized**?

While different kinds of plants require different fertilizer timing, there are some general rules for fertilizing. Plants need fertilizer during periods of active growth. Therefore, when a plant's buds are opening in the spring, they should be fertilized. During the growing season, a plant should be fertilized when it appears to be slowing in its growth or if growth appears to be weak. During very hot or very cold weather such as during the summer or winter months, plants can become dormant and don't need to be fed. They don't even need to be fed in the fall, since this would spur them to keep growing when it's time for them to slow down in preparation for dormancy.

What is an **organic fertilizer**?

Technically speaking, an organic fertilizer contains the element carbon. More commonly, however, an organic fertilizer is made from once-living organisms.

What are some **organic fertilizers** and their uses?

Bonemeal is high in nitrogen and commonly used when planting tulips and other bulbs. Cottonseed meal is also high in nitrogen but is very acidic and should only be used on plants that thrive in acid soil, such as rhododendron and azalea (both *Rhododendron* spp.), heather (*Calluna* and *Erica* spp.), dog's tooth violet or trout lily (*Erythronium* spp.), primrose (*Primula vulgaris*), Russell lupine (*Lupinus* 'Russell Hybrids'), and camellia (*Camellia* spp.). Cattle and chicken manure in large amounts are good sources of nitrogen but should be composted first. Fish scrap is another good source of nitrogen and is also high in phosphorus. Although fish emulsion is commonly sold as fertilizer, it is relatively weak in nutrients.

What is a foliar fertilizer?

A foliar fertilizer is a fertilizer applied to a plant's leaves. Plants absorb nutrients and water through their root hairs and their leaf pores. If a plant is unable to absorb nutrients through its roots due to compacted soil or stress, foliar fertilizing may be a good alternative. Foliar fertilizers can perk up fast-growing plants and some are thought to work as catalysts in plants, increasing their uptake of nutrients through their roots. Some organic foliar fertilizers include fish emulsion, compost tea, and seaweed extract.

What are some **organic sources of phosphorous**?

The phosphorous content of soil is much more stable than nitrogen. A good soil test should help you determine the level of phosphorous in your soil. Some organic sources of phosphorous include phosphate rock, bonemeal, dried blood, and cotton-seed meal. The most frequently used source of phosphorous for the home gardener is bonemeal, which has a phosphorous content of over 20 percent. However, it decomposes fairly slowly so is best used for plants like tulips or crocuses whose bulbs take in their nutrients over a longer period of time.

What are some **organic sources of potassium**?

Potassium or potash can be found in natural mineral sources like greensand and granite dust. It also makes up 6 to 10 percent of wood ash. If you have a fireplace or can have bonfires on your property, wood ashes would be an easily available source of potassium. If you live close to the ocean, seaweed and seaweed extract can also be used to increase potassium levels. While the potassium is not available for plant uptake until the seaweed decomposes, this occurs fairly quickly. Finally, manures and compost as well as hay and leaves have a small percentage of potassium.

What is **green manure**?

A green manure or cover crop is a crop that is sown for the purpose of being turned under to enrich the soil. A cover crop also prevents weed seeds from taking root and soil from eroding.

When do I **turn my cover crop under**?

Most cover crops should be turned under before they're six inches tall. Once they're taller than that, or worse yet, have gone to seed, they're harder to work into the soil.

You can mow the crop with a mulching mower first if you'd like to chop up the green matter more thoroughly.

COMPOSTING

What is **compost**?

Simply put, compost is what's left after garden debris and vegetative material decay to a state that is similar to soil. The result is a rich organic material. Although it depends on the material that has decomposed, compost from yard waste tends to have a pH of between 7.5 to 8.5. The level of macro- and micronutrients in compost also varies, but the nitrogen level tends to be low.

My neighborhood offers curbside pickup of leaves and grass clippings, and my kitchen is equipped with a garbage disposal. Why should I bother with **composting**?

There are two main reasons to set aside those modern conveniences and build a compost pile: what it can do for the earth, and what it can do for you. A large percentage of curbside waste is compostable organic matter, and the landfills where this material goes are filling up at an alarming rate. Rather than disposing of things like leaves, grass clippings, and kitchen waste, why not recycle them and conserve all the plant nutrients they contain? At the most basic level, composting is a responsible and efficient way to manage your home and garden. It allows you not only to return something to the earth, but to create a valuable product to improve your garden or landscape. Compost improves soil texture and structure, helping it to retain nutrients and moisture and improve its aeration. It also moderates the pH levels of soil and helps control weeds, reducing the need to purchase expensive soil improvements, fertilizers, and pesticides. For the little bit of effort that composting requires, you get a healthy garden and a lot of satisfaction.

What sorts of materials make **good compost**? Is there anything I shouldn't put in my compost pile?

Just about anything organic will decompose eventually in a compost pile, but what goes into a pile does affect the quality of what comes out. The key is to use a wide variety of materials in order to encourage quick and complete breakdown and to create a finished product with high nutrient value. Some common compostable materials include grass clippings (but not those treated with chemical fertilizers or weed killers), flowers and other garden refuse (but be careful of weeds that have gone to seed and diseased plants), dead leaves, manure (but not human or pet waste, which can contain organisms that cause disease), hair—both human (unless chemically treated) and animal, feathers, sawdust, straw, corn stalks, soil, shredded paper, wood ashes, dried blood, and bonemeal. Kitchen waste—including fruit and vegetable peelings, eggshells, bread products, coffee grounds and filters, and tea grounds and leaves—is another important source of compostable materials. When adding kitchen scraps, be sure to chop or shred large pieces, mix them into the pile well, and add sawdust, leaves, or another dry, brown material to offset their moisture. There are also a number of things that you should avoid putting in your compost pile. Don't use dairy products, meat or fish, fatty foods, or bones because they are hard to break down and may attract critters. It is also best to avoid using cat litter, charcoal briquets, and coal ashes because they are often chemically treated. Finally, never compost anything that may have been treated with a chemical pesticide or herbicide.

What goes on **inside a compost pile**?

Some people are a bit squeamish about the decomposition process. It may be helpful to know a bit more about the intricate community of organisms that convert complex compostable materials into a useable form for plants. Decomposition occurs in a compost pile thanks to microorganisms (invisible things like bacteria and fungi) and macroorganisms (visible things like earthworms and insects) that break down organic materials to release the nutrients plants need. Several types of bacteria participate in the decomposition process. Aerobes are an efficient type of bacteria that handle decomposition when plenty of oxygen is available (this process is known as aerobic decomposition). Another, less efficient type called anaerobes take over when not enough oxygen is available (this process, which is much slower, is known as anaerobic decomposition).

Different types of bacteria also prefer different temperature ranges. The first wave of aerobic bacteria to hit a new compost pile, psychrophiles, prefer cooler temperatures—down to 28 degrees Fahrenheit. They break down carbon materials and release nutrients and heat. As the pile begins to heat up, another type of bacteria called mesophiles take over. The mesophiles like temperatures of 70 to 90 degrees, but as they continue the work of decomposition they release even more heat. When the temperature of a pile reaches around 100 degrees, a type of bacteria known as thermophiles take over. Thermophiles maintain a high level of activity and may raise temperatures up to 160 degrees Fahrenheit for a time. All these types of bacteria also release enzymes that continue to aid in the breakdown of organic materials long after the bacteria have died.

There are also a variety of fungi at work during the composting process. Their main job is to break down cellulose and lignin—the tough materials in woody stems

A compost pile with a healthy supply of red earthworms to aid in decomposition. (Robert J. Huffman/Field Mark Publications)

and paper. Macroorganisms—visible creatures like earthworms, mites, grubs, centipedes, snails, spiders, beetles, ants, and flies—are another important component of decomposition. These critters mainly chew, digest, and mix compost materials to make the work of bacteria and fungi easier. Sometimes they eat each other or bacteria and fungi. Earthworms are particularly important in an efficient composting system because they do a lot of the preliminary digesting for bacteria, munching their way through the pile and producing fertile excrement known as castings. Overall, decomposition is the most natural of processes, and all of these creatures are simply links in the chain of life.

What are **brown and green materials**? What proportion of each should I put in my compost pile?

The microorganisms that control the decomposition process need both carbon and nitrogen—as well as air and moisture—in order to do their work. Materials that provide high levels of carbon are known as brown materials because they are generally brown, dry, coarse, and bulky. These materials include dried leaves, wood chips, sawdust, and cornstalks. Carbonaceous materials give mass to a compost pile, aid in aeration, and provide energy to microorganisms. Materials that provide high levels of nitrogen are known as green materials because they are generally green, moist, and dense. These materials include grass clippings, fresh garden weeds, manure, and bloodmeal. Nitrogenous materials mainly aid in the reproduction and growth of microorganisms. Ideally, composters should aim for a ratio of brown to green materials between 25:1 and 30:1. Some common compostable materials—such as clover, food scraps, and manure mixed with bedding—will already have a ratio near the ideal range. At any rate, there is no need to take precise measurements, because piles with very different ratios will decompose eventually.

What's the difference between **hot composting and cold composting**?

The many different methods of composting can be placed on a continuum from hot (fast) to cold (slow). The best method of composting depends upon the space you have available, your need for compost, the amount of time and energy you're willing to

An example of hot composting at 150 degrees Fahrenheit. (Robert J. Huffman/Field Mark Publications)

commit to the project, and the sort of equipment and compostable materials you have on hand. Hot composting methods require more effort and attention but also produce finished compost quickly—generally in less than eight weeks. But in order to maintain the temperatures needed for fast decomposition to occur (113 to 158 degrees Fahrenheit), you must provide the right combination of brown and green materials, control moisture carefully, and aerate frequently. Hot composting methods are recommended for those who have a large garden or a strong need to improve their soil conditions. Cold composting methods are considerably less trouble but also produce finished compost slowly—generally in six months to two years. Cold piles require little maintenance and allow you to add materials a little at a time. However, due to the low temperatures, they may also allow weed seeds to survive and later sprout in your garden. Cold composting methods are recommended for those who have lots of room for composting but little time to spend.

Are there any advantages to shredding or chopping up **bulky plant material** before adding it to the compost pile?

By shredding small branches and woody plant material before adding them to the compost pile, you speed up the process of decomposition. If you have a great deal of wood or bulky plant material in your compost pile and are using the cold method of composition, you can wait over a year for those materials to break down. Even in a hot

71

pile, remnants of thicker branches and especially stringy stems may remain. It is better to reduce these materials before you even place them in the pile. The same goes for kitchen scraps, such as fruit and vegetables, that have started their decomposition process in your fridge.

I've had a **compost pile** going for a couple of months now and nothing seems to be happening. Why not?

With the right combination of materials, your pile should begin to heat up and show signs of decomposition within a few weeks. If your pile is just sitting there, with all the materials you've added still intact, there are several possible causes. For example, it may be too dry. Microorganisms require evenly moist, but not really wet, conditions to do their best work. If this seems to be the problem with your pile, poke holes in several locations, insert a garden hose, and water. If the moisture level seems okay, the problem may be a lack of nitrogen. Try mixing in green materials such as grass clippings, fresh manure, or bloodmeal to get things started. Another way to speed up the process is to add oxygen to the pile by turning it with a pitchfork. Finally, if nothing else seems to work, your pile may simply be too small to maintain heat effectively. Gather more materials until it reaches dimensions of at least one cubic yard.

My **compost pile smells bad**. What's the problem?

A good compost pile, even in its early stages of decomposition, should smell mildly earthy. An unpleasant odor emanating from a compost heap usually indicates some sort of imbalance. For example, an ammonia smell means that the pile is too heavy on nitrogen (green) materials. To correct the problem, add carbon (brown) materials such as leaves or wood chips and aerate the pile with a pitchfork. Another common cause of odor is a lack of oxygen, either due to compaction of the pile or excess moisture (ideally, a compost pile should be about as moist as a damp sponge). If your pile is a wet, clumpy mass, add carbon materials and aerate. To prevent unpleasant smells in the first place, aerate your pile on a weekly basis and remember that too much of any one material is never a good thing when it comes to composting.

How do I know when my **compost is finished**?

Finished compost should appear dark and crumbly, with no large, readily identifiable chunks of the original source materials left over (although traces of fibrous materials, like straw, are okay as long as they can be easily crushed between your fingers). The consistency will usually be a bit more porous and fluffy than regular dirt. Finished compost should also smell rich and earthy rather than moldy or rotten. When compost is ready to be used, the temperature of the pile should be the same as the air around it. If the middle is still warm, more decomposition time is needed.

What is compost tea?

It is definitely not something to be consumed in the afternoon with scones, but rather an easy, organic alternative to chemical fertilizers and pesticides. Compost tea can be used to give a quick fix to unhealthy plants, to promote growth of transplants or seedlings, or even to help get a new compost pile started. For a small batch, put equal parts finished compost and water into a watering can, stir, and let the mixture sit for a day or so. For a larger batch, place compost in a burlap bag or old pillowcase, tie it at the top, and suspend it in a large bucket or barrel full of water for a week or so. The resulting nutrient-rich, tea-colored liquid can be poured on the roots of plants as a fertilizer or sprayed on leaves to discourage pests, mold, and mildew. Use the same compost for a few batches of tea, then return it to the compost pile or dig it into the garden (it will still have value because not all nutrients in compost are water soluble). The same methods can also be used to make manure tea or weed tea, which are similarly high in nutrients.

What types of **bins or containers** are used for composting?

Although nature eventually will take its course when compostable materials are just dumped into a pile on the ground, many people choose to contain their compost to give it a more aesthetic appearance, to conserve space, or to speed decomposition. Compost containers range from simple enclosures of chicken wire to elaborate, three-bin wood structures. Perhaps the simplest container to make is a circular pen of woven-wire fencing. You just fasten the two ends of the fencing together to form an upright cylinder large enough to hold the compost heap. Then add compost materials in layers almost to the top of the fencing and drive a stake into the middle to help maintain the shape of the pile and direct water into its center. Whenever the pile needs turning, simply disassemble the enclosure, reassemble it a few feet away, and shovel the compost back in. Similar pens can be made by attaching chicken wire to a rectangular series of wooden tomato stakes placed about one foot apart. Although wire pens are slightly less attractive and create finished compost more slowly than some other containers, they are affordable and allow for good air circulation.

A more permanent type of compost container is a bin made of wood, plastic, or concrete. One well-known version is a Lehigh bin, made of alternating horizontal two-by-fours held together by vertical three-eighths-inch rods through the corners. Lehigh-style bins are attractive, portable, adjustable, and allow for good ventilation. Another common type of bin is a chimneylike structure made of stacked cinder blocks or bricks. In most cases, the blocks are stacked with some space between them to allow for air circulation, and they are not mortared together so they can be moved if

What is sheet composting?

Sheet composting is the practice of spreading raw organic material over a field or plot and allowing it to decay before the next crop is planted. The material is spread evenly over the area and then worked into the top few inches of the soil, allowing air to reach the decaying material. This can be impractical for the home gardener since it can take the area out of "active production" for several months while the material breaks down. However, by applying material in the fall, you allow the material to decompose at a time when the garden is inactive (not always true in the warm zones, however). Spreading shredded leaves in a thin layer over your garden is an excellent example of this. Green manure or cover crops are also methods of sheet composting.

needed. Other simple, inexpensive compost containers can be made using shipping pallets, wooden snow fencing, prefabricated picket fence sections, or even old window screens assembled into a square around fence posts. Smaller composting systems can be created out of a metal garbage can or 55-gallon drum. A wide variety of commercial compost containers are also available. The best type of compost container to use depends upon the space and materials you have available, your need to protect the pile from critters or hide it from irritable neighbors, and your personal preference.

Why doesn't my compost look anything like the **lovely compost** made by my county waste authority?

Municipal or commercially made compost is a truly beautiful thing. Its rich brown color and fine texture make you think you're looking at topsoil. The secret is that, unlike your backyard "cold pile," commercial compost goes through several stages of decomposition at very high temperatures. At the end, the finished compost is then screened. This filters out the larger chunks of not-quite-decomposed compost, creating the lovely loamy stuff you can pile into the back of your pickup every spring.

I'd like to use the compost my city makes from the yard waste of city residents but I'm concerned because my neighbor uses **pesticides**. Should I be?

Current research on the topic seems to suggest that most pesticides used in backyards break down during the composting process. Many municipal composters also test their compost on an infrequent basis to determine the pesticide level, if any. Check with your city or county waste authority to see if they have recent results.

Compost can be kept in many different kinds of containers. (Robert J. Huffman/Field Mark Publications)

We're having another cold winter and it looks like my **compost pile is frozen**. What can I do next year to prevent this?

The microbes that do the job of composting for you stop working when the temperature drops below 40 degrees Fahrenheit. If you want to keep your pile going over the winter, make sure that it is large enough (at least four feet high, four feet wide, and four feet deep) and that it has enough green materials (nitrogen fodder) and water to keep it going. You should also consider turning the pile less frequently over the winter in order to keep the center of the pile as warm as possible.

My neighbors have been complaining about the **critters near my compost pile**. What am I doing wrong?

Critters aren't normally attracted to a properly built compost pile, but they may be attracted to any kitchen waste on top. Eggshells can be particularly appealing, and for best results should be crushed before being added to the pile. After placing any kitchen materials onto a pile, be sure to cover them up with a layer of brown or carbon materials such as leaves. Turning the pile regularly should keep the critters away as well.

WEEDING

What is a **weed**?

A common definition of a weed is a plant that is in the wrong place.

If I'm only going to **weed once a season**, when is the best time to do it?

Weeding done during the first few weeks of spring when the weeds are still small will help keep them down all season. Don't forget to attack the areas surrounding your garden or beds too. Ideally, however, weeding should be done at least weekly to keep on top of unwanted plants.

What are some methods of **weed prevention**?

By spacing plants closer together, you eliminate space where weeds can land and limit the amount of sunlight existing weed seeds may receive. Using mulch also keeps weeds from taking root in the soil and can smother any weeds that already exist in the bed. Plastic, metal, or wood edgings around your beds help prevent grass and other weeds from taking root in your garden.

What are some **perennial weeds**?

Perennial weeds include dandelion (*Taraxacum officinale*), bindweed (*Convolvulus arveosis*), burdock (*Arctium*), goldenrod (*Soldiago* spp.), ground ivy (*Glechoma hederacea*), poison ivy (*Rhus radicana*), bentgrass (*Agrostis tenuis*), quack or couch grass (*Agropyron repens*), smoot bromegrass, timothy (*Phleum pratense*), tall fescue, zoysia grass, bermuda grass (*Cynodon dactylon*), creeping bellflower (*Campanula rampunculoides*), plantain (*plantago major*), stinging nettle (*Urtica dioica*), wild strawberry (*Fragaria vesca*), and wild garlic (*Allium vineale*). Perennial weeds are usually more difficult to pry from the ground due to their stubborn root systems or sneaky reproduction. A mature dandelion's taproot runs deep and has a tendency to snap if not dug to the bottom. Quack or couch grass spreads via stolons and by seed, making it difficult to eradicate. Ground ivy creeps through your grass and garden by sending off runners.

When is the **best time to pull perennial weeds**?

Since most perennial weeds have a taproot, they are difficult to pull when the soil is dry. The taproot has an annoying tendency to snap in two, leaving you with a weed in your hand and its healthy root left in the soil where it will come back to haunt you.

Instead, head out to your garden the day after a rain. The plants will be dry (and you won't risk spreading disease) but the ground will still be moist. Those persnickety taproots will soon give in to your persistent tugging.

What are some **annual weeds**?

Chickweed (*Stellaria media*), crabgrass (*Digitaria* spp.), jewelweed or snapweed, lamb's quarters (*Chenopodium album*), ragweed (*Ambrosia artemisiifolia*), and shepherd's purse (*Capsella bursa-pastoris*) are some annual weeds. Annual weeds are usually easier to pull from the ground since they have shallower root systems. However, many of them go to seed quickly in order to increase their numbers. Try to nab these unwanted plants before that happens and you'll save time later.

A weed is a plant that is in the wrong place. (Steven Nikkila/Perennial Favorites)

Why should I bother **pulling up annual weeds in the fall** since they're just going to die anyway?

That's just it—the annual weeds will die but their progeny will live on! The decreasing amount of daylight in the fall is a signal to annual plants to set seed before the frost hits. By removing the annual weeds before they seed themselves, you deny their offspring the opportunity to plague your garden next year. You also turn up any weed seeds (and insects, for that matter) that are lying in wait in the soil for the wonderful warmth of spring. By tilling in the fall, these pests can be brought to the surface for a frosty death.

> ### Can the weeds I pull up be used as mulch—
> ### laid back on the soil to decompose?
>
> **Y**es and no. If it is a dry, sunny day and the weeds you have pulled don't have any seedheads, go ahead and leave them on the ground as mulch or to be tilled back into the ground eventually. However, if it is a cool and cloudy day or an out-and-out rainy day, don't leave your weeds on the ground—they're liable to slide their freshly pulled roots right back into that nice, moist soil. If the weeds have seedheads, you should have pulled them by now. You can redeem yourself by pitching any remainders rather than leaving them lying on the bed.

How can **precise watering and fertilizing** reduce the amount of weeding I have to do?

Weeds are like any other plant—they need water and nutrients to survive. If you use a sprinkler to water your garden, you are also sprinkling the weeds and enabling them to live a little longer. By watering your plants at their roots using a watering can, a drip irrigation system, or a slow-dripping hose, you conserve water and deny that excess water to your plant's weedy neighbors. And by fertilizing your plants just when they need it, you eliminate the possibility of excess nutrients hanging around in the soil waiting for a weed to walk in.

What can I use to get rid of the **weeds in the cracks** of my sidewalk?

Weeds in these places are among the toughest to get rid of. They can be impossible to pull. Try using hot water! By soaking a weed with hot water (vinegar works too), you break down the plant's cell walls, which cause it to die or become severely weakened. Unfortunately, this technique isn't selective—it will kill your favorite flower as well— so use it only in isolated areas.

MULCHING

What is **mulch**?

Mulch is any material laid around the crown and root system of a plant in order to retain moisture around the roots and prevent weeds from forming. Mulching materials range from cocoa hulls or pea gravel to white rocks and black plastic.

What is the **purpose of mulch**?

Mulch keeps weeds down by preventing weed seeds from taking root in the soil and blocking existing weeds from light and air. It also retains water, keeping plant crowns and roots moist. Mulch reduces soil erosion and compaction by protecting the soil from water runoff and the effects of weather. From a design point of view, mulch improves your garden's appearance by providing texture and a uniform backdrop for your plantings. Organic mulches also improve the soil as they decay

What are some **organic mulches** I can use?

Compost, grass clippings, shredded leaves, shredded cocoa hulls, pine needles, straw, and shredded wood or bark chips all make fine organic mulches.

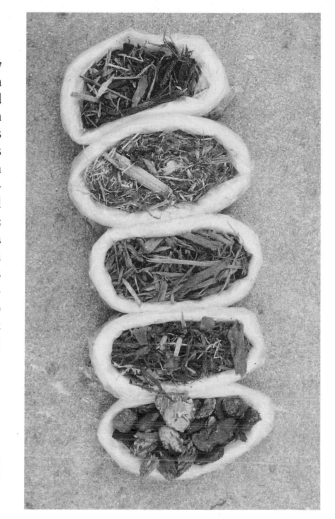

Mulches conserve moisture, hold down weeds, and, as they break down, improve the soil. Available through landscaping suppliers, mulch can be made from a variety of materials—hay, bean hulls, grass clippings, stone, or, as pictured here, tree bark or ground pallets. (Robert J. Huffman/Field Mark Publications)

I used **grass clippings** to mulch my vegetable garden but it began to smell quite nasty. How can I avoid this in the future?

Grass clippings provide a good source of mulch, if you are not already mowing your clippings back into your lawn. Used on your vegetable and flower beds, grass clippings should be spread thinly and allowed to dry somewhat before being used so that they are not decomposing on your beds. Don't use lawn clippings that have been treated with herbicides for at least a month and a half since they have been sprayed. Otherwise, the herbicides may begin to work their black magic on your garden.

79

Decomposed grass clippings are a good source for mulching vegetable and flower beds. (Robert J. Huffman/Field Mark Publications)

What are the benefits of using **compost as a mulch**?

Compost biodegrades over time and adds humus to the soil. It fertilizes at the same time that it suppresses weeds, and actually warms the soil. It should be applied when you plant your garden and periodically throughout the growing season to feed and mulch your plants.

Is it safe to use **newspaper as a mulch**?

Most newspapers today use soy-based, biodegradable inks and solvents as opposed to the metallic inks and toxic solvents of the previous generation. Therefore, they tend to be safe. You might consider soaking the paper first and placing another type of mulch on top in order to keep it in place, however.

I just love the use of **black plastic covered in white rock** as a mulch! Is there any place I can't use it?

Black plastic can be very effective as a mulch as it heats up quickly and provides a barrier to weeds. Although it retains any soil moisture, it also prevents any rainwater from getting in, forcing the gardener to use either a drip irrigation system or to place a hose underneath it to bring water to plant roots. You can slice holes in the plastic in addition to your planting holes, but this does defeat its purpose as a weed barrier

I noticed that the mulch around my tree has become moldy. Is this harmful to the tree in any way?

Mold can sometimes form on mulch that is in a moist, shady area of a yard. But it doesn't harm the tree at all—it just means the mulch is starting to decompose. To get rid of the mold, just turn the mulch over so that it is properly aerated.

somewhat. In places where water conservation is required or needed, it might be wise to think twice about using black plastic.

Also, black plastic should not be used under shrubs and trees. Since moisture (and air) are unable to penetrate the plastic, plant roots grow close to the surface in order to find water and oxygen. Roots are then exposed to extremes in temperature brought on by the plastic or can become girdled, causing the plants to decline and eventually die.

What are some disadvantages to using **peat moss as a mulch**?

Peat moss is lovely to look at and, when wet, retains an enormous amount of water. When mixed with soil or compost, peat gives the soil mix a boost due to this water-holding capability. However, as a mulch, this is a liability. When peat moss dries out, it forms a hard crust on the ground. This prevents rain from penetrating the soil underneath—not the ideal characteristic for a good mulch. On top of that, peat moss is fairly expensive—making it impractical to be used on large areas.

I live in North Carolina and have heard of using **tobacco stems as mulch**. Are there any problems associated with this?

Tobacco stems can provide an additional source of compost to the soil and may help in repelling rodents and many insects. However, tobacco needs to be cured or weathered prior to its use as a mulch since it gives off an offensive odor as it decomposes. It should also be used with care on the vegetable garden since the tobacco may be a carrier of tobacco mosaic, which can affect tomatoes and other plants.

Why do I need to **remove mulch** from my Michigan garden in the fall if I'm only going to put it back on again in a few months?

It is a common belief that mulch keeps plants warm in the winter. However, mulch actually keeps plants cold. You need to remove mulch from your planting bed in order

81

to allow the ground to freeze. Once that has occurred, place the mulch back onto the bed. This prevents the ground from thawing and freezing, which can heave tender plant roots out of the soil, exposing them to damaging frigid air.

GARDEN TOOLS

What are some things to consider when **purchasing a hose**?

A good garden hose can last you a lifetime. But not all hoses are alike! The most obvious difference between a plastic garden hose and a rubber garden hose is in price. A good rubber garden hose can be fairly expensive, compared to the same length made from plastic. However, rubber garden hoses will last much longer (as long as you take care of them) and are less prone to kinking, creasing, and twisting. They also don't tend to spring leaks as easily as plastic and cheap vinyl hoses. For all hoses, the larger the diameter of the hose, the more water it can send out in a shorter period of time.

What is a **garden cloche**?

No, it's not a trendy garden hat—at least, not worn by the gardener. Garden cloches are small plant coverings that raise the air temperature around a plant or group of plants by trapping the sun's heat. Traditionally, they are lovely bell-shaped glass objects treasured by collectors. But even the ubiquitous Wall O' Waters are modern versions of the cloche. The Wall O' Waters use narrow plastic tubes filled with water to trap the sun's warmth. You can make your own cloche by cutting the bottom from a plastic milk jug and placing it over the plant (small side up). Be careful to remove or prop up your cloches on sunny or warm days. Otherwise, you might cook your plants.

What is a **dibble**?

A dibble is a tool shaped like a "t" that is used for planting small bulbs or making holes for large seeds. It is more commonly found in England although there are U.S. dibble fans as well.

What is a **homi**?

A homi is a garden gadget adopted from Korea where it has been in use for hundreds of years. *Homi*, loosely translated from Korean, means "little ground spear." It is short-handled, with its blade at a curving right angle to the handle. The narrow and

A garden cloche can act as protection for transplants and seedlings. (Robert J. Huffman/Field Mark Publications)

triangular blade ends in a point that can be used to make holes for planting or to break up soil clods. The flat edges of the blade can be used for weeding, similar to a hoe. When used to dig small holes, the homi's tip is worked into the ground and the tool is pulled back, saving a gardener's wrists from the strain of pushing and lifting.

How does a **spading fork differ from a pitchfork**?

A spading or digging fork has thick, flat tines and is used for loosening soil or prying perennial clumps from the ground. A pitchfork has three or four slender tines, making it useful only for light loads like hay or straw.

What is a **cold frame**?

A cold frame is a small garden structure that, like a garden cloche, uses the sun's warmth to heat plants. They are essentially bottomless boxes with slanted lids made of glass or translucent plastic that normally sit partially underground. A gardener can either place pots inside the cold frame or prepare the soil in the frame for planting. By opening or closing the lid, a gardener regulates the temperature inside the frame. During the heat of the day, the window is opened to vent the frame and ensure seedlings don't burn in the high heat. In the late afternoon, the window is closed to trap the warmth for the cool night ahead. In early spring, cold frames can be used to

83

A homi is a Korean garden tool. (Robert J. Huffman/Field Mark Publications)

start seeds. The combination of warm sun along with slightly cooler temperatures will result in seedlings that are strong and sturdy.

Measure the length and width of your window. This will be the ultimate size of your cold frame. Use concrete blocks or lumber to create a box the length and width of your window. In order to maximize the amount of light coming into the cold frame, the top of it should slant at a 45-degree angle, with the taller side being roughly one-and-a-half feet tall. Secure the window to the taller side of the frame using two hinges to enable the frame to be opened and closed easily. Fasten a rope or chain on one end to the window and the other end to the frame, so that the window doesn't blow open on a windy day. A dowel can be used to prop open the window, allowing air to circulate when temperatures rise in the frame at midday. Place the frame into the hole, packing the backfill around the frame to insulate it from drafts. When you're ready to plant, you can either place several inches of soil over the drainage layer and plant directly in it, or place containers of plants onto the gravel and sand mix.

What is the difference between an **anvil set of pruners and a bypass set of pruners**?

Anvil pruners have just one moving blade that closes against the material being cut. They tend to be inexpensive and readily available at your local garden center. They work for most garden jobs (cutting open a bag of peat, minor pruning) but tend to crush stems, which can be a real problem when you're working on a prized ornamental. Bypass pruners have two moving blades (similar to a pair of scissors) and cut much more cleanly and closely. However, a quality set tends to run around 40 to 50 dollars through mail order (although with the gardening boom, more and more local stores carry them).

What is a **trowel**?

A trowel or hand digger is a short-handled tool with a small blade similar to a long-nosed shovel. It is used to dig small holes, transplant, lift plants, mix soil, weed, and cultivate. In short, it's the one tool you can't live without.

What is the difference between a **spade and a shovel**?

A spade has a fairly flat, rectangular blade, while a shovel has a curved blade that usually ends in a point. A spade is a more precise tool that makes a

Cold frames save gardeners money by allowing them to grow plants from seed where they would otherwise not have a long enough season. (Robert J. Huffman/Field Mark Publications)

clean cut in the earth. It can be used to edge beds, dig up perennials and ornamentals, and divide plants with a large root ball, among other things. A shovel is best for lifting and digging large quantities of soil or manure since the size and curve of the blade allow it to carry more weight, although it can also be used to dig up perennials and ornamentals.

What is a **rototiller** and why would I use one?

A rototiller is a gas-powered machine that has a wheel with triangular blades on it. As a rototiller is pushed or pulled across a planting bed, the blades dig into and turn over

> ## What should I do to prepare my hand tools for winter?
>
> **B**egin by thoroughly cleaning and drying them (something you should do after every use!). Then polish the blades and metal parts of your tools using steel wool and oil them thoroughly to prevent any rust from forming. Place a few drops of lubricating oil on any moving parts and sharpen the blades. Store tools in a dry place.

the soil, or turn under organic matter. The larger ones can also be used to turn under sod. They make quick work of gardens that can take hours to turn by hand. They can be rented from tool rental shops or garden centers or you may choose to purchase one. Some of the newer rototillers have additional blades you can purchase to convert the tiller into an edger or aerator as well.

I've never gardened before. What are the **top ten garden tools** I should have?

Everyone has their favorites but the following items come in handy just about every time you step into your backyard paradise:

Trowel You'll be using this often for tasks ranging from planting bulbs to mixing soil. Be sure to find one you like.

Spade See discussion above.

Pruners See discussion above.

Bucket The large white buckets used by construction workers come in handy during marathon weeding sessions, to haul water to an area, or to sit down on during gardening breaks. You can cart your hand tools around in them too. But you can also use a small bucket normally used for cleaning (of course, you can't sit on it).

Wheelbarrow or garden cart For hauling dirt and compost, moving plants, and major weeding.

The above items are probably the most crucial. The following are helpful, too, depending on where and how you're gardening:

Shovel See discussion above.

Gloves (unless you don't mind getting your hands dirty). You can go expensive and buy the yummy kidskin gloves that will fall apart by the end of the season and don't take kindly to washing, or you can purchase a sturdy canvas or cotton pair and use them as rags (if there's anything left) every month or so. Purchase something heftier if you'll be pruning roses or picky ornamentals.

Watering can Buy one with a simple spout rather than a sprinkling head to aim water at the plant's root system. Useful for containers or your vegetable garden.

Garden hose To get water from your spout to where your garden needs it, of course. Gardening centers often carry mini-hoses that can be attached to a kitchen sink in order to water houseplants or a terrace garden.

Leaf rake If you have leaves that need to be raked, the plastic or rubber ones are less expensive, but sometimes break during overzealous raking on cold days.

Selecting garden tools is a highly personal decision. Experts recommend purchasing the best quality trowel, spade, and pruners that you can afford as you will have them forever and use them constantly.

OTHER MAINTENANCE

Why do plants need to be **staked or supported**?

The most important reason for staking or supporting a plant is to reduce the incidence of disease. Since many diseases are soil borne, keeping plants off the ground can keep them healthier. It also keeps them free and clear of garden pests looking for an easy meal and a place to nap afterward. In the case of vegetables and fruits, staking and supporting plants can increase the amount of fruit grown in an area. Stakes and supports prevent tall or spindly plants from being damaged by wind or rain and, although a matter of opinion, they can improve the appearance of some plants.

What is the **proper method for single-staking** a plant?

Staking needs to occur fairly early in a plant's growth or when the plant is not much taller than six inches. Choose a stake that will be nearly the size as the mature plant— a top-heavy plant staked too short can be worse off than one not staked at all. Place the stake in the ground close to the stem, carefully avoiding the root ball if possible. Loosely tie the plant's stem to the stake, roughly in the shape of a figure eight. As the plant grows, add additional ties every six to eight inches.

What is the proper method for using **multiple stakes** to support a plant?

Following the guidelines listed in the previous question, sink four to six stakes around the circumference of the plant at the early stages of its growth. Tie twine between the stakes to create a rough circle or square around the plant. As the plant grows, continue to add ties every six tio eight inches, weaving the twine across the plant to keep the it supported.

What is a **wire ring support**?

A wire ring support is commonly used to keep heavier, bushy plants like peonies in bounds. They consist of two to three metal rings connected by metal stakes that are pushed into the ground. They need to be inserted into the ground just as the plant is sending out its spring growth, otherwise it is impossible to fit them over the plant without damaging it.

How do I **stake a tomato** plant?

In order to stake a tomato plant, it must be trained to a single stem. When it is still a young transplant, begin by pruning any suckers that appear. A sucker is a sprout that grows between the main plant stem and a leaf axil or "branch." Follow the directions noted previously for single-staking a plant. Tomatoes require a sturdy, tall support: a stake not less than roughly one to two inches in diameter and five feet high. As the plant grows, it will need to be tied to the stake every foot or so. Long strips of fabric used as ties are sturdy enough for the weight of the plant, yet gentle enough to avoid damaging the main stem. Once the plant reaches the top of the stake, pinch back the growing tip.

What is the advantage of **staking a tomato plant over caging one**?

While staked plants can produce fewer tomatoes per plant, they can be planted much more closely which means a higher yield per square foot. Staked plants may also suffer less disease since they receive better air circulation (the plant is more exposed) and fewer insect problems because they have fewer hiding places.

Red clover (*Trifolium pratense*) has a long taproot system and can grow to be one to two feet in height. While some gardeners like to weed it from their beds, it is known for its soil improvement qualities. (Robert J. Huffman/Field Mark Publications)

What are some **garden tasks** that should be done in the spring?

Pruning and planting of trees and shrubs should be done in the spring. Spring is also a good time to divide perennials and plant them. Mulch should be removed from bulbs and perennials in order to allow beds to dry out and to disrupt any insects that have overwintered in your mulch hotel. Apply a fresh layer of mulch before the summer heat kicks in. Early spring is a good time to aerate and reseed the lawn. Finally, give your bulb garden a good once-over and make note of what worked and what didn't for next year. If you need to make changes in terms of color, mark them now before your plant's leaves disappear.

What are some **garden tasks** that should be done in the fall?

Compost all leaves, twigs, and debris in your garden. Remove mulch from beds. Once your beds are bare, dig in soil amendments such as compost or peat. Turn the soil over, digging six inches where beds are empty and more shallowly near perennials and woody ornamentals. The goal is to expose any insects and weed seeds to the cooler temperatures. Let the soil lie for a few weeks then rake it gently again. Apply mulch once the ground has frozen thoroughly. The point of mulch in the winter is not to keep your plants warm but to keep them cold—preventing them from heaving out of the ground or starting new growth before the weather has stabilized. Fall is the best time to prepare new beds—there just isn't enough time in the spring. Fall is also a good time to aerate and reseed the lawn.

What are some **garden tasks** that should be done in the summer?

Some garden tasks that should be done in the summer include pruning spring-blooming shrubs and trees, deadheading and pinching back annuals and perennials, shearing hedges, weeding, watering, harvesting, and planting extra crops for cooler weather. Before you begin harvesting anything, make notes of where you planted your vegetables so that you can rotate your crops the following year.

What are some **garden tasks** that should be done in the winter?

Some garden tasks that should be done in the winter include applying winter mulch once the ground has frozen (but prior to snow if possible), watering (in dry winters), pruning all trees and shrubs except spring-bloomers and "bleeders," brushing heavy snow off tree limbs after a storm, and tamping plants back into their spots if they've heaved out due to freezing and thawing. Finally, on a clear day, walk around your yard and make notes of any bare spots where you could add woody ornamentals with "winter interest." Trees and shrubs with brightly colored stems or bark or that have an unusual shape can perk up lonesome corners of the yard.

I didn't have time to put my garden to bed before winter hit. What should I do in the spring?

Get your running shoes on, you're going to move fast. If you have a dry day before the ground thaws, begin by raking any leaves from your lawn. The grass may look dead in spots but by removing leaves before it begins growing again, you may give it a fighting chance. Next, clear out any remaining plant debris in your beds. Much of it may have begun breaking down in the beds, but place anything still intact in the compost pile. Cut down dead topgrowth on perennials to their crowns to make way for new growth. If the soil has warmed slightly, you might consider sowing a cover crop that will germinate in cool weather. This will act as competition for any weeds that may still be lingering in your neglected soil and can be tilled in to provide a nitrogen boost for spring planting. You'll need to be especially vigilant of any disease or insect infestations—these probably overwintered near or on your plants and so may come out in full force as soon as the warm weather hits.

Dig in some compost or other organic matter into your beds as soon as the soil can be worked. Leave the beds for a few weeks after you've dug them to expose any larvae or overwintering weed seeds to the elements. Once the weed seeds have sprouted, go back in and clear them out before planting anything. It will pay off in the long run. All this, of course, and you still need to do regular spring tasks!

PROBLEMS

FOUR-LEGGED PESTS

How can I figure out what kind of **four-legged pest** I've got?

It takes a bit of sleuthing to determine which animal is responsible for munching on your garden. But by doing so, you can take the proper steps to deter it. You should begin by looking for animal tracks and droppings. When and how the munching was done can also be a clue as to what kind of critter you've got. For example, rabbits usually nibble in the early morning and late afternoon and don't like to leave a leaf untouched. Deer generally feed at dawn and dusk. The leaves they've chewed on have a tell-tale jagged edge. Groundhogs, skunks, and raccoons tend to be a bit sloppy in their work. A call to your local Extension Service office or the consultation of an animal tracking book can help you diagnose your critter once you have these characteristics nailed down (see question in the Gardens, Gardeners, and Gardening chapter for more information on the Cooperative Extension Service).

I live near a woods and a cornfield. It's a beautiful area but there are deer everywhere. I'd like to have a perennial garden. Are there any **plants the deer won't eat**?

While a proper fit depends on the conditions of the area you'd like to plant in (amount of sun received each day, soil pH and texture, your planting region), some plants that deer don't seem to care for include foxglove (*Digitalis purpurea*), blue monkshood (*Aconitum napellus*), Jacob's ladder (*Polemonium caeruleum*), American holly (*Ilex opaca*), barberry (*Berberis* spp.), boxwood (*Buxus* spp.), clematis (*Clematis* spp.), Colorado blue spruce (*Picea pungens*), columbine (*Aquilegia* spp.), lilac (*Syringa vulgaris*), delphinium (*Delphinium* spp.), and iris (*Iris* spp.)

There are various organic and chemical repellants on the market that claim to repel deer by changing the odor or taste of the plants. You can also throw fine netting over the plants although this can quickly become expensive. However, the best way to prevent having deer munch on your beloved plants is to build a tall (10-feet-high) fence around them.

What kinds of garden **plants do deer prefer**?

It depends on the area and just how hungry the deer are. However, deer have been known to have a hankering for arborvitae (*Thuja* spp.), azalea (*Rhododendron* spp.), euonymus (*Euonymus* spp.), hosta (*Hosta* spp.), impatiens (*Impatiens wallerana*), roses (*Rosa* spp.), crabapples (*Malus* spp.) and other fruit trees, and yews (*Taxus* spp.). Be forewarned, however, that if a deer's usual food source has vanished (like vegetation in open fields and wooded areas before housing development) and they're hungry, they'll eat anything voraciously!

Every year I plant bulbs, and every year **squirrels** munch them up before they bloom. What can I do to discourage them?

You can spray a repellant directly on the bulbs or place screening around bulb groups to discourage their digging. You might consider domestic pets to discourage them as well—my dog loves to chase squirrels, although the cats seem less interested.

How can I **keep rabbits out** of my garden?

The best method is to erect a chicken-wire fence around your garden, making sure the mesh is tightly woven to keep rabbits from prying their way in.

I've moved to a house in the country and the neighbor says she can't grow a garden because of the **raccoons**. Is there any way to keep them out?

Raccoons are among the most persistent of the four-legged pests. They will climb fences, nearby trees, and sheds to get at your garden treasures (corn is a favorite). Unfortunately, the best way to keep them out of a garden is to use an electric fence. While this won't harm the cute robbers, it will discourage them from trying again. You will also need to use fiberglass posts, since the raccoons will scale wooden ones.

What's the difference between **a vole and a mole**?

A vole looks similar to a mouse and is active year-round. They will eat anything green and will also attack the base of trees, nibbling away at the bark. You can try wrapping

Red squirrels prefer conifers, with conifer seeds being a favorite food source. They also enjoy cones, nuts, buds, sap, and some mushrooms, but other than nibbling the occasional pine saplings, red squirrels pose little threat to gardeners. Its larger cousin, the fox squirrel, however, is a persistent garden pest. (Robert J. Huffman/Field Mark Publications)

the base of young trees in the winter to discourage this. Although moles create havoc by tunneling under your lawn and garden, they actually eat Japanese beetles and other grubs. If you get rid of your grub problem, you may well get rid of your moles.

I seem to be having a **problem with skunks** in my garden. How can I keep them away?

Skunks sometimes eat garden plants. If this is the case, you might try erecting a chicken-wire fence around your garden. Like moles, skunks also love to munch on grubs. Check your lawn for grubs (see Japanese beetle question later in this chapter) and apply beneficial nematodes (tiny wormlike organisms) if feasible. Once the grubs have left the lawn, the skunks will most likely leave for grubbier pastures.

I'm sure I had a garden yesterday but when I went to check out my lovely carrot crop today, there was **nothing but holes** where the carrots were. What happened?

Sounds like gophers. Gophers love any of the root crops such as carrots, potatoes, radishes, garlic, and onions. They actually work from underground, digging complex networks of tunnels and then pulling down roots and sometimes whole plants for their meals. The best deterrent is a buried fence. Its aboveground height only needs to be around one foot high, but dig down about 18 inches and bend your barrier outward from the garden to foil their digging attempts.

INSECTS

I live in a heavily wooded area in the Midwest and we just received a flier from the county notifying us that they will be **spraying for gypsy moth**. What is the gypsy moth and what will be sprayed?

The gypsy moth is a non-native insect that feeds on the leaves of a number of hardwood trees such as oaks (*Quercus* spp.), aspens (*Populus* spp.), and conifers such as pine (*Pinus* spp.), juniper (*Juniperus* spp.), and spruce (*Picea* spp.). Egg masses (averaging 400–500 eggs per mass) are laid during late summer in protected areas such as woodpiles, underneath loose bark, and even under boat tarps and house eaves. After hatching, the larvae climb trees, dropping threads like spiders in order to be scattered by the wind. Once the larvae find a suitable host, they eat heartily and can defoliate a tree in a matter of days. Gypsy moth is commonly confused with eastern tent caterpillars, which create silken tents in which they lay their eggs. Gypsy moths, however, don't spin webs or tents when they feed.

Gypsy moth defoliation itself does not kill a hardwood tree; it causes stress as the energy a tree uses to generate a new set of leaves weakens it. Conifers, on the other hand, are unable to fully recover from a complete loss of needles and therefore may die as a result.

Slugs are active by night and consume low-lying parts of many crops. They are attracted to stale beer, and will drown in baited saucers. (Robert J. Huffman/Field Mark Publications)

My roses have yellowed, curled leaves and I've seen swarms of tiny, soft-bodied bugs clustered on the rosebuds and new leaves. What are they and how can I get rid of them?

It sounds like you have aphids. These pesky little bugs suck the juice from plants, leaving them a little shriveled and stressed. An easy method of getting rid of them is to knock them from the plants with a strong spray of water from your hose. Keep it up over several days and you should dispel the population. Also, try to make your yard friendly to aphid-eating insects like ladybugs (see Special Gardens chapter).

If your county is heavily infested, it will probably receive aerial sprays of Bacillus thuringiensis (Bt). Bt is a biological pesticide made from a common soil bacteria. It is known to be toxic only to the caterpillars of moths and butterflies, with rare allergic reactions in some humans. While this makes it more selective than other controls, it is still generally only used when the gypsy moth population has grown large enough to be considered a major nuisance. In many heavily forested areas, the population is monitored but not actively combatted with spraying. This is to avoid interfering with a forest's natural defenses and possibly extending the outbreak.

The best thing a homeowner can do to discourage gypsy moths is to keep trees and shrubs well watered and fertilized. A healthy plant almost always withstands outbreaks of disease and insects as it is not already in a weakened state.

My hostas appear to be under siege. They had lovely whole green leaves yesterday but this morning I discovered huge holes had been chewed in them. What should I do?

It sounds like you have slugs. These soft-bodied slimy creatures are the scourge of gardeners with lovely, shady, cool, damp beds and appealing green plants like hostas (*Hostas*). Slugs generally feed at night, leaving telltale holes and sometimes a sticky slug trail in their wake.

Try pulling any mulch back from the crown of the plant about three to four inches. Slugs love to hide in mulch and this will at least lengthen their trip to your plants. If this doesn't keep them away, place saucers of the cheapest beer you can find in the ground so that the lip of the saucer is even with the ground. Slugs will be attracted by the yeast and drown themselves. Diatomaceous earth (made of the crushed bodies of tiny sea creatures) can also be spread around the plants. The slugs will scratch up their bodies as they attempt to scooch over it and will eventually die. Finally, you can also go on slug patrol at night—knocking slugs into a waiting pail of soapy water.

What is a **Japanese beetle**?

A Japanese beetle is a rather pretty-looking beetle with a metallic green body and copper-colored wings. Its larvae spend their winters in your lawn, chewing on grass roots. If their population becomes large enough, you will notice large dead spots in your lawn. As adults, they feast on leaves and flowers, with roses being a favorite delicacy.

In order to get rid of the larvae, you can purchase beneficial nematodes (tiny wormlike organisms) which will burrow into the beetles, releasing bacteria that kills the grubs. You can also choose to pick them off of the affected plants, knocking them into a pail of soapy water.

Are there any plants that **Japanese beetles** won't eat?

In a study performed by a United States Department of Agriculture (USDA) scientist, Japanese beetles seemed to prefer other plants over asparagus, alfalfa (*Medicago sativa*), rhubarb (*Rheum rhaponticum*), and crimson clover (*Trifolium incarnatum*). And while they munched on the silks of corn plants, they tended to leave the foliage alone.

I just transplanted the tender little **pepper plants** that I had grown from seed into my garden. Now they all look like they've been knocked over. What happened?

Cutworms are to blame. These insects live in the soil of your garden waiting for a tender young stem to nibble on, like that of your pepper plants. They feed at night, severing stems below the soil line. The best way to protect young seedlings is to place a barrier around the base of the stem—a collar cut from cardboard works fine.

My lilac bushes have **blotchy leaves** that look almost burned. What's wrong?

Lilac leafminer larvae have infested your lilac (*Syringa vulgaris*), burrowing between the upper and lower leaf surface and eating their way through them. Once they are mature, they will spin webs around the leaves and continue to eat until the leaves have been skeletonized. In order to get rid of them, you need to remove any infested leaves and burn them. Cut the branches back to unaffected areas. Finally, before the larvae matures in midsummer, spray the shrub with an insecticidal soap.

99

Destructive caterpillars of most butterflies and moths can be hand picked from a small garden as part of an integrated pest management system. (Robert J. Huffman/Field Mark Publications)

I noticed a canopy filled with **small caterpillars** turning up on a lot of my trees. What are they?

You have tentworms. These caterpillars are very destructive. They chew holes in the leaves of woody ornamentals, skeletonizing the leaves and even defoliating the tree. Remove the tents carefully now and destroy the tents by burning or smashing them. These worms are also sensitive to the biological pesticide Bt, so if you have access to this, you might consider spraying your trees thoroughly.

I found a **rolly-polly eating my tomatoes**. I thought these bugs were helpful! What happened?

Rolly-pollys (also known as pillbugs) eat decaying plant matter, which makes them quite useful in the garden for taking care of not-quite-fully-composted compost and helping in the general breakdown of organic material in the soil. However, they also sometimes eat fruit if it is lying on the ground. Try to keep your tomatoes staked, to avoid rotting.

What is the difference between a **pillbug and a sowbug**?

Pillbugs and sowbugs look awfully similar. They are both oval-shaped insects with what looks like their own miniature set of armor on their back. Pillbugs (better known

Is scale a bug or a disease?

Scales are insects, though they're known for passing disease on to plants. Some types of scales also excrete honeydew, which can become covered in gray mold. They resemble small oval bumps without legs (they lose them upon maturity), and they suck sap from a plant. They especially love fruit trees, houseplants, and roses. As immature pests (when they have legs), they can be knocked off plants with a hard stream of water. You should also destroy any tree branches affected by scale to keep them from infecting other trees. Ladybugs love to prey on scales so encourage them to drop in on your garden.

in some areas as rolly-pollys) will curl into a ball when touched—their own defense mechanism against predators—while sowbugs can't.

When I brought home my new plant from the nursery and placed it on the table, I noticed a **cloud of tiny-winged insects** flying away from it. What were they?

Unfortunately, they were whiteflies. These pests live outside in the South and in greenhouses up North and are frequently transferred from plant to plant when a new infested plant is introduced to others. They suck the juices from plants, leaving them yellow and dying. With serious infestations, the plant will weaken and die. You can spray infested plants with insecticidal soap but if the plant is new, I would return it to the nursery or compost it.

I've discovered some **prehistoric-looking beetles** with horns on their heads and behinds underneath the mulch in my planting beds. Should I be concerned about my plants?

The insects you've described sound like earwigs. Earwigs are part of the scavenger insect population. They eat dead or decaying plant material and like to hang out in moist, cool areas such as mulched beds or under decks and stones. They've also been known to eat green plant material, but their innate shyness (they are normally active only at night) usually limits their impact.

Since they make mostly positive contributions to your garden in the form of munching up debris, it's best to leave them be. If you find they've been chewing up your prized hosta (*Hosta* spp.), consider moving your mulch back from the crown of the plant in order to make it harder for them to reach it.

Which insects caused the **decline of elm trees** in North America?

The native elm bark beetle and the European bark beetle were two beetles that caused the decline of thousands of elm trees in the United States. The pests carried the Dutch elm disease fungus, which quickly spread from tree to tree. The native elm bark beetle is a small black beetle with a wide body who lays its eggs in the depressions that run across the grain of wood. To reduce the incidence of the disease, gardeners were encouraged to prune healthy limbs in moderation and to remove dead or dying trees immediately to eliminate habitat for bark beetles.

DISEASE

My tomatoes have come down with a nasty case of something called **verticillium wilt**. How can I cure it?

Verticillium wilt is a long-lived soil-borne fungus (derived from the genus *Verticillium*) that affects a variety of plants in the nightshade family, including tomatoes, potatoes, eggplant, and peppers. Infected plants wilt (hence, the name) and may turn yellow. There is no cure per se, but it can be controlled by regularly rotating your plants, watering at the base of the plant (in order to limit the amount of soil that splashes up on the leaves), and choosing wilt-resistant plant varieties. You can also try soil solarization on new plant beds. This entails loosening up the top layer of soil with a spading fork, then watering it heavily and allowing the bed to sit overnight. The following day, cover the soil with a layer of clear plastic, covering the edges of the plastic with soil so the bed is airtight. After the bed has sat for a month or so, you may remove the plastic and plant in the bed. The solarization process has been found to pasteurize the soil while leaving many beneficial organisms alone.

As for your current tomato plants, remove them from the garden and place them out with the trash to avoid infecting other plants in your garden.

Which **plants are affected by verticillium wilt**?

The number of plant species affected by verticillium wilt is over 200—too lengthy to list here. But some of the more commonly grown plants susceptible to verticillium wilt are tomatoes, potatoes, strawberries, and Japanese maples (*Acer japonicum*). Try to select resistant varieties where they are available.

Leaf spot is a fungus that can be controlled by keeping water off of foliage and using sulfur or another fungicide product. (Steven Nikkila/Perennial Favorites)

What is the difference between **verticillium wilt and fusarium wilt**?

Both wilts have similar symptoms—mainly a yellowing and eventual death of leaves and stems. Verticillium wilt and fusarium wilt are also both caused by soil-dwelling fungi (although different ones), which means they can persist in the soil for several years. Verticillium wilt, however, tends to be more intense during cooler weather while fusarium wilt is more of a hot-weather fungus. For both wilts, the use of resistant plants is key. Fusarium-resistant varieties have an *F* after their name, while verticillium wilt resistant varieties have a *V*.

My roses have funky **black and yellow circles on the leaves** and some of the leaves are turning yellow and falling off. What's wrong with them and what can I do?

Your roses have black spot—one of the major fungi that affect roses. Affected leaves have black circles with yellow edges. When the plant is heavily infected, it can lose all of its leaves and become weak and subject to other problems. Black spot is spread by water that remains on the leaves of the plant, so be sure to water the root zone carefully to avoid splashing water up on the leaves. Also, provide roses with air circulation—keep them well spaced and away from walls and buildings.

To decrease the impact of the fungus, remove any infected canes in the spring. You can also apply a fungicide (try one that is sulfur based) once the leaves have formed, continuing to apply it weekly through the growing season.

What is **rust**?

Rust refers to a fungus whose different species infect a wide assortment of backyard crops such as asparagus, apples, beans, carrots, corn, and onions. A plant with rust has reddish-brown or rusty-looking spots on its leaves and stem. Eventually, the leaves turn yellow and the plant's growth is stunted. It thrives in areas with little wind, so be sure your plants have good air circulation around them. If your plants succumb to rust, get rid of them or the affected part to avoid spreading it to other plants.

My beautiful **spirea bushes** appear to be dying back—some of the leaves and twigs are dying and look like they've been burnt. What can I do?

Unfortunately, not too much. Your spirea (*Spirea*) has fallen prey to fire blight—a disease transferred by rain and insects. Caused by a bacteria, the blight makes leaves on affected shoots die and droop. Dying branches look scorched. You can prune below the affected areas and hope it will pass or apply an antibiotic. In the future, try not to over-fertilize your spireas as this makes them more susceptible to fire blight.

How do I get rid of the **grayish-white powderlike substance** on my bee balm?

You've described powdery mildew—a fungus that appears as white, powdery masses of spores on leaves. Bee balm (*Monarda didyma*) is highly susceptible to this fungus, which can almost completely defoliate the plant by the end of the summer. It is spread through the air and can overwinter on leaves and infected plants. If the mildew is severe enough, you may have premature leaf drop. Be sure your plant receives a good amount of air circulation by placing it away from buildings and keeping its center open through pruning. Remove any infected leaves and stems and dispose of them. You may choose to spray a sulfur-based fungicide but can also ignore a few mildewed leaves without causing harm to the plant.

Which plants can be affected by **powdery mildew**?

Roses (*Rosa* spp.), phlox (*Phlox paniculata*), dahlias (*Dahlias*), beans, peas, small fruits and fruit trees, Kentucky bluegrass (*Roa pratensis*), grapes (*Vitis*), and members of the Cucurbitaceae family, such as squash, pumpkin, melon, and cucumber, are all highly susceptible to powdery mildew. Investigate mildew-resistant plant varieties where available. If any of your plants become plagued with mildew, remove and dispose of all affected foilage immediately and keep the area around the plants well circu-

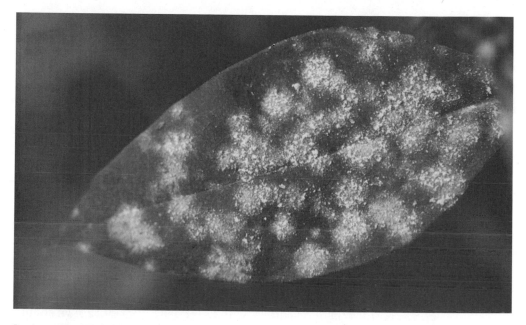

Powdery mildew like that found on this phlox (*Phlox* spp.) leaf can be prevented or controlled by proper sanitation, removal of diseased plants, and selection of fungus-resistant varieties. (Robert J. Huffman/Field Mark Publications)

lated and free of debris. If it appears you are losing the battle on that particular plant, remove and dispose of it.

How can I prevent **potato scab**?

The fungus that causes potato scab is less likely to grow in an acidic soil. By amending your soil to a pH of less than 5.5 or allowing it to remain in its naturally acidic state, you can discourage this disease from affecting your potato crop.

My **oak tree has started dying from the top down**—the leaves are turning dull and wilting before curling up and dropping off. What can I do?

It sounds as if your oak has been stricken with oak wilt. Unfortunately there is nothing you can do to treat this disease once your tree has been infected. The tree will eventually die. Oak wilt is a fungal disease that kills a tree by blocking its water-conducting vessels. It is spread by contact between healthy and sick roots and by oak bark beetles. You should remove and destroy your tree, including the stump, to avoid contaminating other trees. In the future, look for a wilt-resistant variety. Also, practice good pruning techniques such as avoiding pruning in the spring when the beetles are active.

What is clubroot?

Clubroot is a condition caused by a soilborne fungus. It strikes members of the Brassica family including cabbage, broccoli, and Brussels sprouts. While a yellowing of the plant's foliage may occur, you may not actually detect clubroot until you get rid of your crop. Roots of the plant become very large and distorted, which reduces yield in the long run. You can select clubroot-resistant plant varieties to reduce the incidence of the fungus in your garden.

My lawn service said I have **fairy rings**—are they for real?

Fungi known as fairy rings appear as a ring of dark green grass, sometimes edged by small mushrooms. They grow on organic matter in the soil, as opposed to the grass itself, but may reduce the amount of moisture in a lawn. Fairy rings thrive in warm, humid weather. To get rid of them, soak them with water daily. The entire lawn should be aerated, watered well, and fertilized in order to green it up, hiding the damage quickly.

This year my tomatoes had something called **blossom-end rot**. What can I do to prevent this next year?

When tomatoes develop a dark, recessed area on the bottom of the fruit, it is known as blossom-end rot. Blossom-end rot is a nonparasitic disease found in nearly all areas of the country. It usually occurs when the tomato plant has been growing in prime conditions and is subjected to a period of drought at about the same time the fruit is starting to develop. Lack of water causes the cells at the end of the fruit to die, eventually extending up to half the fruit. Blossom-end rot can also result from too much moisture or cultivation, which damages the fine roots of the plant, impairing its ability to take on water. Finally, blossom-end rot can be a symptom of insufficient calcium in the soil.

To avoid this problem next year, do a soil test this year or early in the season next year to determine if you have enough calcium for your tomatoes. You might also choose a variety that is less susceptible to blossom-end rot. Finally, be sure the soil is properly aerated prior to planting, which should aid water and nutrient uptake, and add mulch to preserve moisture around the plant.

DISEASE AND PEST CONTROL

What is the difference between **integrated pest management and organic pest management**?

Integrated pest management (IPM) is an approach to disease and insect problems in the garden that considers suitable and prudent solutions to keep these problem to acceptable levels with the least possible impact on the environment. Pesticides and chemical controls are considered, but only as a last resort. What is deemed an acceptable level may vary from area to area, from gardener to gardener, and from plant to plant! For example, while I will tolerate a certain amount of dandelions (*Taraxacum officinale*) in my lawn (I use one of those weed pullers to yank most of them), my neighbor on one side might be out squirting an herbicide on each plant while the neighbor on the other cultivates "dandies" for salads. Organic pest management (OPM) uses a purely organic approach to gardening with an emphasis on prevention by building up nutrients in the soil, proper plant culture, and preventative pest control. Organically acceptable chemical controls such as pheromone traps and insecticidal soaps are considered, but again only as a last resort.

What is **biocontrol**?

Biocontrol is the use of natural enemies to regulate agricultural and horticultural pest populations. These natural enemies include predators and parasites. The first biocontrol projects began in the 1880s and continued until World War II. At this time, pesticides came into general use as the preferred method for pest control. Since the 1960s and 1970s, however, biocontrol has regained popularity as information about the dangers of pesticides has been more widely disseminated.

What is considered an **ideal biocontrol insect**?

The ideal biocontrol insect is one whose diet is limited to a specific plant. Testing this requires researchers to quarantine the prospective bug and test its appetite not only for the targeted plant itself, but for its botanical relatives, and finally, for other plant species that would be found in the environment where the insect would be released.

What are some potential **drawbacks to the use of biocontrol insects on invasive plant species**?

The research and testing of biocontrol insects is very time consuming. That's because it's necessary to take every precaution that would-be predators do not have an appetite for anything else in their release area. Then once they are released, they are subject to the whims of Mother Nature—climate, other predators, and disease—which can mean

A birch tree being treated with pesticide. (Robert J. Huffman/Field Mark Publications)

the insect fails to establish and do its deed of consuming an invasive plant species. Finally, not all invasive species will merit research on and release of biocontrol insects. A majority of funding goes to biocontrol of species that are impacting farming, ranching, or fishing.

How does a **botanical pesticide** differ from an organic one?

An organic pesticide is one that contains carbon. Contrary to the popular usage of the term, however, it is not "natural" but usually manmade or synthetic. Organic pesticides have been in frequent use in agriculture since the 1940s, and while inexpensive and fairly precise, they have been associated with a number of health and environmental problems as well as misuse. Inorganic pesticides (those without carbon) tend to be more expensive and are not nearly as precise in their action (which means they can be toxic to a wide range of things). A botanical pesticide is a type of organic pesticide that is derived directly from plants. Some examples of botanical pesticides include rotenone, nicotine, pyrethrum, and strychnine. Some botanicals seem to have less impact on the environment. However, just because a pesticide is derived from a plant does not necessarily make it less harmful to humans. Many poisons occur naturally.

What are **nematodes**?

Nematodes are microscopic parasitic worms that feed on plants and are always present in the soil. There are good or beneficial nematodes that burrow inside the grubs of

> ## What is a pheromone trap?
>
> A pheromone trap usually contains sex pheromones—manmade chemicals similar to those found naturally in insects that affect the behavior of other members of the same species. The trap consists of a lure covered with or injected with the pheromones. Once the insect has entered the trap, it is prevented from leaving due to the shape of the opening of the trap or a sticky coating that entangles its feet. The traps are generally ineffective at capturing pests since only males are attracted to the lure, and often more pests are attracted than the traps can handle. They can also be used to disrupt the mating of insects, confusing them through sensory overload. Their best purpose is to monitor insect populations.

some insect pests in order to reproduce, causing the host insect to die. The beneficial nematodes may be used to combat sod webworms, Japanese beetle grubs, flea beetles, gypsy moths, chinch bugs, and other insects. As an added benefit, they don't bother beneficial insects and earthworms in the process. Sold in packages, nematodes look like powder and are combined with water when applied.

The bad or pest nematodes can weaken plants (sometimes forming galls on plant roots) or infect them with viral diseases. The pest nematodes can be combatted by top-dressing plants with compost. The compost attracts organisms that will in turn attack the nematodes. Fish emulsion also repels or kills nematodes.

Is **insecticidal soap** the same thing as dish soap?

No. Insecticidal soap is a commercial product that was developed to kill certain insects while not harming beneficial ones. It is biodegradable and safe to use with pets and people. In order to be effective, insects must come in direct contact with the soap. Insecticidal soap contains unsaturated fatty acids that dissolve the skin of insects. It is most effective against soft-bodied insects, but can kill some hard-shelled insects if they're completely doused with the soap. Insecticidal soap is only effective if it is in a liquid form when it makes contact with bugs. Once it has dried, it is useless.

What are some **disadvantages of insecticidal soap**?

Insecticidal soap breaks down quickly (within a couple of weeks), which means it is better for humans and the environment but bad if it breaks down before affecting the insect population. It is also more expensive and not as widely available as some synthetic insecticides. Insecticidal soap can also burn the leaves of some plants so you should test a few

109

leaves of the plant you're intending to use it on, then wait 48 hours for any adverse reaction. Finally, although it is less toxic than many synthetic insecticides, it is still toxic.

How can a **birdbath** help me solve my insect problems?

Birds are a natural predator of many garden insect pests. In luring birds to your garden for bath time, you can entice them to stay for lunch, dinner, and breakfast the following day!

What is **Bt**?

Bacillus thuringiensis or Bt is a pathogen that paralyzes and eventually destroys the stomach cells of any insects that ingest it. It is usually mixed with a formula to encourage insects to consume more of it. Since it doesn't reproduce itself, it must be reapplied in order to prevent additional outbreaks. It is available in different strains to control different types of pests. The Bt caterpillar toxin is also toxic to the caterpillars of butterflies, so it should be used with care. Other strains include *Bt san diego,* which affects some types of beetles, and *Bt israelensis,* which affects mosquitos, black flies, and fungus gnat.

What is a **summer oil**?

A summer oil (also called superior oil or verdant oil) is a lighter horticultural oil used to kill insects and mites by either smothering them or interfering with their membrane functions. Traditional horticultural oils had to be applied during the fall or winter as they would burn or kill plants if applied during the growing season. Summer oils are a lighter formulation and most can be used throughout the year. Even at a lighter formulation, however, summer oils can burn plants with sensitive leaves, so you need to test the oil on a small portion of the plant, then wait 48 hours before spraying all of it. Plants suffering from moisture stress should not be sprayed. To be on the safe side, don't spray your plants at all on very hot days.

What is diatomaceous earth and how does it work?

Diatomaceous earth is made up of the fossilized remains of teeny prehistoric creatures called diatoms. These fossils have been ground up into what appears to be flour, but is actually similar to finely crushed glass. Soft-bodied pests like earwigs, aphids, and slugs lose fluids and eventually die when they come into contact with diatomaceous earth. It can either be sprinkled around the base of the plant in a three-inch band or applied directly to foliage. In either case, it must be reapplied after a heavy rain.

It should be noted that horticultural oils are not selective—they kill both harmful and beneficial insects. Proper diagnosis of a plant's problem should be the first step before using any oil. Once you have identified the insect causing deterioration in your plant, carefully apply the oil to those infestations only—not randomly to whatever insects are nearby.

Are **pyrethrum, pyrethrin, and pyrethroid** the same thing?

No. Pyrethrum and pyrethrin are botanical pesticides—natural products. They kill pests by paralyzing them on contact and are quite toxic. Pyrethrum is a dust made from the flower of the pyrethrum daisy (*Tanacetum cinerariifolium*). Pyrethrins are toxins that are extracted from the seed of the pyrethrum daisy. Pyrethrum products can be toxic to beneficial insects as well as pests but they break down after a few hours of exposure to sunlight. They will also poison aquatic life and so should not be used near water. Pyrethroid is a synthetic pesticide. It is more toxic than either pyrethrum or pyrethrin and remains in the environment for much longer.

My grandmother always said a **good spray with the hose** would take care of most bugs. Was she right?

A strong blast of water from a hose can knock off many insect pests like mealybugs, spittlebugs, and aphids. It will also keep away other pests like spider mites, which thrive on dirty, dry plants. Remember that a water blast is indiscriminate—it will knock away the good bugs with the bad—so be sure to identify your insect before knocking it silly. When hosing down your plants, be firm but gentle so that you don't damage the plant. Don't forget to spray under the leaves since that's where most bugs like to hide. Finally, spray for pests in the morning so that the plants have time to dry off before dark.

What is an **LD50 rating**?

The LD50 rating is a number given to a pesticide based on the amount needed to kill half of a test population. The higher the rating, the less toxic the pesticide. Many naturally occurring toxins are far more poisonous than synthetic toxins. However, natural toxins generally dissipate much more quickly than synthetic ones. Insecticidal soap and Bt are two examples of pesticides with relatively low levels of toxicity. Highly toxic pesticides include rotenone and nicotine sulfate.

How does a **scarecrow** work?

Maybe the question should be, Does a scarecrow work? Scarecrows attempt to foil birds and other critters from munching on your crops by serving as a stand-in for the gardener. Trouble is, few scarecrows (except for the one in *The Wizard of Oz*) flap their arms like a gardener does when he or she sees the birds pecking away at precious crops. In the best-case scenario, scarecrows need to be rotated frequently with other deterrent tactics in order to keep the critters guessing. In most cases, unfortunately, those pests don't blink an eye at your stuffed-shirt stand-in. And remember, for the most part birds are a good thing to have in a garden.

What is a **trap crop**

A trap crop is a crop that is planted for the specific purpose of luring bad bugs away from your plants. With this technique, you can either sacrifice the trap crop or nab the pesky pests while they're noshing. Your trap crop can either be the crop you'd like to eventually keep, but planted earlier, or you can use a different crop that attracts your particular insect adversary. It is best to plant the crops close to, but not next to, the plants you want to keep. Otherwise, when they're done with the trap, they might move on to the rest of your garden!

ENVIRONMENTAL/ CULTURAL PROBLEMS

What are the most common causes of **environmental or cultural problems**?

Physical damage to a plant's bark or roots, improper watering, improper fertilization, pH and mineral imbalances, and improper light intensity are the most common causes of cultural problems.

How can I tell if I have enough **nitrogen** in my soil?

Determing whether your soil has enough nitrogen is a tricky thing. Since nitrogen can be bound up and unavailable to plants or can be used heavily at certain times, a soil test can be misleading. However, your plants will tip you off. Look for pale green or yellowed foliage, rather than a nice deep green. On some plants, young leaves may curl upward or look stunted. Fruit may be small and flower buds may drop early. Too much nitrogen can be a bad thing too. Plants that have lots of dark green, healthy-looking foliage but no fruit may be suffering from an overload of nitrogen.

How can I tell if I have enough **phosphorus** in my soil?

Phosphorus deficiencies can be detected by a soil test. You can also watch your plants for signs such as stunted or very slow growth (especially with seedlings), purplish-colored leaf tips, and smaller fruit than usual. If you already have a phosphorus deficiency and your pH is at one extreme or the other (either very acid or very alkaline), your phosphorus problem may be worsened. Microorganisms responsible for the release of phosphorus from the soil to the plants are inhibited by extremes in pH.

How can I tell if I have enough **potassium** in my soil?

Again, a soil test is the best way to determine potassium levels. Since potassium is responsible for developing healthy root systems, if your plants appear to have weak root systems or stalks, they may be potassium deficient. Other signs of potassium deficiency include foliage that looks scorched or brown, fruits that fall too early, and slow or stunted growth.

How can I detect **root rot** in my plants?

Once you've detected the symptoms of root rot in your plants, it's probably too late. Plants that are stressed usually fall prey to root rot, which is caused by a soil-borne fungus that enters the plant through a wound. The plant looks stunted, then turns yellow, wilts, and quickly dies. To avoid this, make sure that your garden bed has good drainage and that you water carefully to avoid over- or underwatering plants. If you catch them quickly enough, you can try to save plants suffering from root rot by burying healthy plant stems to spur them to generate new roots.

What is **desiccation**?

Desiccation refers to the drying out of plants, usually through wind. Evergreen plants such as rhododendrons and azaleas (both *Rhododendron* spp.) may be prone to this at the outer reaches of their hardiness zone.

113

Be careful! Many bamboos such as common bamboo (*Bambusa vulgaris*), Buddha's belly bamboo (*Bambusa ventricosa*), and golden bamboo (*Phyllostachys aurea*) can be quite invasive, elbowing other plants with their vigorous growth habit. Invasive plants may be exotics like bamboo or innocents like tansy (*Tanacetum vulgare*). In any case, these plants are very vigorous and beat out most other plants in the competition for resources. If you want to grow an invasive plant, be sure to take precautions like planting it in a container or placing an underground barrier around it to prevent it from overtaking your lawn.

How do I prevent **winter burn**?

Winter burn is also known as desiccation or the drying out of a plant's leaves. Evergreen foliage killed by winter burn looks as though it has been scorched. It can be prevented by keeping the plant well watered until the ground freezes, and by mulching the plant well to prevent the ground from freezing deeply. While you can spray antidesiccants on the leaves or protect the plants with a screen of burlap, these practices are really only necessary for plants that are too tender for the area they're planted in. Remember—right plant, right place!

What is **lawn mower blight**?

Lawn mower blight refers to the damage done by lawn mowers and weed whackers when they are used too close to the base of a tree. The blades or wire can cut into the tree trunk, causing severe damage and eventually killing the tree.

What impact does a **black walnut tree** have on tomatoes?

It can kill them. The roots of a black walnut produce a toxin called juglone, which will poison tomato plants.

I planted azalea bushes near my house and they don't look happy—they haven't grown much and their **leaves are turning yellow**. What should I do?

The chlorosis or yellowing of the leaves could be caused either by winter injury or by an iron deficiency in the soil. Do a soil test to determine the pH of the azalea bed. Azaleas and other rhododendrons (both *Rhododendron* spp.) thrive in acidic soil; a

> ## What is girdling and how does it affect a tree?
>
> **A** tree becomes girdled when a tree root wraps itself around a major root or even the entire tree trunk, slowly strangling the tree as it grows. Girdling can occur either above or below ground. A frequent cause of girdling is the failure to remove the burlap and as much of the wire basket as possible on balled-and-burlapped trees. It can also be caused by wrapping or staking a tree trunk too tightly or by not removing the wrap or the staking materials as the tree grows. Overzealous lawn mowing or weed whacking can also cause girdling. Symptoms of girdling include thin or skimpy growth at the top of the tree, underdeveloped bark, or even a slight discoloration of the leaves on one side of the tree. The trunk may appear to be concave on one side or swollen looking. A tree trunk that appears to grow straight up from the ground rather than flared slightly at the bottom can also be girdled.

more alkaline soil can cause an iron deficiency, which in turn causes chlorosis. You may improve your soil's acidity over time by adding a couple of inches of compost a year but if you have another bed in your yard that is more acidic—say, under a stand of pine trees—it might make sense to move the shrubs to that location.

The two beautiful cherry trees that were here when I purchased my house looked great but the fruit began cracking and splitting. I haven't seen any bugs or varmints—what happened?

It sounds like a water problem. When fruit trees and tomatoes receive insufficient moisture or a fluctuating amount of water during the growing season, their fruits can split. Next year, be sure to water your trees (and the rest of your garden) thoroughly during dry weather. Watering between one and two inches per week if there is no rain should be sufficient.

PROBLEM PREVENTION

How can **tilling** the soil help to keep insect pests out of my garden?

Tilling or turning over the soil can expose the grubs or soil-dwelling stage of many insects to cold, light, and hungry birds. You don't need to do an intense double-digging session—just loosen the soil with a spading fork, hoe, or tiller to a depth of six inches or so. Turning over the soil in the fall can be especially fruitful as many insects lay their eggs in the ground to mature over the winter.

What are the advantages of **crop rotation**?

Crop rotation is the practice of moving a vegetable crop to a different location in your garden from year to year. Because many diseases are soil borne, this practice limits the effect of disease organisms on plants by not allowing them to build up in the soil. Crop rotation also reduces the number of insect pests that overwinter near a host plant, since you are moving their food source.

What is **companion planting**?

Companion planting refers to the practice of placing plants in close proximity to each other based on the beneficial effects this will have. Actual scientific evidence of this concept is somewhat scarce, but some research indicates that companion planting may attract beneficial insects by providing hiding places or food sources for the insects. Certain plants may also lure insect pests away from other plants or confuse a pest with its scent. Marigolds (*Tagetes* spp.) are thought by many to repel certain insects due to their strong scent. Nasturtiums (*Tropaeolum* spp.) may lure aphids away from other garden plants such as roses (*Rosa* spp.).

How can I **prevent diseases** in my garden?

Keeping plants healthy is a matter of good garden habits. Water your garden in the morning, at least before noon, in order to allow the garden plenty of time to dry out before night when diseases thrive in the cool, moist conditions. Also water your plants at their root zone to avoid transmitting soil-borne diseases to plants through soil splash. By the same token, stay out of your garden when it is wet to avoid spreading disease yourself. Mulch can also help keep soil-borne diseases down as well as keeping plants cool and moist. Keep your tools clean, wiping them with a weak bleach solution after removing any extra dirt to avoid spreading diseases between plants. While this may seem extreme, at least clean the tool after using it on a plant you suspect is not healthy. Carefully inspect a plant before introducing it and its troubles to your garden—avoid sickly looking specimens when purchasing them. While nursing a plant back to health may sound noble, chances are good you won't be able to cure its ills and you'll just end up infecting the rest of your clan. The most important method of prevention is to make sure your plants receive the proper amount of fertilizer, water, and sunlight. A plant under stress or weakened from improper conditions is always more susceptible to problems.

The ladybug is the best-known beneficial insect in the garden. Both adults and larvae are an important contribution to managing pests without the use of chemicals. Ladybugs, praying mantis, and other beneficial insects can be purchased from garden centers and mail-order sources. (Robert J. Huffman/Field Mark Publications)

What is the benefit of **cleaning up my garden in the fall**?

Cleaning up your garden in the fall removes possible sources of disease or mold from your plants and disrupts or destroys areas for insects to overwinter. By removing diseased plant material along with your spent annuals and vegetables, removing mulch until the ground freezes, and composting or shredding leaves, you pave the way for a healthier garden next spring.

How can I keep the **iris borer** from decimating my iris border?

The best way to keep the iris borer from ruining your irises is to keep it out of your border to begin with. This means paying close attention to the tender iris spears in the spring for signs of the larvae (they will leave leaf tunnels). If you find the larvae, crush them. They are small—around two inches—and pink with brown heads. In the fall when you dig up and divide your irises, get rid of any rhizomes that are mushy or appear diseased. Clean up the dying leaves and any other plant debris around your irises in the fall as these make warm homes for the eggs.

Does **mulch help keep pests away** or does it invite them in?

While mulch placed too close to a plant can lure such pests as slugs, one of the benefits of properly placed mulch is its ability to repel or confuse some insects. Keep the mulch away from the crown of the plant; its real importance is keeping the root system cool and moist, so four to five inches is sufficient for most plants. Some success stories include using aluminum foil to keep aphids away from squash plants and straw mulch to confuse Colorado potato beetles from their favorite food.

What are **beneficial insects** and how can I attract them to my garden?

Beneficial insects are insects that contribute positively to the garden environment. Bees, wasps, and some flies pollinate plants. Lacewings, dragonflies, ground beetles, fireflies, and beloved ladybugs prey on other insects. Spiders and mites (although not technically insects) are also predators. In order to entice beneficial insects to your backyard, avoid using chemicals altogether or use them only when a plant is under siege and only on that plant. Provide them with alternate food sources by leaving some weeds (only the prettiest, of course), and fill a large bowl or birdbath with water. Plants such as dill (*Anethum graveolens*) and yarrow (*Achillea millefolium*) provide them with extra food in the form of nectar. A brick or rock-edged path provides beneficial insects with a place to lurk.

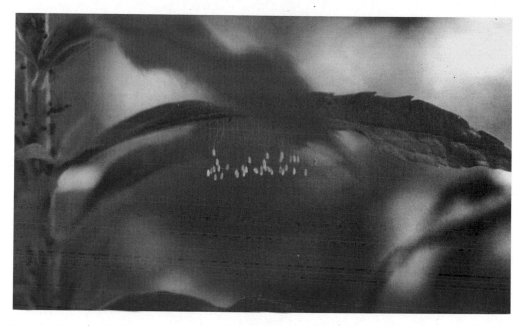

Lacewing flies are beneficial insects that feed on aphids. Lacewing eggs, like those above, can be obtained from mail-order seed companies or garden centers (Steven Nikkila/Perennial Favorites)

I've discovered a million **ants in my vegetable garden**. Should I be concerned they'll eat up my harvest?

Ants in your garden are a good thing— ants aerate the soil, allowing air and water to reach plant roots. Ants are also responsible for moving seeds from place to place (the rapid spread of violets in a garden is an example of ants at work). They generally don't mess with vegetables.

What are the advantages of **plant diversity** in the garden?

A greater variety of plants in the garden means you provide a diversity of habitats for wildlife, including beneficial insects and animals, throughout the year. In addition, by selecting plants from a variety of plant families, you will still have a few plants left standing when a scourge of pests or disease that attacks a whole plant family invades your neighborhood.

GARDEN DESIGN

GARDEN MAKING

What are some characteristics of a **formal garden**?

A formal garden is based on symmetry—although you can have either a symmetrical formal garden or an asymmetrical one. The shapes of beds and features of both types of gardens tend to be regular—rectangles or ovals—and the paths are straight. Plants of the same type are normally used to create symmetry—for example, two globes of common boxwood (*Buxus sempervirens*) marking each side of a doorway. One important element of a symmetrically formal garden is the use of two main axes that intersect at the midpoint of the garden, dividing it into areas that match symmetrically. In an asymmetrical formal garden, the plan is still geometrical, but the axes intersect at a point other than the midpoint, dividing the garden into areas that can be used differently. Small or urban gardens take well to a formal design.

What are some characteristics of an **informal garden**?

Informal gardens usually have irregularly shaped beds with curving edges and paths. In an informal garden, there are no axes—no symmetry. The garden slowly reveals constantly changing views. If the shape of your plot is regular but you like the informal look, use plantings to hide boundaries. There is an absence of manmade structures or, if deemed necessary, they are made of natural materials that blend in with their surroundings. Irregularly shaped lots, yards with an uneven slope, or larger gardens may be shaped informally.

An informal garden with winding paths. (Robert J. Huffman/Field Mark Publications)

What elements do I need to consider when **designing my garden**?

First consider the function of your garden. Do the children need a place to play soccer? Are you looking for a corner for garden parties or quiet solitude? Then consider the existing conditions of the site. I would strongly advise a soil test in order to determine the pH of your bed and which soil amendments (if any) are needed. Then look at other conditions such as amount of sunlight, wind, impact of buildings, slope or low areas, existing plants, moisture and texture of the soil, and the proximity of water and the compost pile. Finally, decide how much maintenance you are willing to do—frame this question to yourself in terms of hours per week to really nail this down.

What is a **focal point**?

The focal point is an interesting element where the eye comes to rest when viewing the garden. The focal point of a garden may be a bench, a striking Japanese maple, a garden sculpture, or your neighbor's majestic oak. There should be only one focal point to any view, but a series of focal points can take the visitor from area to area in a garden. This creates movement, a crucial element to any garden.

What is a **vista**?

A vista is a narrow view through an opening, such as through a gate or a break in a series of hedges. By eliminating the distraction of the wider landscape or surroundings, a garden designer can focus a visitor's attention on a particular object. To call further attention to the object, a designer might choose to gently frame the object with foliage. For example, one could use the arch of a cherry blossom branch in the foreground to curl around the distant spire of a church.

What is the concept of **movement** in a garden and how can it be expressed?

Movement in a garden refers to the use of different shapes or plantings to nudge a visitor (and his or her eye) from place to place in the garden. As noted above, the use of a series of focal points can create movement in a garden. Also, the shape of a garden room or area can have meaning. A narrow room ushers a visitor through quickly, even more so if it has vertical structures that become taller as he or she walks through. A broader room gives guests the chance to stroll and meander. A round or square area is restful, serving as a stopping point for body and soul.

What are the basic principles of **garden design**?

Garden design is founded on basic principles: balance, proportion, repetition or unity, and contrast. Balance consists of providing elements of similar size and weight to each

> ## What does the density of a plant have to do with garden design?
>
> **A** plant's density or visual weight creates a great deal of impact in a garden. For example, consider an evergreen tree, as opposed to a deciduous one. Even in the middle of summer, the evergreen tree tends to have more visual weight than the deciduous one. This means these plants should be considered carefully in developing your garden picture. Used as specimen plants, they will garner a great deal of attention. Used in groupings, they can serve as a dark background for a plant of finer texture.

side of a focal point. If these elements are the same shape (usually the same plant), it is symmetrical. Proportion considers the relationship between the size of one element in a garden with the size of another. Unity or the repetition of an element (shape, color, texture, or even the same plant) throughout a garden ties it together. Contrast provides an element of surprise or variation to your garden. Using two plants with similar sizes but different textures or placing a strong-colored element against a pale background can be appealing. It is usually important to keep some element of similarity between plants in order to provide unity to a garden picture, but that shouldn't stop you from experimenting to create your own signature look.

I've figured out how I'm going to use the garden, I know the soil and other conditions of the area, and I've decided how many hours per week I want to work. How do I establish my **design**?

Based on the conditions of your garden (hours of sun per day, soil pH and texture, slope, wind, and moisture), come up with a list of plants (trees, shrubs, perennials, and annuals) that suit those conditions. Use garden publications, plant encyclopedias, even pictures of other people's gardens for ideas, but always choose a plant that fits the site, rather than trying to make the site fit the plant. You have a much better chance of healthy, happy plants this way and you won't need to spend your time and energy trying to improve conditions for a lagging plant.

Next, decide whether you're interested in a formal or informal garden design (see questions above for description of each). If you're designing a large space, begin by breaking it down into areas based on function. Break this down even further by beginning with a visual focus for each area. This might be a wonderful old apple tree, the view of a pond, or even your freshly painted yardhouse or shed. If you can't find a great focal point (or even worse, have something to hide!), consider "borrowing" a view from your neighbor or surrounding area. For example, a large utility pole stands at the edge of my property but to the left of that, in the distance, is an old cemetery with a huge majestic linden tree. By focusing on that tree and planning my garden out from it, visitors to my garden see the tree, not the utility pole. If you still can't find a visual focus, create one using a plant from your list or perhaps a garden seat or interesting old pot. The plant should be a tree or shrub or a perennial that has some winter interest so that your focal point doesn't disappear when the cold weather sets in.

Using your plant list and the elements of plant design (balance, proportion, and repetition), add plants to frame your visual focus. Some ideas include using contrasting foliage to make the focus "pop" more, choosing colors that complement the focus, and using plants in odd (not even) amounts. Although smaller plants are usually placed in front of larger ones, mix things up a bit. Remember, too, the finer or "cooler" in color the plant is, the more of it you'll need in order for it to stand out. Before you ever put a shovel into the soil, do a dress rehearsal of your ideas. You can either sketch them out on graph paper, or use garden hose to mark the bed and various garden and household flotsam and jetsam (an overturned pail, a burlap bag over a tomato cage) to appropriate plants at their various heights. Be sure to plan for plants at their mature height and width so that you'll place them properly. This all takes some practice, but relax and have fun. And remember, you can always move things around later.

How do **vertical elements** such as climbing plants, walls, and fences affect a garden's design?

Vertical elements affect a garden in a variety of ways. The higher a fence or hedge, the smaller the enclosed space appears. Accordingly, the smaller the garden, the more the vertical elements predominate the area. In small yards, then, it is crucial to consider your vertical elements carefully. Using trellising or a nonsolid fence can give a small garden structure while still allowing light in. In a large yard, vertical elements can give a sense of intimacy and security by dividing the space into garden rooms.

What are some design basics for a **small yard**?

In order to make a small garden or yard feel larger, you should definitely consider blurring the lines between garden and house. Consider not only the room that opens into the garden, but also any views from other floors or windows. Try to match any structural materials in the garden to that of the house. You could even paint walls the same color inside and out. Place container-grown plants in the room leading to the garden to extend the outdoors in.

Avoid cluttering the garden with too many types of plants and too many objects. Just like with interior design, by keeping the number of objects, colors, and styles to a minimum and using oversized structures, you create the feeling of space. Many small

Arrange potted plants around the garden to "try out" a design. (Steven Nikkila/Perennial Favorites)

gardens are shaded by buildings, so try to take advantage of any sunshine that does exist by creating an open space for it or highlighting it with a specimen plant positioned where it will receive the most light. Privacy can be at a premium in a small town garden so consider methods of screening that can provide a sense of enclosure without making the space too narrow or dark. Trellises or finely textured plants are good choices.

Generally speaking, strong colors can be difficult to use in a small garden as they tend to overwhelm it. But if your favorite color is hot pink, use it as a highlight in small spaces and temper it with whites and blue-greys. While you may want to plant everything at once, you should really try to nail down your plan first as a small garden can be overwhelmed quickly by haphazard planting.

What are some design basics for a **large garden**?

The most important element to consider in a large garden is the surrounding area. With a large garden, you have a greater visual expanse to cover. Unless you chose to wall everything in with a large hedge or walls, garden visitors will also view the landscape nearby. Consider focusing on a few outstanding views and build small garden pictures or rooms around them.

Woody ornamentals are an important part of your design as well. You have a much broader selection to choose from than gardeners with a small yard. However, with choice comes responsibility: Don't spread tiny groups of plantings out over the entire yard. If you can't afford to plant the entire garden at once (and really, who can?), choose a couple of key areas to focus on and build outward from them. Eventually, you will be able to link these areas together into a unified whole.

In a large garden, a rainbow of colors can be used at your discretion. However, just as in a smaller garden, you might want to choose a palette of a few colors or some "signature plants" such as groundcovers that will unify your diverse plantings. You may choose to plant each room in a particular palette that complements its sun and light characteristics: for instance, grey-leaved and brightly colored flowers in a sunny exposure; dark green and paler-colored flowers in shadier areas. These could then be tied together using signature plants or by gradually transitioning the color scheme where two rooms meet.

What are some design tips for a **shady garden**?

Shady gardens can be challenging—not just in getting plants to grow properly in them, but in making them look fresh and interesting. Begin by mapping (either on paper or in your head) the areas of sunlight in your yard (yes—there have to be some!). These areas can be used to plant flowering plants that do well in partial shade. However, the most important element of a shade garden is plant shape and texture. Interest is achieved mainly through foliage. Combine different leaf shapes and textures throughout the garden. Many shade plants tend to be low-growers so make a conscious effort to select plants in varying heights to mimic the levels of a forest (groundcover, understory, and canopy). Try to spread your blooming plants (such as ephemerals and bulbs) throughout the garden, instead of positioning them in one area. This way you can avoid a gap in your garden in the later part of the growing season. For most of your color, you will need to depend on plants with colored foliage. Not to worry, many plants such as hostas (*Hosta* spp.) and Japanese maples (*Acer japonicum*) actually show their best color in the shade. And don't forget plants with variegated foliage to add "color" (actually, the absence of color) to a garden. Variegated foliage can be overdone, but when used as highlights throughout the garden it can bring the appearance of light to dark corners. Lastly, shady gardens can tend to look small. Use plants with bright colors or bold textures in the foreground of your plantings and place paler colors and finer textures in the rear in order to provide the appearance of depth in your yard.

What are some design tips for a **sunny garden**?

Gardeners with sunny yards certainly have a vast number of plants to choose from, but sometimes all you want is a little shade for contrast and relief. You might consider creating your own shade with structures like arbors or pergolas covered in vines or by planting trees and shrubs. These are also good elements from a design standpoint in

What can I do to make my flat, rectangular yard look more interesting?

There are several options for adding depth and interest to an uninterestingly shaped (but definitely typical) yard. Place the entrance to the garden on an angle or on the lower half of a long side. This creates immediate interest by giving visitors an unexpected perspective as they enter the yard. Next, if practical, place your entertainment area (barbecue, patio, terrace) in a location away from the house for the same reason. Or use decking to create different levels, creating more interest for the eye. If you have a very small yard, you might consider hardscaping most of the yard (using pavers, brick, or stones), with maybe a small portion of lawn as a kind of carpet. Consider creating levels to your plantings, similar to a forest, with a canopy, understory, and groundcover. This gives the eye layers to look at and eliminates the flatness of the landscape. Raised beds can add height and interest to a flat garden and are practical for gardening in as well (easier to weed and maintain and they warm up faster in the spring).

that they provide "bones" for the yard. The main challenge in designing for a sunny yard is to keep things interesting. One strategy is to play up the amount of light in the yard with light-colored plants. Grey-leaved plants such as lamb's ear (*Stachys byzantia*), lavender (*Lavandula* spp.), and carnations or pinks (*Dianthus* spp.) can be used to great effect in a sunny exposure. Consider, too, the different types of light your garden receives throughout the day. Emphasizing the dusky tones of sunset with plants that receive the full light of day's end is a wonderful way to work with nature.

Mulch is essential in a sunny garden—both from the perspective of maintenance (less frequent watering is needed) and in order to tie plantings together. Dark-colored mulch will give a solid grounding to your plantings but gravel might unify a xeriscape (dry garden) concept.

I live in the city and have a **very small yard** connected to my terrace that I'd like to garden. What can I do?

In dealing with such a small space, it's important to prioritize your needs and wants. Do you plan on entertaining there? While you could set up seating on the terrace, setting up a table and chairs in a secluded corner of the garden will draw guests into the space and help to create depth—crucial in a smaller space. Are you interested in puttering with flowers or vegetables or is a low-maintenance, all-green landscape more to your liking?

In a small space, you should consider your planting scheme carefully in order to allow enough space for the plants to grow properly and be shown off to their full advantage. You may also want to limit your color scheme to provide a more unified look. If you're interested in puttering, look for ways to maximize the space you have in order to gain more room to garden. For very small yards, consider getting rid of the lawn (you don't have room for a mower!) and using paving to establish different garden rooms (or a single room). You can even grow plants between the chinks of the pavers or bricks. Also, think vertically. Climbing plants offer endless possibilities to provide your yard with vertical interest. Although tree and shrub possibilities are limited by your space, don't despair! Dwarf varieties and slower-growing trees such as Japanese maples (*Acer japonicum*) can, and should, be used to provide focal points. Or perhaps a favorite sculpture or other garden art can be showcased in your yard. Water in the form of a small fountain, pond, or even a shallow bowl filled with aquatic plants can give your small space an elegant intimacy. Think of your yard as an extension of your home and consider decorating it to complement your interior.

I just moved to the suburbs after having a terraced apartment and have a whole **acre to garden** on! But there is little to no existing landscape and the yard looks so empty. Where do I begin?

The first thing to do is consider how you will be using the yard. While all that space can be intimidating, starting with its functions will help you break up the space into separate rooms. Once this has been established, consider using hardscaping such as walls, fences, and paving to outline and connect these areas. Your first consideration in plantings should be trees and shrubs to provide shelter, focus, and structure. Repeating a theme such as a color, a shape, or a specific plant provides the yard with unity, which is crucial in a larger area. Other possibilities include establishing a small orchard or grove of trees, a water feature or pool, or a pergola or deck—large-scale projects that are almost impossible for smaller yards. And while it may be impractical (and expensive) to give up your lawn entirely, you may want to consider letting parts of it grow long and allowing wildflowers and grasses to creep in.

How can I design my garden to look good **year-round**?

Begin by studying your garden in the winter. In most regions of the United States in the winter, the structure or bones of a garden are bared to the world. Without the buds of spring, blooms of summer, and rich foliage of fall, elements like trees, shrubs, fences, and buildings become more prominent. Even the demarcation between the lawn or groundcover and the planted beds becomes more pronounced. Start by balancing the scene between evergreens that provide year-round foliage and deciduous trees and shrubs with pronounced shapes, interesting growth patterns, or colorful bark. Then work forward through each season, following basic design principles to fill

129

Examine how your garden and surrounding areas will look in winter. (Steven Nikkila/Perennial Favorites)

in the bed with perennials, annuals, and bulbs that bloom or provide foliage to complement each season. If you are starting from scratch, a good rule of thumb to follow for trees and shrubs is to plant one winter ornamental for each summer or spring ornamental.

How do I design a **low-maintenance garden**?

Start by getting rid of your lawn, or reducing it in size. Even if you're somewhat lax about fertilizing and weed control, lawns have to be mowed and watered frequently. When deciding on plants, choose those that fit your site conditions and narrow this list even further to those that "thrive on neglect" or don't mind going long stretches without being watered. Select plants that need little (if any) pruning, deadheading, pinching back, or coddling whatsoever to look decent. Try to strike a balance between plant diversity (which keeps disease and insects down) and choosing too many plants (which are bound to have different maintenance needs). About a dozen varieties is plenty in the average yard.

Before you plant anything, prepare the soil. Turn it under to about a foot and remove all weeds and weed parts. Anything left will be back to haunt you later. Use mulch everywhere! It will keep down weeds, retain moisture around plant roots, and prevent soil erosion. Finally, keep it manageable by only taking on what you know you can keep up. As mentioned earlier in the chapter, frame your commitment in terms of hours per week to know how much time you can realistically devote to your garden.

How can a **black and white** photograph help me to define my garden?

You see your garden every day. You work hard at it. And yet somehow, it all just feels kind of blah. I know that feeling. And the difficult thing is, you can't quite pinpoint what's wrong. Try taking a picture. But instead of using color, which will mask certain characteristics of your yard and meld everything together, use black and white. Black and white film is brutal—the "bones" of your garden will stand out—if they exist. And errors in judgment (with the exception of color, of course) should pop out instantly.

What are some good **sources of inspiration** for garden design?

While the gardens pictured in glossy magazines and fabulous coffee-table books can be fun to look at, it can sometimes be difficult to apply their ideas to one's own yard. Nearby botanical gardens and arboretums can give you a better sense of how a plant or tree grows (height, width, and visual weight) and, better yet, how well it does in your area. Garden tours sponsored by your local garden club or Master Gardener society can be better sources of inspiration by showing real-life gardeners in yards similar to your own. Even tooling around your own neighborhood can provide you with ideas on plantings that complement (or foil) the housing in your area. Most importantly, look

Use varying plant height and different colors to make a border garden design more interesting. (Steven Nikkila/Perennial Favorites)

to nature for inspiration. By paying close attention to how plants grow together naturally, you recreate these vignettes and provide proper growing companions for your plants. Walks in the woods or nearby meadows can yield a dozen "a-ha's!"

My **garden budget is small**. How can I maximize the impact of my garden with the least amount of cash?

Begin with a plan. First, spend your dollars wisely by investing in elements that will have a large impact. Consider hardscaping and woody ornamentals first. While these items tend to be the most costly, they will also give your garden a basic structure. If you plan on staying in your house for several years, purchase younger trees and shrubs. Their price escalates in direct proportion to their age and size. And don't forget: right plant, right place. Over the long run, you will spend less time and money on a tree or shrub that suits your yard's conditions. In terms of hardscaping, spend your money where it will make the most impact and difference in how you use your yard. For instance, although you may be smitten with a privacy fence with a lattice work accent at the top, do you need to extend this around your entire yard? Or can you use it on the end of the fence you view most often and finish the remaining fence in a simple style?

Once your hard elements and trees and shrubs are in, then you can consider the rest of your plantings. You may choose to limit these plantings to a few annuals for

> **Because my house was built in a former cornfield and has no neighbors or trees, the site gets pretty windy. What can I do to block or temper the effect of the wind on the property?**
>
> Avoid putting up a solid wall or fence—this actually increases wind speeds, which can cause wind chill and turbulence on the inside of the fence, damaging plants. Solid fences are also more likely to blow over. A hedge is a better option; the thicker it becomes, the better it is at dissipating the wind. Hedges also bend with the wind and are less likely to be uprooted. The best option is a wide planting of shrubs and trees. Start with low plantings facing the wind and gradually increase your plantings in height to trees. This forces the wind up and over the tops of the trees, leaving the other side sheltered. For additional protection, you could install a nonsolid fence on the other side of the trees.

color during the first few expensive years when the basic structure of your garden is being laid. When purchasing perennials, buy smaller, hardier plants and fill in with annuals. These will quickly fill out. With a little forethought, you can select ones to be divided and spread out over your garden.

How can I block the sight of a **utility pole** in the corner of my yard?

In city and suburban neighborhoods, utility poles can be a necessary part of a yard, but confounding for a gardener to contend with. There are several ways to go about screening this view. If the top of the pole is screened out by a nearby tree canopy, try a small, spreading shrub or small tree such as a smoke bush (*Continus coggygria*) or one of the multilimbed amelanchiers (such as *Amelanchier grandiflora*) to cover the lower half of the pole. If you need to screen out the entire pole, begin by determining your main viewing point of that area. Then plant a tall, spreading tree like an oak or pine between the pole and your viewing point. If you don't have room for a large tree, a narrow, cylindrical-shaped shrub such as an arborvitae (*Thuja occidentalis* 'Nigra') is an excellent choice.

While I love my **container plants**, I'm tired of seeing them in their usual pots on the patio steps. Any suggestions?

Rather than relegate your potted plants to your patio, move them into your garden. Placing potted plants on pedestals or small pillars of bricks (with foliage conveniently hiding your handiwork) provides you with an instant focal point or dash of color where you need it. In addition, you can mix plants together that normally wouldn't thrive in the same environments, such as a potted azalea (*Rhododendron* spp.) in the

133

middle of your alkaline-loving pasque flowers (*Pulsatilla vulgaris*). Containers can also add height to low beds or provide a fill-in for a dead plant or bare spot.

My yard has a natural **slope** to it. Should I have it regraded?

Not necessarily. If the yard slopes toward the house, you may consider grading it away from the house for purposes of drainage. In terms of design, however, a sloped yard can be very attractive. Take advantage of the slope by placing a focal point where the garden begins to slope downward. If the slope runs from side to side in the yard, you might consider repositioning the garden entrance to the side of the yard.

I've figured out the **shapes of the beds** that I want to create. How do I go about marking these?

In order to create straight lines or edges, tie a section of twine around a peg or stick and secure the end to another peg or stick. Place the stick in the ground where the corner of the bed will be and secure the other stick at the other edge of the bed. Use a sharp spade to cut along the line created by the twine. To mark curves, bend a garden hose to the curve you want and use the spade to cut along it (being careful not to slice your hose!). Another option is to use nontoxic spray paint to "draw" your bed edges freehand on your sod or even on hardpan (hard soil).

I've just moved to an **old house** where the previous owner gardened a bit and I want to start gardening right away. What should I do first?

Sit and wait. Although it may kill you to do it, give yourself a year to watch the light, the wind, the shade, and the moisture content of the soil. Identify all plants on the property and determine how they're doing (Right spot? Healthy? Overgrown?). Then decide whether you want to keep them in their current spot or get rid of them altogether. Take a soil test and make any amendments as needed. Use this information to begin planning your garden for the following year. You'll be happy you did.

PLANT SHAPES, TEXTURES, AND COLORS

How does **color** affect garden design?

Colors can influence perspective when viewing the garden from a distance. Cool colors, such as blue forget-me-not (*Brunnera macrophylla*) and green hosta (*Hosta*),

Conifers arranged in a symmetrical landscape design show use of plant shape. (Robert J. Huffman/Field Mark Publications)

recede into a landscape while hot colors, such as pink geraniums (*Pelargonium*) and red-flowered cannas (*Canna*), come forward into a scene. Colors can also be used to create repetition or a theme in a garden or to set a mood.

I love **brightly colored flowers**. How can I use them in my garden without it looking like a circus?

You are not alone! For many gardeners, planting the biggest, brightest blooms they can find is the main point of gardening. In order to break up the color somewhat, you can choose colors in the same family such as pink and red. Look at a color wheel to get some ideas. Or you can limit your palette to three to four colors with one of those colors being a neutral such as white or gray. Don't forget to consider the background your plants will be appearing against. Another way to create unity among a variety of colors is to choose plants with similar shapes or textures. Or select the same plant in a variety of colors.

What are some **common shapes** of plants?

Plants grow in a wide variety of shapes. Some plants, like the Yoshino cherry (*Prunus yedoensis* 'Pendula') and willow (*Salix babylonica*), have a weeping growth habit. Forsythia (*Forsythia* 'Beatrix Farrand') and orange-eye butterfly bush (*Buddleia davidii*)

135

grow in a vaselike shape. Poplar trees (*Populus* spp.) and gas plants (*Dictamnus albus*) form tall columns in the landscape. Red maple 'Autumn Flame' (*Acer rubrum* 'Autumn Flame') and *Sedum spectabile* 'Autumn Joy' are more rounded, whereas the red maple 'Gerling' (*A. rubrum* 'Gerling') and the Colorado blue spruce (*Picea pungens*) take on a more pyramidal shape. The limbs of the magnificent tupelo (*Nyssa*) and lovely Sargent crabapple (*Malus sargentii*) have a spreading growth habit. The paperbark and sugar maples (*Acer griseum* and *A. saccharum*) are oval in shape. Finally, many groundcovers such as common thyme (*Thymus vulgaris*) and dianthus (*Dianthus*) have a mat-forming growth habit.

How do particular plant **shapes impact garden design**?

Columnar or vertical shapes are used as exclamation points or focal points in a garden, primarily because they are not often found in nature and so one's eye is drawn to them. Rounded, horizontal shapes are more frequently found in nature and so become a more soothing pattern. By repeating a form or shape, a gardener can create a feeling of unity or flow to the garden. These repeated shapes must be balanced by other forms, however, in order to avoid becoming monotonous.

How does **plant texture** affect garden design?

Soft, flat-appearing plants such as beech (*Fagus*) and hornbeam (*Carnipus*) serve as perfect backdrops for flowering plants or those with more decorative foliage. Glossy-leaved plants tend to come to the forefront of a garden picture and can therefore be used to focus attention or emphasize a particular area. Plants with different textures can be used to offset each other. However, too much contrast can be too much of a good thing. Keep it simple.

What are some **glossy-leaved** plants?

Glossy-leaved plants work wonders in shady areas of the yard since their reflective surfaces take advantage of the indirect light. A more common glossy-leaved plant is the herb angelica (*Angelica archangelica*). Other choices include bear's breeches (*Acanthus moontanus*), skunk cabbage (*Lysichiton americanum*), and *Senecio smithii*.

What is a **coarse-textured plant**?

A plant that has large, widely spaced leaves is said to have coarse texture. Sometimes a plant's texture does not appear coarse unless placed with plants of finer texture.

What are some **coarse-textured** plants?

Canna (*Canna* spp.), hosta (*Hosta* spp.), iris (*Iris* spp.), large-leaf (elepidote) evergreen rhododendrons (such as *Rhododendron catawbiense* and its cultivars), water lilies (*Nymphaea*), golden groundsel (*Ligularia dentata*), pigsqueak (*Bergenia cordifolia*), peony (*Paeonia* spp.), holly (*Ilex* spp.), daylilies (*Hemerocallis*), yucca (*Yucca* spp.), camellia (*Camellia* spp.), nasturtium (*Tropaeolum* spp.), and *Sedum spectabile* 'Autumn Joy' are some examples of coarse-textured plants.

What is a **fine-textured plant**?

A plant that has small, closely spaced leaves is said to have fine texture.

What are some **fine-textured plants**?

Various ferns such as maidenhair fern (*Adiantum* spp.) and Christmas fern (*Polystichum acrostichoides*), grasses such as *Miscanthus sinesis* 'Gracillimus', as well as bleeding heart (*Dicentra* spp.), Japanese maple (*Acer japonicum*), heavenly bamboo (*Nandina domestica*), red osier dogwood (*Cornus stolinifera*), wormwood (*Artemisia* spp.), and witch hazel (*Hamamelis* spp.) are some examples of fine-textured plants.

A yucca is an example of a coarse-textured plant. (Robert J. Huffman/ Field Mark Publications)

What is a **variegated leaf**?

A variegated leaf has an irregular arrangement of color on it with the most common being green and white or ivory. Other color combinations include: green, white, and yellow; pink and green; brown and pink; brown and green.

Variegation refers to white or colored markings such as stripes, bars, or blotches on a leaf, flower, or stem. (Robert J. Huffman/Field Mark Publications)

What are some **plants with variegated leaves**?

There are a number of pelargoniums (also known as geraniums) with variegated leaves, including *Pelargonium hortorum* 'Mrs. Henry Cox', *P. hortorum* 'Caroline Schmidt', and *P. Hortorum* 'Happy Thought'. Coleus is also available in variegated forms such as *Coleus blumei* 'Carefree Mixture'. Japanese spindle tree (*Euonymus japonicus*) has several variegated forms that are fairly common, including 'Albo-marginatus' and 'Aureo-variegatus'. Other plants with variegated leaves include ribbon grass or gardeners' garters (*Phalaris arundinacea* picta), hostas such as *Hosta undulata*, *H. fortunei*, and *H. crispula*; Bethlehem sage (*Pulmonaria saccharata*), and some of the spotted deadnettles such as *Lamium maculatum* 'Roseum' and *L. maculatum* 'Beacon Silver'.

What are some **architectural plants**?

Architectural plants tend to have a very strong form due to their dramatic leaves, stems, or branches. While they make excellent focal points, they can also be used to provide structure to a planting of finer-textured plants. Agave (*Agave* spp.), yucca (*Yucca* spp.), iris (*Iris* spp.), and hosta (*Hosta* spp.) are all strongly architectural plants. Some lesser-known (or considered) choices include Chinese rhubarb (*Rheum palmatum*), phormium (*Phormium* spp.), bergenia (*Bergenia cordifolia*), the euphorbias (*Euphorbia* spp.), and rodgersia (*Rodgersia podophylla*).

What are some design elements of a white garden?

White gardens are most effective when they are comprised of green- and grey-leaved plants that serve to offset white flowers or plants with variegated foliage. In a white garden, contrasting foliage textures are important to provide interest in green-on-green areas. Garden structures in the form of walls, fences, or hedges are also important in order to frame a scene or provide a background for white blooms.

Are there any **plants that are black**?

This is a matter of opinion. Most plants that gardeners see as "black" are actually deep purple or deep burgundy, but no matter. Amongst these are sweet potato vine (*Ipomoea batatus* 'Blackie'), chocolate cosmos (*Cosmos astrosanguineus*), fountain grass (*Pennisetum setaceum* 'Rubrum'), 'Dark Opal' basil (*Ocimum* 'Dark Opal'), *Iris* 'Ruby Chimes', smoke bush (*Cotinus coggygria* 'Royal Purple'), *Penstemon digitalis*, *Tulipa* 'Black Parrot', *Viola tricolor* 'Bowles Black', and black bachelor's buttons (*Centaruea cyanus* 'Black Ball').

Is it possible to create an **all-green garden**?

All-green gardens can be the most difficult to put together but the most rewarding to look at. Keep in mind that there are practically as many shades of green as there are plants. There is the grey-green of lamb's ear (*Stachys byzantina*), the acid-green of spurge (*Euphorbia polychroma*), and of course the hundreds of variegated choices. When considering variegated plants, choose selectively as too many of these can take away from the sense of surprise they provide. For all greens, you might experiment by taking leaves from a number of plants and creating your own color wheel. This will give you some idea of the variation between greens and give you ideas on how to play up these contrasts. Finally, don't ignore leaf shape and plant structure: A green garden gains much from the use of a variety of textures and shapes to keep it interesting.

How do plant **colors affect perspective**?

Just as in art, colors in a garden have an enormous impact on perspective. Pale colors tend to recede. Blue especially makes a garden feel serene. If you plant a drift of blue flowers at the back of a bed, you can make the bed appear deeper than it actually is. White and pale pink can brighten up shady areas, bringing the corners of beds forward. Likewise, bright colors such as yellow, orange, and red also jump out at you. While they can make a distant garden come forward, they can also make a small garden feel smaller, so use them with some caution. If you have a narrow bed or yard, yellow or red plants placed at the corners can "square it up."

GARDEN DESIGNS

How do I plan a **perennial border**?

Begin by preparing the soil in the border, amending the soil to a pH of around 6.0 to 7.5 and digging in plenty of compost to provide plants with a good head start. In such conditions, most perennials show their appreciation by filling out quickly. When creating the size of the bed, remember that borders look best if they are no smaller than five feet wide and at least twice as long. However, your ability to maintain the bed should be the overriding factor in your decision. A perennial or herbaceous border is usually plotted against a fence or wall (hence the "border" notation), but poor air circulation can lead to disease and bacteria problems. Leave a path of a foot or so between fence and plants in order to provide circulation as well as an "invisible" path from which to do maintenance tasks like weeding and watering.

Draw up a list of plants that thrive in your area, given the conditions of your bed. Then narrow the list down to about a dozen plants, making sure to include plants that flower at different times throughout the season. Use paper and pencil to place bubbles (indicating the plant's mature width) on a diagram of your border. Start with the tallest plants first, placing these mostly at the back of the bed. Then, review the elements of garden design and consider how each plant you add will affect the previous one. Think of color and texture combinations, flowering times, and foliage. A symmetrical plan is nice to start with, but feel free to mix things up a little. Work toward the front of the bed using plants in descending height. Don't forget vining plants to add height or to creep over the straggling foliage of early bloomers. Consider including annuals in your border as well, especially in the first few years as your perennials are growing (they usually take several years to reach mature, wonderful-looking status). Then go ahead and plant. If the effect seems too studied (two silver mounds on either side of two asters clumped around the shasta daisies), go back and move things around slightly until you're happy with the arrangement. (Mind you, this will take the rest of your life.)

How do I create a **hedgerow**?

Keep in mind that a hedgerow works best in a larger lot, removed from houses or outbuildings, so that the shrubs have the chance to achieve their mature size without impinging on the rest of the yard or eating the house. The key to a natural-looking hedgerow is using a mixture of varieties of shrubs. Think of a hedgerow as a border of shrubs (which is essentially what it is). Design the bed for year-round interest by including evergreens for density, early- and late-flowering shrubs for color, a variety of foliage texture and color, and a mixture of shapes to keep things interesting. Place plants of similar upkeep and site needs together to simplify maintenance and achieve coherence. Keeping the number of different plants small and repeating a few key plants throughout the border will also unify the planting. If your goal is to create a privacy barrier instantly, include shrubs such as forsythia (*Forsythia* 'Beatrix Farrand') that grow quickly. Complete the look by planting some bulbs or perennials to naturalize just under the hedgerow.

My property runs along the edge of a **woods**. I love the wildness, but how can I tame it without tampering with it too much?

Begin by taking stock of what you have: plants, trees, shrubs, and soil. Use a field guide to identify the major plants and watch out for poison ivy (*Rhus radicana*)! Then take note of any plant that catches your eye. It doesn't have to be a majestic oak; it could be a small, attractive dogwood. These plants will serve as focal points. In order to call attention to them, remove underbrush and possibly some lower limbs from taller trees around these focal points. Based on your knowledge of the site conditions, develop a list of native and exotic plants that will grow well in your woods. Check with your local native plant society for suggestions and lists of invasive exotics to avoid. Select a few plants to enhance your woodland focal points. Consider mowing or maintaining paths that lead to these features, but try to follow the makeup of the woods, rather than felling any trees. Your primary goal is to enhance the woods, not overshadow it.

What is **Intensive gardening**?

The intensive method of gardening features vegetables planted closely together in broad, raised beds. Initial soil preparation builds up the organic content of the soil using compost, rock phosphate, and other materials. Compost is used throughout the growing season to maintain the fertility level of the soil. Crops are planted in succession, with cover crops planted when the soil is not in use. Crops are also rotated to maintain soil nutrients. Types of intensive gardening include the biodynamic method, French intensive, and square-foot gardening. If executed properly, intensive gardening can produce higher yields than traditional row planting. But it requires long hours and heavy labor at the outset as well as continual soil improvements in order to maintain it.

What other plants are traditionally planted in **rose gardens**?

A formal rose garden usually includes a hedge of boxwood (*Buxus* spp.), yew (*Taxus* spp.), hemlock (*Tsuga* spp.), or false cypress (*Chamaecyparis lawsonia*). If you live in a warm enough climate, lavender (*Lavandula officinalis*) or rosemary (*Rosmarinus officinalis*) can also be used to create a hedge. Blowzy or airy old-fashioned flowers

141

Coneflowers (*Rudbeckia* spp.) surrounding this bluebird box unify this natural garden and attract birds and other wildlife. (Robert J. Huffman/Field Mark Publications)

such as peonies (*Paeonia officinalis*), violas (*Viola* spp.), foxglove (*Digitalis purpurea*), baby's breath (*Gypsophila paniculata*), and veronica (*Veronica*) will enhance your roses with pale colors that echo their shades.

I don't have the space for both a **vegetable garden and an ornamental one.** Can I combine the two?

Of course! Edibles can be among the most colorful and sculptural plants of all. But since they are edible and have a tendency to disappear from the garden at various points in the growing season, along with being completely absent during winter, you need to incorporate some structure as well. Box hedges are a traditional potager selection, but any evergreen that doesn't mind serving as a hedge will work. And don't forget the shrubby grey-leaved herbs like English lavender (*Lavandula angustifolia*) and rosemary (*Rosemarinus officinalis*) as long as they're hardy in your area. If your prospective garden is next to the house, consider using fruit trees and evergreens or shrubby herbs as starting points and then working outward with your edibles. Finally, incorporate some decorative but hardworking paths since they'll be used frequently to water, pick, and visit your garden.

The choices of ornamental edibles are endless. Rhubarb (*Rheum hybridum*) makes a fine focal point, as do artichoke and cardoon. Climbers include beans (scarlet runner is a good choice), ornamental gourds, and golden hops (*Humulus lupulus* 'Aureus'). Colorful leaf lettuces can serve as groundcovers, as can the feathery tops of carrots. Bronze-leafed fennel, dill, and asparagus fronds are also fernlike in their own right. Cabbage, broccoli, brussels sprouts, and chard add color and shape to the garden. Toss in a few self-seeding annuals like sweet alyssum (*Lobularia maritama*) to attract bees and provide additional color.

Since this is an edible garden, after all, you will harvest some plants, but consider thinning and overseeding where you can to keep the show going. And at the end of the season there is nothing prettier (to my mind) than thyme leaves (*Thymus vulgaris*) turning deep purple, arugula and lettuce bolting to seed, and the squash vine turning bright yellow before it succumbs to a frosty death. Leave some seedheads here and there both for winter interest and the start of next year's garden in the form of self-seeded seedlings (but be sure to get rid of any diseased plants).

I have an **enormous, ugly wall** at the back of my shallow city yard that I need to keep for the security. Any suggestions on how to make it attractive?

If you're artistic or know someone who is, the wall could be painted as a garden scene using *trompe l'oeil* (optical illusion) to give your plot a "borrowed" view as well as depth. Or you could put up a large trellis (or several small inexpensive ones) and plant some quick-growing climbers such as silver lace vine (*Fallopia aubertii*) or the beautiful hop (*Humulus lupulus aurea*). These selections might be invasive in some gardens but that's the goal here. Another option, depending on your climate, would be to place container-grown bamboo (*Bambusa* spp.) plants at the foot of the wall. Their delicate but vigorous limbs could shield the ugly view while providing your yard with a certain exotic mystique.

What lightweight container can I use to grow an **alpine garden** on my terrace?

Your terrace most likely has conditions that alpine plants are used to: windy and dry. Try using a plastic pedestal birdbath. The shape bestows an elegant importance on the planting, while the lightweight plastic tends to overcome any weight restrictions. Fill the bottom inch or so of the bowl with small pebbles for drainage, then fill the remainder with a light scree (see related question in Special Gardens chapter). Place slightly taller plants in the middle and gently modulate the soil line to dip toward the edge of the bowl, so that the planting can be seen from all sides. Start with easily grown plants such as hens and chicks (*Sempervivum hirtum*), then experiment to see which plants thrive in your location.

You keep talking about **"borrowing a view"** from a surrounding landscape. How do I do this?

Borrowing a view refers to the practice of focusing a garden visitor's attention on a point outside the garden. This might be a lovely tree, a view of the mountains, or a striking building. When "borrowing a view," you need to have a clear sight path or axis to the view itself. Beautiful pictures need framing and a view is no exception: The foliage color and texture of trees or shrubs that edge your focal point should be complementary to it, while not being so colorful that they distract from the view. In the rest of your plantings, you may select a very few plants that gently repeat the shape of the outside focal point and place them sparingly to complement the view. In this way, you can develop a theme for a garden that flows from its surroundings.

How can I hide the **dying foliage** of spring-blooming bulbs and perennials in the middle of summer?

The yellowing leaves of tulips (*Tulipa* spp.) and other bulbous plants that were at their peak a mere month before is indeed a sad sight. One way to mask their death is to overplant with a groundcover or summer- and fall-blooming perennials. An easy example of this is daffodils (*Narcissus* spp.) overplanted with tiger lillies (*Lilium tigrinum*). A similar difficulty comes into play with perennials such as delphiniums (*Delphinium* spp.), which put on a beautiful temporary show but whose foliage tends to become ratty-looking with each passing day. A later-blooming vine such as sweet pea (*Lathyrus odoratus*) can be grown close to the delphinium. With a little assistance, it can scramble over the shards of its predecessor, all but eliminating it from the landscape until next year.

GARDEN HARDSCAPING

What is **hardscaping**?

The term hardscaping refers to nonplant materials that are used to provide structure in a garden, such as walls, fences, terracing, paths and walkways, arbors, and pergolas.

What is a **ha-ha**?

A ha-ha is a radical slope—a trough really—placed at the edge of a garden. Its historical purpose was to keep farm animals from invading the house garden.

What is a **pergola**?

A pergola is a garden structure with an open, trellised roof for vines. Pergolas are usually fairly substantial in size, compared to an arch or arbor. They are sometimes attached to buildings to provide a shaded area of seclusion.

145

An example of a pergola at Henry Ford Estate, Fair Lane, in Dearborn, Michigan. (Robert J. Huffman/Field Mark Publications)

What kind of materials can be used to create **garden paths**?

A path needs to be easy to maintain and durable enough to hold up to foot traffic. Both the tone (formal or informal) and composition of the garden should be considered. Grass makes a simple, though maintenance-heavy, path, which looks right at home flanked by perennial flower beds. It is also impractical in drought-stricken areas. Pea gravel provides a pleasant crunching sound when you walk on it and can be counted on to look good without too much effort. Brick—either pavers or classic brick, depending on your region—can be used to create a more permanent path that would hold up to foot and wheelbarrow traffic. Bluestone creates a lovely, though expensive, look. If the path meanders through trees, consider using pine needles or finely shredded bark to imitate the forest floor. You might also consider changing materials as the path wanders from area to area, or combining materials such as stones set into a background of shredded bark.

What is a **nursery bed**?

A nursery bed or holding bed is a plant bed in which smaller plants are held until they're large enough to go into the main garden. Nursery beds are also useful to keep plants you're unsure of what do to with until a permanent place in the garden is found for them.

What is an **island bed**?

An island bed is a bed that is placed so that observers may view the plants from all sides of the bed. They are designed with taller plants in the middle of the bed (with the height of the plants no more than half the width of the bed) and smaller plants around the edges of the bed.

What is an **alpine bed**?

An alpine bed is comprised of plants that grow naturally in mountainous regions. As such, they do not like their feet wet! Alpine plants tend to be spreading and creeping in nature, and thrive in rocky, well-drained soil that is high in organic matter. Alpine plants include alpine liver wort (*Erinus alpinus*), cranesbill (*Geranium dalmaticum* and *G. sanguineum*), rock jasmine (*Androsace* spp.), myrtle spurge (*Euphorbia myrsinites*), alpine poppy (*Papaver alpinum*), and mossy saxifrage (*Saxifraga* 'Bob Hawkins' or *S. moschata*).

Garden paths may be permanent and are often made of brick, cobblestone, gravel, stone slabs, or concrete paving blocks. (Robert J. Huffman/Field Mark Publications)

What is **carpet bedding**?

Carpet bedding dates back to Victorian England when gardeners planted enormous beds with thousands of tender, exotic plants in patterns that resembled the highly colored and exotic carpets that were fashionable at the time. A subdued, modern version of this can be found in almost every yard in the United States, where row upon row of garden geranium (*Pelargonium*) is interrupted only by a row of dusty miller (*Artemisia stelleriana*). The term "bedding plants" refers to the tender perennials and

147

The many windows of a greenhouse (also known as a glass house) allow the maximum amount of sunlight to enter. The sunlight enters as short-wave radiation, which is able to pass through glass. After the sunlight is reflected by the plants and soil, it becomes long-wave radiation, which cannot pass back through the glass. This allows heat to build up inside the greenhouse, keeping out extremely cold temperatures. Additional heat can be supplied by space heaters or a small furnace, but many plants only need to be kept above freezing in order to survive the winter (although they won't flower). These include annual geraniums (*Pelargonium* spp.) and fuchsias (*Fuchsia* spp.).

annuals such as geranium (*Pelargonium* spp.), dusty miller (*Senecio cineraria*), ageratum (*Agaratum houstonianum*), marigold (*Tagetes* spp.), salvia (*Salvia* spp.), dahlia (*Dahlia* spp.), petuna (*Petunia* spp.), cockscomb (*Celosia cristata*), and snapdragon (*Antirrhinum* spp.) that are used in similar fashion.

What is an **alpine house**?

An alpine house is an unheated greenhouse that has additional venilation at its sides. In a true alpine house, this would take the form of continuously open windows along the sides. Alpine plants don't mind cold weather—the problem is humidity. By ensuring the maximum amount of venilation, the alpine plants (and their gardener) remain happy.

What is the difference between a **greenhouse** and a **conservatory**?

The most important difference between a greenhouse and a conservatory is that a greenhouse is meant for plants, while a conservatory is meant for people. This means conditions in a greenhouse tend to be damper and warmer than is comfortable for most people, but these same conditions make plants housed there very happy. A conservatory may have some plants growing in it, but its space is designed for human living. Often, conservatories are attached to the house, while a greenhouse may be freestanding, although this varies based on the preferences of the gardener.

What is a **drift**?

A drift is a large and usually irregularly shaped mass of one type of plant. The concept, credited to landscape designer Gertrude Jekyll, creates instant impact in a garden— much more than, say, a dozen different plants in the same bed.

> ## I have just built a new house and don't want to spend the money on a concrete driveway that will just look ugly. What are some other options?
>
> **D**riveways are such a common part of American yardscapes that most folks don't consider their impact. Some other, less obtrusive options for driveway material include gravel, unmortared brick, and wood chips. Another newer material is a grid made of cement or steel that has spacers for growing grass or groundcover. These are attractive and natural looking, but are sturdy enough for cars. Additionally, they prevent the driveway from becoming a mudhole when it rains.

What is a **lense**?

A lense is a planting in which the middle of the bed is wide and the ends taper gently, giving an undulating effect to the bed. You can choose to emphasize this quality further by creating a crescendo effect with your color selection, moving from cool whites, greys, and blues to fiery pinks and oranges.

I am considering buying a **sculpture** for my garden and need some suggestions on where I might place one.

Sculpture adds a very personal element to a garden. No matter where it is placed, it will set a tone for the particular space it resides in, so placement should be considered carefully. If you'd like the piece to be the focal point for an area, place it by itself in a central location. If you'd like to call equal attention to a natural element nearby, place it to the side of the other element, making sure that both pieces have roughly the same visual weight. If the sculpture is quieter, or you'd like it to play a part in a larger grouping of plants, position the piece in the foreground. This can take much thought and adjusting so you may wish to substitute a lightweight pot as a stand-in until you are fairly sure of the final position.

What is an **allee**?

An allee is a tunnel made of living plants. Roses scrambling up arches that jut over a path or nut trees trained to curve over a walkway are examples of allees.

What are some benefits of using **materials other than concrete or macadam** to construct a driveway?

Gravel or even wood chips can provide a homeowner with additional traction in winter, without need for shovel or plow. They can also be cheaper—both in terms of materials and labor (you can lay your own fairly easily). They are environmentally advantageous too—a porous material sends rainwater back to water table, rather than to storm drains. Finally, these materials are more attractive, their natural beauty fitting peacefully into the rest of your landscape.

How can **gravel** be used in a garden?

Besides its standard use as a driveway, gravel is actually a versatile surface for a garden. Gravel can be used as a groundcover or mulch. Bulbs, herbs, shrub, and perennials can grow through a thin layer (no more than four inches or so) of gravel. For dry gardens or xeriscapes, gravel can create a very relaxed look while tying things together. Gravel creates a unique texture that can be left to lie as it chooses or raked, as the Japanese do, to provide more order to the material or to create patterns in it. Gravel can also serve as an alternative to bricks or pavers for a patio or path—pea gravel especially makes a wonderfully satisfying sound when stepped on. In areas of high use or low light, gravel can also be considered as an alternative to grass. Wherever gravel is used, it requires a retaining edge to keep it from spilling into areas it shouldn't.

Are there any inexpensive methods of **edging** around beds other than that black plastic strip?

There is one that's free for the doing—creating a trench between the bed and the lawn. This provides a nice, finished but natural look to your bed. Although you can purchase a half-moon edger for this purpose, a sharp spade (or even a shovel if you don't mind a rougher edge) works nicely. Sink the spade down to its blade depth and push forward slightly, creating a trench around six inches wide. Since grass spreads via rhizomes, it will be unable to ford the trench. This should be done at least once a year, and looks best if done a couple of times during the growing season.

What is **wattling**?

Wattling is a traditional type of fencing, often used by English farmers to create permanent or temporary barriers. A wattle generally consists of a frame of strong support stakes interwoven with flexible branches. It can be created from hazel, willow, osier, or bamboo.

GARDENS, GARDENERS, AND GARDENING

FAMOUS GARDENERS

I receive the magazine *Organic Gardening* and noticed the name of J. I. Rodale on its masthead. Who was Rodale?

Jerome Irving Rodale (1898–1971), founder of the organic farming movement in the United States, was best known for his magazines *Prevention* and *Organic Gardening and Farming.* As a young child, Rodale was frequently ill. Bodybuilding and self-improvement classes gave him a new lease on life and provided an inkling as to his adult interests. Rodale, however, had an inauspicious start in publishing, having begun as a writer and would-be publisher of humor magazines. The company he founded in 1930 to publish his humor magazines, Rodale Press, has since developed into a successful and respected publisher of health and gardening publications.

After purchasing a farm in Emmaus, Pennsylvania, with his wife, Anna, in 1940, Rodale began to study and use the theories of Sir Albert Howard. Howard was a British agronomist who believed that crops raised with fertilizer from animals and vegetables (manure and compost) were healthier than those raised with chemical fertilizers. Rodale took Howard's theories to heart and hearth by using them on his own farm. Using Howard's theories along with his own ideas on the connection between soil health and plant health, Rodale developed the organic method of farming. That same year, Rodale published the first issue of *Organic Gardening and Farming,* in which he discussed such concepts as companion planting, beneficial insects and earthworms, and problems relating to the use of pesticides. Rodale became a powerful advocate for organically grown, natural foods and products through his Soil and Health Foundation. Interestingly enough, Rodale was more interested in organic farming from a health perspective than in actually digging in the dirt. His magazine *Prevention* detailed the latest medical and scientific findings about human health and advocated a healthy diet in combination with vitamins and minerals.

I recently visited Monticello, the beautiful former estate of **Thomas Jefferson**. What other contributions to American horticulture did Jefferson make?

The third president of the United States, Thomas Jefferson (1743–1826) was an avid gardener, landscape designer, and naturalist. Perhaps his most significant contribution to American horticulture and botany was his sponsorship of the Lewis and Clark expedition to the westernmost regions of the United States, crossing the great Mississippi and blazing a trail all the way to the Pacific Ocean. Jefferson's secretary, Meriwether Lewis, and Lewis's friend William Clark uncovered many key native American plants such as the Oregon grape (*Mahonia aquifolium*) and the giant redwood trees during their two-year journey. The pair were also immortalized by two wildflowers they discovered—*Lewisia* (also known as bitterroot) and *Clarkia* (sometimes called Rocky Mountain garland). Lewis and Clark added four new genera and over two hundred species to the catalog of wildflowers.

Among other horticultural accomplishments, Jefferson also helped to popularize the idea of crop rotation; promoted the use of native plants in the landscape; introduced such current garden staples as the tomato to American farmers and gardeners; and befriended many landscape designers and agriculturalists, including William Hamilton and Bernard McMahon.

Jefferson's estate, Monticello, served as his own botanical garden and outdoor laboratory. Located on a mountaintop near Charlottesville, Virginia, Monticello was a working farm of 5,000 acres. In his eight-acre orchard and enormous terraced vegetable garden, Jefferson experimented with such diverse plants as rice, wine grapes, and peas. He meticulously documented all of his findings in garden diaries (this, during the peak of the American Revolution!), some of which were later published in 1944 as *Garden Book*.

Of course, such a gardener also deserves to have a plant named after him. Indeed, Jefferson received an entire genus! The genus *Jeffersonia* was named in his honor and features the wildflower *Jeffersonia diphylla* or American twinleaf. It is a woodland perennial that bears white flowers in early spring, close to Jefferson's birthday on April 13th.

Who is known as the **father of American landscape architecture**?

Frederick Law Olmsted (1822–1903) coined the term *landscape architecture,* as opposed to landscape gardening, in order to better describe the craft's roots in architecture. Olmsted founded a landscape design firm based in Brookline, Massachusetts. Along with other landscape architects, Olmsted helped to popularize the naturalistic landscape gardening style that features broad sweeps of lawn, trees in their natural

American twinleaf (*Jeffersonia diphylla*), named in honor of Thomas Jefferson. (Robert J. Huffman/Field Mark Publications)

state (more or less unpruned), and herbaceous plants (perennials). He promoted the idea of parks as functional green spaces in urban areas. This effort culminated in what is perhaps the grandest park in the United States—New York City's Central Park, which Olmsted and landscape architect Calvert Vaux designed in 1858. Among his other projects was his design of the grounds of the U.S. Capitol in the 1870s.

Who was **William Robinson**?

William Robinson (1839–1906) was an influential garden writer in the late nineteenth century and a contemporary of landscape designer Gertrude Jekyll (see related question below). Born in Ireland in 1839, Robinson began working as a gardener in his teens, eventually working his way up to foreman in charge of the perennial borders at the Royal Botanic Society's garden in London. He was known for his temper, which flared during one of his early horticulture jobs: After a falling out with his employer, Robinson extinguished the fires that heated the greenhouse under his care, then opened all the windows in the place, thereby allowing the plants to freeze to death.

This same temper was to surface again later in his life. Robinson began formulating ideas on gardening that were much different from the gardening that was in vogue in Victorian England at the time. In an era of "bedding out," woody ornamental standards, knot gardens, and other formal shapes, Robinson pushed for shrubs left unpruned, climbers scrambling up buildings and terraces, the use of native plants, and,

155

most importantly, the herbaceous or perennial border. He became a passionate advocate for this naturalistic style of gardening and promoted his ideas in his books and magazines, including *The Wild Garden, The English Flower Garden, Gardening Illustrated,* and *Farm and Home.* In fact, Robinson went so far as to admonish the administrators of the Royal Botanical Gardens at Kew (see question below) to label plants with only their common (not scientific) names. He also shrewdly aimed his pronouncements at a new group of gardeners—the lower and middle classes—and received a tidy profit from his publications. With his earnings, he purchased a 200-acre estate in Sussex called Gravetye that became his living laboratory. Gertrude Jekyll took up Robinson's cause (albeit in a gentler fashion), and gardening has never been the same.

Who was **Gertrude Jekyll** and what were some of her gardening principles?

Gertrude Jekyll (1849–1939) was a noted English landscape designer. She was born in London to a modestly well-to-do family and studied painting at the South Kensington School of Art. She began her career as a painter but retained her interest in plants and flowers from childhood. After reading the words of William Robinson, she befriended him and began writing for his publications. She also began dabbling in landscape design on the side, working with with the young architect Edwin Lutyens (who was a neighbor) on a number of projects, eventually including her own estate, Munstead Wood. After having trouble with her eyes, she needed to give up painting and so began working as a landscape designer full time. Considered the mother of perennial borders, Jekyll also contributed a number of ideas on landscapes, such as:

- using grey-leaved plants to highlight sunny areas (those facing south and west) and green-leaved plants to highlight shadier areas (those facing north and east) in the garden

- designing wild gardens that connect formal landscapes to the country surrounding them

- planting in "drifts" or long, flowing groups similar to brushstrokes in a painting

- designing "hot" and "cool" areas of a garden, with hot areas featuring red, yellow, and orange flowers, and cool ones white, pale blue, and yellow ones.

Which **British father and son gardening duo** have names synonymous with successful flower gardening?

Alan (1900–) and Adrian (1920–) Bloom are famous for their 150-acre nursery, Blooms of Bressingham, which produces over three million pots of perennials every year. They have been responsible for plant introductions such as *Achillea* 'Moonshine', *Phlox paniculata* 'Franz Schubert', and *Fragaria* 'Pink Panda' strawberry. Alan Bloom also popularized the concept of the island bed (see related question in chapter

This border with its "hot" colors would be offset by a soothing "cool" border of flowers in pastel or softer tones in a Gertrude Jekyll planting scheme. (Steven Nikkila/Perennial Favorites)

on Garden Design), while his son Adrian is frequently a featured guest on gardening television programs such as *The Victory Garden*.

Who was **Jens Jensen**?

Jens Jensen (1860–1951) was a Danish landscape architect known as the father of the Chicago park system and for the movement toward native plantings in parks and gardens. He was born and received his training in Denmark, but came to the United States at the age of 24 to escape the "soulless" formality of European gardens. After working in the Chicago parks for several years, he planted an "American garden" featuring native shrubs and wildflowers in Union Park. He served as general superintendent and consultant to the Chicago park system for nearly 30 years. Following his retirement from the park system, he designed private gardens for such famous families as the Fords and the Florsheims. Jensen also founded a school called the Clearing, which served as a "school of the soil" for budding landscape architects and artists. He worked for the preservation of native landscapes as well as for the establishment of parks in crowded cities.

Who was **Ellen Biddle Shipman**?

Ellen Biddle Shipman (1869–1950) was called the "dean of American women landscape architects." In the early twentieth century, most women working in landscape design were relegated to the flower beds. Known for her heavily textured plantings that bloomed from April through October, Shipman began her career in 1912, working with architect Charles Platt. They worked on a number of projects through the 1920s when Shipman then began working with another well-known landscape architect, Warren Manning. Shipman and Manning did several jobs in the Midwest, particularly the Cleveland area. One of their commissions, a private estate outside of Cleveland known as Halfred Farms, remains almost the same as when it was first designed. Over her lifetime, Shipman designed over 600 gardens.

What are some trademarks of gardens designed by **Oehme** and **van Sweden**?

Wolfgang Oehme and James van Sweden are partners in a Baltimore-based landscape firm. Oehme is known as a master plantsman, while van Sweden develops the sweeping designs for which they are known. The duo have been at the vanguard of the perennial gardening movement since the 1960s. Their gardens feature little or no lawn; drifts of North American native perennials such as purple cornflower (*Echinacea purpurea*), *Sedum spectabile* 'Autumn Joy', Joe-pye weed (*Eupatorium purpurem*), and black-eyed Susan (*Rudbeckia hirta* 'Goldstrum'); and bold ornamental grasses, along with a few key woody ornamentals to create natural-looking landscapes. These landscapes have been copied throughout the country not only for their attractiveness but also for their relatively low level of maintenance. Their designs can be viewed at the Smithsonian's National Zoological Park in Washington, D.C.; Hudson River Park in Battery City Park, New York; German-American Friendship Garden, Washington, D.C.; and Francis Scott Key Park in Washington, D.C.

Who was **Le Notre**?

Andre Le Notre (1613–1689) is best known as the French designer of the gardens at Versailles. It seems his future as a gardener was predestined: Andre was the son of Jean Le Notre, royal master gardener, and grandson of Pierre Le Notre, gardener-in-chief of the Parterres of the Tuileries. At the tender age of 27, he was appointed designer in ordinary of the king's gardens for none other than Louis XIV, a tough client if ever there was one. Le Notre's first major project, however, was the gardens at Vaux-le-Vicomte for Nicolas Fouquet. Consisting of an unprecedented 1,000 acres of garden and park, it attracted the attention of Louis XIV, unfortunately for Fouquet. Le Notre and the architect and designer were quickly snatched by Louis for the design and development of Versailles.

Le Notre's gardens are exemplary for their composition along a central axis. Unlike previous gardeners, Le Notre took all features of the gardens (fountains, terraces, orchards, etc.) and fit them together as a cohesive unit. Prior to this, the features were planned somewhat haphazardly and without unity. Le Notre's gardens stressed symmetry and elegance.

Who was Edward Augustus Bowles?

Edward Augustus Bowles (1865–1956) was known as the greatest amateur gardener of his time. He was also a rabid plant collector who traveled the globe, bringing back many rare and wonderful plants to his garden. In addition, Bowles developed his own plant hybrids, published scholarly papers on his findings, assembled vast collections of certain plants, and painted botanical portraits of them in watercolor. Most importantly, however, he wrote books detailing his efforts in his own gardens: *My Garden in Spring, My Garden in Summer,* and *My Garden in Autumn and Winter.*

Who is considered to be the **father of botany**?

Theophrastus of Lesbos, born around 373 B.C., is considered to be the father of botany. He studied under Plato with Aristotle. Both Aristotle and Theophrastus left Plato's Academy to found the Lyceum, where the two oversaw the publication of many important scientific and philosophical works. One of the most important, penned by Theophrastus, was *An Enquiry into Plants*. This was the first known attempt to classify plants. He was also a gardener, so much so that his will specified arrangements for the maintenance of his garden after his death.

Who was **Pliny the naturalist**?

Caius Plinius Secundus (died circa A.D. 79), known as Pliny the naturalist, wrote a book called *The Natural History*. Among other information, the book provides in exquisite detail the plants and gardens of the Romans during the first century after the birth of Christ, which included lilies and 12 kinds of roses. Pliny tells us that the Romans were as deft at co-opting the art of gardening as they were at doing so for nearly every other custom they came upon. When *The Natural History* was translated into English during the reign of Queen Elizabeth I, Pliny's work became well known and often used.

Who was **tradescantia** named after?

Tradescantia or spiderwort was named after John Tradescant the younger (1608–1662). There were two John Tradescants, father and son, who played important roles in the early development of gardening in England. They were among the earliest known plant collectors. John Tradescant Sr. helped to finance an expedition to the then-new colony of Virginia so that he could receive new plants being collected. Among these was spiderwort or *Tradescantia,* which was named for his son. John Sr.

Who was Carolus Linnaeus?

Carolus Linnaeus (1707–1771) was a Swedish botanist who developed an enormous collection of plants. He is said to have had a powerful memory and excellent eyesight, which allowed him to catalog these plants along with detailed descriptions. In doing so, Linnaeus came up with the system known as binomial nomenclature, in which every plant is identified (primarily) in Latin by the genus it belongs to as well as the species of the particular plant. Up until this point, plants had names that amounted to descriptions—in a terse Latin, of course. By giving each plant a genus and species, Linnaeus endowed each plant with a unique name. While many plants have common names, these can vary from region to region. In some instances, different plants can have the same common name. It is Linnaeus' system that is used internationally to bring order to the plant kingdom.

later traveled throughout Europe, bringing back mulberries, grapes, peaches, and figs to England. He also ventured to Russia, making what is thought to be the first known list of Russian plants. He settled down as royal gardener to Charles I and established the first English museum, called the Ark, which featured a garden filled with rare trees and plants. John Jr. also traveled on plant-collecting expeditions, returning after his father's death to serve as royal gardener and run the Ark.

Who was **Gregor Mendel**?

Gregor Johan Mendel (1822–1884) was a priest and schoolteacher who became known as the father of modern genetics. An avid amateur gardener, Mendel conducted a series of experiments on sweet peas (*Lathyrus odoratus*) in his garden at the monastery of St. Thomas in Vienna, beginning in 1856. After almost 10 years of study and research, Mendel presented his results to a small local scientific society, the Brunn Society for the Study of Natural Science. Though his work did not become famous until after his death, it was eventually learned that humble Mendel discovered the principles of the laws of inheritance. By crossing plants with different traits and examining the results, Mendel saw that there were dominant traits and recessive traits in plants (and, as we learned later, in people and animals as well). Although he did not discover what caused this to occur, he was able to show that the results were consistent from generation to generation.

Who was **Thomas Church**?

Thomas Church (1902–1982) was an American architect who worked in California in the 1930s and 1940s. He wrote a book on his modern approach to gardening called

Who wrote and illustrated *The Secret Garden*?

Frances Hodgson Burnett (1849–1924) wrote *The Secret Garden* in 1911. Originally from Manchester, England, her family moved to Knoxville, Tennessee, in 1865. Hodgson Burnett began writing for magazines soon after. In addition to *The Secret Garden* Hodgson Burnett also penned the children's classics *Little Lord Fauntleroy* and *A Little Princess*. During her lifetime, however, Hodgson Burnett was best known for her romance novels. Perhaps the best known and most loved edition of *The Secret Garden* is the one beautifully illustrated by artist Tasha Tudor. Tudor has an extraordinary garden herself, revealed in *Tasha Tudor's Garden* by Tovah Martin.

Gardens Are for People. Church saw that the English landscape style didn't survive in the heat of California. Borrowing the idea of fusing indoors with outdoors from both the Japanese and the Spaniards, Church redefined the garden or yard as a play space with a swimming pool, sandbox, and deck for entertaining—an attitude that has prevailed throughout the country even today. While Church didn't ban plants, he considered practicality their main purpose. His primary use of trees was for shade. Flowers were used sparingly for decoration and tall hedges were employed for privacy. Church's approach was rapidly adapted in other parts of the country and the world.

Who was **Andrew Jackson Downing**?

Andrew Jackson Downing (1815–1852) was a landscape designer and writer in the mid-nineteenth century. He is perhaps best known for his adaptation of British landscape design for American gardens. Born in Newburgh, New York, Downing began working at his family's nursery at a relatively young age. Writing for horticultural publications in his teens and twenties, he helped to publish an American edition of *Theory of Horticulture*, which was a key horticulture volume in Britain. At 26, he published his own work, *A Treatise on the Theory and Practice of Landscape Gardening, Adapted to North America*. Downing was an early proponent of the use of native plants in gardens and encouraged gardeners to manage simple, restrained gardens. He became editor of *The Horticulturist* in 1846 and contributed to the plan to create New York City's Central Park. His ideas on gardening are being returned to today, as a result of a heightened interest in native plants and an American style of gardening.

Who was **Alice Harding**?

Alice Harding was the author of two classic volumes on peonies: *The Book of the Peony* and *Peonies in the Little Garden*. These volumes are still considered the definitive works on peonies. An outstanding amateur gardener, Harding collected and bred dozens of plants, including her favorite peonies. A wealthy woman, she donated plant specimens to botanical gardens and provided funding for horticultural competitions (though never entered her own plants).

Who was **John Bartram**?

John Bartram (1699–1777) was the first American botanist and naturalist. Born to Quaker parents, Bartram was largely self-taught through observation, reading, and correspondence. He traveled the eastern half of the United States in search of plants and natural history specimens for his own botanic garden. Among his discoveries was the *Franklinia,* named for his friend Benjamin Franklin, but which was never found again in the wild. Established in 1731, the Philadelphia Botanical Garden, better known as Bartram's Garden, is the oldest botanic garden in the United States. Bartram and his son William identified and introduced for cultivation over 200 native American Plants. In 1765, he was given the title of royal botanist by King George III, which he held until his death in 1771.

FAMOUS GARDENS

What is a **botanical garden**?

A botanical garden is a collection of living plants, maintained and displayed for the dual purposes of education and research. Botanical gardening organizations may feature their research in publications or provide speakers on selected topics. Many botanical gardens also manage endangered native plant species and seek to educate others on these species. All plants, native and exotic, are clearly labeled for visitors and researchers. The garden may be affiliated with a university, a government, or a private group and may be comprised of a conservatory, research greenhouses, display and trial gardens, or an arboretum. As dry as they may sound, most botanical gardens are actually quite beautiful, designed not only to educate but to engage. They provide a unique opportunity to view and learn about an enormous number of plants that are suited to the area.

What is the **oldest botanical garden in the United States**?

Bartram's Garden or the Philadelphia Botanical Garden in Philadelphia, Pennsylvania, was established in 1731 by naturalist John Bartram and continues to be enjoyed by garden lovers from around the world even today. Other long-lived botanical gardens

A view of beautiful Balboa Park, San Diego, California. (Robert J. Huffman/Field Mark Publications)

The Arnold Arboretum in Boston, Massachusetts, is home to many different varieties of trees, including the grey birch and weeping willow. It is the oldest and largest arboretum in the United States. (Steven Nikkila/Perennial Favorites)

still in use are the U.S. Botanic Garden in Washington, D.C. (founded in 1950), the Missouri Botanical Garden in St. Louis (founded in 1859), and the Cincinnati Zoo and Botanical Garden in Ohio (founded in 1875).

Where was the **first botanic garden** established?

The first botanic garden was established at Padua, near Venice, Italy, around 1543. Prior to this time, any gardens that had been established for study were used exclusively for the purpose of medical healing. The botanic garden at Padua, known as the Orto Botanico, featured many exotic plants. The Orto Botanico was also among the first botanic gardens to sponsor a series of plant-hunting expeditions. These explorations were quite fruitful in bringing plants such as the first tulips and some of the earliest hyacinths to Europe.

What is an **arboretum**?

An arboretum is a collection of trees established and maintained for the purposes of both education and research. It may feature trees native to the local area or from other climates. Besides being a place of research, an arboretum is a beautiful place to learn about and appreciate woody ornamentals.

Where is the **Arnold Arboretum**?

The Arnold Arboretum is located in Jamaica Plain, Massachusetts, and was named for its original benefactor, James Arnold. Founded in 1872, it is the oldest and largest arboretum in the United States. The Arboretum houses vast collections of hardy trees, shrubs, and vines, including many exotic plants, on over 265 acres and is considered one of the largest and best documented woody plant collections in the world. Despite the scientific nature of the site, the Arnold Arboretum has the feel of a natural landscape or park and was, in fact, designed by landscape architect Frederick Law Olmstead, who collaborated with the Arboretum's first director, Charles Sprague Sargent.

Where is the **most famous white garden**?

The White Garden at Sissinghurst in Kent, England, is probably the most famous white garden. It was designed by Vita Sackville-West and her husband, Sir Harold Nicolson, in 1939 but was not actually planted until 10 years later. Sackville-West and Nicolson were wealthy amateur gardeners who considered a white garden the epitome of good taste, as opposed to the blowzy, colorful herbaceous borders of the cottage style that was popular in Great Britain and elsewhere.

Where is the **largest bulb garden**?

The fantastic Keukenhof Garden in Lisse, Holland, is arguably the world's largest bulb garden. Previously an estate garden, Keukenhof was developed by market-savvy Dutch bulb growers in 1949 as a showcase for their work. Keukenhof is comprised of 70 acres of lawns, ponds, and of course, bulbs, and is a key stopping point on European garden tours. The Keukenhof Garden is famous for its "rivers of bloom," including a river of blue muscari weaving through banks of red tulips and yellow daffodils. The beds are actually redesigned every year; between 6 and 7 million bulbs are planted each fall, then dug up following their bloom and replanted the next year.

Which **famous golf course** is also the site of botanical gardens?

St. Andrews in Scotland, home of golf's British Open, can also boast of its own botanic garden. The lovely St. Andrews Botanic Garden was founded in 1889 to provide botanical specimens for teaching and research in the University of St. Andrews.

Which **French impressionist** established gardens at Giverny from which he drew inspiration?

Impressionist painter Claude Monet (1840–1926) settled in Giverny, France, after a series of events, including the death of his wife and the bankruptcy of his most enthusiastic collector, forced him to seek a quiet place to care for his family and to paint. With limited

165

funds, Monet rented a pink stucco house and, over many years, developed a series of gardens that were rooted in his artist's knowledge of color and proportion. He established the Clos Normand Garden, which features three acres of flowers, and the Grande Allee, as well as a two-acre water lily garden that was inspired by the artist's collection of Japanese woodblock prints. The gardens became Monet's living studio, featured in many of his paintings. Following Monet's death, the extraordinary gardens were cared for by family members but became neglected with their passing. In 1977, they were restored. The gardens at Giverny have become a shrine for fans of Monet's landscapes as well as experienced garden designers, and are visited by thousands of art and garden lovers annually.

Which famous gardening event takes place in **Chelsea, England**?

The Chelsea Flower Show has been an annual international horticulture exhibition and high society social event since 1913, except for temporary hiatuses during the First and Second World Wars. Sponsored by the Royal Horticultural Society, the show has also traditionally marked the beginning of England's social season for those who observe such things. The show holds a private viewing for members of the Society, followed by three days open to the public. For regular gardeners, Chelsea is known for its fantastic exhibitions and competitions by nurserypersons as well as amateurs. The Flower Show also includes scientific exhibits, tools and equipment, and flower-arranging competitions. Members of the Royal Family traditionally attend a private viewing of the show. The highlight of Chelsea is the close of the show, when all plants and assorted paraphernalia from the exhibitions are for sale. Entire exhibits have been carted off as pieces to be installed in someone's yard.

Which public garden has established a **catalog of U.S. landscape records**?

Wave Hill in the Bronx, New York, is a 28-acre estate that features an alpine garden, a wild garden, woodlands, flower gardens, a conservatory, and a monocot garden. In its quest to educate the public on the history of gardening and landscapes in the United States, Wave Hill established a database called the CATALOG of Landscape Records in the United States in 1986. The CATALOG records information on the location and content of landscape and horticulture documents such as maps, planting plans, nursery catalogs, personal or business archives, photographs, postcards, and real estate documents. This information is used by landscape historians and preservationists and other interested parties. In addition to this useful source, Wave Hill is known for its creative mix of colorful plants and flowers, courtesy of its former director, Marco Polo Stufano.

Where is the **first garden designed for the blind**?

The Fragrance Garden is part of the Brooklyn Botanic Garden (BBG) in Brooklyn, New York. It was designed by Alice R. Ireys in 1955 and features raised beds planted with

The sight and sound of water in the garden is attractive to humans as well as wild visitors. This water garden is located at the Henry Ford Estate, Fair Lane, in Dearborn, Michigan. (Robert J. Huffman/Field Mark Publications)

fragrant flowers and plants with textured foliage, as well as culinary herbs. The BBG also houses the Cranford Rose Garden, the Osborne Garden (which is in the Italianate style), a children's garden, the Discovery Garden, an herb garden, the Japanese Hill-and-Pond Garden, the Lily Pool Terrace, a native garden, a Shakespeare garden, and a rock garden.

I recently moved to the Southwest from the East Coast and am interested in finding the **Desert Botanical Garden** to learn to about gardening in this new climate. Where is it located?

The Desert Botanical Garden is located in the heart of the American desert, Phoenix, Arizona. It covers 145 acres and features over 20,000 desert plants representing 4,000 species, all planted in their natural habits. A resource like this should assist you in learning more about the plants that will grow in your new home.

Which garden estate was designed in part by **Henry Francis du Pont**?

H. F. du Pont inherited his birthplace, Winterthur, in 1928. The estate had been occupied by the du Pont family since 1810. Du Pont collaborated with Marian Cruger Coffin, a landscape architect, to create 60 acres of garden surrounding his childhood home. Winterthur features a quarry garden, Azalea Woods, a reflecting pool, a sundial garden, and the Pinetum. In creating his naturalistic landscapes, du Pont was careful to preserve both native species as well as key specimen trees his parents had planted. Winterthur is located in Delaware and is open to the public.

I'm interested in planting a native grass bed in my yard. Where can I go to see **collections or gardens of native grasses** to get some design and plant ideas?

A number of collections of native grasses happen to be located in the Midwest and West—home of the original tallgrass prairie. The arboretum at the University of Wisconsin at Madison maintains a number of restored prairies. They include the Curtis Prairie, which is the oldest restored tall-grass prairie in the world. Nebraska is also home to large grasslands, including the Ogallala National Grassland in Sioux and Dowes counties. In Morris, Illinois, the Goose Lake Prairie State Park is the home of a remnant of the original tall-grass prairie that stretched from Minnesota to Texas.

I have seen pictures of a **garden** in Japan that features large stones in a huge bed of gravel. What is the garden and where is it located?

The Ryoan-Ji is a monastery in Japan that houses a garden in the style for which the Japanese are famous. This type of garden is known as a dry landscape. Built in 1490,

> ### How did Kenilworth Aquatic Gardens in Washington, D.C., become a national park?
>
> Kenilworth Aquatic Gardens in Washington, D.C., was formerly the largest commercial water gardening supplier in the United States. The gardens were originally established by Walter Shaw in 1882, who transplanted water lilies (*Nymphaea* spp.) from his former home in Maine to his property on the Anacostia River. He established over 40 ponds containing aquatic plants, and began propagating and selling his plants for planting in water gardens. Kenilworth Aquatic Gardens were purchased by the East National Capital Parks system in 1938 and today continue the work of Walter Shaw in breeding new varieties of water lilies.

the landscape is made up of a walled area in which fifteen large stones are set into a bed of gravel. The gravel is precisely raked on a daily basis by one of the monks, with the pattern made to imitate the waves of the sea. The garden can only be viewed from a platform running alongside it. Thousands of visitors have pondered its meaning over the centuries.

What is the **Villa Lante**?

The Villa Lante is a garden near Rome—perhaps one of the best examples of a garden in the Italian style. It was commissioned by Cardinal Gambara in 1566 as a country villa and garden. The cardinal was interested in placing the focus on the garden, as opposed to the house, so the building is actually broken into two at the garden's entrance. It features waterworks of every shape and kind including fountains, rills, and a channel of water in the middle of a dining table (to cool wine).

Where are some examples of **American Japanese gardens**?

While obviously the finest examples of the Japanese method of gardenmaking are found in Japan itself, many beautiful Japanese gardens exist in the United States. The Bloedel Reserve on Bainbridge Island in Washington includes three beautiful Japanese gardens: a stroll garden, a Zen meditation garden, and a moss garden. The Japanese hill-and-pond garden at the Brooklyn Botanic Garden in New York is another lovely example. The Japanese garden in Portland, Oregon, was built by Japanese garden master Takuma Tono in the late 1960s. A number of botanical gardens in the United States also contain a Japanese garden, including the Denver Botanic Garden, the Missouri Botanical Garden, the Chicago Botanic Garden, and the Huntington Botanical Garden (in California).

CAREERS IN GARDENING

What is a **Master Gardener**?

The Master Gardening program was first established by the Cooperative Extension Service in the state of Washington in 1972. The purpose of the Master Gardening program is to provide current information on horticulture and pest management to participants who will extend that knowledge into their communities. A certified Master Gardener is someone who has taken the Master Gardening certification program through the Cooperative Extension Service. A Master Gardener candidate normally attends classes and takes graded exams in botany, garden design, and lawns, among other topics. In addition to this, a candidate must serve in a volunteer capacity for a certain number of hours to be certified. At least part of this time is usually tied to projects sponsored by the Extension Service, such as answering questions at a Master Gardener booth at local nurseries or farmers markets. The remainder of volunteer hours can be fulfilled in a variety of ways, including speaking on gardening to groups and leading gardening projects for the elderly and children. After their initial certification, Master Gardeners must continue to pursue a set number of educational and volunteer hours in order to retain their annual certification. If you're interested in becoming a Master Gardener, contact your local Cooperative Extension Service for more information.

What is the **Cooperative Extension Service**?

The Cooperative Extension Service was established by the Smith-Lever Act of 1914. Smith-Lever provided an annual $10,000 grant to each state to develop a county-based Cooperative Extension Service. These Extension Services work with land grant institutions (whose mission is to "promote liberal and practical education of the industrial classes in the several pursuits and professions of life") and the United States Department of Agriculture (USDA) to communicate practical information on agriculture to their communities. Although agricultural agents initially worked primarily with farmers, the program eventually expanded to reach out to suburban and urban populations. The Master Gardening program is an example of this.

Which areas of study does a **student in landscape architecture** cover?

While specific curriculums vary from university to university, students in landscape architecture take a wide range of courses. These include landscape and site planning, design, construction, graphics, landscape horticulture and ecology, architecture, computer-aided design, and professional practice. Students may choose to focus on environmental planning and design as well.

> **While I love gardening, I would like to hire a professional to develop an initial landscape design for the yard of the new house I am building. What is the difference between a landscape designer and a landscape architect?**
>
> **B**oth landscape designers and architects may create planting schemes and plans for garden structures such as fences, walls, gazebos, and greenhouses. A landscape architect, however, has received formal training (usually through a university program) and is generally licensed in his or her state of practice. A landscape architect may be proficient in aspects of landscape design such as exterior design and construction. A landscape designer may or may not have received formal training and tends to focus more on plantings than on buildings and structures.

What is **horticulture**?

Horticulture is the study of cultivated plants such as ornamental trees and shrubs, flowers, vegetables, and fruit. It has its roots in the Latin word *hortus,* which means garden. Along with science, horticulture involves a certain amount of art as well.

What is **olericulture**?

Olericulture is the study of vegetables.

What is **floriculture**?

Floriculture is the study of flowers.

I live in the city and have no area to garden, and I'm interested in learning more about **community gardens**. How do they work?

A community garden is one that is planned, established, and cared for by a group of people in that community. Individuals share time, space, and energy to make the garden fruitful. Community gardens have been around since the First and Second World Wars when neighbors shared land and water in so-called victory gardens. According to *Rodale's Encyclopedia of Organic Gardening,* victory gardens grew 40 percent of the United States' produce during 1944, which was their peak production year. Community gardens have been established on vacant lots, in neighborhood parks, on private

Community gardens are an excellent way for gardeners with little space in their own yards to increase their harvest. (Robert J. Huffman/Field Mark Publications)

property, and in the middle of cities. Neighbors can choose to maintain the property as a group or subdivide it into individual plots for neighbors to maintain. In some areas, cities or neighborhoods set up lotteries in order to award individuals a plot; in other areas, participants may pay a small annual membership fee. Produce grown on these plots may be taken home by families, sold for profits, or shared with the less fortunate. Although many community gardens feature vegetables, fruits, and herbs, some beds are designed for the sole purpose of neighborhood beautification.

GARDENING LORE

When did **gardening** begin?

According to archaeologists, the origins of gardening can be found in two areas of the world. It is believed that gardening began in both Egypt and China at around the same time—roughly 2000 B.C. The first Chinese gardens were actually hunting parks for the early emperors. China had a great wealth and diversity of plants—representing practically every genus native to the northern hemisphere—since it was left relatively untouched by the Ice Ages. These hunting parks consisted of adding elements such as bridges or gates to areas of natural beauty without removing plants or moving earth. Later, as the population expanded and nature began to be impinged on, the Chinese emperors used myths as inspiration for carving up the landscape. The lake-and-island garden, which is the basis of Asian gardens even today, has its roots in a Chinese myth.

The inhabitants of the Egyptian desert were entirely dependent on a system of canals and reservoirs that carried water from the Nile. In order to efficiently irrigate crops and provide drinking water, the system was designed along straight lines and a central axis. Gardens evolved from a few trees planted alongside these reservoirs and canals to greater plantings with areas for respite and recreation. Persia adapted and refined the Egyptian garden, retaining its innate formality. The garden became walled in—sheltering its inhabitants from a hot sky and cooling them with rills and pools that divided the garden into four areas representing the four quarters of the universe.

How did the **formal style** of gardening develop?

The formal or architectural style of gardening evolved from the original Egyptian and Persian gardens. These were built along central axes to take advantage of water that flowed in pools and rills. High walls were built and trees were planted to protect people from the sun. Gradually, these so-called paradise gardens or *pardes* became more elaborate, with plantings and seating—true garden escapes. The Greeks, Romans, Italians, and French all built gardens that were variations on the theme of these original gardens, each people incorporating elements of their culture. Roman gardens were rooted in the beautiful and thoughtful architecture for which they are known—villas located to take advantage of extraordinary natural views, fountains and statuary incorporated into the design, and the like. Later, Italian gardens continued to incorporate fine masonry and elaborate water features into their garden design, while the French adopted and enlarged—in a serious way—previously used formal conceits. From the beginning, then, formal gardens revolved around a particular form or design, rather than around the plants.

How did the **naturalistic or informal style** of gardening develop?

The naturalistic or informal style of gardening has its roots in China. Unlike much of the world in 2000 B.C., China had a wealth of natural beauty that needed little embellishment. Chinese hunting parks were, in essence, natural landscapes, with features such as bridges and terraces added to make the hunt more comfortable. Later, these natural landscapes were tweaked slightly by emperors who wanted to evoke mythical significance in nature. Gardens as reproductions of myths, such as the lake-and-island garden, are still relevant in Chinese and Japanese landscapes today. At some point during the eighteenth century, the English, who had been gardening formally like everyone else in Europe, began to garden informally. With the influential voices of individuals like William Robinson and Gertrude Jekyll spurring everyone onward, the gardening world became interested in emphasizing the plants in a garden, rather than the design itself. Here we have the beginnings of the herbaceous or perennial border and cottage gardens. From this point forward, the English informal style has become the predominant garden design, although landscape design has continued to change with the current emphasis on native plants and low-maintenance and drought-tolerant landscapes.

What are the elements of a **Japanese tea garden**?

The most important feature of a Japanese tea garden or *roji*—which translates loosely as "dewy path" garden—is the use of stepping stones leading to the teahouse. Originally, these were needed to keep visitors' feet out of the mud. Their placement is important to give visitors pause at certain aspects of the garden. The path is entered through a portal and is lit at night by stone moon lanterns. It leads to a water basin where visitors clean hands and mouth before entering the teahouse. A final element is the bamboo pipe that brings water into the basin, which symbolizes fresh water flowing from a stream.

What is the connection between *feng shui* and Chinese gardens?

Feng shui, also known as *kan yu*, is about living in harmony with nature. The belief is that by living in harmony, people can harness natural energies to better their lives. Feng shui is a basic element in Chinese garden design. Gardens are sited along the energy lines of *feng shui* in order to distill energy from nature herself.

What is the **Victorian style of gardening**?

Gardens in Victorian England were showcases for their owners' wealth and taste (although the latter was questionable at times). Much effort and expense went into the care and cultivation of exotics in glasshouses, which were then "bedded out" in great, gaudy carpet beds. Gardening was done on a very large scale: a typical country house might have 10 different gardening areas including a rose garden, perennial borders, and water gardens, with 10 gardeners per area. The hew and cry of the day seemed to be, "The more tender a plant, the more desirable," and "Let unity of form and color go to heck."

What is a *pardes*?

A *pardes* or paradise garden was a walled garden originally developed in Persia around 2000 B.C. It usually had four rills or water courses that met in the center to provide irrigation and respite from the heat. It was planted with trees and built with porticoes to provide additional relief from the sun.

Which **American native plants** are used by gardeners in other countries?

Hardy perennials such as purple coneflower (*Echinacea purpurea*), Joe-pye weed (*Eupatorium purpureum*), goldenrod (*Solidago* spp.), bee balm (*Monarda didyma*), blanket flower (*Gaillardia pulchella*), Michaelmas daisy (*Aster novi-belgii*), phlox (*Phlox carolina*), black-eyed Susan (*Rudbeckia hirta*), gayfeather (*Liatris* spp.), tickseed (*Coreopsis* spp.), and California poppy (*Eschscholtzia californica*) have been embraced by gardeners around the world for their use in herbaceous borders. Virginia creeper (*Parthenocissus quinquefolia*) and virgin's bower (*Clematis virginiana*) have scrambled up walls in other parts of the world. Finally, beautiful American native woodys such as flowering dogwood (*Cornus florida*), red, silver, and sugar maples

(*Acer rubrum, A. saccharinum,* and *A. saccharum*), Colorado blue spruce (*Picea pungens*), and Douglas fir (*Pseudotsuga menziesii*) have found a home in foreign forests.

Which wildflowers, commonly thought of as native since they have naturalized themselves through most of the United States, are actually **introduced plants**?

The lovely Queen Anne's lace (*Anthriscus sylvestris*) that appears in vacant lots and along roadsides actually originated in parts of Europe, Turkey, and northwest Africa. The beautiful blue flowers of chicory (*Cichorium intybus*) are visitors from dry, sunny areas of Ethiopia, the Mediterranean, and Europe. Even the beloved tiger or ditch lily (*Lilium tigrinum*) was introduced to the United States from abroad. While it dots drainage ditches throughout the Midwest, the tiger lily originated in marshy and meadowland areas of Japan, Korea, and China.

Which plant used to be the **only known remedy for malaria**?

The bark of the cinchona tree, native to South America, is used to make quinine. In the 1600s it was discovered that this substance would cure malaria, allowing further colonization of tropical areas of the world. Quinine is also, of course, the key ingredient in tonic water.

I seem to get poison ivy every year in my backyard and am concerned about infecting others with it when I have it. Can you spread the itch of **poison ivy** from person to person?

No. Urushiol—the oil given off by the poison ivy (*Rhus radicana*) plant—bonds to the skin and changes to a harmless form of it. However, you can become infected from any residues left on garden tools over the winter (another good reason to clean up your tools in the fall). The best treatment for poison ivy is to rub the area with rubbing alcohol and rinse thoroughly with water soon after being exposed. But as of this writing, there is no cure for poison ivy.

> ## When was the first lawnmower invented?
>
> In 1830, Edwin Budding invented the first lawnmower in England. Budding worked as an engineer at a textile factory. He realized that textile machinery used to cut cloth could be improvised into a machine that cut grass. Budding's lawnmower wasn't imported to the United States until 1855.

Which museum hosts the **largest collection of toy lawnmowers**?

For all you mower fetishists out there—the British Lawnmower Museum in Lancashire, England, houses the world's largest collection of toy lawnmowers. The venerable BLM is also home to a variety of adult-sized mowers as well, ranging from the original pushmowers from the 1830s to the modern, gas-powered beauties of today.

What motor sport involves a **basic backyard tool**?

Yes, it's true, there is such a thing as lawnmower racing! Billed as "The Alternative Motor Sport" by its fans, lawnmower racing originally began in West Sussex, England, in 1973. The mowers are self-propelled (including riding mowers, "run-behind" mowers, and towed-seat mowers) and were all originally designed and sold just to mow lawns. Participants maneuver their mowers around grassy fields at speeds of up to 35 mph, according to the British Lawnmower Museum website. Various local and national championships culminate in a two-day International World Championship Lawnmower Event. As of this writing, lawnmower racing has not become an Olympic sport.

What is the **world's largest grass**?

Despite its resemblance to many woody ornamentals, bamboo (*Bambusa* and *Phyllostachys* spp.) is considered to be the world's largest grass. It is a large evergreen grass that produces a woody trunk. Rapidly reproducing itself via either clumps or runners, bamboo can live a long time.

What is the **most popularly grown rose**?

The hybrid tea rose "Peace" (*Rosa* 'Peace') is probably the world's most frequently grown rose. Its pastel petals change with the colors of the day—pale yellow at dawn with the tips flushing deep pink at noon and then quietly fading again at dusk. "Peace" was named during World War II on the day that Berlin fell, May 2, 1945.

SPECIAL GARDENS

CONTAINER GARDENS

What are some advantages of **container gardening**?

With containers, you can garden in small spaces—especially handy for apartment dwellers or those gardeners with more inclination than yard. Container planting also allows the adventurous gardener to experiment with plants ill-suited to his or her backyard environment or region. For example, a gardener with alkaline clay soil can grow acid-loving azaleas (*Rhododendron* spp.) in pots. Plants in pots are also mobile—allowing the gardener to change the garden's look on a daily basis or to move plants indoors when frost hits. This mobility also means you can correct errors of placement—a plant can easily be moved from an area that is too shady or sunny. Containers are also wonderful for gardeners with physical difficulties that prevent them from working the soil. By placing containers on pedestals or tables, you can bring the garden to the gardener.

How do I select the **proper-sized container** for my plant?

A good rule of thumb is to choose a container that is about two inches larger in diameter than the root ball of the plant (or group of plants). Plant roots need room to grow and breath. In order to provide proper support to the plant, the container should also be around one-third to one-half the height of the mature plant. If you select a pot that is too large, the potting mix will tend to stay wet, which can lead to fungal diseases or rotted roots. If the pot is too small, the plant's growth is stifled and it can become stressed, making it an easy target for disease and pests.

What is the proper **spacing** for plants in a container?

Plants in containers should be planted much more closely than you would plant them in a bed—start with half the recommended spacing. Adjust as seems appropriate. Some gardeners plant root ball against root ball, although they begin by loosening the root ball of each plant before placing it in the container. This gives the containers a full, lush look immediately, but it can also stress the plants as their root systems don't have room to absorb water and nutrients efficiently. Experiment with different approaches and go with what works for you.

What can I do to be sure my pot provides proper **drainage**?

Start with a container that has a hole (or holes, if it's large) in the bottom. If there isn't one, you can use a drill and a masonry bit to drill one. If the holes are large, use shards from broken clay pots or a bit of screen over them to prevent soil from draining out of the container. If you're unable to drill a hole in the container, plant in another container that does have a hole in it (plastic works just fine). Line the original container with pebbles or broken pot shards to ensure the pot doesn't sit in water and place the potted plant inside.

How do I properly **water plants in pots**?

The best way to water container plants is to soak the potting medium thoroughly, allowing any excess to drain through the bottom (this means, of course, that you need to provide proper drainage to begin with). This allows water to reach the roots, making them grow deeper and stronger and the plant more drought resistant and less susceptible to problems. However, remember most plants are overwatered, rather than underwatered. You can check to see if your container plant needs water by sticking your finger in the soil an inch or so below the surface. If it feels dry, it's time to water.

What sort of regular **maintenance** do container gardens require?

Container gardens are actually more labor intensive than gardens planted in the soil. Since the plants live in an artificial environment, they can become stressed. Containers need to be watered regularly and deeply in order to promote a good root system and keep the plants from wilting. They also need to be fertilized regularly—monthly is not too often—since nutrients tend to leach from the containers. Many foliage plants benefit from a foliar fertilizer such as fish emulsion and water, which keeps their leaves glossy as it nourishes them. They also need regular grooming to look their best since they are a focal point in a garden. Pinch out the growing tips of the plants to keep them bushy looking and promote flowering. Remove faded flowers and leaves as soon as they appear.

A selection of hanging plants and beds of plants at a greenhouse at Henry Ford Estate, Fair Lane, in Dearborn, Michigan. (Robert J. Huffman/Field Mark Publications)

What are the advantages and disadvantages of **clay pots versus plastic pots**?

The main difference between clay and plastic containers is how they hold water. Plastic pots retain water better, making them much more convenient for gardeners who aren't able to water frequently in hot weather. When the weather is dry, clay pots may require watering twice a day! Plastic pots are also lightweight and easier to move around. Unfortunately, plastic pots take longer to dry out when they've been filled during periods of heavy rain or overwatering—bad news for plants that don't like their feet wet. Finally, many gardeners just aren't willing to trade the classic look of clay pots, even for plastic lookalikes. A compromise is to use a plastic container to hold a plant and slip a clay pot over it for aesthetics.

I live in a very dry area and the **soil has turned white** at the tops of my containers, causing the pots to be stained. What happened?

You are describing the problem of salt buildup, which is commonly associated with houseplants but also occurs in dry regions of the country. The salt is left behind when water and fertilizer evaporate. In order to keep your plants healthy, flush the soil thoroughly with lots of water to dissolve and drain out the salt. This should be done every three to six months or whenever you notice the soil surface becoming a crusty white.

181

Use a very weak solution of bleach and water to scrub out empty containers. Rinse them thoroughly before planting in them again.

How should a **window box garden** be designed?

The most important thing to remember about a window box garden is that it is meant to be viewed from both outside and inside. Therefore, you should consider planting either end of the window box with taller plants than those in the middle (allowing the viewer inside to see both the garden and outdoors). Other elements that make a window box garden special are combinations of plants of tall and medium heights as well as trailing plants. Scale is an important consideration as well—you don't want to use plants that are much taller than twice the height of the window box. Like other containers, window boxes should be stuffed full in order to look their best. Regular maintenance such as deadheading, picking off browned or dead foliage, fertilizing, and adequate watering will keep them looking good.

I'd like to **grow vegetables** but just have a small terrace off my apartment. What can I do?

Almost any vegetable can be grown in a container. Look for dwarf or "patio" varieties of plants and think vertical as well as horizontal. A salad garden could be created using a window box filled with a variety of cutting lettuces and greens such as 'Royal Oakleaf', arugula, and radicchio. Red and green chard in a crock would be lovely to look at and eat. "Patio" tomatoes such as 'Superb Super' bush tomato or 'Sweet Million' cherry tomato could be grown in deep pots. Try using a strawberry pot (a pot with "planting pockets" along its sides), filling it with annual herbs such as thyme (*Thymus vulgaris*), chives (*Allium schoenoprasum*), and dill (*Anethum graveolens*). Plant pole beans and peas in a pot with a trellis or allow them to scramble up a roof support. Bush varieties of beans, cucumbers, and squash as well as okra and broccoli also work well in containers.

When growing larger vegetables, be sure to use a large enough container for the plant's root system. Tomatoes like room to grow. If you're concerned about your terrace's ability to bear weight (and you should be), consider using some of the new "looks-like-clay-but-it's-not" pots. Made from polyethylene resin, these pots look great but weigh next to nothing.

Can I grow plants in **containers other than pots**?

Growing plants in containers other than pots is very chic. Try recycling items such as old pails, a bathtub, a kitchen sink, or that backyard classic—the used tire! Almost anything can be used as a container as long as it is large enough for the root system of the plant you're planning on putting in it. You will also need to monitor the plant's moisture intake

Containers of all sorts can be used to grow a variety of plants. (Steven Nikkila/Perennial Favorites)

and ensure the roots don't get waterlogged. Plan on either drilling a hole in the base of the item or lining it with gravel or broken pot shards in order to provide proper drainage.

I love those **English troughs** that are used as rock gardens but I haven't seen any old sinks for sale around here. How can I make one?

You can easily make your own trough using a mold and a homemade mix called "hypertufa." Create a mold or form using one of the following: two cardboard boxes; two plastic containers; two homemade boxes. These should nest inside one another, leaving about two inches of space in between them and deep enough so that the trough will be at least six inches deep. Prepare the hypertufa using one part Portland cement, two parts moist peat moss, and one part coarse sand. Mix well, and then add enough water until the mix is thick but somewhat fluid. Pour the mortar into the mold and tamp it into place. Let it set a day and remove the mold, then let it sit a few days longer before planting.

I love the look of **moss growing on clay pots**. Is there any way to encourage this process?

Moss does add a certain air of faded elegance to containers and garden statuary. To encourage moss, try brushing your pots with a solution of buttermilk. Keep them cool and moist for a few weeks and your pots should take on a distinctly mossy character.

183

Which **herbs** grow well in containers?

Herbs seem to be tailor-made for containers. If you only have room for a window box or pots on a windowsill, look for low-growing herbs such as chive (*Allium schoenoprasum*), basil (*Ocimum basilicum*), parsley (*Petroselinum crispum*), and thyme (*Thymus vulgaris*). If you have a terrace or balcony, almost any herb will do. A larger pot planted with herbs in the same culinary family works well. Try an Italian mix of oregano (*Origanum vulgare*), parsley, basil, and rosemary (*Rosemarinus officinalis*) or Asian specialties such as "Siam" basil (*Ocimum basilicum* 'Siam'), cilantro (*Coriandrum satirum*), and Oriental chive. You can even experiment with sweet bay tree (*Laurus nobilis*) or rosemary topiary (*Rosemarinus officinalis*) in pots, moving them into the house when frost hits.

I've planted **annuals** in pots the last few years but they never seem to look as good as they do in the nurseries. What am I doing wrong?

A common design mistake with containers is planting too few plants. Pack those pots full! By the end of the summer, you shouldn't be able to see any of the top edge of the pot. Try something different by planting a perennial in a pot such as English lavender (*Lavandula angustifolia*) or even a variegated hosta (*Hosta* spp.). Or start with your basic pink geranium (*Pelargonium* 'Mrs. Henry Cox' is lovely) and jazz it up with a new cascading petunia (*Petunia* 'Purple Wave' is a recent introduction), lamb's ear (*Stachys olimpica*), one of the trailing ivies such as *Hedera helix* 'Asterix' or *Hedera helix* 'Diana', and a dwarf, creeping thyme such as *Thymus leucotrichus* for good measure.

You can also keep things interesting by changing the makeup of your pots throughout the year. Start with a large pot. Plant large bulbs such as tulips (*Tulipa* spp.) toward the bottom of the container and smaller bulbs such as crocus (*Crocus* spp.) just above those, following guidelines for bulb depth. Place a perennial plant or small woody ornamental at the center of the pot. Then, with each season, plant annuals. For spring, plant pansies (*Viola tricolor hortensis*) or other cold-tolerant annuals. When the weather heats up, compost the pansies and switch to a summer palate of heat-tolerant annuals such as geraniums (*Pelargoniums* spp.) and petunias (*Petunia* spp.). As summer draws to a close, compost those heat-lovers and add fall-blooming mums (*Chrysanthemum* spp.) or asters (*Aster* spp.). In the winter, the perennial (if it is evergreen) or shrub will provide winter interest.

Can I **reuse the soil** I have in my containers from year to year or should I start fresh every year?

You can replant in the soil you have in a container for up to three years, unless the plants develop some kind of disease. Start fresh if the plants become diseased or just aren't thriving.

> ## What kind of soil should I use in containers?
>
> **D**o not use garden soil in your pots—it will be too heavy and filled with weed seeds. A light soilless mix ensures air and nutrients reach plant roots. Try a 1:1:1 mixture of soil, peat, and compost, with perlite or vermiculite thrown in to keep it loose, or use a premixed potting soil. Since these mixes tend to dry out quickly, be sure to monitor the moisture in your pots, especially if they are made of clay.

I purchased a lovely **wire planter** that hangs on my brick wall. How can I water it without losing dirt, soil, and plants in the process?

Be sure you've properly prepared the planter to begin with—lining it with plastic and/or peat moss to retain water, soil, and plants. Rather than using a can to water this fragile arrangement, try crushed ice. The ice will provide moisture to your plants without seeping out of the container. Since the ice is crushed, it will quickly melt without damaging the plants.

How do I care for my plants in **hanging baskets**?

Plants in hanging baskets tend to dry out much more quickly than other types of container-grown plants. Water hanging baskets daily, soaking them thoroughly. To avoid soaking yourself or any innocent bystanders, it's best to bring these plants to ground level before starting to water. Plants in hanging baskets also tend to be heavy feeders, so plan on fertilizing once a month or so when watering. Remove spent flowers and dying foliage to encourage the plant to send out new growth, and monitor the health of the roots. If they become mushy or the plant becomes wilted (even though the soil is moist), you are probably overwatering. If the roots become overcrowded and begin to spill out of the container's drainage holes, use your fingers to carefully loosen them, allowing oxygen in.

I live in zone 4. Can I grow **trees and shrubs in containers**?

If you will be keeping your woody ornamentals outside for the winter, you shouldn't consider growing trees and shrubs in outdoor containers in your area. While many trees and shrubs can withstand cold temperatures above ground, their root systems are more tender. So while a tree may be hardy to 15 degrees Fahrenheit below zero, its roots may only be hardy to 15 degrees Fahrenheit above zero. The soil in a container has roughly the same temperature as the air, whereas the soil in the ground only freezes to a depth of six inches or so in most cold areas. You may be able to keep them

> ### I live in an area where temperatures generally remain above 20 degrees Fahrenheit in the winter. What do I need to do to keep my potted trees going through the winter?
>
> **W**hile you should be able to sustain trees and shrubs in containers over the winter in your area, the cold will still affect them. When first planting, choose a large container. This will allow the root system to develop more fully, providing good support for the plant and keeping it healthy. Over the winter, keep the tree or shrub well watered and mulch it heavily at the beginning of the season. The most common reason for container-grown trees and shrubs to die over the winter (provided they are in a warm enough zone) is lack of water. You also might consider wrapping evergreens with burlap to protect them from the drying wind.

going in the winter if you are able to move the trees and shrubs to a garage, unheated porch, or other sheltered area. Mulch them well and wrap their pots with burlap. Don't forget to water them regularly! They will surely perish if their root systems dry out in cold temperatures.

I have a terrace garden and would like to add some trees to my plantings. What are some good **trees or shrubs** to grow in containers?

In selecting trees to be grown in containers, consider the ultimate height and width of the tree and its moisture requirements. Dwarf tree specimens are an obvious choice but you could also select a shrub that could be pruned to imitate a tree. Consider, too, some of the bamboos such as golden bamboo (*Phyllostachyas aurea*) or black bamboo (*P. nigra*) which, while technically grasses, provide the height and feeling of trees. Some actual trees to consider include European fan palm (*Chamaerops humilis*) and pygmy date palm (*Phoenix roebelinii*) in zones 9 and 10, fringe tree (*Chionanthus virginicus*), crape myrtle (*Lagerstroemia indica*), European white birch (*Betula pendula* 'Dwarf'), and California redbud (*Cercis occidentalis*). Shrubs that make for nice container plants include boxwood (*Buxus* spp.), compact inkberry (*Pyracantha* 'Tiny Tim'), Japanese barberry (*Berberis thunbergii* 'Atropurpurea'), Van Houtte spirea (*Spiraea x vanhouttei*), Chinese witch hazel (*Hamamelis mollis*), and agave (*Agave spp.*) and Japanese aralia (*Fatsia japonica*) in zones 9 and 10.

Can I keep my containers of **flowering plants outdoors** over the winter?

There's really no sense in keeping annuals going, even in zones warmer than 7, since they will eventually succumb to the elements. Better to compost them, along with the soil in their pots. If you're growing perennials in your containers and you live in a cold zone, move the plants into the garden for the winter so that their roots will be protected and they will go dormant. Empty pots should be cleaned, dried, and stored in a frost-free place like your garage. If you live in zone 7 or higher, you can bury your containers in the ground for the winter.

My container garden is kind of a **hodgepodge of plants and pots**. How can I get it to look more unified?

This is a common conundrum with many gardens—not just ones planted in containers. Begin by bringing all of your containers together in one place. When they are scattered about, they don't have the same effect as a colorful grouping. Next, group similar containers together, such as square containers, clay containers, gray containers. If you have a few odd pots out that are large, these can be left to stand by themselves. The larger the pot, the more eye-catching it is. The smaller ones can be filled with trailing plants so you don't see the pot itself. Dramatically shaped pots such as urns may even be left empty. Then consider your plantings. The containers in each grouping should have plants that complement one another. You could try a collection of succulents in one area and small woody ornamentals in another, but try mixing things up as well, bringing plants together through complementary leaf color or shape. If an arrangement looks too studied, you can easily pull a container out of the group and replace it with another one. Experiment!

How can containers serve as **design elements** in my garden?

Containers do a great job of framing a view or a focal point. A common use of containers is to frame the front door of a house. Consider using them to frame any entrance in your garden such as between garden rooms or on both sides of a path, an arch, or a set of steps. Unusual containers can serve as focal points in and of themselves—try a large copper pot or a pottery bowl set on a pedestal. Modern-looking, simple pots can appear sculptural left empty or filled with a simple, architectural plant. The materials of the container itself give a garden a certain feel. Plants in baskets or strawberry pots have a romantic feel to them. A classic, formal garden might use concrete urns or faux lead pots to give a feeling of antiquity. Containers provide a gardener with the freedom to pursue different effects from year to year or season to season.

A monarch butterfly stops briefly on a blooming flower. (Robert J. Huffman/Field Mark Publications)

WILDLIFE, WILDFLOWER, AND NATIVE PLANT GARDENS

I'd like to attract **butterflies** to my yard. Which plants should I use?

There are a large number of plants that can be used to attract butterflies. Among the most common are yarrow (*Achillea*), pot marigold (*Calendula officinalis*), purple coneflower (*Echinacea purpurea*), blanket flower (*Gaillardia pulchella*), black-eyed Susan (*Rudbeckia hirta*), nasturtium (*Tropaeolum*), sweet alyssum (*Lobularia maritima*), lupine (*Lupinus*), hollyhock (*Alcea rosea*), salvia (*Salvia*), cosmos (*Cosmos bipinnatus*), thyme (*Thymus vulgaris*), showy sedum (*Sedum spectabile*), spiderflower (*Cleome*), bee balm (*Monarda didyma*), and, of course, orange-eye butterfly bush (*Buddleia davidii*).

Which kinds of plants do **butterfly larvae** live in?

Spiderflower (*Cleome*), asters (*Aster* spp.), false indigo (*Baptisia*), columbine (*Aquilegia* spp.), lupine (*Lupinus*), perennial pea vine (*Lathyrus latifolius*), hollyhock (*Alcea rosea*), and the wild plum and cherry (*Prunus* spp.) and oak (*Quercus* spp.) trees are among the plants that host butterfly larvae.

What is a **snag**?

A snag is a dead tree that is still standing. For wildlife gardeners, snags are important as they host beetles and borers, which attract birds and other predators. Tree hollows also form nesting areas for birds and other mammals.

What is a **forb**?

A forb is a nongrass herbaceous plant, generally referring to those that are native to an area. Forbs include milkweed (*Asclepias* spp.), false indigo (*Baptisia* spp.), gayfeather (*Liatris* spp.), spiderwort (*Tradescantia* spp.), smartweed (*Polygonum* spp.), goldenrod (*Solidago* spp.), pitcher plants (*Sarracenia* spp.), lobelia (*Lobelia* spp.), Joe-pye weed (*Eupatorium purpureum*), blanket flower (*Gaillardia pulchella*), sneezeweed (*Helenium* spp.), black-eyed Susans (*Rudbeckia hirta*), prickly-pear cactus (*Opuntia ficus-indica*), dutchman's pipe (*Aristolochia durior*), Alleghany spurge (*Pachysandra procumbens*), wild ginger (*Asarum canadense*), and mayapple (*Podophyllum peltatum*).

I'd like to attract **birds** to my backyard in the winter without a feeder. What kinds of plants can I grow?

Look for plants that retain their seedheads in the winter. These would include globe thistle (*Echinops* spp.), purple coneflower (*Echinacea purpurea*), plains coreopsis (*Coreopsis tinctoria*), safflower (*Carthamus tinctorius*), sunflowers (*Helianthus*—if left standing and uneaten by squirrels), bachelor's button (*Centaurea cyanus*), cosmos (*Cosmos bipinnatus*), and marigolds (*Tagetes* spp.). Evergreens or thickets of deciduous woody ornamentals provide cover and nesting material for birds. Don't forget to have a source of fresh water for the birds. While a birdbath is nice, even a shallow frostproof bowl sunk into the soil works wonders.

What kinds of trees and shrubs **attract birds**?

Trees and shrubs with berries are sure-fire bird magnets. Viburnum (*Viburnum* spp.), serviceberry (*Amelanchier* spp.), highbush blueberry (*Vaccinium corymbosum*), American elderberry (*Sambucus canadensis*), currant (*Ribes* spp.), cherry (*Prunus* spp.), crabapple (*Malus* spp.), dogwood (*Cornus florida, C. racemosa,* and *C. kousa*), Oregon grape holly (*Mahonia* spp.), and sumac (*Rhus glabra* and *R. typhina*) are all good choices. Also, don't forget to include some evergreens in your "bird forest" to provide protection from the elements and predators. American holly (*Ilex opaca*), scarlet firethorn (*Pyracantha coccinea*), inkberry (*Ilex glabra*), Eastern red cedar (*Juniperus virginiana*), dwarf mugo pine (*Pinus mugo* 'Mugo'), yew (*Taxus* spp.), Norway spruce (*Picea abies*), and, in zones 7 through 10, Carolina cherry-laurel (*Prunus caroliniana*) are all favored by birds for nesting.

What kind of flowers are **hummingbirds** attracted to?

Try hollyhock (*Alcea rosea*), bougainvillea (*Bougainvillea*), orange-eye butterfly bush (*Buddleia davidii*), canna (*Cannas*), spiderflower (*Cleome*), iris (*Iris* spp.), daylily (*Hemerocallis* spp.), cardinal flower (*Lobelia cardinalis*), rhododendron (*Rhododendron* spp.), salvia (*Salvia* spp.), gladiolus (*Gladiolus* spp.), wisteria (*Wisteria* spp.), and honeysuckle (*Lonicera* spp.).

What are **beneficial insects**?

For the gardener, beneficial insects are those bugs whose presence assists the home gardener. They provide a number of positive functions such as pollinating flowers, eating other pest insects or killing them by means of a parasitic relationship, breaking down decaying material, or serving as food for birds or other animals that provide additional benefit to the garden. Beneficial insects include bees, flies and some moths, parasitic wasps, yellow jackets, ground beetles, lacewings, and dragonflies.

A colorful feeder or colorful plants will help attract hummingbirds. (Robert J. Huffman/Field Mark Publications)

What does my garden need to attract **wildlife**?

The basic elements of a wildlife garden are a source of water, a mixture of both sunny and shady areas for different types of wildlife to congregate, a wide variety of plants and habitats for different wildlife, and natural as opposed to chemical methods of pest and weed control. Although a small pond or creek would be ideal, a birdbath or even a shal-

The damselfly catches flying insects by making a basketlike trap of its legs. (Robert J. Huffman/Field Mark Publications)

low mud puddle creates an oasis for butterflies and birds. If your yard lacks trees, consider planting a few fast-growing evergreens or thick deciduous shrubs to provide cover and perches for songbirds and squirrels. With a smaller lot, vines and trailing plants can create thickets for nesting. If your yard is full of shade, try pruning or thinning some of the trees and shrubs to provide a sunlit area for butterflies and meadow birds. A diverse garden with a wide variety of plants (even exotic ones) and habitats attracts a diverse number of insects and animals. Most importantly, stop using chemicals of any kind in your yard. Fertilizers, fungicides, pesticides, and most herbicides can kill garden creatures. Use compost and mulch and learn to live with a few bugs. Many are beneficial and others at the very least provide food for birds and critters.

How can I lure **toads to my pond**?

If you have a pond, toads will come. But to keep them there, you need to make your pond toad and frog friendly. The edge of your pond should be gently sloped to help the frogs and toads hop in and out of the water. Pebbles or water lilies around the edges will give them something to jump to. These critters also need the protection of reeds, cattails, and other plants in order to have a place to hide and lay their eggs. Toads like to stay cool and damp at night so provide them with habitat such as rock piles or boards sunk in the mud for their snoozing hours.

What is the difference between **a native plant and an exotic one**?

A native plant is a species that grows naturally in a region, while exotics have been brought into an area where they were not originally found.

What are the advantages of using **native plants in a wildlife garden**?

While you can attract wildlife to your backyard with exotics, plants indigenous to an area tend to attract more wildlife within that area. Another reason to consider using native plants is that birds and other wildlife tend to scatter the seed they eat through their droppings. Many exotic plants have "escaped" into the wild this way, wreaking havoc in fragile ecosystems.

How do **invasive exotic plants affect native ones**?

Invasive exotics like kudzu vine (*Pueraria lobata*) have wreaked havoc in both the cultured and natural landscapes where they have been introduced. Invasive exotics don't just take up extra space in your garden, they also take up space in the wild. Even when a gardener is careful to contain a particular exotic using underground barriers or by planting it in a pot, the seeds of the plant can be carried by animals and weather. Once

> ### Can I have a wildlife garden without having a yard?
>
> If you have sun on your terrace or patio, you can have a wildlife garden. Plant large containers chock-full of plants like purple coneflower (*Echinacea purpurea*), Joe-pye weed (*Eupatorium purpureum*), butterfly bush (*Buddleia* spp.), and milkweed (*Asclepias* spp.). Don't forget to include some grasses and sedges such as little bluestem (*Schizachyrium scoparium*), big bluestem (*Andropogon gerardii*), Indian grass (*Sorghastrum nutans*), umbrella sedges (*Cyperus* spp.), Morrow's sedge (*Carex morrowii*), and grass nut (*Triteleia laxa*). Group your pots tightly to provide cover for butterflies and birds. Consider adding seed and nectar feeders as well as a birdbath. All this and there might be a small corner left for you to sit in!

in the wild, these exotics compete with fragile native plants for nutrients and water. And of course, there is no gardener to pull them up. If enough exotics multiply in a particular area, they can crowd out the natives permanently, reducing diversity in the landscape and bringing unforeseen consequences to the ecosystem.

What are some examples of **native plants that have been endangered by exotic species**?

Purple loosestrife (*Lythrum salicaria*) is an example of an invasive plant that has escaped into the wild. It has wreaked havoc by nudging out native cattails in wetland and boggy areas. As a result, it has been banned for sale in many states. Current eradication efforts are focusing on the use of biocontrol insects (insects whose diet consists of loosestrife) to eliminate loosestrife from the landscape. The kudzu vine (*Pueraria lobata*) is infamous in southern landscapes for choking the life out of other vegetation. Other exotic species with invasive tendencies include California, Japanese, and Chinese privet (*Ligustrum ovalifolium*, *L. japonicum*, and *L. sinese*), Chinese tallow tree (*Sapium sebiferum*), crown vetch (*Coronilla varia*), Russian olive (*Elaeagnus angustifolius*), and heavenly bamboo (*Nandina domestica*). These plants and many others vary in their invasiveness from area to area, so you should check with your local Extension Service office for additional information.

How can I reduce the possibility of **invasive exotic plants escaping** into the wild?

The best way to reduce the risk of invasive exotics leaving your garden for Nature is to stop purchasing any plant that is known to be invasive in the wild and eliminate any

Parry's century plant or mescal (*Agave parryi*) is not a cactus, but it is a desert plant and requires many years to flower. This one was photographed at the Arizona-Sonora Desert Museum. (Robert J. Huffman/Field Mark Publications)

others from your landscape. For invasive exotics that spread through runners or division only, you can attempt to curtail this by keeping them in containers or surrounding them with underground barriers. However, many plants also reproduce through seed, which can be spread by humans, wind, rain, and animals. Unless your plant is sterile, it will most likely appear elsewhere despite your best efforts.

Are there any native plants that can be used for **groundcover**?

For shady areas, plants such as Alleghany spurge (*Pachysandra procumbens*), creeping phlox (*Phlox stolonifera*), American barrenwort (*Vancouveria hexandra*), and Allegheny foamflower (*Tiarella cordifolia*) are all evergreen groundcovers that are native to the United States. Goldenstar (*Chrysogonum virginianum* var. *australe*), native junipers (*Juniperus horizontalis* and *J. communis*), and pachistima (*Paxistima canbyi*) are native groundcovers that enjoy sunny spaces.

What native plants are **related to carrots**?

The Umbellifera or Apiaceae family includes not only carrots and parsley, but also hairy angelica (*Angelica venenosa*), rattlesnake-master (*Eryngium yuccifolium*), pennywort

(*Hydrocotyle americana*), golden parsnip (*Zizia aptera*), and golden zizia (*Z. aurea*). Members of the carrot family serve as host plants for the larvae of black swallowtail butterflies. Introduced Umbellifera members include Queen Anne's lace (*Anthriscus sylvestris*), bishop's weed (*Ammi majus*), and fennel (*Foeniculum vulgare*).

I live in the desert. What are some **desert natives** that I can grow in my landscape?

Saguaro cactus (*Carnegica giganta*) is a well-known American desert native but it is rapidly disappearing from its natural habitats due to collection by unscrupulous plant dealers. Other choices are the buckhorn cholla (*Opuntia acanthocarpa*), creosote bush (*Larrea tridentata*), various penstemons, and Chuparosa honeysuckle (*Justicta californica*).

I have a large, sunny bit of lawn that I'd like to convert to a **meadow**. How do I start?

Contact your local Extension Service office to determine native plant possibilities, then select plants based on the type of soil you have as well as the site. Remember, meadows usually include both flowers and grasses. Grasses are important because they add movement and sound to your meadow, so plan on keeping the percentage of grasses higher than the percentage of flowers. Meadow plants include yarrow (*Achillea millefolium*), prairie onion (*Allium stellatum*), anemone (*Anemone* spp.), pussytoes (*Antennaria* spp.), columbine (*Aquilegia* spp.), aster (*Aster* spp.), Indian paintbrush (*Castilleja* spp.), Queen Anne's lace (*Anthriscus sylvestris*), purple coneflower (*Echinacea purpurea*), California poppy (*Eschscholtzia californica*), Joe-pye weed (*Eupatorium purpureum*), queen-of-the-prairie (*Filipendula rubra*), prairie smoke (*Geum*), hairy star-grass (*Hypoxis*), *Houstonia* spp., oxeye daisy (*Heliopsis* spp.), tidy tips (*Layia elegans*), gayfeather (*Liatris* spp.), wood lily (*Trillium* spp.), Texas bluebonnet (*Lupinus texensis*), annual phlox (*Phlox drummondii*), obedient plant (*Physostegia virginiana*), meadow beauty (*Rhexia* spp.), black-eyed Susan (*Rudbeckia hirta*), goldenrod (*Solidago* spp.), blue-eyed grass (*Sisyrinchium graminoides*), desert zinnia (*Zinnia haageana*), atamasco lily (*Zephyranthes atamasco*), milkweed (*Asclepias syriaca*), sage (*Salvia* spp.), sneezeweed (*Helenium* spp.), and false indigo (*Baptisia*). Meadow grasses include little bluestem (*Schizachyrium scoparium*), big bluestem (*Andropogon gerardii*), Indian grass (*Sorghastrum nutans*), dropseed (*Sporobolus* spp.), witch grass (*Panicum virgatum*), and love grass (*Eragrostis* spp.).

Your next step depends on whether you have more time or energy. If you have time, you can till the grass under. You'll need to do this several times every few weeks for as long as it takes (it could be a year) until there are no more grass seedlings sprouting. If you have energy, remove the sod and compost it. If you want, you can add

195

Wildflowers growing in natural areas can carpet the landscape. Gardeners often plant flowers in masses to recreate this striking image. (Robert J. Huffman/Field Mark Publications)

more topsoil to restore the soil line. You can use either transplants or seeds to create your meadow. If you choose to seed your meadow, begin by raking the soil level, then broadcast the seeds evenly by hand, making sure to keep off of the bed to avoid soil compaction. Rake and water the bed gently, then wait for the seeds to sprout.

Another option would be to stop mowing the lawn and see what happens. If you live in a neighborhood, you may want to check city ordinances and alert your neighbors that you're planning a meadow. To keep the area from looking too wild, mow a wide grass border around it, which gives it a maintained look. After a year of letting the lawn grow out, mow the soon-to-be-meadow in early spring and leave the cuttings. Then overseed or place plantings throughout the bed. Keep the new seeds or plants well watered so that they will germinate. In order to prevent woody plants from taking over, you must be vigilant in weeding out small seedlings. Also, remove any other plants that don't meet with your approval.

Once the meadow is established, you will need to cut it (or burn it, if you're out in the country) every spring, followed by a raking. This assists the plants with reseeding and provides those sprouting with more access to sun and rain. Finally, remember that the "wild look" is in name only. A meadow requires regular maintenance to prevent it from becoming a forest.

I'm interested in growing **native plants**. Can I just go to the woods and dig them up?

No. Not only is digging up native plants unethical, it may be illegal depending on the plant you choose and the area you live in. These plants are also usually very particular about the environment they grow in and will most likely die when transplanted. Unscrupulous nurseries remove plants from the wild, drastically decreasing or even eliminating their populations. Finding more than one kind of wildflower in a pot or a plant loose in its container (indicating it may not have been grown in that container) may signify that the plant has been collected, rather than propagated. Choose instead to purchase plants that have been propagated by a reliable nursery. Doing a little research to discover which plants are most easily propagated will also help to determine whether a plant has been collected. Try to find plants that have been propagated and grown close to home. They will have adapted to conditions closest to your own backyard.

The exception to this rule is in areas where land development threatens native plant populations. Plant societies and interested individuals often band together to rescue plants from destruction by earthmovers. In order to make these moves successful, try to move wildflowers when they aren't blooming. They're less fragile. Younger plants are also more likely to withstand the shock of transplanting. As with other transplanting, choose a cloudy, misty day to move plants and keep the plant roots moist in order to prevent them from drying out. Include lots of the original soil

Purple loosestrife (*Lythrum salicaria*) has escaped from gardens and become a serious threat to native species in marshes, where it tends to crowd out cattails. (Robert J. Huffman/Field Mark Publications)

around the roots when you dig up the plant so its new home feels like its old one. Try to replant the specimen the same day that you've dug it up. Finally, keep the new plant well watered in its new environment as it recovers from the shock.

WATER GARDENS

What is a **bog garden**?

A bog is a continually wet area whose bottom consists of peat, as opposed to a swamp whose bottom consists of mud and decayed plants. Due to the peat, bog soil tends to be more acidic. If you have a low-lying area on your property that never completely dries, try creating a bog garden. Add peat and humus to the area, then select plants. Be sure to keep the area moist.

What kinds of plants grow in **bogs**?

Marginal or bog plants grow in saturated soil that is above the water line. Many of them are grown for their foliage as they tend to be inconsistent bloomers. Astilbe (*Astilbe* spp.), gunnera (*Gunnera magellanica*), and water mint (*Mentha aquatica*) all have beautiful foliage. Bog plants with lovely flowers include marsh marigold (*Caltha palustris*), swamp rose mallow (*Hibiscus moscheutos*), pitcher plant (*Sarracenia* spp.), Joe-pye weed (*Eupatorium purpureum*), yellow flag (*Iris pseudacorus*), sweet flag (*Acorus calamus*), and American blue flag (*Iris versicolor*). Chinese water chestnut (*Eleocharis dulcis*) is an edible bog plant. Papyrus (*Cyperus papyrus*) may be grown in tropical areas or brought indoors for the winter.

I have a very small yard—how can I **create a pond**?

A pond or small pool can be created using half of a whiskey barrel (found at most garden centers). Begin by removing any loose wood and clean the barrel thoroughly. Once it is dry, coat the inside with a water sealer that is not toxic to plants or fish. Once the sealant has dried, fill the barrel with water and let sit overnight. Empty out the water to get rid of any remaining residue, then fill with water. Select small water plants such as the petite, hardy water lily 'Indiana' (*Nymphaea* 'Indiana') or variegated sweet flag (*Acorus calamus* 'Variegatus'), while avoiding those like water hyacinth (*Eichhornia crassipes*) and curled pondweed (*Potamogeton crispus*), which can be invasive. Plant those that need soil in plastic mesh containers using a special soil mix for aquatic plants. Floating plants can be placed on top of the water. Maintenance is

199

Fragrant water-lily (*Nymphaea odorata*) on a pond. (Robert J. Huffman/Field Mark Publications)

important in a pond. Keep it clear of weeds, algae, and dead leaves and divide plants as they outgrow their containers. If you live in a cold climate, you will need to empty the pond and store it for winter.

How do I decide where to **dig a pond** in my yard?

For purely aesthetic reasons, you should place your pond in an area of the yard where you can view it from the house and patio. Although it could be picturesque to have your pond surrounded by trees, this is actually an unwise choice. While light shade reduces the incidence of algae in a pond, leaves falling from trees can increase algae due to their own nitrates and phosphates. And tree roots wreak havoc by breaking through the bottom of the pond liner. A better choice is to find a sunny area and keep roughly two-thirds of your pond covered with floating plants, which also help keep algae out. If you plan on growing water lilies (*Nymphaea* spp.), they need at least four hours of sun to flower well.

You also need to consider the slope of your yard. While it may seem counterintuitive to dig your pond in a flat area of the yard, rather than that low-lying spot, it is important to do so. Surface water can contaminate a pond with debris. In addition, any natural water pressure in the ground can push up on the liner, causing problems underneath your pond. Also, try to keep your pond away (or sloping away) from your house, just in case it overflows during a heavy rain.

Is it better to have a **large pond or a small one**?

This depends on your budget and the size of your yard, but generally speaking it is best to build the largest pond you can maintain. In a smaller pond, the water temperature fluctuates more frequently, which is hard on both the animals and the plants in your little water paradise. This also makes a small pond more labor intensive. If you want to overwinter plants or fish, your pond also needs to be at least two feet deep. However, many cities have restrictions on the depth of ponds (usually no deeper than three feet) in order to prevent drowning accidents.

What kinds of plants **grow in water**?

Water plants can be divided between those that need to be planted and those that float. Floating plants help to discourage algae and provide shade. They include water hyacinth (*Eichhornia crassipes*), duckweed (*Lemna minor*), and water soldier (*Stratiotes aloides*). Plants that need to be planted in a pond include water lilies (*Nymphaea, Nuphar,* and *Victoria* spp.), as well as floating heart (*Nymphoides peltatum*), cape pondweed (*Aponogeton distachyus*), yellow pond lily (*Nuphar lutea*), sweet flag (*Acorus calamus*), iris (*Iris* spp.), flowering rush (*Butomus* spp.), and pickerel weed (*Pontederia cordata*).

What is an **oxygenator**?

An oxygenator is a type of water plant that is used to absorb salts and release oxygen into the water, allowing for the healthy growth of water plants and preventing algae from forming. Oxygenating plants include elodea (*Anacharis canadenis*), fairy moss, (*Azolla filiculoides*), water starwort (*Callitriche* spp.), water violet (*Hottonia palustris*), water crowfoot (*Ranunculus aquatilis*), curled pondweed (*Potamogeton crispus*), and hornwort (*Ceratophyllums demersum*).

Why are **deep water plants** like water lilies important in a pond?

Water lilies are so lovely to look at—it is hard to imagine needing any other reason for keeping them in a pond. However, water lilies and other deep water plants also perform an important function in a pond. With their root systems growing between one and three feet below the water line and their foliage and flowers on top of the water, their leaves cast shade over a good percentage of the pond. This helps reduce the level of light underwater, which in turn helps reduce algae. However, if more than two-thirds of the pond is covered by these floaters, the balance of the pond can be disrupted.

What types of maintenance are required for an **established pond**?

An established pond needs to have its plants pruned on a regular basis, removing brown or yellow leaves. It also needs to be cleaned twice a year (spring and fall are good times) in order to remove decayed vegetation. Removal of foliage, even if it is dead, needs to be done gradually so as not to upset the fragile balance of your pond's ecosystem. Aquatic plants also need dividing on a regular basis to keep them healthy and ensure they refrain from taking over your pond paradise. In cold-weather areas, you may need to heat your pond in the winter to make sure plants and fish survive.

What is the **best time of year to plant aquatic plants**?

The best time of year to plant aquatic plants is in the late spring or early summer. At this point, the plants are just starting to grow vigorously. Given the remainder of the summer and fall, they will be able to establish a strong root system that allows them to survive cold weather. While this is most important for areas where the plants will be wintering outdoors (in ponds or pools at least two feet deep), it makes for hardier plants in all water features.

How and when do I **divide aquatic plants**?

The best time to divide aquatic plants is when you empty and clean your pond, ideally in late spring. The plants should be washed thoroughly first. Then remove any spindly or weak-looking growth. Tubers should be cut into pieces, leaving one healthy crown for each plant. The tuber should be short with the old, fleshy roots removed.

What kind of environment do **water lilies** need in order to **bloom** throughout the season?

Water lilies need lots of sun—at least four hours in warm climates, but really six or more in most areas. Water lilies are heavy feeders—their soil should be fertile and they should be fed monthly throughout the growing season. Finally, the level of still water that they reside in is important: water lilies need a pond in that is at least 18 inches deep, with two to three feet being preferable.

How do I **overwinter my water lilies**?

This depends on the type of water lilies you have, and the depth of the water in your pond. Hardy water lilies will survive in areas as cold as zone 4. They need to be kept in ponds that are deep enough to allow the plants to stay alive in water that has remained unfrozen under a layer of ice. If you have tropical water lilies, these are normally kept

> ## How do I plant water lilies?
>
> Use a planting basket, lined with burlap, available at nurseries that sell aquatic plants. This allows the plant to sit in water, while being planted in a medium that provides them with nutrients. Water lilies require rich soil since they are heavy feeders. A good soil is made up of roughly six parts loam and one part manure or bonemeal. The lilies should be planted with the crown of their root just above soil level. Before sinking the container in water, place a layer of pebbles or gravel on top to keep the soil from spilling into the water.

as annuals in any zone colder than zone 10 (most of the United States), although they may be nursed along in a tub of water kept in a greenhouse or sun porch.

I have planted all my aquatic plants in my pond. What is the proper method for **filling the pond with water?**

A pond should be filled gradually over a period of several days in order to reduce the effects of shock on the plants. Run the water slowly and aim it at an empty pot set in the bottom of the pond to avoid stirring up any mud. Fill the pool to the point where the crowns of the plants are covered by water. Then wait a few days for the plants to recover before filling it to the top.

What are the advantages and disadvantages to **keeping fish in a pond**?

Fish eat mosquito larvae and add color and life to your pond. Unfortunately, they also eat tadpoles, amphibian eggs, and dragonfly larvae and attract life to your pond—in the form of fish-eating birds and frogs (kind of neat) and raccoons (not always so neat). You shouldn't feed the fish in your pond very often. That way, they will nibble on the mosquito larvae, the algae, and even the plants, which will help to keep the ecosystem in balance. Overfed fish contribute to the algae problem through their excrement, which contains nitrates (algae food).

Can I have both **fish and plants in my pond**?

You can keep both fish and plants in a pond but you need to consider the type of fish you're putting in the pond and a proper balance between fish and plants. Japanese koi are beautiful, but they have an annoying tendency to dig in the bottom of a pond, uprooting all of those hundred-dollar water lilies you just purchased. A better choice would be goldfish. The ones labeled "feeder fish" at the pet store are just fine. Keep the number of fish relatively low—an inch of fish per square foot of pond surface is about the right proportion. Otherwise, you risk encouraging algae.

What is a **rain garden**?

A rain garden is a garden that is planned in a low-lying area of a yard. A rain garden takes advantage of the regular soaking of this area (through rain and runoff) to feature bog plants and other moisture-loving plants. Most importantly, however, a rain garden is installed to reduce the amount of runoff into storm drains.

What is a **swale**?

A swale is an area where rainwater flows. In arid parts of the country, swales may be bone dry for most of the year. But during the rainy season, a barren swale may become a raging torrent of water. Since these natural depressions are important for carrying stormwater, gardeners with larger pieces of property (and even those with smaller ones) need to carefully consider planting in any swales on their property. You might consider leaving them alone or planting them with plants that don't mind wet feet. Another option is to line them with rocks to create a kind of dry riverbed (which will be wet, of course, when it rains).

How can I make my **swimming pool** a part of my garden?

The current fashion used to incorporate swimming pools into a garden landscape is to paint the inside of an in-ground pool with black paint. While this enables the swimming pool to double as a romantic reflecting pool, it is certainly not the safest practice for a pool which will be swum in. (How will you know which end is the deep one and what else awaits you when you dive in?) And if you're not going to swim in your pool, why not just create a reflecting pond?

Another trendy option is to plant perennials—ornamental grasses or romantic perennial flowers—right next to the pool edge. This again makes it tricky for the pool to function as a pool. Obviously, gardens and pools that receive regular use have a hard time co-existing. By choosing an interesting paving around the pool, you could integrate it with other parts of the garden such as paths or terraces. Placing interesting containers of sun-loving plants near the pool is a classic method of gardening with pools. Or you might instead screen the pool with a tall hedge or decorative fence and do your gardening in a different area.

OTHER SPECIALTY GARDENS

What is **hydroponic gardening**?

Hydroponics refers to the practice of growing plants without soil. Plants can be grown in water, aggregates, or even humid air, but the most important element is a nutrient solution. Crops such as tomatoes, squash, sweet peppers, hot chiles, lettuce, spinach, chard, cucumbers, broccoli, and beans, as well as herbs, flowers, and houseplants, have all been grown hydroponically.

Which kinds of plants grow in a **moon garden**?

A moon garden is one that is planted to be viewed at twilight or evening. In the dusky twilight, white-flowered and grey-leaved plants tend to make the strongest impact. You might start by creating a moon-shaped bed. Gray-leaved plants such as English lavender (*Lavandula angustifolia*), rosemary (*Rosmarinus officinalis*), and lamb's ear (*Stachys byzantina*) could be used as structure or edging, along with boxwood (*Buxus* spp.) or even holly (*Ilex* spp.) for daytime viewers. In the spring, white tulips (*Tulipa* 'White Emperor') could be featured. Later, poet's jasmine (*Jasminum officinale*), sweet alyssum (*Lobularia maritima*), evening stock (*Matthiola bicornis*), four o'clocks (*Mirabilis longiflora*), or even a small star magnolia tree (*Magnolia stellata*) provide the garden with both scent and flowers, adding romance to your nocturnal strollings. Flowering tobacco (*Nicotiana*), evening primrose (*Oenothera biennis*), angel's trumpet (*Datura arborea*), moonflower vine (*Ipomoea alba*), night-blooming cereus (*Hylocereus undatus*), and abronia (*Abronia* spp.) all bloom in the late afternoon or evening. 'New Dawn' and 'Nevada' are pale-flowered roses that work well in the night garden, along with 'Pallida', which has a sweet fragrance. Silver mound (*Artemisia*

Herb gardens, such as the Elizabethan knot garden, are typically laid out in a formal design. (Steven Nikkila/Perennial Favorites)

schmidtiana), artemisia (*Artemisia* spp.), and senecio (*Senecio* spp.) provide a finishing glimmer of silver in the dusk.

Another interpretation of a moon garden is rooted in feminist thinking. These gardens might include herbs and flowers traditionally associated with women, such as pennyroyal (*Mentha pulegium*) and shepherd's purse (*Capsella bursa-pastoris*).

What is a **knot garden**?

A knot garden is an herb garden design that dates back to the 1500s. Elizabethan gardeners used herbs or boxwood to create hedges with flowing lines and sharp angles that appeared to be woven together. This type of garden requires a great deal of time spent with clippers in order to preserve its precise design.

What is a **potager**?

Potager means "kitchen garden" in French. It is a vegetable garden in which flowers and herbs intertwine with vegetables to create a colorful design. The plants are laid out in rectangular beds, adding an element of formality to the design. A potager features vegetables that are chosen for their appearance as much as their flavor, such as scarlet runner beans (*Phaseolus coccineus*) or okra (*Hibiscus escutlentus*).

What is a **jardin du curé**?

Jardin du curé translates from the French as "priest's garden," and refers to a small, informal version of a potager.

What is a **cutting garden**?

A cutting garden is one that is planted and laid with flower arrangements in mind. It might include plants for drying such as statice (*Limonium* spp.) and sweet Annie (*Artemisia annua*). Annuals such as flowering tobacco (*Nicotiana*), pot marigold (*Calendula officinalis*), zinnia (*Zinnia* spp.), and stock (*Matthiola incana*) stand up to cutting. Oriental poppies (*Papaver orientale*) are beautiful, but need to have their ends seared in order to last. Bulbs and corms such as tulips (*Tulipa* spp.), narcissus (*Narcissus* spp.), anemones (*Anemone* spp.), gladiolus (*Gladiolus* spp.), and allium (*Allium* spp.) are essentials in the early spring. Black-eyed Susans (*Rudbeckia hirta*), aster (*Aster* spp.), coreopsis (*Coreopsis* spp.), dianthus (*Dianthus* spp.), and roses (*Rosa* spp.) are other great possibilities. Try plants with unusual growing habits such as blanket flower (*Gaillardia pulchella*), whose stems curl toward the sun for interesting arrangements.

The hibiscus-like flowers of okra are appealing to both eye and palate, making it the perfect candidate for planting in a potager. (Robert J. Huffman/Field Mark Publications)

How can a garden be adapted for **gardeners in wheelchairs**?

A garden can be adapted for gardeners in wheelchairs by raising a garden high enough above the ground so that a wheelchair can fit under it. Create or purchase planter boxes and place them on old card tables or a table created from plywood and sawhorses. Consider purchasing a lightweight hose set, similar to those used in greenhouses, and locate the garden near a spigot. Garden supplies should be at the ready, placed on waist-high shelving. Follow guidelines for container gardening in order to successfully maintain the garden. Gardeners with back problems can also use this type of garden, adjusting the height of the garden so that they can stand or sit while gardening.

What is a **Shakespeare garden**?

In his sonnets and plays, Shakespeare mentions several hundred different plants widely used in the rural society that was sixteenth-century Elizabethan England. Shakespeare lovers everywhere have designed Shakespeare gardens that feature plants such as wormwood (*Artemisia absinthium*), primrose (*Primula* spp.), thyme (*Thymus vulgaris*), violets (*Viola odorata*), honesty or money plant (*Lunaria annua*), and lavender (*Lavandula officinalis*).

What is an **alpine garden**?

An alpine garden is one that mimics the growing conditions above the tree line on a mountain. The soil is gravelly though fertile (a mixture known as scree) and the bed may even include larger rocks for plants to spread out on. An alpine garden may feature plants native to alpine environments (see related question in Perennials chapter) or those that appreciate the same growing conditions, such as hens-n-chicks (*Sempervivum tectorum*), stonecrop (*Sedum* spp.), and even small cacti.

What is a **xeriscape**?

A xeriscape is a landscape that is water efficient. It does not necessarily include cactus and yucca or exclude lawns and flowers. Instead, it makes the most of the natural rainfall or water sources in an area and keeps plants that need additional water to a minimum, siting them together for maximum efficiency.

What are some ideas for planting a **children's garden**?

Children and gardening are a natural combination—being outdoors and with beautiful plants makes learning fun and easy. Older kids can be provided with their own plot to plant seeds and watch them grow (see related question in Seeding, Propagation, and Planting chapter). All kids love bright colors and interesting shapes. Look for fun plants and plant projects like creating giant sunflower forests, growing tepees of pole beans or morning glories, raising giant pumpkins for jack-o-lanterns (see related question in Fruits and Vegetables chapter), and developing a fragrance or vegetable garden. Consider selecting sturdy varieties of plants that thrive on neglect and choose some smaller varieties that will be more on a child's scale. Keep paths between beds

> ## What is a cottage garden?
>
> The original cottage garden is an appropriation of cottager's gardens in England. A cottager's garden was a loose collection of plants that evoked a country or romantic feeling independent of its surroundings. These were planted without much thought to design, but were beautiful for their color harmonies. The definition has broadened a bit to include any garden that is romantic or country in feel. Curved beds, integrating herbs with flowers, scrambling roses over an arbor—these are all features of a cottage garden. Landscape artist Gertrude Jekyll was said to have borrowed heavily from the cottage gardens that surrounded her estate.

wide to allow children easy access. Make sure your garden is cleared of any poisonous plants and always provide supervision.

What is a **collector's garden**?

A plant collector is someone who falls in love with a plant for its own inimitable characteristics, as opposed to purchasing plants as part of a landscape or garden design. Many gardeners are plant collectors and their gardens are wonderful reflections of that. The garden of a collector can be a hodgepodge of species or it can be a true collection of as many cultivars of one species as yard and wallet will allow. A rose garden is a type of collector's garden, as is an iris garden, a hosta garden, a primrose garden, and the like. The downside, obviously, of this type of garden is that many of these plants have but one blooming season and the garden hangs its head the rest of the year. But collections don't need to be helter-skelter or purely row upon row of the same species—the best have some thought put into them regarding structure and color, as well as year-long interest.

What Is a **sunken garden**?

A sunken garden is a garden that is built into an excavated area in the ground. One could be constructed from an old foundation or cellar, as long as steps are built into it. They are usually designed in a formal style, given their rectangular shape and "unnaturalness." These gardens can normally house plants that are marginally hardy for the area, since they are protected from cold winds.

PERENNIALS

PERENNIAL PLANT CARE

What is a **perennial**?

A perennial plant is one that flowers and sets seeds for two or more seasons. Perennials such as American columbine (*Aquilegia candensis*) only live for a few years. Others such as peonies (*Paeonia officinalis*) may live for 100 years or more.

What is a **tender perennial**?

A tender perennial is a plant that is perennial in tropical or subtropical regions but that can't survive winter temperatures in other regions. A geranium (*Pelargonium* spp.) is an example of a tender perennial.

How do **tender perennials** differ from annuals?

Tender perennials differ from annuals in that, obviously, many tender perennials continue to grow and rebloom in frost-free areas, whereas annuals eventually die. Like annuals, however, many tender perennials also bloom in their first year when grown from seed. Cold-hardy perennials tend to take a few seasons to establish before blooming.

What is a **hardy perennial**?

A hardy perennial is a perennial that tolerates frost. A chrysanthemum (*Chrysanthemum* spp.) is an example of a hardy perennial.

The marsh marigold (*Caltha palustris*), often called cowslip, is a member of the buttercup family and thrives in wet conditions. (Robert J. Huffman/Field Mark Publications)

What **growing conditions** are required for most perennials?

As a rule of thumb, most perennials need loamy, evenly moist soil with a pH between 5.5 and 6.5. The site should receive full sun (at least six to eight hours) during the day. However, there are many exceptions to this rule because it is possible to find a number of perennials that grow in drier or wetter soil, well-shaded areas, and clay or sandy soil.

How do I prepare my **perennial bed**?

A perennial bed should receive careful preparation, since unlike with annuals, you have only one chance to get it right! The bed should be dug deeply to at least a foot (if not deeper) with all weeds removed, clods broken up, and the soil level. You might consider double digging the bed to ensure loose soil, which will enable your plants to develop strong root systems. A soil test should be done, with soil amendments added to bring the soil to 5.5 to 6.5 pH. Plenty of organic matter such as compost should be dug so that your plants will thrive.

How and when should I **plant perennials**?

Perennials can be planted throughout the growing season. The ideal planting time, however, is when the plant is first breaking its dormancy during early spring and the

The black-eyed Susan (*Rudbeckia hirta*), or gloriosa daisy, is a self-seeder. (Robert J. Huffman/Field Mark Publications)

ground is ready to be worked. Fall would be the next best time, as the cooler temperatures place less stress on plants. As with other ornamentals, try to plant your perennials on an overcast or misty day or at least avoid overly hot or windy days.

Be sure you have your bed prepared before you purchase your plants. This will help you buy the right plant for the right site and will ensure the plant doesn't wither away on your deck awaiting your day off. Loosen the soil in your perennial bed to at least a foot deep, breaking up any large clods, and incorporate any necessary soil amendments, along with a liberal dose of compost. The hole should be wide and deep enough to accommodate the root ball of the plant. If the perennial has fibrous roots, loosen these up and place the plant in the hole so that the crown or base of the plant is at the soil surface and the roots are spread out around it. Other plants vary in their needs. Plants with taproots such as Oriental poppies (*Papaver orientale*) need a hole dug deep enough for the taproot to extend down. The rhizomes of bearded irises, such as *Iris* 'Conjuration', 'Brown Lasso', and 'Dark Vader', need to be placed just at the soil surface, while peonies (*Paeonia officinalis*) need to have their eyes or buds planted no lower than 1 to 2 inches below the surface. Fill the hole and add water immediately, adding a tad more soil if needed.

Remove any flower buds on your plant. During this first season, you want the plant to spend its energy building a strong root system. Monitor the plant carefully for the next few weeks, keeping it well watered. A one-inch layer of mulch applied a few inches away from the crown of your plant will help keep moisture at the root ball and weeds from competing with the new plant.

I'd like to **plant some perennials around some large trees** in my yard but I'm afraid of damaging the trees. What can I do?

You're right to consider the tree's needs. The most important tree roots lie in the top six to 12 inches of soil, so it is important to avoid damaging these roots by rototilling or even double digging a large bed. Instead, plant young perennials individually in small planting holes. Choose perennial varieties that have a habit of spreading or that will reproduce by self-seeding for the best chance of success. Fill in with compost and water frequently until the plants become established.

When is the best time to **divide my perennials** and how mature does the plant need to be to do it?

Generally speaking, most perennials are divided in the spring, just as the new growth is starting to emerge but before they begin to bud or are in full bloom. However, some perennials such as Oriental poppies (*Papaver orientale*) and herbaceous peonies (*Paeonia* spp.) like to be divided and planted in the fall. Other perennials that bloom very early in the spring such as bleeding heart (*Dicentra spectabilis*) should probably be divided and planted in the fall in order to preserve their flowers.

A perennial normally does not need to be divided for a year or two after being transplanted. There are some signs that indicate a plant might need to be divided. When Shasta daisies (*Leucantheum superbum*) have fewer blooms and begin to die out in the middle, it's time to divide them (usually every other year). Pinks or carnations (*Dianthus* spp.) also tend to die out if they aren't divided every few years. Other perennials such as bee balm or bergamot (*Monarda didyma*) will quickly spread through your garden if they are not divided every two years or so. Hostas (*Hosta* spp.) can be divided every few years (each new rosette forming a new plant), but they provide more visual weight to your garden if they are left to grow larger. In addition to

Butterfly milkweed (*Ascleplas tuberosa*) Is a native perennial that is difficult to transplant due to its extremely long taproot. (Robert J. Huffman/Field Mark Publications)

encouraging more vigorous growth and bloom, dividing plants also ensures you will regularly check them for bugs and disease.

How do I **divide a perennial**?

It depends on the root system of the perennial. Bearded iris (such as *Iris aphylla* or *I. pallida*) and other perennials with rhizomes should be cut apart so that there are buds (knobby-looking growth) on each new plant. Perennials with fibrous roots can be dug up and gently teased apart with your hands. Larger plants with tougher root clumps can be pried apart using digging forks or by making a clean cut with a spade. Chrysanthemums (*Chrysanthemum* spp.) and other plants that become woody when they mature should be dug up with new plants created from the growth around the edges. Compost the remaining woody growth in the center. Before dividing plants, it is best to know where you'll be putting the new plants so they can be back in the ground with their roots covered in soil and soaked well with water in no time.

I divided my **peony bush** but it hasn't bloomed since and it has been two years! What did I do wrong?

Peonies (*Paeonia officinalis*) don't generally like to be disturbed, so it takes them a few years to get back to blooming. They can also be planted too deep. When planting your new peony division, be sure the eyes (the pink buds on the root system) are planted just one to two inches below the soil surface. During the first few years after planting, you should consider removing any flower buds that do appear so that the energy of the plant goes into growing strong roots. Once the plant is mature and has healthy foliage, be sure the plant is receiving at least six hours of sun per day and that it isn't receiving too much nitrogen, which can also decrease blooms.

When should I cut back the **foliage on my peonies**?

Peonies (*Paeonia officinalis*) are glorious in full bloom, but their flowers last a short period of time. Fortunately, their beautiful verdant foliage remains green through most of the summer. Once the leaves start to fade and turn brown (usually in the late fall), the foliage should be cut back to the ground and composted to prevent insects and disease from seeking shelter over the winter. If you have already had problems with disease or insects over the summer, you should consider removing the foliage when it is still green and placing it in the trash instead.

Why do **chrysanthemums** need to be pinched back?

Removing the top or apical bud from a stem, also known as pinching back, causes the mum to send off new branches below the bud. This results in a plant that is fuller looking with better blooms (see apical dominance question in the Plant and Soil Science chapter). Generally speaking, mums should be pinched every month or so during the growing season up until the end of July. Other plants that require pinching back include aster (*Aster* spp.), delphinium (*Delphinium* spp.), and phlox (*Phlox carolina*).

How do I **stake my perennials**?

In staking soft-stemmed plants, it's important to remember to be gentle with them. The goal here is to provide support without mangling your plant. In your quest for a beautiful garden, you should also refrain from using any staking materials that are obvious or just plain ugly. In general, the plant support should be at least three-fourths as tall as the plant to provide proper support. For tall plants such as delphinium (*Delphinium* spp.), place a stake near the crown of the plant, being careful not to damage the plant roots. Using garden twine or other soft and inconspicuous material, loosely tie the plant to the stake. You can also purchase stakes that are flexible so they bend with the plant without letting it break, or stakes with a U-shaped end to hold the plant steady. Twigs can provide a rustic-looking support for smaller, lighter plants. For broader plants with weighty blooms such as peonies (*Paeonia officinalis*), plant rings or several stakes with twine wrapped around the stake and the plant provide sturdy support. Remember to place plant supports early in the season before your perennials actually need them to avoid plant mangling.

How often should I fertilize my perennials?

Something to consider when fertilizing perennials is that they will be in the ground longer than annuals. While this sounds self-evident, it has implications for how often you want to fertilize them. While perennials need nitrogen to grow, you may want to consider fertilizing them only one to two times per season. Plants can become fertilizer dependent—needing that quick fix of 15–15–15 in order to bloom at all. But if you properly prepare and regularly amend the soil and have chosen a perennial that appreciates your site conditions, it should do well and be better adapted to survive periods of your life where you don't feel much like gardening.

How do I **mulch my perennials**?

Perennials generally need a layer of one to two inches of mulch. If you use a mulch that decomposes quickly like grass clippings, you may consider a slightly thicker layer. Place the mulch around the plant, being careful to leave space around the crown to reduce the possibility of disease and damage from slugs. Perennials should be mulched after the soil warms up in the spring in order to keep the roots of the plant moist and weed free. In the fall, remove the mulch until after the ground has frozen. Then replace it to keep the soil around the root ball from freezing and thawing, which can damage the plant.

What should I do to get my **perennial beds in order for the winter**?

Perennial borders do require regular maintenance in order to look their best. In the fall, divide any plants that are in need of it and replant those divisions, digging additional compost into the planting hole. Cut any remaining shoots down to the base of the plant. You may choose to leave the seedheads or stems of some plants for winter interest. Also, in areas of severe winter cold, leaving the plants unpruned can help to protect the crown of the plant. A thin layer (one to two inches) of compost can be applied as a topdressing to the bed. An additional light mulching is optional (although recommended in colder areas), but it should be applied after the ground has frozen. Clean up any plant debris (fallen or diseased foliage, faded flowers, and prunings) around the plant and weed the border well. Weeding at this time is crucial to get a jump start on next season. Besides, the weeds are much easier to spot at this time of year, rather than during the peak of the season. Compost the remaining plant material and settle into your winter reading chair with a good plant catalog!

Jack-in-the-pulpit (*Arisaema triphyllum*) is a wildflower that grows well in shady areas. (Robert J. Huffman/Field Mark Publications)

What sort of maintenance do **bearded irises** require?

Bearded irises (such as *Iris aphylla* or *I. pallida*) do require some looking after, since they are prone to damage from wind and rain during their blooming period (late spring, early summer), as well as from the dreaded iris borer. You can reduce the incidence of weather damage by planting them in an area of your yard that receives some shelter, but with good air circulation. After blooming, cut down their flower stalks and knifelike foliage two to three inches from the ground, with the cut foliage creating a small "fan." In the fall, all irises should be dug up and divided. Get rid of any rhizomes that are mushy or diseased and clean up any remaining plant debris around them. The new rhizome clumps should be replanted shallowly—only an inch or two into the soil. In the spring, remove any plants (rhizomes and all) that have tunnels mined by iris borer larvae. This may help prevent them from infesting your entire bed.

What is the advantage of **perennials over annuals**?

Although you might think perennials are cheaper in the long run, since you only purchase them once every few years, they do require more labor and cost more (in terms of soil amendments and compost as well as the price tag of the plant) at the outset than annuals do. The main advantage of perennials in cooler climates is that they can extend the growing season. Many annuals require temperatures above freezing in order to survive and thrive. Some perennials need cooler temperatures to flower and some remain green throughout much of the year.

Now that I've successfully grown perennial flowers, I'd like to cut a few for **bouquets**. Are there any guidelines I should follow?

The best time to cut flowers is in the early morning. Use a set of sharp scissors or pruners and cut the stems as long as possible down to a bud or leaf node that is facing the outside of the plant. By cutting flowers in a variety of budding and blooming stages, you make your bouquet more interesting and lifelike. Carry a bucket of luke-warm water with you and plunge the stems into the water immediately after cutting. For hollow-stemmed flowers like Oriental poppies (*Papaver orientale*), use a match or lighter to sear the end of the stem in order to keep water inside.

PERENNIAL SELECTION

Which perennials grow in **dry and shady conditions**?

Perennials that grow or thrive in dry and shady or partially shady sites include the celandine poppy (*Chelidonium majus*), candytuft (*Iberis sempervirens*), gas plant (*Dictamnus albus*), pinks (*Dianthus* spp.), bishop's hat (*Epimedium var. versicolor*), lungwort (*Pulmonaria* spp.), big blue lily turf (*Liriope muscari*), Solomon's seal (*Polygonatum* spp.), and Gladwin iris (*Iris foetidissima*).

Which perennials will grow in **moist and shady conditions**?

Fern, primrose (*Primula* spp.), comfrey (*Symphytum uplandicum*), columbine (*Aquilegia* spp.), astilbe (*Astilbe* spp.), bergenia (*Bergenia cordifolia*), bleeding heart (*Dicentra spactabilis*), hellebore (*Helleborus* spp.), epimedium (*Epimedium perralderianum*), and hosta (*Hosta* spp.) are just a few of the perennials that thrive under moist and shady conditions.

Which perennials grow in **dry and sunny conditions**?

Think meadow flowers for dry and sunny areas: purple coneflower (*Echinacea puppurea*), *Coreopis*, sage (*Salvia* spp.), golden rod (*Soldiago* spp.), globe thistle (*Echinops ritro*), yarrow (*Achillea millefolium*), blanket flower (*Gaillardia pulchella*), daylilies (*Hemerocallis* spp.), perennial flax (*Lineum perenne*), and gayfeather (*Liatris* spp.). Artemisia (*Artemisia* spp.), baptisia (*Baptisia* spp.), *Scabiosa* spp., thrift (*Armeria*), golden marguerite (*Anthemis tinctora*), spike speedwell (*Veronica spicata*), English

Hostas (*Hosta* spp.) are grown mainly for their striking foliage and grow well in moist and shady conditions. They are hardy perennials that usually do well on their own, but can be multiplied easily by dividing and replanting. (Steven Nikkila/Perennial Favorites)

lavender (*Lavandula angustifolia*), lamb's ear (*Stachys byzantina*), pinks (*Dianthus* spp.), sedum (*Sedum* spp.), spurge (*Euphorbia polychroma*), statice (*Limonium* spp.), foxtail lily (*Eremurus* spp.), and yucca (*Yucca* spp.) also thrive in these areas.

Which perennials grow in **moist and sunny conditions**?

Think of swamps and wetlands: cardinal flower (*Lobelia cardinalis*), spiderwort (*Tradescantia* spp.), white turtlehead (*Chelone glabra*), yellow flag (*Iris pseudacorus*), marsh marigold (*Caltha palustris*), meadowsweet (*Spiraea latifolia*), meadow rue (*Thalictrum*), bee balm (*Monarda didyma*), sneezeweed (*Helenium autumnale*), loosestrifes (choose members of the *Lysimachia* genus rather than *Lythrum*), and Virginia bluebell (*Mertensia pulmonarioides*) all thrive in moist and sunny areas. Goat's beard (*Aruncus dioicus*), Japanese iris (*Iris ensata*) and Siberian iris (*Iris forrestii*), hibiscus (*Hibiscus* spp.), Himalayan cowslip (*Primula sikkimensis*), geum (*Geum* spp.), and rodgersia (*Rodgersia* spp.) also love moist soil.

Which perennials grow well in **acidic soil**?

Primrose (*Primula* spp.), Virginia bluebell (*Mertensia pulmonarioides*), Gentian (*Gentiana* spp.), toad-lily (*Trycytris* spp.), Himalayan cowslip (*Primula sikkimensis*),

Bee balm (*Monarda didyma*) will grow well in moist and sunny conditions. (Robert J. Huffman/Field Mark Publications)

Lupine (*Lupinus* spp.) is a member of the Pea family and grows well in acidic soil. It blooms in early and midsummer. (Steven Nikkila/Perennial Favorites)

Lilium speciosum and tiger lily (*Lilium tigrinum*), lupine (*Lupinus* spp.), slipperwort (*Calceolaria rugosa*), Scottish flame flower (*Tropaeolum speciosum*), heath (*Erica* spp.) and heather (*Calluna* spp.), stinkwort (*Helleborus foetidus*), and milkweed (*Asclepias*) are among the perennials that will flourish in acidic soil.

Which perennials grow well in **alkaline soil**?

Although gardeners with alkaline soil often curse it, a number of beautiful perennials thrive in this type of soil. Orange-eye butterfly bush (*Buddleia davidii*), foxtail lily (*Eremurus* spp.), globe thistle (*Echinops ritro*), verbascum (*Verbascum* spp.), Oriental poppy (*Papaver orientale*), purple toadflax (*Linaria purpurea*), Russian sage (*Perovskia atriplicifolia*), *Salvia x. superba*, yarrow 'Cerise Queen' (*Achillea millefolium* 'Cerise Queen'), gas plant (*Dictamnus albus*), pincushion flower (*Scabiosa caucasica*), *Sedum spectabile* 'Autumn Joy', threadleaf coreopsis (*Coreopsis verticillata*), red valerian (*Centranthus ruber*), pinks (*Dianthus* spp.), strawflower (*Helichrysum bracteatum*), pasque flower (*Pulsatilla vulgaris*), and baby's breath (*Gypsophila paniculata*) all love alkaline soil.

What are some **tender perennials**?

Tender perennials include plants in genera such as *Tradescantia, Lantana , Senecio, Lobelia, Petunia, Pennisetum, Vinca, Tropaeolum, Salvia, Helichrysum, Heliotropi-*

Cosmos 'Sensation'
Which annuals are easiest to grow for a beginning gardener? See page 264. (Robert J. Huffman/Field Mark Publications)

California poppy (*Eschscholzia californica*)
What are some annuals that will grow in dry soil?
See page 261. (Robert J. Huffman/Field Mark Publications)

Salvia 'Flare Path'
What are warm-weather annuals? See page 250.
(Robert J. Huffman/Field Mark Publications)

Coleus spp.
What are some annuals that are grown for their foliage? See page 270.
(Robert J. Huffman/Field Mark Publications)

American robin
What does my garden need to attract wildlife? See page 190. (Robert J. Huffman/Field Mark Publications)

Tagetes erecta
I'd like to attract birds to my backyard in the winter without a feeder. What kinds of plants can I grow? See page 189.
(Steven Nikkila/Perennial Favorites)

Iris spp.
What kind of flowers are hummingbirds attracted to?
See page 190. (Robert J. Huffman/Field Mark Publications)

Blue cohosh
What are some different arrangements of plant leaves? See page 9.
(Robert J. Huffman/Field Mark Publications)

Dusty Miller (*Senecio cineraria*)
What impact do leaf characteristics such as color and texture have on a plant's survival? See page 10.
(Robert J. Huffman/Field Mark Publications)

Compass-plant
What are the functions of a plant's leaves? See page 9.
(Robert J. Huffman/Field Mark Publications)

Squirrel corn
What determines leaf color in a plant? See page 9.
(Robert J. Huffman/Field Mark Publications)

False Solomon's seal (*Polygonatum* spp.)
Which perennials will grow in dry and shady
conditions? See page 219.
(Robert J. Huffman/Field Mark Publications)

Bee Balm (*Monarda didyma*)
Which perennials will grow in moist and sunny
conditions? See page 220.
(Robert J. Huffman/Field Mark Publications)

Bracken fern
Which perennials will grow in moist and shady
conditions? See page 219.
(Robert J. Huffman/Field Mark Publications)

Purple coneflower (*Echinacea purpurea*)
Which perennials will grow in dry and sunny
conditions? See page 219.
(Robert J. Huffman/Field Mark Publications)

Black swallowtail larvae
What is the difference between integrated pest management and organic pest management? See page 107.
(Robert J. Huffman/Field Mark Publications)

Japanese beetle on plant
Are there any plants that Japanese beetles won't eat? See page 99.
(Steven Nikkila/Perennial Favorites)

What kind of soil should I use in containers? See page 185.
(Steven Nikkila/Perennial Favorites)

I live in the desert. What are some desert natives that I can grow
in my landscape? See page 195.
(Robert J. Huffman/Field Mark Publications)

Lupinus spp.
Which kinds of plants do butterfly larvae live in? See page 188. (Robert J. Huffman/Field Mark Publications)

Sedum spurium 'Dragon's Heart'
What are some perennials that can be left unpruned for winter interest? See page 229. (Steven Nikkila/Perennial Favorites)

Zinnia spp.
What are some annuals that bloom in the late summer or early fall? See page 269. (Robert J. Huffman/Field Mark Publications)

What are some characteristics of an informal garden? See page 121.
(Steven Nikkila/Perennial Favorites)

Western wallflower
What are some spring-flowering annuals? See page 269.
(Robert J. Huffman/Field Mark Publications)

What are some characteristics of a formal garden? See
page 121. (Steven Nikkila/Perennial Favorites)

Michigan lily
What are some summer-blooming bulbs?
See page 238.
(Robert J. Huffman/Field Mark Publications)

Tulip (*Tulipa* spp.)
What are some spring-blooming bulbs? See
page 238. (Steven Nikkila/Perennial Favorites)

Closed Gentian (*Gentiana* spp.)
Which perennials will grow in acidic soil?
See page 220.
(Robert J. Huffman/Field Mark Publications)

Globe thistle (*Echinops ritro*)
Which perennials will grow in alkaline soil?
See page 222.
(Robert J. Huffman/Field Mark Publications)

Can strawberries really be grown in a strawberry pot? See page 298.
(Robert J. Huffman/Field Mark Publications)

How do I plan my vegetable garden?
See page 276.
(Robert J. Huffman/Field Mark Publications)

What's the proper method for harvesting berries? See page 300.
(Robert J. Huffman/Field Mark Publications)

When is the proper time to harvest green beans? See page 290.
(Robert J. Huffman/Field Mark Publications)

Holly (*Ilex* spp.)
What types of shrubs can be kept as hedges? See page 310. (Robert J. Huffman/Field Mark Publications)

Pussywillow (*Salix discolor*)
How can I force a branch to bloom? See page 327.
(Robert J. Huffman/Field Mark Publications)

Acer saccharinum
When is the best time of year to fertilize my tree?
See page 322. (Steven Nikkila/Perennial Favorites)

Sweet woodruff (*Galium odoratum*)
What are some herbs that are used to flavor drinks?
See page 384. (Robert J. Huffman/Field Mark Publications)

Borage (*Borago officinalis*)
What are some reputed healing qualities of borage?
See page 386. (Robert J. Huffman/Field Mark Publications)

Sage (*Salvia officinalis*)
What are some traditional uses of sage? See page 389. (Robert J. Huffman/Field Mark Publications)

Heliotropium arborescens 'Marine'
What is heliotrope? See page 273. (Steven Nikkila/Perennial Favorites)

Virginia bluebells (*Mertenesia pulmonaioides*) bloom in the spring. They enjoy moist, rich, humusy soil and partial shade.
(Robert J. Huffman/Field Mark Publications)

um, Hibiscus, Begonia, Canna, Dianthus, Ipomoea, Dahlia, Lablab, and, of course, *Pelargonium.*

Which perennials **bloom in the spring**?

Consider spring a showcase season for perennials, since it is still generally too cool in most areas for annuals to make a big display. A majority of hardy perennials bloom during April and early May. Spring-blooming bulbs are obviously the main show, with tulips (*Tulipa* spp.) and daffodils (*Narcissus* spp.) being the featured stars. Supporting performances by bulbs include grape hyacinth (*Muscari* spp.), ornamental onion (*Allium* spp.), and English bluebell (*Hyacinthoides non-scripta*). Spring-blooming plants include violet (*Viola* spp.), spurge (*Euphorbia polychroma*), bleeding heart (*Dicentra spectabilis*), perennial forget-me-not (*Brunnera macrophylla*), blue lungwort (*Pulmonaria angustifolia*), *Geranium* 'Johnson's Blue', columbine (*Aquilegia* spp.), candytuft (*Iberis sempervirens*), false indigo (*Baptisia australis*), perennial thrift (*Armeria maritima*), Siberian iris (*Iris sibirica*), oxeye daisy (*Heliopsis* spp.), and angel's trumpet (*Datura arborea*). Tender spring-bloomers for warmer areas include gazania (*Gazania* spp.), weeping lantana (*Lantana montevidensis*), and ice plants such as *Drosantheum roseum.*

Which perennials **bloom in the summer**?

In summer, the paler colors of spring make way for bolder colors. Summer-blooming perennials include spiderwort (*Tradescantia* spp.), balloon flower (*Platycodon grandiflorum*), delphinium (*Delphinium* spp.), bearded iris (such as *Iris pallida*), peony (*Paeonia* spp.), Oriental poppy (*Papaver orientale*), catmint (*Nepeta* spp.), *Phlox paniculata* 'Eva Cullum', Shasta daisy (*Leucantheum superbum*), *Coreopsis verticillata* 'Moonbeam', 'Stella de Oro' daylily and other daylilies (*Hemerocallis* spp.), bee balm (*Monarda* spp.), lavender cotton (*Santolina chamaecyparissus*), sneezeweed (*Helenium autumnale*), bugbane (*Cimifuga racemosa*), gas plant (*Dictamnus albus*), purple coneflower (*Echinacea purpurea*), black-eyed Susan (*Rudbeckia hirta*), lady's mantle (*Alchemilla vulgaris*), and verbascum (*Verbascum* spp.).

Which perennials **bloom in the fall**?

Autumn is another extraordinary season for perennials. While many annuals succumb to the first frosts of fall, there are many perennials that continue blooming after a light frost. Chrysanthemums (*Chrysanthemum* spp.) are a commonly used fall-bloomer. Others include asters (*Aster* spp.), bellflower (*Campanula* spp.), leadwort (*Ceratostigma plumbaginoides*), autumn monkshood (*Aconitum carmichaelii*), obedient plant (*Physostegia virginiana*), *Ligularia dentata* 'Desdemona', sneezeweed (*Hele-*

Bellflower (*Campanula* spp.) blooms in the fall and can be used nicely in a three-season border design. (Steven Nikkila/ Perennial Favorites)

nium autumnale), autumn-blooming candytuft (*Iberis sempervirens* 'Autumn Snow'), plume poppy (*Macleaya cordata*), Joe-pye weed (*Eupatorium purpureum*), goldenrod (*Solidago* spp.), and *Sedum spectabile* 'Autumn Joy'. A tender fall-bloomer for warmer climates is *Crassula* 'Campfire'. Most areas are also suitable for the fall-blooming crocus (*Colchicum speciosum*) and cyclamen (*Cyclamen coum*).

Which perennials **bloom in the winter**?

The beautiful blooms of bulbs such as winter aconite (*Eranthis hyemalis*), crocus (*Crocus* spp.), and snowdrops (*Galanthus nivalis*) peep through melting snow. Christmas and Lenten roses (*Helleborus niger* and *H. orientalis*) also bloom in the winter and have lovely foliage as well.

Are there any perennials with **grey or silver foliage**?

Grey- and silver-leaved plants act as an excellent foil for bright or pastel-colored flowers and can provide contrast to darker-leaved plants, lighting up areas of a garden. Meadow rue (*Thalictrum aquilegifolium*), *Hosta* 'Sieboldiana', lamb's ear (*Stachys byzantina*), plume poppy (*Macleaya cordata* 'Kelway's Coral Plume'), dusty miller (*Senecio cineraria*—used as an annual except in zones 8 through 10), silver mound (*Artemisia schmidtiana* 'Nana'), rue (*Ruta graveolens* 'Jackman's Blue'), yarrow (*Achillea millefoli-*

225

um 'Moonshine'), Turkish mullein (*Verbascum bombyciferum*), wormwood (*Artemisia absinthium* 'Lambrook Silver'), blue oat grass (*Helictotrichon sempervirens*), and *Buddleia fallowiana* are some of the perennials with grey or silver foliage.

What are some perennials that could be used as **focal points**?

Yucca (*Yucca* spp.) provides an exciting focal point to a garden—its knife-like leaves making an exclamation point in a garden. Plume poppy (*Macleaya cordata*) can also serve as a subtler focal point with its salmon-colored flowers rising from its large leaves. Any of the hostas (*Hosta* spp.), when large enough, can be used as a focal point in a low-growing bed. For the summer garden, consider using cannas (*Canna* spp.), whose large, tropical good looks provide emphasis to a perennial border, or globe thistle (*Echinops ritro*) for the wild garden. *Ligularia dentata* 'Desdemona', sometimes known as golden groundsel, rises to three feet at maturity and has wonderful dark green leaves that are plum-colored underneath, setting off its deep orange flowers. You might consider using a vining plant such as clematis (*Clematis* spp.) on a tuteur or other upright support to create interest in the garden as well. In the winter, the tuteur could be left bare to provide something for the eye to rest on. In drier parts of the country, look for tall, native plants such as cacti in the *Opuntia* genus to provide focus in a desert landscape.

Violets (*Viola* spp.) are a popular fragrant flower. (Robert J. Huffman/Field Mark Publications)

Which perennials were commonly used by the English landscape designer **Gertrude Jekyll** in her plantings?

Roses (*Rosa* spp.), lamb's ear (*Stachys byzantina*), bergenia (*Bergenia cordifolia*), clematis (*Clematis montana* and *Clematis* 'Jackmanii'), Oriental poppy (*Papaver orientalis*), delphinium (*Delphinium* spp.), perennial baby's breath (*Gypsophila paniculata*), a variety of ferns and epimediums, candytuft (*Iberis sempervirens*), a variety of irises (*Iris* spp.), and geraniums (both perennial and pelargoniums) are among the many Jekyll-favored perennials.

What are some perennials that have **fragrant flowers**?

Although they are considered shrubs, not flowers, roses (*Rosa* spp.) are the obvious choice. Other perennials with fragrant flowers include pinks (*Dianthus* spp.), *Iris graminea*, clematis (*Clematis recta* and *Clematis integrifolia* 'Hendersonii'), perennial pea (*Lathyrus sylvestris*), sweet rocket (*Hesperis matronalis*), Himalayan cowslip (*Primula sikkimensis*), peony (*Paeonia* spp.), and violets (*Viola* spp.) all have fragrant flowers.

What are some **blue-flowered perennials**?

Taller blue-flowered perennials include delphiniums (*Delphinium* spp.), the taller *Veronica* species, Stokes aster (*Stokesia* spp.), Russian sage (*Perovskia atriplicifolia*)

The lance-leaved coneflower (*Rudbeckia triloba*) is also called the thin-leaved coneflower. It is similar to a black-eyed Susan, but it has smaller, more numerous flowers with shorter, fewer rays. (Robert J. Huffman/Field Mark Publications)

and other sages, Michaelmas daisy (*Aster frikartii* and *Aster novi-belgi* 'Marie Ballard'), cupid's dart (*Catananche caerulea*), the herb hyssop (*Hyssopus* spp.), a blue-flowered bellflower (*Campanula garganica* 'Telham Beauty' and *Campanula glomerata* 'Superba'), and false indigo (*Baptisia australis*). Lower-growing perennials include *Geranium* 'Johnson Blue', spreading veronica (*Veronica prostrata*), perennial forget-me-not (*Brunnera macrophylla*), *Gentiana septemfida*, the groundcover ajuga (*Ajuga* spp.), and bellflower.

What are some perennials that **self-seed**?

Plants such as lady's mantle (*Alchemilla vulgaris*), columbine (*Aquilegia* spp.), golden marguerite (*Anthemis tinctoria*), spurge (*Euphorbia polychroma*), and lanceleaf coreopsis (*Coreopsis lanceolata*) are all prolific self-seeders.

Are there any perennials that **don't have to be deadheaded**?

There are a number of perennials that will continue to bloom throughout the summer without constant deadheading. Threadleaf coreopsis (*Coreopsis verticillata* 'Moonbeam'), Russian sage (*Perovskia atriplicifolia*), purple coneflower (*Echinacea purpurea*), yarrow (*Achillea millefolium*), and grayleaf cranesbill (*Geranium cinereum*) all bloom throughout the summer without deadheading. In addition, the seedheads of purple coneflower are a favorite finch food.

What are some perennials that have **beautiful leaf color** in the fall?

Many members of the *Carex* spp. fade to a beautiful buff color that they retain throughout the winter. *Euphorbia polychroma* gradually changes its leaf color over the year from a limy green in the spring to pinky red stems accented by yellow leaves in the fall. The foliage of *Geranium macrorrhizum* 'Album' takes on a purplish pigment in the fall. The pale green foliage of showy sedum (*Sedum spectabile*) changes to a sharp yellow in the fall, which complements its earthy-colored seedheads. When conditions are right (cool nights and warm days), *Hosta* cultivars turn a lovely shade of gold before fading into the earth. And two perennial members of the edible garden—rhubarb (*Rheum hybridum*) and asparagus (*Asparagus officinalis*)—have foliage interest in the autumn. Before dying back for the winter, the big green leaves of the rhubarb plant change to butter yellow, complementing their red stems. Likewise, the ferny fronds of asparagus fade to a pale yellow.

What are some perennials that can be left unpruned for **winter interest**?

Any perennials with interesting or edible seedheads such as purple coneflower (*Echinacea purpurea*), black-eyed Susan (*Rudbeckia hirta*), yarrow (*Achillea millefolium*),

229

What is the difference between a tree peony and your standard issue backyard peony?

"Backyard" peonies, such as the fernleaf peony (*Paeonia tenuifolia*) and the common peony (*Paeonia officinalis*), are herbaceous perennials, meaning they die back to the ground each year. Tree peonies, such as the Tibetan peony (*Paeonia lutea ludlowii*) or the Mouton peony (*Paeonia suffruticosa*), are more shrub than tree, but are considered woody ornamentals with their woody stems and slightly lax branches. Tree peonies bloom earlier than herbaceous ones and have larger flowers. Common peonies do, however, retain their foliage for most of the summer until it sadly shrivels in the fall. They are also slightly more cold hardy than tree peonies, surviving in zones 3 through 8, as opposed to a tree peony in zones 4 through 8.

and showy sedum (*Sedum spectabile*) are best left standing for the winter garden. Even the low-standing seedheads of the groundcover sedum will provide interest before the heavy snows hit. Many heathers (*Calluna* spp.) actually bloom in the winter, and those that don't at least remain evergreen in certain climates.

I keep seeing goldenrod being featured in perennial borders. Doesn't **goldenrod cause hayfever**?

No—goldenrod (*Soldiago* spp.) is commonly confused with ragweed (*Ambrosia artemisiifolia*), which blooms at the same time of the year as goldenrod. Ragweed's blooms aren't as visible as those of goldenrod so goldenrod gets the blame for your sniffing and sneezing. Ragweed generates pollen that is airborn for reproduction, while goldenrod is pollinated by insects.

What are **alpine plants**?

Alpine plants are those that are adapted to growing above the tree line on a mountain. In the garden, however, they include any plant that grows in a rock garden or trough garden. They like a gravelly, fertile, well-drained soil similar to their natural habitat. Some alpine plants include woolly yarrow (*Achillea tomentosa*), sea thrifts (*Armeria juniperfolia* and *Armeria maritima*), *Euryops acraeus*, purple rockcress (*Aubrieta deltoidea* 'Variegata'), *Hypericum olympicum*, and Amur adonis (*Adonis amurensis*).

What are some perennials with **striking foliage**?

A design element of perennials that is often overlooked is their foliage. Perennials with variegated foliage include purple moorgrass (*Molinia caerulea* 'Variegata'), ribbon grass (*Phalaris arundinacea picta*), *Hosta undulata*, golden balm (*Melissa officinalis* 'Aurea'), zebra grass (*Miscanthus sinensis* 'Zebrinus'), maiden grass (*Miscanthus sinesis* 'Gracillimus'), Japanese iris (*Iris kaempferi* 'Variegata') and sweet iris (*Iris pallida* 'Variegata'), variegated Japanese Solomon's seal (*Polygonatum odoratum* 'Variegatum'), lungwort (*Pulmonaria saccharata*), and snow-on-the-mountain (*Euphorbia marginata*). For a different effect, perennials such as spotted dead nettle (*Lamium maculatum* 'Aureaum'), Bowles' golden grass (*Milium effusum* 'Aureum'), *Hosta fortunei* 'Aurea', spurge (*Euphorbia polychroma*), common oregano (*Origanum vulgare* 'Aureum'), and lady's mantle (*Alchemilla vulgaris*) feature yellow or acid green leaves. Some perennials even change colors later in the season, including the previously mentioned spurge, a number of heaths and heathers (*Erica* spp. and *Calluna* spp.), hardy plumbago (*Ceratostigma plumbaginoides*), bishop's hat (*Epimedium niveum*), meadow geraniums (*Geranium pratense* 'Album' and *Geranium pratense* 'Mrs. Kendall's Clarke'), and vines like Virginia creeper (*Parthenocissus quinquefolia*) and Boston ivy (*P. tricuspidata*). See the previous question on gray- and silver-leaved plants for additional color ideas.

Finally, some perennials have foliage that is beautiful in form. Consider any and all ferns, bergenia (*Bergenia cordifolia*), rodgersia (*Rodgersia tabularis*), astilbe (*Astilbe* spp.), herbaceous peony (*Paeonia* spp.) for a short while, *Gunnera manicata*, plume poppy (*Macleaya cordata*), and the bamboos such as *Arundinaria murieliae*.

I live in an area that has been undergoing **droughtlike conditions** over the past several years. Are there any perennials that can survive this?

With weather patterns shifting and more regions limiting the amount of water available for outdoor use, it is smart to consider making a switch to perennials that will thrive under these conditions. Drought-tolerant perennials include rock cress (*Arabis procurrens*), aster (*Aster* spp.), baptisia (*Baptisia perfoliata*), globe centaurea (*Centaurea macrocephala*), threadleaf coreopsis (*Coreopsis verticillata*), a number of the spurges or Euphorbia genus, including *E. corollata*, *E. cyparissias*, *E. epithymoides*, and *E. myrsinites*, prickly pear cactus (*Opuntia humifusa*), showy sedum or stonecrop (*Sedum spectabile* and *S. spurium*), *Iris* 'Pacific Coast', blanket flower (*Gaillardia pulchella*), hollyhock mallow (*Malva alcea*), bee balm (*Monarda didyma*), and English lavender (*Lavandula angustifolia*).

Which flower means **"first rose"**?

Primrose or *prima rosa* is said to be the first rose of the year. Wild primroses (*Primula vulgaris*) are also said to represent first or new love.

Though once considered to be a common weed, the New England hardy aster (*Aster novae-angliae*) is becoming more popular in wildflower gardens, mainly because it can stand drought-like conditions. (Robert J. Huffman/Field Mark Publications)

How was **daisy** named?

The daisy's botanical name, *Bellis perennis*, originates in the Latin word for "beautiful." The Old English term *daeges-eaye* or "day's-eye" describes the way in which the flowers open and close with the sun.

BULBS

What is a **bulb**?

The term *bulb* has one meaning, but two uses. A bulb is the swollen underground stem that is made up of food surrounding a bud. The food enables the bulb to survive periods of cold and drought. Bulbs multiply by generating bulblets from the mother bulb. The resulting plant, such as a tulip, that comes up from a bulb is also usually referred to as a bulb, although the correct term is *bulbous plant*. Growers often refer to plants and plant structures that are actually corms and tubers as bulbs as well but, technically, they are different (see related question in Plant and Soil Science chapter for more information).

My tulips are done blooming and look so straggly. Can I **remove the leaves**?

If you'd like to have beautiful tulips (*Tulipa* spp.) next year, it's best not to. Removing the leaves disrupts the cycle of the bulb, preventing it from storing energy for the next year. If you wait until the leaves have shriveled and turned brown, you can help this process along. While some people place rubber bands over the leaves and various other contraptions, the most beautiful method of hiding the wilting leaves is by planting a spring-flowering plant or beautiful groundcover over the bulbs.

What is a **naturalizing bulb**?

A naturalizing bulb is a bulb that grows vigorously and multiplies itself if it is planted in an area where it can hold its own against other plants such as grasses or groundcovers. When you want your bulbs to naturalize, you usually plant them in drifts or large groups. If you plant them in a lawn, remember that you need to hold off mowing until the foliage has turned brown. Some examples of naturalizing bulbs include narcissus and daffodil varieties (both *Narcissus* spp.), Siberian squill (*Scilla siberica*) and striped squill (*Puschkinia scilloides*), glory-of-the-snow (*Chionodoxa*), snowdrops (*Galanthus nivalis*), crocus (*Crocus* spp.), and winter aconite (*Eranthis hyemalis*).

Crocus (*Crocus* spp.) bulbs ready to be planted. (Robert J. Huffman/Field Mark Publications)

What **growing conditions** do bulbs require?

Most require a period of either cold or drought in order to break dormancy. They also require full sun, for the most part, but this is not normally a difficult requirement for spring-flowering bulbs as the leaves have yet to fill out on the trees. Bulbs planted in warmer parts of your yard will bloom earlier than cooler areas, so you may want to consider scattering them in different portions of your yard to extend the show or to provide a psychological boost a few weeks sooner than usual. Bulbs do not like being waterlogged, so be sure the soil they are planted in is well drained, if not sandy.

How can I tell **which end is "up" on a bulb**?

For larger bulbs such as tulips and daffodils, it is relatively easy to find the tapered end, which should be planted up. This end sometimes has a shoot growing out of it. The "down" end of a bulb will sometimes have remnants of dried roots. With very small bulbs, look for a slight tapering at the top of the bulb and don't sweat it too much. Chances are the bulb will right itself in time for blooming.

How do I **plant bulbs**?

On average, bulbs need to be planted three times their own depth. Although you can use either a bulb planter or a dibble to plant single bulbs, most bulbs look best when planted in groups or drifts. Try using a spade or trowel to dig a small bed, then place a light dusting of bonemeal in the bed followed by a half-inch of backfill at the bottom. Then, scatter your bulbs (growing tip up) through the bed, attempting to keep at least one to two bulbs' width between them. After backfilling with the remaining dirt, water the area thoroughly.

How do I **plant bulbs in my lawn**?

You can plant bulbs singly (which is more time consuming) or in groups. To plant them singly, sprinkle the bulbs across the lawn. Then, using a trowel or a bulb planter, lift up a core of sod to the depth required by the bulb, creating a hole for each bulb. Sprinkle a small amount of bonemeal into the hole and mix gently, then pop the bulb in with the tip up. If you plant a large group of bulbs, cut away a square of sod. Loosen the soil underneath to the depth required by the bulbs and scratch some bonemeal into it. Then place the bulbs at least a bulb's width from each other and replace the sod.

What are some good **bulbs to plant in lawns**?

When selecting bulbs to be planted in lawns, consider the fact that you will not wish to mow the lawn in that area until the bulb foliage has shriveled and browned. Choose early-bloomers such as crocus (*Crocus* spp.), daffodils (*Narcissus* spp.), and early tulips (*Tulipa* spp.), or else your lawn may become tall enough to go to seed in that area.

When should I **divide my daffodil bulbs**?

Since daffodil bulbs naturalize freely, they should only be divided when they fail to bloom as profusely as they used to. Dig up the bulbs and separate the bulbils from the main bulbs and replant. This can be done any time after the leaves have died down.

How can I get my tulips to **reflower** every year? I'm tired of planting them again and again.

Tulips do have a shorter life expectancy than, say, narcissus, which tend to be naturalizers. Planting tulips deeper (say to five times their own depth) can help ensure the tulips will produce flowers for more years. Also, by refraining from removing the foliage before it turns brown, you allow the bulb to continue growing, putting its energy toward storing more food. Deadheading after the bulb has finished flowering prevents the plant from putting its energy into seed formation. Finally, you might consider planting species tulips, such as *Tulipa praestans*, which are "naturalizing tulips." Hybrids of *Tulipa kaufmanniana* tend to live longer than other species.

235

Do bulbs need to be **fertilized**?

Yes—for the best and most consistent blooming, bulbs do need to be fertilized. Before planting bulbs, place bone-meal in the planting hole, then cover lightly with the backfill before setting the bulb in. Most spring-flowering bulbs also appreciate a small amount of bonemeal scratched into the soil around them in the early spring, just as the leaves begin to come up. If you have sandy or infertile soil, you may choose to apply a second treatment of bonemeal once the flowers have faded.

How do I **force bulbs** to bloom inside my house?

Some bulbs are easier to "force" than others. These include paperwhites and other *Narcissus tazetta*, hyacinth (*Hyacinthus* spp.), and crocus (*Crocus* spp.). In order to have a bulb blooming at a particular time, you must consider both the time the bulb needs to

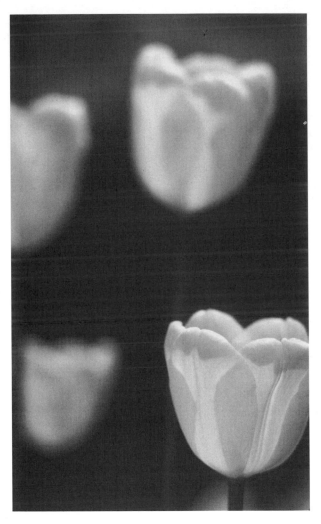

Tulips (*Tulipa* spp.) look lovely when interplanted with other flowers, but tulips of similar color planted together in beds or borders produce striking effects. (Robert J. Huffman/Field Mark Publications)

spend in the dark (on average about three months but this varies from bulb to bulb), and the time the bulb needs to spend in the light (usually around a month). Count backward from the desired bloom date to determine the "potting up" date. "Potting up" consists of filling containers with a 1:1 mixture of potting soil and topsoil (for its mois-ture-retentiveness), then placing the bulbs in the container with their tips just showing above the soil line. Fertilize lightly with a liquid fertilizer, then place the container in a cool, dark area that stays right around 40 degrees Fahrenheit. Once they have complet-ed their "dark" phase, gradually bring the container into the light and water occasion-ally to keep the bulbs moist. Some bulbs like paperwhites, hyacinth, and crocus can be

> ## What is bonemeal and how is it used?
>
> **B**onemeal is an organic fertilizer derived from animal bones that supplies bulbs, fruit trees, and shrubs with a good source of phosphorus. It is most commonly used when planting or topdressing bulbs.

grown in water. These can be purchased in planting "kits" that include the bulb and container.

Can **forced bulbs** be replanted?

The process of "forcing" bulbs does require more energy from a bulb than if it were planted in the ground. These bulbs won't successfully "re-force," but they can be replanted in the garden if they are properly treated in their containers. This means deadheading and allowing the foliage to wither, just as you would if the plant were outdoors. Keep them moist initially, but reduce your watering until the foliage has withered. After being replanted in your garden, it may take several seasons for them to recover.

It's January in zone 5 and I **didn't have time to plant my bulbs in the fall**. Can I plant them now?

If you've had a mild winter up to this point and the ground has not yet frozen, you can go ahead and plant. But if your ground has already frozen, it's probably pretty difficult to dig through frozen ground (let alone the ice and snow). If that's the case, try giving your bulbs a "refrigerator winter." Place the bulbs in your fridge, wrapped well in paper towels. This will help keep them dry so that they don't mold. Bring them out to plant once the ground has thawed enough to dig. Most bulbs need roughly 10 to 12 weeks of cold in order to bloom. With any luck, your bulbs will flower this spring. If not, they should flower the following one.

How do I plant a mixture of **bulbs in containers**?

The best way to plant a variety of bulbs in containers is to plant in layers, beginning with the largest bulbs at the bottom of the container. All bulbs should be planted three to four times their depth. For example, start with tulip and narcissus bulbs at the lower part of the container, followed by hyacinth, then crocus.

237

What are the **earliest tulips** to bloom?

Among the earliest tulips to bloom are the botanical or species tulips. These tulips are shorter stemmed and smaller flowered but are lovely to see when they appear. Their stockiness makes them somewhat more weather resistant than their fragile hybrid cousins, and they also tend to come back year after year. Some examples of botanical or species tulips include *Tulipa kaufmanniana* and its hybrids, *T. greigii* and its hybrids, and *T. praestans* and its hybrids.

What are the **latest tulips to bloom**?

Parrot tulips are usually the last tulips to bloom. They are known as parrot tulips for their brightly colored and irregularly cut tepals (or petals), which resemble those of a bird. These showy hybrids can be blooming at the same time as some spring-blooming perennials. 'Bird of Paradise', 'Flaming Parrot', 'Orange Favorite', and 'Rococo' are a few of the many parrot tulips available.

What are some **summer-blooming bulbs**?

Summer-flowering bulbs include gladiolus (*Gladiolus* spp.), lilies (*Lilium* spp.), some cyclamens (*Cyclamen* spp.), tuberous begonias (*Begonia x. tuberhybrida*), allium (*Allium* spp.), dahlia (*Dahlia* spp.), ranunculus (*Ranunculus* spp.), canna (*Canna* spp.), agapanthus (*Agapanthus* spp.), and oxalis (*Oxalis* spp.).

What are some **spring-blooming bulbs**?

Spring-flowering bulbs include tulip (*Tulipa* spp.), narcissus (*Narcissus* spp.), hyacinth (*Hyacinthus* spp.), bulb iris (such as *Iris histrioides* and *I. Graeberiana*), glory-of-the-snow (*Chionodoxa*), squill (*Scilla* spp.), winter aconite (*Eranthis hye-*

Grape hyacinth (*Muscari* spp.) is a spring-flowering bulb. Its flowers are bright blue to purple. (Robert J. Huffman/Field Mark Publications)

malis), snowdrops (*Galanthus nivalis*), fritillaria (*Fritillaria* spp.), and anemones (*Anemone* spp.).

Are there any **fall-blooming bulbs**?

Fall-blooming bulbs are less commonly offered by garden centers and usually need to be ordered by mail. The most common fall-blooming bulb is the autumn-flowering crocus (*Colchicum speciosum*). Hardy cyclamens (*Cyclamen coum*) also bloom in the fall, along with some species of allium (*Allium* spp.).

I love **gladiolus** but they never seem to look right in my garden with other plants. What am I doing wrong?

Due to their distinctive shape and flower, gladiolus (*Gladiolus* spp.) are one of those rare plants that look better in the vase than in the garden. They are best grown in a cutting garden where they can be planted far enough apart to yield nice-sized flowers. If grown in a flower border they look better planted close together, but this has an adverse affect on their bloom.

What should I do with my **cannas** in order to keep them for next year?

Wait to dig up your cannas (*Cannas* spp.) from the ground or container until after the first frost. Then, carefully dig up the bulbs and remove any dirt from them. Inspect them carefully and discard or compost any diseased or unhealthy-looking bulbs. Separate any bulbs that will do so easily, then place the bulbs in a paper bag packed loosely with paper and store them in a cool, dry place for next year.

CLIMBING AND VINING PERENNIALS

What are the different ways **vines** climb?

Vines climb by twining their stems around trees, pillars, and posts. When a twining vine touches an object, its sensitive plant tissue reacts by growing more cells at that spot, causing the vine to twist and bend around the object. Other vines climb by means of tendrils—delicate structures that wrap themselves around things. Scandent or trailing plants have long stems that may or may not attach themselves loosely to their support. These vines need to be tied to their support in order to "climb" it. Other vines produce plant structures that will cling to an object upon touching it. The structures are usually either small rootlets, shooting off either side of a stem, which burrow into the cracks of whatever they are climbing, or adhesive disks that adhere to a building through suction. Many ivies cling using their rootlets, while vines like Virginia creeper (*Parthenocissus quinquefolia*) attach with adhesive disks.

How do I **plant my perennial climber**?

Climbing plants need to be planted properly so that they will be well positioned to do their climbing. An ill-placed climber may mean one that doesn't climb its support, refuses to flower, or, once established, breaks from the weight of its unsupported limbs. All climbers should be planted at least a foot and a half from the wall or fence they will be covering so that they will be watered during rain showers. As is true for most other perennials, many climbers need to have their planting holes dug just deep enough so that the top of their root balls will be at the same level as the soil when planted. Clematis (*Clematis* spp.) are one exception (see below).

Climbers with adhesive pads or aerial roots can be left to establish themselves against their support, without any training (though sometimes a slight nudge in the right direction helps). Perennials that climb by twining need a little more direction. If the plant needs additional support against the wall or fence (something to twine through), secure your support roughly a foot above the soil line and several inches out from the wall. Otherwise, your plant may be trained directly onto a fence. Soak the root ball thoroughly before planting. Twining climbers should be placed in their planting holes so that they angle toward the support. Each shoot should be staked to the bottom of the support or fence, with new shoots staked in as they appear. Be careful to tie the shoots loosely to their stakes in order to avoid damaging them. Mulch the plant with a couple of inches of compost and water thoroughly. While your climber is being established, be sure to keep it well watered and mulched, and topdress it with compost in the early spring for the first few seasons.

When should I prune my **spring-flowering clematis** vine?

Spring-flowering clematis such as *Clematis montana, C. armandii,* and *C. alpina* all bear flowers on the previous year's shoots in the spring. If you prune them in the spring, you will most certainly remove the flowers. Instead, these clematis should be pruned immediately after their blooming period is over. Remove any dead or broken stems and shorten other stems, where needed for space. Otherwise, these clematis should be pruned only occasionally to keep the plant in shape.

When should I prune my **summer-flowering clematis** vine?

Summer-flowering clematis such as *Clematis florida, C.* 'Henryi', and *C.* 'Nelly Moser' do benefit from a light pruning yearly. They should be pruned of their dead or broken **241** stems in the early spring, before they begin growing. Any remaining stems should be pruned back to strong, new buds. After blooming, their spent flowers can be removed to encourage additional flowering. These clematis appreciate pruning, as they bloom on these same shoots the following year.

When should I prune my **autumn-flowering clematis** vine?

Clematis 'Ernest Markham', *C.* 'Jackmanii', *C. flammula,* and other autumn-flowering clematis require a thorough pruning annually. Autumn-flowering and herbaceous clematis only bloom on the current year's growth. Without pruning, they won't flower. In the early spring, before new growth begins, cut back all the previous year's stems to a pair of healthy buds six inches above the soil.

How should I **plant my clematis**?

Clematis need to be planted more deeply than other climbers in order to become properly established. Place the plant in the soil so that the top of its root ball is several inches below the soil line. This encourages the plant to send out strong shoots from below the soil level. Deciduous clematis such as marsh clematis (*Clematis crispa*), *C. languinosa* 'Candida', and *C. spooneri* should be cut back to a strong set of buds located about a foot above the soil level. All clematis should be staked and loosely tied until they are established and climbing by themselves.

When do I prune my **woody vine**?

Woody vines should be pruned on a regular basis to keep them looking neat and to avoid having to hack them to ugliness when they've become too large. An initial pruning of broken or dead stems and roots should take place immediately after planting the vine. While they may require some pinching back in their first few months after planting (see below), most woody vines should be pruned just once a year. Vines grown for their foliage should be pruned in the late winter or early spring. Flowering vines are dependent on their season of bloom. Vines such as wisteria (*Wisteria* spp.) that bloom in the spring from the previous year's buds should be pruned immediately after blooming. Vines that bloom later in the summer or in early fall should be pruned in the early spring, before new growth begins.

How do I prune my **woody vine**?

Use a good set of bypass prunes to cut off broken or dead stems back to the main stem before planting, and prune anytime the plant is damaged. Once your woody vine begins growing up its support, you may choose to pinch back the tips of its stems to just above any new growth (buds) so that the vine will branch out and look more lush. Without

What site conditions are proper for a clematis?

Clematis like to have their heads in the sun and their roots in the shade. Look for a location that receives at least a half-day's sun for the best flowering. In order to keep the roots cool and moist, plant your clematis vine behind another plant, under heavy mulch, or in a partially-shaded spot that will receive a half-day's sun. They enjoy fertile, well-drained soil with a layer of compost applied around them in late winter. Avoid applying the compost directly to the crown of the plant.

this pinching back, many vines will end up looking bare at their base. Watch for any suckers that appear at the base of the plant and prune them out immediately. To thin the vine, take out individual branches down to the base of the plant, rather than shearing it. A flowering vine that has become overly lush with foliage can be root-pruned to encourage it to flower more. Use a sharp spade to cut around the plant roughly a foot for each inch of the stem's diameter. Heavily overgrown nonflowering vines can also be cut back to their base in the early spring in order to stimulate new growth.

What are some climbing perennials that have **year-round interest**?

Boston ivy (*Parthenocissus tricuspidata*), Virginia creeper (*P. quinquefolia*), climbing hydrangea (*Hydrangea petiolaris*), and grape vine (*Vitis* spp.) all have at least three seasons of interest. The lush foliage, lovely tendrils, and edible fruit of grape vines make them beautiful in spring and summer. In the fall, the foliage of crimson vine (*V. coignetiae*) changes to a coppery red. In the winter, the browned and curling tendrils and stems make a beautiful sculpture. The climbing hydrangea has gorgeous dark green foliage and white flower clusters in the summer. In the winter, the older woody stems of the climbing hydrangea have red, shredding bark. The verdant-leafed *Parthenocissus* species is a common sight in the East on university structures and historic buildings. In the fall, they also bear dark blue berries near their russet, crimson, and burgundy leaves. Once the leaves fall, the remaining woody stems trace delicate webs on brick walls.

What are some vines that I can grow in **shade**?

English ivy (*Hedera helix*) is the most commonly grown ivy for the shade. Related Algerian cousins, *H. canariensis* and *H. canariensis* 'Variegata', have lovely wine-red stems to accent their beautiful foliage and will also tolerate shady spots. In areas warmer than zone 9, baby's tears (*Soleirolia soleirolii*) makes a lovely groundcover.

What are some climbers for **acid soil**?

Most vines tend to appreciate a soil with a pH around 6.5 to 7.0, which is on the acid end of the scale. Boston ivy (*Parthenocissus tricuspidata*) appreciates an even more acidic soil. Scottish flame flower (*Tropaeolum speciosum*) is another acid-lover in warmer climates.

Which vines **grow by twining**?

There are two types of twining vines. Vines like the passionflower (*Passiflora racemosa*) use their tendrils to fix themselves around a support or climb up into a shrub. Clematis (*Clematis* spp.) use leaf stalks to spiral around supports via tendrils. Other twining vines include climbing jasmine (*Jasminum officinale*), wisteria (*Wisteria* spp.), and perennial sweet pea (*Lathyrus latifolius*).

Which vines grow by **clinging**?

There are two types of clinging vines. They cling either through self-adhesive pads or by aerial roots, both of which extend from the end of a shoot or at a node. Boston ivy (*Parthenocissus tricuspidata*) and its cousin Virginia creeper (*P. quinquefolia*) climb using self-adhesive pads, as does climbing hydrangea (*Hydrangea petiolaris*). English ivy (*Hedera helix*) and periwinkle (*Vinca minor*) climb using aerial rootlets. These kinds of vines make the best groundcovers.

What are the **advantages and disadvantages of planting climbing ivy** to grow on a house?

Ivy can add an air of permanence and gracious age to any structure. It can also add architectural interest to a house that lacks it or be used to mask an unfortunate element. When growing ivy on a house, a homeowner should consider its disadvantages as well. Climbers that adhere through tiny rootlets creating suction should be kept off of wood and aluminum-sided houses since the grip of especially strong vines can pry at any existing cracks. They also need to be pruned regularly to be kept away from windows, screens, roofs, and chimneys for the same reason, and because the tiny disks leave their mark on these areas and are close to impossible to remove except with a strong arm and a wire brush. Finally, any ivy growing on a structure creates a habitat for critters and insects—a bonus in the garden but a possible downside if your house is anything but impenetrable.

Poison ivy is an invasive plant that can quickly spread or climb. (Robert J. Huffman/Field Mark Publications)

Doesn't **climbing ivy pull the mortar out** from between bricks?

The many buildings on the East Coast and in England stand testament to the fact that structures can remain standing long after ivy has begun scrambling up their walls. Over a long period of time, self-clinging climbers will begin to erode the lime mortar of old walls. However, modern buildings use a cement mortar that is more resilient. If you're in doubt about your wall or structure's ability to withstand the effects of a climber, ask an expert to examine the wall for any defects or problems that may be exacerbated by the ivy.

I love the look of a **climber scrambling up a tree trunk**—will this hurt the tree?

An ivy scrambling up the trunk of a tree is indeed a beautiful garden picture. When planning to repeat this scene from nature, you need to consider the strength and size of the tree, the manner in which the climber climbs and its vigorousness, and the final height and width of the climber. Obviously, a tree that is already under stress would be underserved by having a vigorous climber choke the last life out of it. On the other hand, if the tree is already on its way out, why not hide that fact with a lovely vine that will give a dead or dying tree the appearance of foliage? However, it is best to avoid any climber that is invasive such as the silver fleece vine (*Polygonum aubertii*). Even if you plant a less invasive climber, you should keep a close eye out for problems since a vigorously growing climber can provide a hiding place for insect pests and mask early evidence of disease on seemingly healthy trees. Steer clear of any ivy that attaches itself with adhesive disks and rootlets. Vining and twining climbers are less stressful on the tree, although they will need to be trained to climb. Your tree should be healthy and mature before sending the climber up, and both the tree and the climber should be kept pruned so that the climber's needs don't overtake the tree's. Choose your climber with care and closely monitor its impact on your tree to avoid harming it.

ANNUALS AND BIENNIALS

ANNUAL PLANT CARE

What is an **annual**?

In the strictest sense, an annual is a plant that completes its life cycle in one year. This means the plant germinates, grows, flowers, sets seed, and dies within the span of a year's time. However, in the nursery trade, many plants known as annuals such as geranium (*Pelargonium* spp.) and heliotrope (*Heliotropium arborescens*) are actually tender perennials. Others, such as foxglove (*Digitalis purpurea*), are actually biennials.

What is a **biennial**?

A biennial is a plant that doesn't bloom or set seed until its second year of life. It may actually survive another season or two, but its flowering isn't nearly as profuse. Biennials include foxglove (*Digitalis purpurea*), columbine (*Aquilegia canadensis*), forget-me-not (*Myosotis sylvatica*), larkspur (*Consolida ajacis*), Canterbury bells (*Campanula medium*), hollyhock (*Alcea rosea*), and sweet William (*Dianthus barbatus*). Some biennials can be sown early in the fall season and spend winters as good-sized plants (foxglove is an example).

What are **hardy annuals**?

Hardy annuals are annual plants that tolerate a fair amount of frost, with the degree of frost tolerance depending on the plant. They grow best in cool weather and with seeds surviving prolonged exposure to cold temperatures. Some examples include pot marigold (*Calendula officinalis*), Iceland poppy (*Papaver nudicaule*), English daisy

Sweet William (*Dianthus barbatus*) is a biennial with flower clusters of red, pink, white, or combinations of these. (Steven Nikkila/Perennial Favorites)

(*Bellis perennis*), monkey flower (*Mimulus x hybridus*), and bachelor's button (*Centaurea cyanus*). Like biennials, hardy annuals can either be sown in the fall (although usually later than biennials) for flowering the following spring, or in the early spring, as soon as the ground can be worked.

What are **half-hardy annuals**?

Half-hardy annuals can take light frost (usually as larger plants, rather than seedlings), but can't withstand continued exposure to temperatures below freezing. As a result, they can't be planted until the spring as they won't "winter over." Some half-hardy annuals include spiderflower (*Cleome* spp.), cosmos (*Cosmos bipinnatus*), and petunia (*Petunia* spp.). It should be noted, however, that in milder winters, these same half-hardy annuals may reseed themselves and survive.

What are **tender annuals**?

Tender annuals can't take any frost at all. These annuals can't be sown outdoors or planted outside until all danger of frost has passed (the frost-free date for your area is the best indication of this). They are mainly started indoors, although a few, such as pot marigold (*Calendula officinalis*) and zinnia (*Zinnia* spp.), grow so quickly that they can be direct seeded outdoors. Other tender annuals include nasturtium (*Tropae-*

Impatiens (*Impatiens* spp.) does best when planted indoors or during warm weather. (Steven Nikkila/Perennial Favorites)

olum *majus*), sweet verbena (*Verbena officinalis*), ageratum (*Ageratum conyzoides*), moss rose (*Portulaca grandiflora*), and scarlet salvia (*Salvia splendens*).

I purchased a packet of bachelor's button and the description on the packet included the notation *cool-weather annual*. What is a **cool-weather annual**?

Cool-weather annuals are those annuals that thrive in cooler temperatures and during the shortened days of late winter and early spring. They tend to wilt, become stunted in their growth, or die during the longer days of summer. Generally speaking, these are half-hardy or hardy annuals such as bachelor's button (*Centaurea cyanus*). Others, such as pot marigold (*Calendula officinalis*), pansy (*Viola tricolor hortensis*), sweet alyssum (*Lobularia maritima*), lobelia (*Lobelia erinus*), sweet pea (*Lathyrus odoratus*), and nasturtium (*Tropaeolum majus*), thrive in that short period in zone 5 known as early summer. In hotter areas, they may be grown in the winter. They can also be preserved through the heat in partially shaded areas that receive regular watering.

I planted **stock** for the first time this year but most of the plants didn't bloom. Why not?

Stock (*Matthiola incana*) is a cool-weather plant. If temperatures are consistently higher than 60 degrees Fahrenheit, the plant will go into a form of dormancy. Try

249

starting your stocks from seed in the early spring and transplant them out when the weather is still cool. This should encourage them to bloom early. Don't forget to have another plant nearby to fill the bare spot they'll leave when they're done blooming in midsummer.

What are **warm-weather annuals**?

Warm-weather annuals are annual plants that thrive in warm weather and sulk or stop growing in cool weather. Biennials, tender perennials, and half-hardy perennials tend to be warm-weather plants. Some of these plants are naturally also more heat resistant than other plants. *Asarina barclayana*, Mexican poppy (*Argemone mexicana*), Malabar gourd (*Cucurbita ficifolia*), angel's trumpet (*Datura arborea*), sweet scabious (*Scabiosa atropurpurea*), zinnia (*Zinnia* spp.), salvia (*Salvia* spp.), morning glory (*Ipomoea purpurea*), impatiens (*Impatiens wallerana*), geranium (*Pelargonium* spp.), and petunia (*Petunia* spp.) all thrive in warm weather.

What are **heat-resistant annuals**?

Heat-resistant annuals are those plants that continue to bloom in the summer in warmer regions of the country, when many plants become stressed by the heat. Ornamental kale (*Brassica oleracea*) is, surprisingly enough, relatively heat resistant. Other reliable heat-resistant annuals include some varieties of ornamental pepper (*Capsicum annuum*), tickseed (*Coreopsis tinctoria*), yellow cosmos (*Cosmos sulphureus*), cigarflower (*Cuphea ignea*), and bluebell or prairie gentian (*Eustoma grandiflorum*).

What **growing conditions** are required by annuals?

The most important requirement of annuals is full sun. Most annuals (with some exceptions noted under shade annuals) need at least six hours of sun per day to keep their blooms blooming. The soil needs to be fertile, moist, and friable with an average pH of between 6.0 and 7.0. Annuals also "feed" a little more heavily than perennials do, so you want to be sure to incorporate compost or manure into your bed.

What do I need to do to prepare an **annual bed**?

Annuals are not as deep-rooted as perennials so they don't require a deeply prepared bed. However, loosening the soil to about a foot will allow moisture to penetrate the roots and drain properly. Many annuals rot easily when their roots sit in water. Add any soil amendments to bring your pH to the average noted previously. Be sure to weed out any perennial or annual weeds to keep out competition for nutrients and water. Also, annuals grow at such a fast rate, weeds can easily be lost among them.

When is the best time to plant annuals?

Hardy and half-hardy annuals that are direct seeded can generally be planted as soon as the soil can be worked in the spring (see Seeding, Propagation, and Planting chapter), although some can be planted the previous fall or even late summer for bloom in early spring. Annuals started from seed should be started according to the packet directions (usually several months before the frost-free date in your area). If you have started plants from seed or have purchased transplants, don't forget that they need to be hardened off before planting. Tender annuals should not be transplanted before the frost-free date in your area. Hardy transplants such as pansies (*Viola tricolor hortensis*) can usually be set out a month or so prior to that, if they have been hardened off.

I seeded a number of annual flowers last year but I didn't **thin them out** at all and they failed to flower well. What is the proper method for thinning annuals and how much space should remain between the seedlings afterwards?

Annual seedlings can be thinned out any time, but try to get them when they are just a few inches high to avoid damaging the remaining plants. The best technique is to use a small pair of scissors to cut off the offending seedling to the soil level. While all plants vary in their spacing requirements, a good rule of thumb is that the distance between plants should be roughly equal to half the height of the mature plant. You may need to thin the plants more than once.

How do I **plant and space annuals** to look their best?

Another term for annuals is "bedding plants," which refers to their propensity for being planted in groups. Annuals planted singly just don't have the same impact on the landscape as the riot of color produced by a large grouping. Obviously, this does not negate planting a single annual in a container, but even there more *is* more. When planting your annuals, pay attention to the instructions on the tag, which usually call for spacing them anywhere from several inches apart to a foot apart, depending on their growth habit. However, if your particular favorite annual has a tendency toward powdery mildew or has a bushy growth habit, consider spacing them even farther apart for air circulation and to enable them to reach their full potential.

Another thing to consider when planting annuals is the pattern in which they are planted. While it is common to plant them in straight lines or in a grid, this can look rather stilted. Try planting them in a group of three—a roughly triangular shape. This is much more natural looking.

251

I planted **bachelor's button** for the first time this year and they came up looking a bit thin and spindly. What should I do differently?

Most likely, you planted the seeds of your bachelor's button (*Centaurea cyanus*) too close together and failed to thin them out. When planting annuals from seed, sow the seed thinly. Once the seedlings pop up, thin them carefully using tweezers or a small pair of scissors, cutting the seedlings off at the soil line. Thin them to the distance apart recommended on the seed packet. This will enable the plants to grow a healthy root system.

Is it necessary to **rotate or change my annuals** or their planting location from year to year?

Most kinds of annuals are not bothered by growing in the same area year after year, such as if you always plant impatiens (*Impatiens wallerana*) under the shade of your maple tree (although, with all the wonderful annuals to choose from, you might consider branching out a little). However, annuals such as marigold (*Tagetes* spp.), snapdragon (*Antirrhinum majus*), and China aster (*Callistephus chinensis*) are prey to certain soil-borne diseases that can be carried over from year to year. If your plants had a disease the previous year, you could infect new transplants when you plant them in your bed. So, be sure to move these garden stars from place to place in your yard each year and take a year off now and again. To be on the safe side, be sure to remove all plant materials from any annual bed at the end of the season in order to reduce the incidence of pests and disease.

How do some plants **self-seed**?

All plants that reproduce sexually "set seed" or "go to seed," which means they all have the *potential* to be self-seeding. But the seed of some plants germinates especially easily without human interference, making these plants known as self-seeders. This can be due either to the large quantity of seed that the plant produces (giving it more opportunities for successful reseeding) or to the size of the seed itself (if it is small, it might not require much in the way of nutrients or soil to thrive).

What is a **volunteer**?

A volunteer is a seedling that has grown of its own volition—self-seeded by its parent plant. Volunteers sometimes spring up in places you don't want them, where they become weeds. But they can easily be dug up and carefully transplanted to an area where they will become a desirable plant again.

What is **deadheading** and why do I have to do it?

"Deadheading" refers to the removing of spent or faded blooms from a plant. When a plant blooms, it is preparing itself to reproduce or go to seed before it dies. This requires a great deal of energy from the plant. You can prolong the bloom (and the life of the plant) by deadheading it. Some plants, such as impatiens (*Impatiens wallerana*), do their own deadheading when flowers drop off the plant. However, most flowers require human intervention. The majority of annual flowers can just be pinched off from a plant by simply using your thumb and index finger. With a large annual planting, you might consider using shears to remove spent flowers. Many perennials that need deadheading require pruners or small scissors to get through their woody stems.

How often should I **fertilize my annuals**?

As noted, annuals tend to be heavier feeders than perennials since much of their life is spent in bloom. If you apply fertilizer when planting out annuals, they shouldn't require any additional fertilizer for a couple of months. When the plants slow in their growth or develop yellow leaves, it may be time to fertilize again. Plants that need a great deal of moisture tend to need more fertilizer as well. Manure tea, or a balanced, water-soluble fertilizer (that is, one that has an even ratio of nitrogen, phosphorus, and potassium), works well.

Which of the **macronutrients** (nitrogen, phosphorus, potassium) is most important for annuals?

Since annuals are prolific bloomers, it is important that they have an adequate supply of phosphorus (the second nutrient listed on a fertilizer label) in order to keep up their colorful show throughout the growing season. In addition, adequate amounts of nitrogen and potassium will ensure that the annuals have strong stems, good leaf color, and general health.

How do I **mulch my annuals**?

Annuals need one to two inches of mulch in order to retain moisture. As with perennials, try to keep the mulch away from the crown of the plant to reduce the incidence of

Since coleus (*Coleus* spp.) is best known for its colorful foliage, its flowers should be pinched back to keep it from getting leggy. (Steven Nikkila/Perennial Favorites)

slugs and other garden pests. You might also consider using an organic mulch that decays and can be turned under at the end of the season, rather than an inorganic one that will need to be disturbed every year during planting and at the end of the season.

What kind of **regular maintenance do annuals** require?

Most annuals need regular watering (at least weekly) to look their best. If they look wilted in the cool of the morning, it's time to water. Deep watering is not as necessary as it is for perennials, since an annual's root system has to last only one season. Fertilizing is important, as many annuals are heavy feeders. Regular weeding is important to reduce competition for water and nutrients and to keep out bugs and disease. Deadheading should be done on a weekly or semiweekly basis in order to encourage the plant to send out new blooms. Pinching back (see related question in Perennials chapter) is necessary for some annuals like impatiens (*Impatiens wallerana*), wax begonia (such as *Begonia schmidtiana*), and coleus (*Coleus* spp.) in order to keep them from getting leggy. Mulching should only be necessary at the beginning of the season. Finally, once your annuals are done blooming, their foliage has died down, or they have been killed by frost, move them to the compost pile—roots and all. This reduces the incidence of insects and disease in your garden.

> ## How do I pot an annual to spend the winter indoors?
>
> It depends on the annual you are bringing inside. For all of them, however, bring them indoors before frost and select younger plants. Pot them up and leave them outside initially before bringing them in. For plants such as zonal geranium (*Pelargonium zonale* or *P. inquinans*), coleus (*Coleus* spp.), petunia (*Petunia* spp.), moss rose (*Portulaca grandiflora*), and wax begonia (such as *Begonia schmidtiana*) you may either cut them back by half, fertilize, and plant in a pot, or take stem cuttings and root them indoors in either a rooting medium or plain water.

What kind of **care do biennials** require in their first year?

Since biennials will be around a second season, they do require a little more attention than annuals if you are growing them from seed. Once your seedlings have sprouted, be vigilant about removing weeds from the bed. No plant likes competition. If you planted the seeds too closely, you will need to thin the bed. This can be done easily with a set of short-bladed scissors to avoid removing all of the plants. Keep them well watered throughout the first year to ensure their survival until the flowering stage. If they have not been planted where they are to bloom, you can move them to their proper location in the fall of the year they are planted, as long as the weather is not too wet or cold. As with perennials, you may want to check the plants for heaving (due to the freezing and thawing of the soil) during the winter, but this is not crucial.

How do I **select annual plants** for purchase?

It's usually best to buy annual transplants without blooms or at least with just buds, rather than in bloom. Some plants such as pelargonium (*Pelargonium* spp.), petunia (*Petunia* spp.), and marigold (*Tagetes* spp.) can be purchased in flower, but look for transplants that are stocky and healthy. Although this makes a gardener more dependent on a nursery to properly tag and identify plants (this is why it's important to go to a good nursery!), nonbudded transplants have not wasted their energy on blooms while growing in their tiny plastic cells.

What are the advantages of **annuals over perennials**?

Annuals have an extended period of bloom (usually from the first frost-free date to the last frost-free date), while perennials usually bloom for several weeks at a time. Annuals also bloom quickly, going from bud to bloom in a few short weeks. And annuals are

> **I have a large whiskey barrel that I'd like to plant with annuals but I don't want to spend a lot of money on soil. Can I fill the barrel with topsoil from my garden?**
>
> Actually, you don't need to fill the barrel completely with soil at all. Use broken pottery, old plastic pots, or what have you to fill the bottom two-thirds (or more) of the barrel. While their root systems do expand over the growing season, annuals still only require a planting depth of roughly six to twelve inches, so just be sure your planting medium meets this requirement. Although you could use topsoil in your barrel, you will get the best results from using a lighter soil mix such as one that contains peat or perlite.

good for the beginner—they don't take much effort to get growing and are rarely bothered by disease.

Can I **transplant** annuals?

Although it is not a common practice in the United States, professionals and gardeners with large areas will sometimes grow annuals in a nursery bed for transplanting later in the season. That way, the annuals don't take up space in a flower border until their color is needed. Other gardeners, who realize too late that a certain color combination is just plain offensive, have also been known to move annuals. In order to transplant your annuals, begin by giving them a solid soaking. Then, dig carefully around the plant to make sure you take as much of the root ball with the plant as possible. Move the plant into its new position and water well.

Some of my weaker-stemmed annuals always seem to fall over in heavy wind and rain. How should they be **staked**?

Just like perennials, some weaker-stemmed annuals appreciate a little staking to look their best. Unfortunately, most ready-made plant supports are too much for small annuals. Rather than hauling out large stakes and heavy twine, try using button thread, loosely tied around the stems of your plants, to provide them with a little support. If they need additional help, tie the thread around twigs stuck into the soil, near the crown of the plants. Larger-stemmed annuals can use the same supports used by perennials (see related question in Perennials chapter).

Is there any way to keep my tender perennials and annuals from freezing when we have an **early frost**?

There is nothing sadder than the sight of a bed of blackened plants in September. For most gardeners, it can almost be too much to bear. You have several options to try to stretch your season out. The tried-and-true approach is to cover plants with an old sheet or newspapers. Cover the plants loosely to avoid breaking their stems and secure the corners on the ground with bricks or stones so that the wind doesn't blow your cover. In the morning, remove the plants' bedclothes so that they don't suffer from lack of oxygen and sunshine. Another approach, more commonly used by farmers to save their crops, is to run your sprinkler all night on your tender bed.

How do I use bedding plants with **mixed colors** in my landscape?

Packets and flats with mixed colors can frequently be cheaper than the same plants all in one color. The trick to using plants in mixed colors is to refrain from planting them with different plants in mixed colors. This creates too much contrast and looks kind of willy-nilly. Instead, use them with plants of complementary colors in containers. Another option is to plant them all in one bed or intersperse them with another plant in one color.

I picked up a bargain flat of annuals that are a little **overgrown**. Do they need to be planted differently from younger transplants?

While it is best to buy transplants that are small, green, and not in bloom, sometimes the thrill of gardening and shopping the sales gets the best of us. To encourage your adolescent transplants to put some of their energy into root growth, gently tease apart the roots. This should only be done if the roots are growing out of the bottom of the container and are spilling out of the top of it. In other words, only if the plant is very pot-bound. Normally, most annuals don't like to have their roots monkeyed around with.

Next, pinch back all leggy growth, blooms, and buds to a node (a little bump on the side of a stem). This will help the plant focus on root growth, rather than blooming, until it is established. Finally, water well and hold off on fertilizer. Chances are, the plant received plenty of fertilizer while it awaited your arrival at the store late in the planting season.

I'd like to use an **annual vine to cover my arbor** in a hurry while I wait for my perennial vine to climb up it. Is there any way to encourage the annual?

This is a great use for annual vines. Since they will scramble up an arbor in a season, they are perfect cover-ups while you wait for your slower-growing perennial to take root. But why fight gravity? Plant the vine on top of the arbor! Use a lightweight plas-

Most geraniums (*Pelargonium* and *Geranium* spp.) are perennials or biennials, but there are a few annual varieties. (Steven Nikkila/ Perennial Favorites)

tic container of a size that will perch comfortably in the trellis of your arbor. Plant the vine inside the container and secure the container to the top of the arbor, letting the lip of the container meet the top of the arbor and the container hang beneath it. Position the pot at the farthest end of your primary line of sight to the arbor to make it less obtrusive while the vine is growing. Then stand back and let it grow! Remember to keep it watered—especially in its first weeks of growth—and be sure to secure it snugly in case of high winds.

Every year I love to plant geraniums, vinca, and lobelia in my window boxes and every year, the **lobelia** seems to shrivel up and die in about a month. What am I doing wrong?

Lovely lobelia (*Lobelia* spp.)—especially the trailing kind—does look wonderful in window boxes. Unfortunately, lobelia is a cool-season annual that tends to fade in the heat of the summer. There are a few tricks you can use to keep your lobelia going, however. Try to overplant your boxes—add verbena (*Verbena* spp.), a small zinnia (*Zinnia angustifolia*), mealy-cup sage (*Salvia farinacea*), and sweet alyssum (*Lobularia maritima*) and plant the lobelia underneath the taller plants. Providing it with extra shade may encourage it to linger longer. Also, keep your window boxes well watered. Lobelia needs a lot of moisture to keep generating those dainty blooms.

> ### What is the proper method for
> ### cutting annual flowers for bouquets?
>
> While cutting flowers from annual plants does not require the same care as cutting flowers from perennials, by cutting properly you can promote additional blooms on your annuals. Cut your flowers in the morning, but wait until after the dew has evaporated to avoid spreading or introducing disease. Rather than cutting just the stem length you need, cut the stem farther down, toward the center of the plant. This will encourage the plant to send out larger new blooms. Remove leaves at the bottom of the stem by stripping them off and place the cut stems in a pail of tepid water. And while you're cutting flowers for your bouquet, remove any spent flowers from the rest of the plant. With annuals especially, spent flowers signal the end of a plant's life.

I live in zone 3. How can I keep my geraniums, er, **pelargoniums going from year to year**?

There are two ways you can keep your pelargoniums (*Pelargonium* spp.) going from year to year. You can overwinter them by digging out the plants in the fall, shaking most of the soil from their roots, and placing them in paper bags (one plant to a bag). Use a second paper bag to cover the top of the first bag and store in a cool, dry place. Check them periodically to be sure they don't rot. In the early spring, remove the last of the dirt, cut down the tops and main stem to a stub, and replant in a fresh pot. Keep them in a sunny window until the weather has warmed enough to bring them outside.

The second method is to take cuttings from your favorite pelargoniums in the late summer or early fall (see related question in Seeding and Planting chapter). Root the cuttings in a damp mix of sand and sphagnum moss and keep them in indirect light (near, but not in a sunny window). Keep the mix moist and after a week or so, tug gently to check to see if it has rooted. Once they've rooted and put out new growth, you can replant them in another container.

I'd like to **grow sunflowers for cutting** but don't want to have a bunch of woody stalks to look at. Any suggestions?

You may choose to continue to grow sunflowers (*Helianthus* spp.) that have a single stem such as 'Sunbeam', 'Giant Sungold', and 'Sunbright'. However, when you plant your sunflowers, also plant seeds of an annual climber such as morning glory (*Ipomoea tricolor* 'Heavenly Blue'). As the climber begins to grow, encourage it to wind its

> **I love zinnias but every year my plants seem to fall prey to powdery mildew. Is there any way to prevent this from happening?**
>
> **Z**innias (*Zinnia* spp.) are wonderfully versatile plants in the garden. They are great for cutting and add an almost formal splotch of color in a bed with their cookie-cutter flowers. If you are sowing your zinnias from seed, you might consider planting them a little later in the spring—wait until it's almost summer. Mildew tends to thrive in the cooler, humid conditions of the spring.

stems around the large sunflower stem. When you need to cut the sunflower, the vine should be there to cover the damage.

Another option is to select from the many varieties of multistemmed or branching sunflowers. Some of these include 'Sunset', 'Chianti', 'Prado Red', 'Lemon Queen', and 'Evening Sun'.

During a trip to my local farmers' market last weekend, I noticed vendors with small, creeping plants that they called **zinnias**. I thought all zinnias were tall and multicolored. What gives?

Actually, there are a number of different species of zinnia (*Zinnia* spp.), including one that actually falls under a different genus. The common zinnia (*Zinnia elegans*) is probably the plant you're used to calling a zinnia. It can range in height from half a foot to three feet tall and shows beautiful multi-colored flowers, usually with tubular or flat petals. Another type of zinnia is sometimes called the classic zinnia (*Zinnia angustifolia*). This zinnia has a spreading habit and usually grows no taller than about a foot. The flowers look more like daisies and the leaves are more narrowly shaped than those of the common zinnia. The creeping zinnia (*Sanvitalia procumbens*) is very low to the ground—roughly half a foot tall—with yellow or orange flowers and dark purple centers and stems. It can be used as an annual groundcover.

I love the ease and **bright color of annuals** but they seem to poop out before the rest of my garden does. How can I stretch out their blooms for a longer period of time?

Although many annuals do bloom over a period of several months, their bright colors do eventually fade. Consider deadheading them more frequently, or better yet, stagger your annual plantings over several weeks rather than all at once. This should stretch out your season a little more.

I've seen some annual plants that have been **grown into standards**. How can I do this?

Technically, these plants are most likely tender perennials. But in any case, plants such as fuchsia (*Fuchsia* spp.) and geranium (*Pelargonium* spp.) may be trained into standards with a little bit of effort. Choose a plant that has a strong, straight stem or train a cutting up a small cane by placing the cane against the cutting and tying them loosely together. Once the plant grows, remove the side shoots from all but the top one-third of the plant. If at any time the plant becomes potbound, move it into a larger pot. Once the plant has reached the desired height, pinch out its growing tip in order to encourage the plant to develop more side shoots. Remove any side shoots that develop in the bottom two-thirds of the plant. When shoots form at the top of the plant, pinch out their growing tips as well.

ANNUALS FOR PARTICULAR USES

What are some annuals that grow in **dry soil**?

Salvia (*Salvia* spp.), globe amaranth (*Gomphrena globosa*), statice (*Limonium* spp.), sweet alyssum (*Lobularia maritima*), calliopsis (*Coreopsis tinctoria*), dusty miller (*Senecio cineraria*), creeping zinnia (*Zinnia angustifolia* 'Persian Carpet'), moss rose (*Portulaca grandiflora*), California poppy (*Eschscholtzia californica*), tithonia or Mexican sunflower (*Tithonia* spp.), and four o'clocks (*Mirabilis longiflora*) all grow well in dry soil.

What are some annuals that grow in **wet soil**?

Most annuals don't care to have their feet wet, but monkey flower (*Mimulus cupreus* 'Red Emperor') and forget-me-not (*Myosotis sylvatica*) thrive in humusy, moist areas.

What are some annuals that grow in **acidic soil**?

Most annuals prefer soil on the more acidic side of neutral, and begonia (*Begonia*) and snapdragon (*Antirrhinum*) thrive in acidic soil that contains plenty of moisture-retaining peat.

261

Dusty miller (*Senecio cineraria*) is grown for its mounded clumps of silvery-gray foliage and is typically used as an accent plant to provide color contrast. It prefers dry soil. (Robert J. Huffman/Field Mark Publications)

> ## While I understand deadheading all annuals is important, this practice is pretty time consuming. Which annuals need to be deadheaded regularly?
>
> Annuals such as pot marigold (*Calendula officinalis*), zinnia (*Zinnia* spp.), cosmos (*Cosmos* spp.), marigold (*Tagetes* spp.), geranium (*Pelargonium* spp.), verbena (*Verbena* spp.), and begonia (*Begonia* spp.) should be deadheaded on a regular basis. Otherwise these beautiful plants may stop flowering altogether.

Which annuals grow well in **alkaline soils**?

A number of annuals thrive in alkaline soils. These include bachelor's button (*Centaurea cyanus*), scarlet salvia (*Salvia splendens*), cosmos (*Cosmos bipinnatus*), clarkia (*Clarkia elegans*), zinnia (*Zinnia elegans*), honesty (*Lunaria annua*), love-in-a-mist (*Nigella damascena*), nemesia (*Nemesia strumosa*), petunia (*Petunia* spp.), lobelia (*Lobelia erinus*), tickseed (*Coreopsis tinctoria*), larkspur (*Consolida ajacis*), and annual sweet pea (*Lathryus odoratus*).

Which annuals flourish in **full sun**?

Sweet alyssum (*Lobularia maritima*), Livingstone daisy (*Dorotheanthus bellidiformis*), moss rose (*Portulaca grandiflora*), rock purslane (*Calandrinia umbellata*), linaria (*Linaria maroccana*), nasturtium (*Tropaeolum majus*), California poppy (*Eschscholtzia californica*), everlasting (*Helipterum manglesii*), and cosmos (*Cosmos bipinnatus*) do well in hot, sunny areas with dry soil.

What are some annuals *besides* begonias and impatiens that will **grow in shade**?

Try flowering tobacco (*Nicotiana alata*)—its white flowers will light up a corner of your yard. Coleus (*Coleus* spp.) has lovely multicolored foilage with varying patterns. Although lobelia (*Lobelia erinus*) is often placed with geraniums (*Pelargonium* spp.) to accent sunny pots, it thrives in shade. The black-eyed Susan vine (*Thunbergia alata*) adds height to your shady garden. Pansies (*Viola tricolor hortensis*) are another tried-and-true shade lover. Look for violet cress (*Ionopsidium acaule*), browallia or sapphire flower (*Browallia* spp.), forget-me-not (*Myotosis sylvatica*), Canterbury bells (*Campanula medium*), honesty or money plant (*Lunaria annua*), Oriental woodruff (*Asperula orientalis*), and foxglove (*Digitalis purpurea*) as well.

263

Which annuals are **easiest to grow for a beginning gardener**?

Although most annuals are relatively pest and disease free except in warm, humid areas of the country, there are a number of annuals that provide the best chance of success for a beginning gardener. Annuals that are easy to seed include bachelor's button (*Centaurea cyanus*), cosmos (*Cosmos bipinnatus*), sunflower (*Helianthus annuus*), flowering tobacco (*Nicotiana alata*), and marigold (*Tagetes* spp.). Annuals that thrive as transplants include zonal geranium (*Pelargonium hortorum*), impatiens (*Impatiens wallerana*), and lantana (*Lantana camara*).

Are there any annuals that are **reliable self-seeders**?

Annuals that reseed themselves dependably are almost like having perennials that bloom all summer! Flowers such as Chinese forget-me-not (*Cynoglossum amabile*), sunflower (*Helianthus annuus*), larkspur (*Consolida ajacis*), cosmos (*Cosmos bipinnatus*), bachelor's button (*Centaurea cyanus*), opium poppy (*Papaver somniferum*), pot marigold (*Calendula officinalis*), sweet alyssum (*Lobularia maritima*), and feverfew (*Chrysanthemum parthenium*) are dependable repeaters (see related question in Seeding, Propagation, and Planting chapter).

I'm planning on growing a **cutting garden** this year. What are some flowering annuals that are good for cutting?

Annuals are the perfect addition to a cutting garden because they provide you with flowers all summer long. Some annuals that are perfect for cutting are dahlia (*Dahlia* spp.) and bells-of-Ireland (*Moluccella laevis*). Annual sweet pea (*Lathyrus odoratus*) is another great addition for the romantic tendrils borne by its stems. Flowers such as bachelor's button (*Centaurea cyanus*), globe amaranth (*Gomphrena globosa*), cockscomb (*Celosia cristata*), strawflower (*Helichrysum bracteatum*), and the smaller, single-stemmed sunflowers (*Helianthus* spp.) are long lasting as well.

Are there any annuals grown mainly for their foliage that can be **used in floral arrangements**?

There are a number of annuals with lovely or unusual foliage that can be used in floral arrangements. Although annual sweet peas (*Lathyrus odoratus*) are often cut for their dainty blooms, their delicate tendrils and quirky stems add a note of interest to any arrangement. Coleus (*Coleus* spp.), with its variegated leaves, works well in arrangements—look for chocolate-leafed varieties to marry with burgundy or lime flowers. Dusty miller (*Senecio cenaria*) and *Helichrysum petiolare* offer a wonderful velvety texture and gray color to bouquets.

While I love the giant sunflowers, my garden isn't quite big enough for them. Are there any other **types of sunflowers**?

There are many shorter varieties of sunflowers that were bred for smaller gardens and containers. These include 'Solar Babies', a mix of lemon- and bronze-colored flowers with single stems that peak at around three feet; 'Sunset', a three-feet-tall sunflower with a dark center and red petals with gold tips; and 'Sonja', which has orange petals and a dark center and grows to three and a half feet tall. Even smaller sunflowers include 'Elf', 'Kid Stuff', and 'Sundance Kid', which range from a foot-and-a-half to two-and-a-half feet tall.

Dahlias (*Dahlia* spp.) are the perfect choice for a cutting garden. (Steven Nikkila/Perennial Favorites)

What are some **blue-flowered annuals**?

There are almost as many blue-flowered annuals as there are shades of blue. Some blue-flowered annuals include edging lobelia (*Lobelia erinus* 'Sapphire'), *Petunia* 'Blue Skies', baby blue-eyes (*Nemophila menziesii*), kingfisher daisy (*Felicia bergeriana*), *Browallia viscosa*, California bluebell (*Phacelia campanularia*), morning glory (*Ipomoea tricolor* 'Heavenly Blue'), common morning glory (*Ipomoea purpurea*), common flax (*Linum usitatissimum*), borage (*Borago officinalis*), apple-of-Peru (*Nicandra physalodes*), prairie gentian (*Eustoma grandiflorum*), Chinese forget-me-not (*Cynoglossum amabile*), bluebonnet (*Lupinus subcarnosus*), larkspur (*Delphinium consolida*), mealycup sage (*Salvia farinacea* 'Victoria'), and Southern star (*Oxypetalum caeruleum*).

This variety of *Zinnia elegans* is known for its orange flower. Zinnias make excellent cut flowers. (Steven Nikkila/Perennial Favorites)

What are some **yellow-flowered annuals**?

There are many yellow-flowered annuals beside the usual marigolds. Try using yellow-flowered annuals with white- and blue-flowered plants to create a fresh look in your garden. Some yellow-flowered annuals include partridge pea (*Cassia fasciculata*), evening primrose (*Oenothera laciniata*), okra (*Abelmoschus esculentus*), black-eyed Susan vine (*Thunbergia alata*), creeping zinnia (*Sanvitalia procumbens*), sweet sultan (*Centaurea moschata* 'Dairy Maid'), greenthreads (*Thelesperma burridgeanum*), Dahlberg daisy (*Thymophylla tenuiloba*), common sunflower (*Helianthus annuus* 'Giganteus'), African marigold (*Tagetes erecta* 'Yellow Climax'), *Tagetes* 'Lemon Gem', cape daisy (*Venidium fastuosum*), *Calceolaria mexicana*, canary-bird flower (*Tropaeolum peregrinum*), annual chrysanthemum (*Chrysanthemum coronarium*), California poppy (*Eschscholtzia californica*), and monkey flower (*Mimulus guttatus*).

What are some **orange-flowered annuals**?

There are many orange-flowered annuals. Some of the more common ones include nasturtium (*Tropaeolum majus*), pot marigold (*Calendula officinalis* 'Orange Coronet'), *Viola* 'Paparadja', and cockscomb (*Celosia cristata* 'Apricot Brandy' and 'Gold Torch'). Some of the more unusual orange-flowered annuals are *Osteospermum hyoseroides*, Mexican sunflower (*Tithonia rotundifolia*), gloriosa daisy (*Rudbeckia* 'Marmalade'), and horned poppy (*Glaucium corniculatum*).

> ## What are some annuals that should be direct seeded?
>
> **M**any annuals can be direct seeded in the fall in warmer regions for bloom in the spring. However, some annuals resent being transplanted or are just easier to direct seed. These include clark (*Clarkia elegans*), love-in-a-mist (*Nigella damascena*), owl's clover (*Orthocarpus purpurascens*), Iceland, corn, and opium poppies (*Papaver nudicaule, P. rhoeas,* and *P. somniferum*), creamcups (*Platystemon californicus*), horned poppy (*Glaucium corniculatum*), annual baby's breath (*Gypsophilia elegans*), larkspur (*Delphinium consolida*), *Centaurium erythraea,* and *Coreopsis atrosanguinea.*

What are some **red-flowered annuals**?

Red-flowered annuals add a wonderful punch to the landscape and combine beautifully with white- and pink-flowered plants. Look for these red-bloomed beauties: *Zinnia* 'Big Red' and 'Peter Pan Scarlet', *Tropaeolum* 'Empress of India', Iceland poppy (*Papaver nudicaule* 'Red Sails'), *Impatiens wallerana* 'Busy Lizzy', *Impatiens* 'New Guinea', *Verbena* 'Showtime Blaze', and scarlet runner bean (*Phaseolus coccineus*).

What are some **pink-flowered annuals**?

Many annuals are pretty in pink. Consider the many, many shades of annual geraniums (*Pelargonium* spp.). Other options include Deptford pink (*Dianthus armeria*), *Verbena* 'Pink Bouquet', pink stock (*Matthiola incana* 'Annua'), butterfly flower (*Schizanthus pinnatus*), English daisy (*Bellis perennis*), Madagascar periwinkle (*Catharanthus roseus* 'Cooler Icy Pink'), basketflower (*Centaurea americana*), hawk's beard (*Crepis rubra*), *Verbena* 'Raspberry Crush', hyacinth bean (*Dolichos lablab*), annual foxglove (*Digitalis purpurea* 'Foxy'), *Clarkia unguiculata, Malope trifida,* honesty or money plant (*Lunaria annua*), globe amaranth (*Gomphrena globosa* 'Rose Pink Improved'), tree mallow (*Lavatera arborea*), *Petunia* 'Pink Satin' and 'Count-Down Warm Pink', and wax begonia (*Begonia* 'Silvermist').

What are some **white-flowered annuals**?

White flowers provide a garden with a certain crispness and can be used to great effect in small gardens. Some white-flowered annuals are curled mallow (*Malva verticillata* 'Crispa'), moonflower (*Ipomoea alba*), angel's trumpet (*Datura arborea*), Madagascar periwinkle (*Catharanthus roseus* 'Albus'), *Lavatera* 'Mont Blanc', feverfew (*Chrysanthemum parthenium*), desert evening primrose (*Oenothera deltoides*), *Zinnia* 'Peter Pan White', cape marigold (*Dimorphotheca pluvialis*), *Helianthus annus* 'Italian

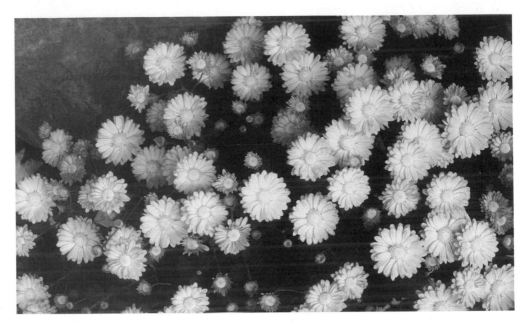

Chrysanthemums are a popular choice for the garden due to their long, colorful blooming cycles. To prevent them from becoming too leggy, they need to be pinched back monthly until they begin to form buds for fall bloom (usually July or August). (Robert J. Huffman/Field Mark Publications)

White', *Iberis pinnata*, statice (*Limonium sinuatum* 'Soiree White'), caraway (*Carum carvi*), white snapdragon (*Antirrhinum* 'Rocket White'), sweet alyssum (*Lobularia maritima* 'Carpet of Snow'), annual baby's breath (*Gypsophila elegans*), rocket candytuft (*Iberis amara*), and flowering tobacco (*Nicotiana alata* 'Niki White').

What are some annuals with **ornamental fruit**?

While vegetables are grown for their edible fruits, many annuals bear fruit that is strictly ornamental. The scarlet seedpods of the hyacinth bean (*Dolichos lablab*) show beautifully against the vine's blue-green leaves. Ornamental peppers (*Capsicum annuum*) look like the real thing and are available with either small, rounded fruits or longer peppers. Caper spurge (*Euphorbia lathyris*) is also known as the mole plant for its supposed ability to repel moles. Finally, the beautiful green flowers of Japanese hops (*Humulus japonicus*) eventually change to conelike fruit whose purpose is not solely ornamental!

What are some annuals traditionally used in **cottage gardens**?

Annuals used in cottage gardens include love-in-a-mist (*Nigella damascena*), morning glory (*Ipomoea* spp.), honesty or money plant (*Lunaria annua*), annual forget-me-not

(*Myosotis sylvatica*), cosmos (*Cosmos bipinnatus*), corn poppy (*Papaver rhoeas*), bachelor's button (*Centaurea cyanus*), pot marigold (*Calendula officinalis*), sweet alyssum (*Lobularia maritima*), browallia (*Browallia* spp.), sweet pea (*Lathyrus odoratus*), sweet William (*Dianthus barbatus*), and spiderflower (*Cleome*).

I'm interested in growing an old-fashioned garden. What are some **heirloom annuals and biennials**?

Heirloom annual flowers have proven the test of time due to their beauty and dependability in many gardens. Cool-weather heirloom annuals include larkspur (*Delphinium consolida*) and annual sweet pea (*Lathyrus odoratus* 'Painted Lady'), which date back to the eighteenth century. 'Painted Lady's' fragrant blooms are rose and cream, while larkspur is known for its beautiful blue flowers (although it also comes in lilac, pink, and white). Warm-weather heirloom annuals include morning glory (*Ipomoea tricolor*), nicotiana (*Nicotiana* spp.), four o'clock (*Mirabilis jalapa*), nasturtium (*Tropaeolum majus*), stock (*Matthiola incana*), and small-flowered zinnias like *Zinnia angustifolia*. Biennial heirlooms include foxglove (*Digitalis purpurea*—also a reliable reseeder), hollyhock (*Alcea* spp.), and Canterbury bells (*Campanula medium*).

What are some **spring-flowering annuals**?

Wallflower (*Cheiranthus cheiri*) and forget-me-not (*Myosotis sylvatica*) provide a lovely contrast of orange (*Cheiranthus cheiri* 'Golden Bedder') and blue in the spring garden. Wallflower has a wide range of colors to choose from, including cream, red, and crimson to complement spring-blooming bulbs.

What are some **summer-flowering annuals**?

Most annuals flower in the summer. Some used less frequently in backyard plantings include nasturtium (*Tropaeolum majus*), Iceland poppy (*Papaver nudicaule*), fernyleafed love-in-a-mist (*Nigella damascena*), heavenly scented stock (*Matthiola incana*), Canterbury bells (*Campanula medium*), small blue-flowered California bluebell (*Phacelia campanularia*), unspectacular but fragrant mignonette (*Reseda odorata*), and bedding dahlias (*Dahlia* spp.). These can be more difficult to find at your local nursery and are often grown from seed.

What are some annuals that **bloom in the late summer or early fall**?

It is always a sad time in the garden when the plants and flowers you've come to love begin to fade as winter approaches. Some annuals, however, seem to reach their peak at the end of summer, giving one last shout before frost hits them. Sunflower (*Helianthus* spp.), spiderflower (*Cleome* spp.), cosmos (*Cosmos* spp.), China aster

269

(*Callistephus chinesis*), pot marigold (*Calendula officinalis*), zinnia (*Zinnia* spp.), scarlet sage (*Salvia splendens*), moss rose (*Portulaca grandiflora*), nicotiana (*Nicotiana alata*), and impatiens (*Impatiens wallerana*) all bloom or retain their bloom in late summer and early fall.

Do any annuals **bloom in the winter**?

Pansy (*Viola tricolor hortensis*) blooms in the late winter/early spring in colder climates and is best grown in the winter in warmer ones. Honesty or money plant (*Lunaria annua*) also flowers in spring but during October through January has striking seed pods that provide a "dry bloom" to a garden.

What are some **vining or climbing annuals**?

One of the easiest ways to beautify a mailbox or a fence post is by sowing some annual vining seeds at its base in the spring. Vining annuals include morning glory (*Ipomoea purpurea*), sweet pea (*Lathyrus odoratus*), black-eyed Susan vine (*Thunbergia alata*), calico flower (*Aristolochia elegans*), balloon vine (*Cardiospermum halicacabum*), Japanese hops (*Humulus japonicus*), moonflower (*Ipomoea alba*), cup-and-saucer vine (*Cobaea scandens*), and hyacinth bean (*Dolichos lablab*).

What are some annuals with a **creeping or prostrate habit**?

Creeping annuals can be used to quickly cover bare or unsightly areas of the garden. They also provide a small sea of color with just a few plants. Creeping annuals include creeping zinnia (*Sanvitalia procumbens*), scarlet pimpernel (*Anagallis arvensis*), ivy geranium (*Pelargonium peltatum*), purslane (*Portulaca oleracea*), canary-bird flower (*Tropaeolum peregrinum*), ice plant (*Mesembryanthemum crystallinum*), baby blue-eyes (*Nemophila menziesii*), *N. maculata*, Kenilworth ivy (*Cymbalaria muralis*), *Portulaca pilosa*, and nasturtium (*Tropaeolum majus*).

What are some annuals that are grown for their **foliage**?

Licorice plant (*Helichrysum petiolare*) and dusty miller (*Senecio cineraria*) have silvery gray foliage. Coleus (*Coleus* spp.), annual fountain grass (*Pennisetum setaceum*), cockscomb (*Celosia* spp.), and sweet potato vine (*Ipomoea butatus* 'Blackie') have lovely dark-leaved varieties. Asparagus fern (*Asparagus densiflorus* 'Sprengeri') and *Vinca major* (along with licorice plant and dusty miller) are commonly used in container plantings. Snow-on-the-mountain (*Euphorbia marginata*) and polka-dot plant (*Hypoestes phyllostachya*) have beautiful variegated leaves. The elephant-ear leaves of *Caladium* (a tuber) come in a wide variety of stunning colors. Although love-in-a-mist (*Nigella damascena*) is mainly grown for its delicate flowers, it also has handsome hazy foliage.

What are some annuals with fragrant flowers?

Heliotrope (*Heliotropium aborescens*), mignonette (*Reseda odorata*), sweet pea (*Lathyrus odoratus*), Oriental woodruff (*Asperula orientalis*), stock (*Matthiola incana*), sweet verbena (*Verbena officinalis*), petunia (*Petunia* spp.), moonflower (*Ipomoea alba*), Swan River daisy (*Brachycome iberidifolia*), *Bartonia aurea*, and wallflower (*Cheiranthus cheiri*) are all scented annuals, with fragrance that ranges from delicate (stock) to overpowering (heliotrope).

What are some annuals with **variegated foliage**?

A number of annuals are grown primarily for their beautiful variegated foliage. Joseph's coat (*Amaranthus tricolor*), *Coleus blumei*, variegated honesty (*Lunaria annua* 'Variegata'), varieties of ornamental cabbage (*Brassica oleracea*), *Phormium tenax* 'Variegatum', and *Canna* 'Striata' all have beautiful variegated foliage. A number of geraniums (*Pelargonium* spp.) also have variegated foliage, including 'L'Elegante', 'A Happy Thought', 'Caroline Schmidt', and 'Mr. Henry Cox'.

What are some annuals that can be used as **focal points**?

Many annuals need to be planted in groups in order to provide enough visual weight in the landscape. For this reason, they are often unlikely candidates to be the focus of a planting. However, canna (*Canna* spp.), ornamental cabbage (*Brassica oleracea*), foxglove (*Digitalis purpurea*), and, of course, pelargonium (*Pelargonium* spp.) shine as focal points.

Which annuals work best for **dried flower arrangements**?

Globe amaranth (*Gomphrena globosa*), annual baby's breath (*Gypsophila elegans*), strawflower (*Helichrysum bracteatum*), cockscomb (*Celosia cristata*), starflower (*Scabiosa stellata*), and bells-of-Ireland (*Moluccella laevis*) all dry well to provide fragile bouquets for the winter months.

I'm looking for some **unusual plants** to fill my containers, but don't have the time or the money to spend on perennials. Are there any annuals with a little more panache than petunias?

As gardening has continued to increase in popularity, plant connoisseurs have sought out unusual annuals to supplement their perennial borders and fill their pots. Some

271

Petunias (*Petunia* spp.) are popular bedding plants and can be wintered indoors. (Steven Nikkila/Perennial Favorites)

nurseries have responded to the challenge by offering these to their customers, but they are still difficult to find. However, plants such as *Helichrysum petiolare* 'Limelight', *Verbena* 'Homestead Purple', *Coleus, Ipomoea batatas* 'Blackie' and 'Margarita', *Artanema fimbriata, Salvia* 'Van-Houttei', and *Petunia integrifolia* 'Alba' are becoming more commonplace.

What were some annuals that **Claude Monet** planted in his gardens at Normandy?

Monet's gardens, as depicted by his marvelous paintings, are known and loved the world around. In particular, his deft use of brightly colored annuals to create extravagant color contrasts has been frequently imitated. A favorite use of trailing nasturtiums (*Tropaeolum majus*) was to erase the edges of flower paths and to bring bright color all the way down to the ground. Other annuals used by Monet include stock (*Matthiola incana*), sweet pea (*Lathyrus odoratus*), snapdragon (*Antirrhinum majus*), pot marigold (*Calendula officinalis*), sunflower (*Helianthus annus*), and Shasta daisy (*Chrysanthemum maximum*).

Are there any annuals that can be **wintered indoors as houseplants**?

Many annuals can be kept as houseplants for either planting out the following summer, or for providing a bit of color during the winter months. Wax begonia (*Begonia*

Which plant was named after the Greek god of the sun?

The sunflower, of course, was named after Helios, the Greek god who became the sun after being drowned by his uncles, the Titans. The botanical name for sunflower is *Helianthus*, which is a literal translation (*anthos* means flower). The sunflower received its name not for its appearance, but rather for its habit of turning in the direction of the sun.

semperflorens cultorum), coleus (*Coleus* spp.), impatiens (*Impatiens wallerana*), zonal geranium (*Pelargonium hortorum*), pansy (*Viola tricolor hortensis*), petunia (*Petunia* spp.), moss rose (*Portulaca* spp.), and verbena (*Verbena* spp.) all take to indoor planting.

Which annuals are **drought-tolerant**?

For cooler weather, annuals such as forget-me-not (*Myosotis sylvatica*), California poppy (*Eschscholtzia californica*), Iceland poppy (*Papaver nudicaule*), Swan River daisy (*Brachycome iberidifolia*), blue marguerite (*Felicia amelloides*), and star of Texas (*Xanthisma texanum*) all thrive in drought conditions. Spiderflower (*Cleome hasslerana*), cosmos (*Cosmos bipinnatus*), moss rose (*Portulaca grandiflora*), and desert evening primrose (*Oenothera deltoides*) are warm-weather annuals that will survive drought.

What is a **pelargonium**?

A pelargonium (*Pelargonium* spp.) is commonly known as a zonal geranium or just plain geranium by most folks. It is a tender perennial much beloved by most gardeners and planted in clay pots and painted tires from Poughkeepsie to Potero. Actually, however, a true geranium is a perennial that is low growing and spreading in habit, with leaves and blooms that are smaller than the pelargonium's. Due to the misnomer of the pelargonium, a true geranium is sometimes known as a hardy geranium.

What is **heliotrope**?

A heliotrope (*Heliotropium* spp.) is an old-fashioned tender perennial, known to most gardeners as an annual. It has wrinkled, dark green leaves and beautiful violet-blue flowers that have an amazingly sweet fragrance.

273

Which tender perennial was named for a **former U.S. ambassador to Mexico**?

The poinsettia (*Euphorbia pulcherrima*) was named for Dr. Joel Roberts Poinsett, who served as U.S. ambassador to Mexico from 1825 to 1829. He brought the plant to the United States from Mexico, where it was used to decorate churches during Christmas time and was known as the "Nativity flower."

Which annual native wildflower was named after the explorer **William Clark**?

The hardy annual clark (*Clarkia*), also known as Rocky Mountain garland, was discovered growing in the West by Lewis and Clark. The species includes *Clarkia amoena*, which is found growing from British Columbia to California. It grows between one and three feet high and features crimson flowers. *C. purpurea* grows to three feet, with red, purple, or pink flowers featuring a dark center. It is found in both Oregon and California. Native to California, *C. unguiculata* ranges in height from one and a half to three feet with purple, rose, or white flowers.

VEGETABLES AND FRUITS

PLANTING AND CARING FOR A VEGETABLE GARDEN

What are the proper **growing conditions** for a vegetable garden?

The most important consideration for a vegetable garden is sunlight. Be sure the location you choose receives a minimum of six hours of direct sunlight per day. If you live in the North, you should choose a southern exposure. If you live in the South, you may want to choose a northern exposure to provide protection for your plants during the heat of the summer. If you are able to do a soil test on the site, the preferred pH of most vegetables is between 6.0 and 7.0. The ideal soil is a sandy loam. Be sure the area is properly drained (no standing water). A low-lying area in your garden could be more susceptible to frost. Finally, have a source of water, your compost pile, and your tools close by so that your garden will receive the attention it needs on a regular basis with little extra effort on your part.

I'm going to a **farmer's market** next weekend to buy vegetable plants for my garden. What should I look for?

While it may be tempting to buy the biggest plants you find, look for transplants that are short, small, and dark green. This means they are sturdy and well nourished. Taller, paler spindly plants may have been under- or overfed or have received an inconsistent amount of light. Try to select plants that don't have any fruit formed yet, or if the healthiest-looking plants have buds, remove these before planting. Vegetables grow most vigorously before they set fruit and transplants need to spend their energy on growing new shoots and sturdier limbs during their first few weeks in your garden.

Finally, carefully inspect the plant's roots—be sure they are white and healthy looking. Mushy or darker roots mean the plant has been in its pot for too long. Plants are healthiest when their growth is not hindered by lack of nutrients, improper temperatures, or growing room.

How do I **plan my vegetable garden**?

Begin by deciding which vegetables you and your family enjoy. Unless you plan on growing extra vegetables for charitable organizations like Plant a Row for the Hungry (a worthy cause), stick to vegetables you know you'll eat fresh or will process right away. If you've never grown vegetables before, start small and expand as you become more proficient or interested. You could even consider planting a theme vegetable garden like a salad garden or an all-Italian garden.

Next, decide how you'll plant your crops—intensively (good for small gardens and growing organically), in rows, or in another configuration. If you have a small plot or are growing your vegetables in containers, don't forget to think vertical. Even in larger plots, cucumbers, squash, and melons can all benefit from being trellised—it keeps fruits/vegetables off the ground and away from pests and disease. In planning your garden, it is important to keep track of where you have planted your crops from year to year. To minimize disease and insect infestations, crop rotation (see related question in Problems chapter) is a must. You also need to consider the sun's angle in relation to your garden. For example, tall crops such as corn can shade smaller crops. This can be a problem for peppers, but will help lettuces, which tend to bolt in hot weather.

I'm planning my **first vegetable garden** but don't have much space. Are there any vegetables I should avoid?

Broccoli, corn, potatoes, and globe artichoke take up a great deal of space. Cucumbers, melons, peas, and winter squash also require large amounts of space, but these plants can be grown vertically (on trellises and poles) in a small garden. Better choices for a small garden are beans (both bush beans and pole beans), carrots, eggplant, lettuce and greens, peppers, tomatoes, turnips, and onions.

What are the advantages of **planting vegetables in raised beds**?

There are many advantages to planting vegetables in raised beds. You can preserve your soil's tilth with raised beds since you won't be stepping on the soil and compacting it. Raised beds also warm up more quickly in the spring—a boon in northern climates. They improve drainage or fertility problems. They tend to be easy to weed, water, and fertilize because of paths placed around these beds. Crop rotation is also easy—you just move your crops from bed to bed.

Raised garden beds are most appropriate in cool, wet climates because they heat up quickly in spring and dry out rapidly in summer. They also work well where the ground is too hard to work. (Robert J. Huffman/Field Mark Publications)

What are the disadvantages of **planting vegetables in raised beds**?

While planting vegetables in raised beds can pay off in the long run, the chores of double digging, adding soil amendments, and building boxes (if you choose to) can make the initial creation of raised beds labor intensive. It is probably too much bother and work to dig raised beds for large crops such as potatoes, corn, and beans. Raised beds also tend to dry out faster than flat ones.

What are the advantages of **planting vegetables in rows**?

Planting in long, straight rows is a time-honored practice that works well with the farm equipment and rolling acres this method was originally designed for. Mounded rows warm faster in the spring and improve drainage. Weeding, watering, and fertilizing are relatively easy to do with a row garden as well.

What are the disadvantages of **planting vegetables in rows**?

While maintenance is simple with rows, for backyard gardeners rows can be less practical. Rows take up more space and produce less vegetable per square foot. When working in rows, you also stand the risk of compacting your soil through repeated stepping in to weed, water, and harvest.

How frequently do I need to water my vegetable garden?

Your vegetables generally need about an inch of water per week. They should be watered early in the day to keep down both the incidence of disease and fungus that occurs with evening watering, and the evaporation that occurs in warmer climates when watering at midday. Be sure to water the plants to their root zone in order to ensure the plants receive the maximum benefit from the watering.

What are the advantages of **planting vegetables intensively or in squares**?

Intensive vegetable gardening produces greater yields from a smaller space. It also minimizes weeds, since they have no place to grow.

What are the disadvantages of **planting vegetables intensively or in squares**?

An intensive garden requires a great deal of work to establish and requires regular soil improvements. It is also more difficult to find space for large, aggressive growers like squash in these spaces unless you trellis them. Due to the close proximity of the plants, an intensive garden is hard to mulch, although technically the plants should serve as a "living mulch" for each other by shading out weeds and keeping roots cool.

Should I **mulch my vegetable garden**?

Yes. Using a light mulch such as straw reduces watering and cuts down on weeds. Begin mulching once the soil has warmed up in the garden. You can also mulch by hilling up soil around the base of a vegetable plant. Vegetables such as corn, potatoes, and tomatoes appreciate this treatment.

Why should I **weed my vegetable garden**?

Weeding a vegetable garden is crucial to prevent weeds from competing with the plants for nutrients and water. Start with a clean bed—remove all perennial and annual weeds from the bed—then keep it up throughout the season. Although you can use a hoe or trowel, you should be careful not to injure tender vegetable plant roots.

How should I **fertilize my vegetable garden**?

Preparing the soil carefully at the beginning of the season by digging in compost and other organic matter gets you off to a good start. Quick-growing crops such as let-

Tomato cages help prevent fruit from touching the ground and allow sprawling plants to grow vertically, using less garden space. (Robert J. Huffman/Field Mark Publications)

tuces and bush beans probably won't need additional fertilization. Longer-season vegetables like tomatoes and peppers should receive an additional boost of compost or manure tea once they've set flower.

What does it mean to **"cage" a tomato plant**?

Tomato plants have a tremendous rate of growth but lack a strong stem to support the weight of their fruit. If left to sprawl on the ground, the tomatoes are more susceptible to soil-borne disease. By placing wire mesh around the plant and staking the plant in the center, you provide support to the plant with room to grow. Be sure to select a mesh with holes large enough to harvest the fruit through!

Last year, I saved seeds from my pumpkin and zucchini plants. When I planted them together this year, they grew **strange-looking vegetables** that weren't quite pumpkins and weren't quite zucchinis. What happened?

The Cucurbitaceae family is a cross-pollinating one. This means that when the plants are planted near each other, they pollinate each other. The resulting seeds/new plants do not maintain their identity. In the future, try to avoid planting them near each other or don't try to save seeds in order to start new plants.

Why don't all of my **cucumber flowers** result in a cucumber?

A cucumber plant is monoecious, which means it has both female (pistillate) and male (staminate) flower structures. However, the pistil and stamen are found on different flowers. Since only a female flower can produce a fruit, the flowers you see that don't result in cucumbers are male flowers.

In the seed catalog I order from, it lists both **determinate and indeterminate tomatoes**. What's the difference?

Determinate tomato plants bear all of their fruit at one time and die after they reach their mature height. They are usually smaller, more compact plants. Indeterminate tomato plants grow and produce fruit throughout the season until frost kills them. As a result, they can grow quite tall. Gardeners who have a shorter growing season or who plan on processing or freezing their harvest might choose to grow a determinate plant.

My **lettuce** has grown tall and leggy and has developed flowers. Is it still good to eat?

You have just described lettuce that has "bolted" or gone to seed. Most lettuces thrive in the cooler temperatures of spring and tend to bolt once

A merchant proudly displays his tomatoes at the farmer's market in Livonia's Wilson Barn in Michigan. For the best in local produce (and some great tips on growing vegetables), visit your local farmer's market. (Robert J. Huffman/Field Mark Publications)

hot weather hits. Once they've begun to flower, lettuces take on a bitter flavor and are best composted. Next time, plant your lettuce earlier or choose a bolt-resistant variety.

When and how do I plant **garlic**?

Garlic should be planted in the fall. The cloves should be planted about an inch deep in the South and two to three inches deep in the North. Keep the bed weed free in order to minimized the effects of competition. At the end of the following summer, your garlic should be ready to be harvested. Carefully dig up the cloves when the green tops have died back. Don't forget to save a few small cloves for next year's planting!

I bought some leek sets to plant and the instructions say they need to be blanched. What does that mean?

Blanching is a process of keeping a plant or part of a plant out of the sun for a period of time in order to whiten or bleach it. For leeks and onions, begin by digging a shallow trench one to two inches deep. Plant the sets in the trench, spacing them accordingly. Cover the roots with a thin layer of soil.

As the sets begin to grow, continue to hoe soil back into the trench. After a week or so, the trench should be filled to the top and the leeks or onions should be ready for a topdressing of compost.

My neighbor is always showing off the large tomatoes he grows. I don't mean to be competitive, but how can I grow bigger tomatoes?

The best way to grow a large tomato is to select the right variety. Beefstake tomatoes, for example, are destined to give sizable fruit. Other varieties, like Romas, aren't meant to be grown large. Before deciding on a tomato variety you may want to seek the advice of your local nursery or Extension Service office to see if there are any new hybrids that can offer you a genetic edge against your neighbor. It's also important to remember that in breeding tomatoes for size, hybridizers sometimes sacrifice flavor in order to achieve the largest tomato.

My largest tomatoes keep splitting while they are still on the vine. Is there some sort of disease causing them to do that?

No, it is not likely a disease causing your tomatoes to go to Splitsville. The problem is more likely your watering regimen. Inconsistent watering can cause your tomatoes to grow at uneven rates—sometimes quickly, other times more slowly—which can make the fruit susceptible to cracking. To reduce the risk of this taking place, try mulching your plants with hay and use a drip hose in order to ensure the most controlled watering possible.

My yard has very few trees, so it tends to get a lot of sun in the summer. Which vegetables like a lot of sun?

Generally speaking, plants that set fruit require the highest amounts of sun. Vegetables that fall into this category include tomatoes, eggplants, peppers, okra, cucumber, squash, corn, melons, and beans.

Cucumber plants are less susceptible to rot and pest problems when grown on a trellis. (Robert J. Huffman/Field Mark Publications)

I'd like to grow a vegetable garden, but my yard is very **shady**. Am I out of luck?

No—you can still grow vegetables in a yard that gets between four and six hours of sunlight a day. In general, vegetables that are either "roots" (growing below the ground) or "shoots" (foliage without flowers or fruit) tolerate shadier conditions than flowers that set fruit. Vegetables that grow in these conditions include lettuce, spinach, collard, kale, asparagus, rhubarb, carrot, beet, radish, green onion, and arugula.

I'd like to minimize **water use in my vegetable garden**. Are there any vegetables that can get by with less water?

Tomatoes, peppers, and beans can get by with less water than vegetables like lettuce, onions, corn, cucumber, and celery, which have a higher water content.

I'm interested in **extending my vegetable garden** into the fall. Which vegetables survive some frost?

Root crops such as beets, carrots, and radishes survive early frosts. Peas, spinach, Swiss chard, lettuce, and parsley can also take some frost. Brussels sprouts and cabbage benefit in flavor and color from a light frost before being harvested.

I've had a hard time getting **carrots** to grow in my garden. What can I do to improve my chances?

To improve your results, try combining the carrot seed with radish seed. Carrot seed is very tiny and notoriously slow to germinate. By mixing it with radish seed, carrot seed is easier to broadcast. Also, radishes germinate first, loosening up the soil for the carrots to follow.

I have seen a lot of **pole bean supports** in the garden catalogs that are pretty expensive. Aren't there any more affordable options?

Pole beans scramble up just about anything—try growing them on a chain-link fence. A decorative option would be to create a rustic tepee of poles or slender tree limbs, allowing the pole beans to climb the poles. An inexpensive option in a vertically challenged garden would be to purchase two small metal posts and use twine to create "rungs" between the two posts. Plant seeds at the base of the bottom-most twine rung and stand back!

I overplanted my carrot patch, but I never got around to **thinning out** the extra seedlings. Is this a big problem?

No—carrots don't necessarily need to be thinned. Go ahead and harvest those carrots that are ready to be eaten. Think of them as "thinnings" if you must. With the space made available through the first harvest, the smaller carrots will have room to grow and can be harvested later.

Help! I planted a million **carrots** and the weather is starting to turn cold. I don't have enough recipes to use my carrots in if I harvest them all at the same time. What should I do?

I have a great recipe for carrot dill soup. . . . Actually, you can go ahead and pick those carrots you'll use right away. Leave the remaining carrots in the ground. When the weather starts to get cold,

Beans come in two basic varieties: bush and pole. Pole beans, shown here, require some type of support and produce heavier yields than bush beans. (Robert J. Huffman/Field Mark Publications)

place a dry mulch such as straw over the growing bed. It will keep the area dry and warm until you're ready to finish eating your carrots.

How do I plant and harvest **asparagus**?

Asparagus is usually started from crowns bought from a local or mail-order nursery. It should be planted in the spring, as soon as the ground can be worked. Make sure your bed is free of any weeds and is well fertilized with compost. A soil test might be a good idea as well, since this planting is "forever" due to the perennial nature of asparagus.

285

Start by digging a foot-deep trench, placing a cup or so of compost at 12-inch intervals and set the crowns out on the compost hill, making sure the roots are spread out and the buds in the center are facing upward. Cover the crowns with a few inches of the soil, then as the season progresses and the shoots begin to come up, gradually add soil to refill the trench. No asparagus should be harvested the first year after planting. At the second year, a few spears thicker than a pencil may be harvested for around two weeks. Snap the spear off near the soil line, being careful not to injure the crown. The third and fourth consecutive years, harvest larger spears for a period of a month to a month and a half, stopping when the spears are thinner than pencil width.

Once the season is over, let the asparagus ferns grow until they are dead, then compost them. In order to limit competition for nutrients and water, try to keep the bed weed-free by picking weeds by hand or using mulch. Using tools to pull weeds may damage the crowns. Fertilize asparagus using a fertilizer high in phosphorus and potassium, applying it when growth starts and at the end of the season.

What is the difference between **snap, snow, and shell peas**?

Snap peas have plump, edible pods—both peas and pods can be eaten. Harvest snap peas when the pods are plump and green. Snow peas—often used in stirfrys—also have edible pods but they tend to be flatter. Snow peas are ready for eating when they are still young and thin—the peas are really secondary here. Shelling peas are grown only for their peas, and their woody pods should be composted. These peas should be picked when the pod is fat but still green. Once it has browned, the seeds have dried and can be kept for planting next year.

What is an **onion set**?

An onion set is a dwarf onion bulb that has been grown from onion seed planted very closely together. Sets allow gardeners in cooler areas to harvest onions sooner. Onions grown from seeds have a long growing period—around 130 days to maturity. However, there is greater selection in seeds than in sets. When selecting onion sets to plant, choose those that are around a half-inch in diameter.

I would love to grow **potatoes** but I live in an apartment building with a terrace. Can potatoes be grown in a pot?

Freshly dug potatoes are one of life's greatest pleasures. Besides, growing your own potatoes gives you the opportunity to try a wider variety of potatoes than you can normally buy at a grocery store. While many people believe that growing potatoes requires a lot of room, you can grow potatoes in a large pot, a half wine barrel, or other large container. You don't even need to purchase a special type of potato. While you can order seed potatoes or new potatoes, any ordinary potato will do.

> **I grew Brussels sprouts for the first time this year but instead of producing beautiful tight sprouts, they all look like half-opened flowers. What did I do wrong?**
>
> **B**russels sprouts are a wonderful crop to pick fresh from the garden but they do require some oversight. A common cause of half-opened sprouts is an inadequate amount of organic material in the bed. Like other brassicas, Brussels sprouts are heavy feeders so be sure to dig in a good amount of compost or other organic material into your soil before planting them.

Fill your container with a soil mixture meant for containers (see Container Gardening section in Special Gardens chapter), stopping short of the top by six inches or so. Place your potatoes on top of the soil so that they are between six and eight inches apart. There is no need to cut the potatoes into pieces so that each piece has an "eye"—just go ahead and plant the whole potato. Cover the potatoes with 4–6 inches of mulch. Water well and that's it! The potatoes will send up their top growth within the next few weeks. Once the top growth dies, your potatoes are ready to be harvested. Just uncover them and enjoy!

How do I **harvest my potatoes** without slicing them in two?

Potatoes must be dug up with some care to avoid slicing them into small pieces (although they're still edible, of course). Check the size of the potatoes to decide if they're ready to harvest. If you want "new" potatoes, they can probably be harvested with the top growth still green and flowers attached (although early varieties should be left until the flowers are completely open). If you want larger potatoes, wait until the top growth has died down. Once this happens, try to follow the dead stems to their originating potato using your hands and a trowel. If this doesn't work, carefully explore the bed using your hands and a small fork. Once you've located a group of potatoes, use the fork or your hands to lift them from the soil. Keep exploring the bed in this manner until you've dug up all your potatoes.

What is the best method for **drying hot peppers** for use in the winter or to create decorative wreaths?

Peppers are actually very easy to dry. Pick the peppers when they're red—they're more colorful and have a spicier flavor. Then place the peppers on a screen left outside in the sun. That's it! The sun will quickly dry the peppers and the screen will ensure ade-

287

> ## I want to grow an enormous pumpkin for Halloween this year. What can I do to help it grow large?
>
> **B**egin by digging plenty of organic matter into your bed. Provide the pumpkin plant with a lot of growing room as pumpkin plants are notorious for their sprawling habit of growth. Thin down the number of pumpkins per vine to just a few to ensure the energy of the plant is focused. Finally, be sure to water the plant abundantly.

quate ventilation. When they're dry, you can preserve them in glass bottles or string them together to make wreaths and roping.

What can I do to ready my vegetable garden for the **winter**?

Begin by composting all spent plants. Any plants that were diseased or insect ridden should be placed with the trash in case your compost pile isn't hot enough to kill these organisms. Next, turn the soil over—leaving large clods on the surface to be broken up during the heaving and thawing that occurs during winter. Lastly, sow a cover crop to prevent soil erosion and keep weeds from taking over your bed. In the spring, a quick turn of the soil and you should be ready to plant again!

I wasn't able to put my vegetable garden to bed before winter. What should I do to ready my vegetable garden in the **spring** for planting?

Start by drawing a quick map of where you had planted your crops last summer. Do this to the best of your recollection. If you're able to determine where your tomatoes were planted because their tangled remains still cling to their rusty cages, then you're one step ahead. Next, remove any remaining plant materials and compost them. If they're already halfway decomposed (and they very well may be) and the soil is ready to be worked, you can cut them into smaller segments and dig them into the soil.

Since you don't really have time to plant a cover crop, spread a 2-inch layer of compost over the entire vegetable bed and turn the soil gently, breaking up large clods with the end of your spade or a hoe. Rake gently so that the bed has an even pitch. This should, of course, be done once the soil is ready to be worked. Then, using your map as a guide toward crop rotation (see related question in Problem Prevention section of the Problems chapter), determine where your vegetables should be planted this year. Look for opportunities to plant nitrogen-fixers like peas and beans and companion planting pairs or trios if you had problems with certain insect pests last year. You

Tending a community vegetable garden at Greenmead Community Garden in Livonia, Michigan. (Robert J. Huffman/Field Mark Publications)

should also plant quick-growing cover crops whenever areas of your vegetable bed lay fallow. This will keep the weeds out and put nutrients back into the soil.

When is the proper time to harvest **winter squash**?

Winter squash is best picked just prior to the first frost. Acorn and butternut squash should be harvested after their undersides change color (from a dark green to orange on the acorn squash) and the skin is hard.

When is the proper time to harvest **zucchini** and other summer squash?

Summer squash is best picked when it is young and small. I repeat, pick the squash when it is young and small. If the squash aren't picked, this causes the plant to stop flowering. In the case of zucchini, you may want to watch for the flowers on the end of the squash to drop off and pick them the next day. On the other hand, if you want to slow the plant's growth, you may consider leaving a few zucchini on the plant.

When is the proper time to harvest **green beans**?

If they are to be eaten immediately, green beans taste wonderful when picked somewhat small. If they'll be used for freezing or eaten after a few days, beans should be harvested before you can see the outline of the individual beans in the pod.

How do I harvest **broccoli** to encourage the plant to produce more shoots?

Most broccoli varieties will keep producing side shoots once its main head is cut. While yellow broccoli flowers are edible, broccoli is at its tenderest and most appealing for the table when the flower buds are green and compact. Harvest the main head near the base of the plant and your broccoli will keep producing side shoots for another month or so.

With a threat of frost, I picked my remaining **green tomatoes** and brought them inside. How can I encourage them to ripen further indoors without going bad?

Inspect your tomatoes for any soft spots or dark areas—these will only "improve" with age and you don't want one bad tomato to spoil the whole bunch! Wrap each individual tomato in newspaper and place them in a cardboard box in one layer only. Keep the box in a cool, dry place. Over the next few weeks, your tomatoes will ripen to a lovely red. Keep checking them while they're ripening and get rid of any tomatoes with signs of decay immediately.

VEGETABLE FAMILIES

Which plants provide **nitrogen** to the soil in a form that is usable by other plants?

Members of the Legume family, such as beans and peas, have a symbiotic relationship with a form of soil bacteria. Legumes work with rhizobia bacteria to extract nitrogen from the atmosphere and convert it to a usable form in the earth. The bacteria live on the roots of the beans or peas, forming nodules that draw nitrogen out of the air and store it as nitrate.

Which kinds of vegetables **grow underground**?

Root vegetables include beet, carrot, parsnip, radish, rutabaga, and turnip. Rutabaga and turnip are also part of the Brassica or cabbage family. Vegetables that grow as bulbs include onion, garlic, shallot, and leek.

Which vegetables are members of the **nightshade family**?

Vegetable members of the nightshade or solanaceous family include tomatoes, potatoes, eggplants, and peppers. With the exception of potatoes, they generally need warm temperatures to germinate and grow. Pests include the potato beetle. Raspberries and strawberries are the fruit cousins of this family.

Which vegetables are members of the **Cucurbitaceae family**?

Cucurbits or gourds include squash, pumpkin, melons, and cucumber. They are vining crops that thrive during the summer (warm-season crops).

291

Beets are perfect for homegrowing, since they are easily grown, resistant to disease and pests, require little space, and store well. (Robert J. Huffman/Field Mark Publications)

What is the difference between **a squash and a pumpkin**?

Botanically speaking, a pumpkin has a hard stem attached to the fruit while a squash has a soft and somewhat spongy stem.

What is the difference between **butterhead lettuce, crisphead lettuce, romaine lettuce, and loose-leaf lettuce**?

Butterhead, crisphead, and romaine lettuces all form heads and are known, of course, as head lettuces. Butterhead lettuces such as 'Buttercrunch' have large leaves with smooth edges. Crisphead lettuces such as the ubiquitous 'Iceberg' have much more rounded heads with curly, crisp leaves. Romaine lettuces like 'Little Gem' grow in an upright, almost football-like shape as opposed to the round shape of butterheads and crispheads. Loose-leaf lettuces—as their name would imply—do not form heads at all but rather send up individual leaves. They are sometimes called "cut-and-come-again" lettuces because they may picked over several weeks rather than being harvested all at once. Many home gardeners choose to grow loose-leaf lettuces because they are so simple to grow and because you can explore a wider variety of lettuces than are available at most grocery stores. I prefer the flavor of leaf lettuce as well. 'Red Oak Leaf' and 'Salad Bowl' are two varieties of loose-leaf lettuces.

Squash is classified by winter and summer varieties, with winter squash having hard rinds, which makes it perfect for storing. (Robert J. Huffman/Field Mark Publications)

What are **cole crops**?

Cole crops are part of the cabbage or Brassica family and include broccoli, Brussels sprouts, cabbage, kale, and cauliflower. They are generally cool-season vegetables and are susceptible to problems such as cabbage worm and clubroot. Research has shown that cole crops contain chemicals that seem to play a role in preventing certain types of cancer.

Are there any **perennial vegetables**?

Vegetables that are perennial in all 11 U.S. growing hardiness zones include asparagus, rhubarb, and the Jerusalem artichoke.

Are **Jerusalem artichokes and globe artichokes** the same thing?

No—Jerusalem artichokes are actually related to sunflowers. They produce small tubers that are harvested in the late fall and early spring. The tubers are replanted in order to start new plants. Globe artichokes are the ones commonly available in the grocery store. These plants produce flower heads that are harvested in the mid- to late summer.

I like spicy foods so I'd like to plant the **hottest pepper** I can find in my garden. Which variety is the hottest?

The question of which pepper packs the most punch is one that is hotly (groan) debated. While there are many opinions on the subject, the hottest of hot peppers appears to be the Scotch bonnet—although the habañero pepper comes in a close second.

I was told the more you abuse your **peppers**, the hotter they get. So last year, when I planted peppers for the first time, I watered them only as they started to droop but the crop just didn't meet my expectations. What did I do wrong?

Peppers like a well-drained soil of average fertility and like to be sited in full sun. While they will tolerate drought, they can turn bitter if they go for extended periods without water.

What is the **easiest vegetable** to grow from seed?

While this is a matter of opinion, radish is a very easy and beautiful vegetable for beginning gardeners to start with. This is because it generally grows well in any type of soil, as long as the bed is in full sun. As a root vegetable, radishes also like to have an adequate amount of phosphorous and potassium in the soil. They germinate very quickly after planting (no more than one week later) and can be direct seeded in the early spring once the soil can be worked. The most important things to remember for radishes is to thin them early on and make sure they get at least an inch of water a week. Harvest spring-sown radishes as soon as they're ready, otherwise they may become too large and woody. Radishes sown in the fall can be left in the ground until after frost, then harvested and stored in a cool, dry place.

What are some varieties of **heirloom or open-pollinated vegetables**?

Heirloom beans include 'Blue Lake', 'Great Northern', 'Scarlet Runner', and 'Kentucky Wonder'. 'Early Pearl', 'Black Aztec', and 'Shoepeg' are heirloom varieties of sweet corn. 'Nantes', 'Danvers Half Long', and 'Chantenay' are heirloom carrots. 'Oak Leaf', 'Salad Bowl', and 'Buttercrunch' are better-known varieties of heirloom lettuce. Heirloom radishes include 'Easter Egg', 'French Breakfast', 'Shunkyo', and 'Rattails'. The well-known 'Brandywine', along with 'Golden Queen', 'Old Wyandotte', 'Ida Gold', and 'San Marzano' are good-tasting heirloom varieties of tomatoes. Finally, 'All-Blue', 'Yukon Gold', and 'Acadia Russet' are some of the heirloom potatoes.

Peppers are classified as either sweet or hot. They are annuals in cold climates, but can be grown as perennials in warmer areas. (Robert J. Huffman/Field Mark Publications)

Although I've seen the term crop rotation mentioned frequently, is this important for all vegetables or just certain families of vegetables?

The idea behind crop rotation is to keep crops that share certain insect pests and have certain nutrient requirements together in a section of the vegetable garden and relocate it from year to year in order to foil the insects and ensure the soil is replenished. The usual plan is to place a garden on a three-year rotation with a fourth area for perennial crops or large crops such as potatoes.

In terms of their nutrient requirements, crops are roughly grouped as follows, from least to most: nitrogen-fixers (peas, beans) and light feeders (onions, garlic); fruiting vegetables (tomatoes, peppers), squash and the Brassica family (broccoli, Brussels sprouts, cabbage, kale, and cauliflower); root crops (carrots, beets, radishes, rutabagas, turnips). By planting a nitrogen-fixer such as peas the year before a nitrogen-needer such as cabbage is planted, you reduce the need for additional fertilizer and keep the soil nutrient level high. Members of the Nightshade family (tomatoes, peppers, and eggplant) should be rotated on a yearly basis due to their susceptiblity to soil-borne disease. By keeping these crops together and moving their location every year, you can reduce the incidence of such diseases as Fusarium wilt and, when they do occur, prevent them from spreading. Short-lived vegetables such as lettuce and spinach can be snuck into beds in between crops or in the shade of large ones.

PLANTING AND CARING FOR FRUITS

What are the proper growing conditions for **ground and bush fruits**?

Ground and bush fruits require a site in full sun that receives some wind to provide good air circulation around the plants. Most do best in light, sandy soils of an average pH (with an exception below) but with plenty of organic matter dug in.

What are the proper growing conditions for a **citrus orchard**?

A citrus orchard requires a location in full sun and heat (obviously only the warmer regions should apply), although oranges will take some cold temperatures. Citrus fruits appreciate being kept out of wind and like a moist but well-drained soil with a slightly acid pH. Oranges like sandy soil while lemons will manage in heavier soils.

What are the proper growing conditions for an **apple orchard**?

Apple trees should be grown in a warm and sunny spot, ideally on a slight slope that faces south or southeast. This provides the trees with the benefit of a sheltered, warm

Though most oranges are grown in the warmest parts of Florida, California, the Mississippi Delta, and the lower Rio Grande Valley, some varieties can be grown by gardeners in greenhouses. (Robert J. Huffman/Field Mark Publications)

home and protection from frost (as long as the trees aren't planted at the base of a steep slope). They need a deeply dug soil that has had all major obstructions (tree roots, old trees, rocks) dug from it and lots of organic matter dug in to provide drainage while retaining some moisture.

How do I plant a **peach tree**?

Review the tree planting question in the Trees and Shrubs chapter and follow those instructions. In addition, peach trees are usually grafted and therefore need to have the bud union placed two to three inches above the soil surface to eliminate suckering. If the union is planted below the soil line, the grafted tree may develop its own roots, which will eliminate the benefits of the rootstock. Be sure to gently but firmly tamp the soil while filling the planting hole and provide a balanced, water-soluble fertilizer to the soil immediately after planting.

How do I plant **strawberries**?

Strawberries need to be rotated, so be sure the bed you choose is large enough to accommodate this. You can choose from a number of different ways to plant your berries, depending on how much time and effort you want to devote to them.

If you want a minimum of effort, use the matted-row system. Berries need to be planted about a foot and a half apart in a row with three to four feet between rows. The runners are allowed to root themselves wherever they like. The gardener maintains order in the patch by removing daughter plants (see page 304) when they grow closer together than six inches or when the row becomes narrower than a foot. This system tends to result in smaller berries but by getting rid of daughter plants first, you can stave this off somewhat.

If you're willing to work a little more and like things neat, try the spaced runner system. Berries are planted at least a foot and a half apart with around two and a half feet between the rows. Keep only a half-dozen runners spaced six inches apart and compost older plants to keep this spacing.

If you don't mind keeping a close watch on your strawberry patch, the hill system is one for you. The berries are planted between 12 and 18 inches apart in all directions and any runners that form are cut. This works best with berries that are poor runners.

Do **strawberry plants** need to be mulched?

While your strawberry bed can be left unmulched, there are several benefits to using a fine layer of straw mulch. A straw mulch will keep the leaves and fruit dry, which will reduce the incidence of disease. Straw also keeps the your berries off of the ground. Otherwise, they risk becoming a fine dessert for your local slug population. Finally, I find that the straw provides a good pale background for the berries, making them easier to see among their deep green leaves. The straw should be applied just as the berries are starting to fruit and should be removed as soon as the plants stop producing.

Can strawberries really be grown in a **strawberry pot**?

Yes—if you lack space but love strawberries, you might consider growing them in this type of container. A strawberry pot is a tall vaselike pot with planting pockets all along its sides. A single strawberry plant is planted in each pocket along with several planted in the top of the pot. The only downside of a strawberry pot is that the strawberry plants on the bottom can sometimes fail to get enough water. This can be solved by placing a length of plastic pipe down the center of the pot and resting it on a piece of broken pottery, before filling the container with soil and plants.

How do I prune my **peach tree**?

After planting, cut back the young peach trees to 18 to 24 inches, leaving two or three vigorous-looking branches close to the cut that have a wide angle between the branch and the main trunk (the angle is known as the crotch). These branches should be fairly long and thick, and of similar size to one another. These will become

> ## I love plums but they're so expensive at the supermarket. Are they easy to grow at home?
>
> In cooler areas of the country, plums are difficult to grow because they often flower early and run the risk of succumbing to the frequent late frosts that occur in these areas. Plums are also heavy feeders. They need a good amount of nitrogen, water, sunlight, and space in order to flourish. While some yards have a few of these, it is the rare one that has all of them in great quantity. Finally, many plums are self-sterile, making it difficult to get them to flower and bear fruit at all. Your best bet is to try an easier fruit tree such as an apple.

your scaffold branches. If the branches are thin, cut them back to short stubs with a few outward-facing buds, and the following year choose scaffold branches from these. If there are no branches with these characteristics, cut back all branches to short stubs. A month later, lightly prune to remove any shoots that appear. Monitor for several weeks and remove additional new growth from the trunk. The following spring, choose additional branches to keep so that the tree develops a nice, rounded shape and cut the scaffolds into equal lengths. This pruning method is known as the open center method.

How do I prune my **grape vines**?

Young grape vines are pruned in order to encourage them to fill out a two-wire trellis quickly. Pruning is done in the early spring, before growth starts. The planted vine is cut back to two or three buds, which will grow into canes. The longest of these canes will form the trunk and should be secured to the trellis. All other canes should be removed in the second year, with two buds left to branch horizontally from the trunk along the top wire, and a strong sucker left at the bottom to create a second trunk at the lower wire. The following years, the top cane should be pruned down to its wire, with growth encouraged along the top and bottom wires. Any fruit that develops during these early growing years should be removed as well. With mature grape vines, select four healthy canes with previous season's growth on them and remove all other growths.

How do I prune my **everbearing raspberry bushes**?

Raspberries are produced on new canes. Everbearing raspberries produce two crops on the same cane—one in the late summer or early fall and one in the late spring of the following year. Once the cane has produced its crop, remove it. If you are renovating a raspberry patch, use a sharp, clean pair of pruners to remove all weak, spindly canes, retaining only four to five strong central canes. If the patch appears to be diseased, get rid of it and start again with new plants.

How frequently should I water my **apple orchard**?

If it is a young orchard, the apple trees should be kept evenly moist with the root system soaked thoroughly when it becomes dry. Mulch can help this process. A more established orchard still needs water, but receives most of it from nature. It should receive additional water if a check of the soil around a tree's root system indicates it is dry. Apples should not need or receive additional water after the early fall in order to prepare for winter dormancy.

How should I **fertilize my brambles**?

Bramble fruits (which grow on thorny canes) should be fertilized in early spring. Compost or manure can be used to topdress brambles or you can apply a balanced fertilizer. If growth is out of control, consider reducing the amount of fertilizer you're using.

What's the proper method for **harvesting berries**?

All berries should be picked in the cool of the morning to maintain fruit quality. Bramble berries (see page 303) should be picked when they have full color, with any overripe or inferior fruit composted. Blueberries should be harvested by running your hand over a cluster and letting any ripe berries fall into a pail. This method is better than picking by color because the berries need to sit on the bush a little longer to ripen after they've turned blue. Strawberries should be harvested when they're fully red. Pick them by the stem to avoid bruising and place them in a shallow basket so that the weight of the topmost berries does not damage those on the bottom.

> ## How else, besides in size, do standard, semidwarf, and dwarf fruit trees vary from one another?
>
> The fruit of dwarf, semidwarf, and standard varieties of trees is equal in size—the characteristic of tree height does not affect the size of the fruit. Dwarf fruit trees bear a moderate amount of fruit. Semidwarf varieties produce fruit on both the inner and outer branches of the tree and, as a result, tend to have very high yields per tree. Standard fruit trees bear their fruit mainly on the outer branches of the tree, which tends to reduce their yields somewhat.

I have an old **apple tree** on my property that's in need of some TLC. What do I do?

Take on this project in the early spring so that the tree will have time to recover during the summer. First, determine if the tree can be saved. The trunk and major limbs should be in good shape (not hollow or rotted). Then look for younger sprouts in the lower part of the tree. The bark on these branches will be very smooth, indicating its youth. These sprouts will be encouraged to create a new structure for the tree. Remove all old, larger limbs to about six inches above the new growth. This is best accomplished through the use of a chainsaw and a professional in order to ensure the removal doesn't damage the younger shoots, the older tree, and any people nearby. The tree will undergo a tremendous amount of new growth that year. During the following spring, remove most of this except those limbs that can be trained or will grow outwardly and horizontally. These limbs should be cut back six inches or so. Additional vigorous growth should result, with most of this removed the following spring. Any desirable branches left should be cut back slightly to encourage outward, rather than upward, growth. During these first few years of renovation, don't fertilize the tree as it is already expending energy on new growth.

Although we've had a very cool spring this year, some of our **early-blooming fruit trees are in full bloom.** Should I be concerned?

Watch for the bees! Fruit trees rely heavily on insects to help them pollinate. If you haven't noticed any insect activity while your fruit trees are in bloom, you may be in danger of losing some or all of the yield from your trees. Fortunately, there are methods to pollinate your trees that can remedy this situation.

How do you go about **hand pollinating** a stand of fruit trees?

With hand pollinating, you are attempting to replicate the normal activity of insects. This doesn't necessarily mean dressing up in a bee costume and antennae, however.

The usual method is to rub the flowers of one tree with a cotton swab or similarly gentle device and then spread that pollen into the flowers of a compatible mate. While this can be a time-consuming task in a sizable orchard, it can be the difference between having a good yield and none at all (see previous question).

I live in a warm part of the country and was told that some fruit trees wouldn't get a long enough **dormancy period** if I planted them here. What does that mean?

Although most people think of winter as a time when plants simply shut down and wait for the coming of spring, fruit trees actually require a dormant period in order to properly set fruit. Therefore, if you live in an area where temperatures rarely fall below 45 degrees Fahrenheit, you will be limited in the varieties of fruit trees you can plant.

I planted watermelon last year and although it was a good year with lots of rain, the **melon just wasn't very sweet.** What should I do differently this year?

While watermelon needs plenty of water during its growing period, it needs a dry period just prior to harvest in order to "sweeten up." This is because with wet soil less oxygen is available in the soil to go to the watermelon plant roots, and photosynthesis slows without sunshine. Both occurrences affect sugar production in the plant. This year, if the same weather prevails, wait for a week or so to harvest. If you've just had a saturating rain and your melons look ripe, give the melons a few days to sweeten up before harvesting.

How can I tell when my **watermelon is ripe** and ready to pick?

There are several things that indicate a watermelon is ripe. When the glossy rind begins to dull, the melon may be ready. Another indication is the drying and browning of the tendril on the vine just opposite of where the watermelon stem is attached. A third method for checking the ripeness of a melon is to turn it over and examine the spot on the bottom of the melon where it rested on the ground. If the spot is greenish-yellow, the melon should be ripe.

FRUIT FAMILIES

What is the difference between **pome fruit and stone fruit**?

Pome (from *pomme,* which means apple in French) fruits, such as apples and pears, have many seeds. Stone fruits, as their name might suggest, have one hard pit. Peaches, plums, and cherries are stone fruits.

Which kinds of grapes will grow in the United States?

American grapes (*Vitis ruscana*), European grapes (*Vitis vinifera*), hybrids between the two, and muscadine grapes (*Vitis rotundifolia*) are all grown in the United States. American grapes tend to be more disease resistant and hardy than European grapes, but are grown mainly for eating and juice. European grapes are also known as wine grapes. Muscadine grapes are grown in warm regions and used mainly for jelly, juice, and wine.

What are the **bramble fruits**?

Bramble fruits are fruits that grow on thorny canes. They are mostly perennial plants that bear fruit on biennial canes. Red, black, and purple raspberries and blackberries are brambles.

Which types of trees are in the *Prunus* genus?

Trees in the *Prunus* genus include both ornamental and edible fruit trees such as almond, cherry, peach, and plum. They are stone fruits.

Which types of trees are in the *Malus* genus?

Apple and crabapple trees are members of the *Malus* genus. They are pome fruits.

Which native fruit grows in **acidic soil**?

Blueberries thrive in acidic soil. Native to North America, blueberries appreciate full sun and soil with a pH between 4.0 and 5.0. In the wild, some varieties of blueberries grow in swamps, while others grow on barren, rocky mountaintops. In the garden, however, they need moist, well-drained soil around their roots.

What is a **dwarf fruit tree**?

A dwarf fruit tree is a fruit tree that has been grafted onto a rootstock that provides the tree with its size characteristics. Dwarfs generally mature at around eight to 10 feet in height. Genetic dwarf fruit trees have their own ability to remain small (they are not grafted onto a different rootstock).

303

What are some advantages of **dwarf fruit trees** over standard fruit trees?

The obvious advantage of dwarf fruit trees over standard fruit trees is that their smaller size allows them to be planted in almost any landscape. Therefore, they will easily fit in most suburban yards. Their smaller size also means that these trees are easier to plant, fertilize, mulch, and harvest than larger trees. Dwarf trees also bear fruit sooner than their standard counterparts. Most dwarf varieties will begin fruiting by their second year while standard varieties can take up to 10 years before fruiting.

What is an **everbearing plant**?

An everbearing plant is one that bears fruit throughout a season, as opposed to a June-bearing variety that bears all of its fruit at one time. For canning and preserving, a June-bearing plant might be preferable.

What is a **high-chill fruit cultivar**?

A high-chill cultivar is a fruit tree that requires longer, colder winters in order to set and yield fruit. Because high-chill fruit trees require a longer period of dormancy, they typically bloom later than their low-chill counterparts.

What is a **low-chill fruit cultivar**?

A low-chill cultivar is a fruit tree that needs fewer cold days of winter dormancy in order to set and yield fruit. A low-chill cultivar is desirable in warmer areas that have mild winter temperatures.

Are there any **fruits that will grow in the shade**?

Many berries prefer shade because that is where they grow in the wild. Alpine strawberries, thimbleberries, salmonberries, lingonberries, and wintergreen prefer shade.

Both red raspberries and blueberries can also tolerate partially shady conditions. Other fruits that grow in the shade include muscadine grapes and certain pear cultivars such as 'Turner Shade' and 'Kieffer'.

TREES AND SHRUBS

WOODY ORNAMENTAL TYPES

What is a **woody ornamental plant**?

A woody ornamental is a perennial plant such as a tree or a shrub that does not die back to the ground each year. Even though a plant may be commonly called a bush or a shrub, such as butterfly bush (*Buddleia* spp.), it may not be a woody ornamental.

What are **deciduous ornamental plants**?

Deciduous ornamentals are plants such as burning bush (*Euonymus alata*), dogwoods (*Cornus* spp.), and maples (*Acer* spp.) that lose their leaves in the fall and remain leafless until the spring. They are used in the landscape for their flowers, their changing foliage color, and the shape and color of their leafless silhouette in the winter.

What are **broadleaf evergreens**?

Broadleaf evergreens are landscape plants that have broad or wide leaves that remain green throughout the year. Some examples of broadleaf evergreen shrubs include boxwood (*Buxus* spp.), rhododendron (*Rhododendron* spp.), and holly (*Ilex* spp.). They are used to provide structure in the garden in winter and are frequently planted near building foundations. Broadleaf evergreens that take well to shearing can be used to create a hedge.

What are **narrowleaf evergreens**?

Narrowleaf evergreens are ornamental plants that have long, slender, needle-shaped leaves that remain green throughout the year. Pine (*Pinus* spp.), fir (*Abies* spp.),

The weeping beech (*Fagus sylvatica* f. *pendula*) is a hardy deciduous tree, used both ornamantally and as a shade tree, because of its lovely, spreading foliage. (Robert J. Huffman/Field Mark Publications)

juniper (*Juniperus* spp.), and cedar (*Cedrus* spp.) are some examples of narrowleaf evergreens. Larger varieties are used in landscaping to screen out unsightly views and noise. They also provide shelter, reducing the effects of wind and sun on buildings.

What is a **conifer**?

Conifer means "cone-bearing." This term refers to primarily evergreen trees and shrubs that have either true cones (such as pines) or arillate fruits (yews).

What are the **layers of a forest**?

A forest can be divided into vertical layers. The canopy or top layer is comprised of all of the tree crowns in an area. The understory is comprised of smaller trees that grow under the canopy. The shrub layer is made up of woody vegetation (shrubs as well as seedling trees) that grows under the understory. The ground layer is made up of small plants such as wildflowers, ferns, and mosses that grow on the forest floor.

What is a **copse**?

A copse or coppice (also see coppicing on page 329) is a stand or grove of small trees. Generally, it consists of a thin planting of standards and open areas of shrubs underneath. A well-designed copse might include flowering trees in the foreground

Examples of a common hedge, used as borders, as fences, to hinder wind, or simply as an attractive ornamental. (Robert J. Huffman/Field Mark Publications)

with trees with good fall color or fruit planted in the rear in order to ensure visual interest year-round.

What is a tree's **drip line**?

The drip line is the circle formed by the outermost branch tips of the tree, where rainwater drips off the tree. The drip line is an important consideration in the care of a tree, since the root system of a tree—particularly the fine, shallow roots that collect most of the moisture and nutrients used by the tree—extend to this point. When mulching, watering, or topdressing a tree, always extend your planting materials out to this point.

What is a **sub-shrub**?

A sub-shrub is a plant that is permanently woody at its base, but whose stems tend to be soft or herbaceous. For this reason, sub-shrubs are considered perennials, as opposed to a true shrub. Plants such as butterfly bush (*Buddleia* spp.), however, may be woody to their tips in warmer areas and herbaceous in colder ones. A broader definition of a sub-shrub is a plant that tends to be shrubby in its growth but low and soft wooded. Ornamentals like rosemary (*Rosmarinus officinalis*) and heather (*Calluna* spp.) are usually considered sub-shrubs.

309

What types of shrubs can be kept as **hedges**?

A number of shrubs can be planted to form a hedge. If you would like to create structure in your garden year-round, try using a shrub that is evergreen. A classic hedge may be created using a variety of boxwood, such as *Buxus sempervirens*. Box requires annual trimming to retain a formal shape. Other evergreen shrubs that make nice formal hedges include common yew (*Taxus baccata*) and common holly (*Ilex aquifolium*). An evergreen hedge also creates immediate privacy and can be used to provide shelter from the wind.

Deciduous shrubs create a more informal-looking hedge, which can also be quite lovely in the garden. Some deciduous shrubs that take well to hedging include rose (*Rosa;* the rugosa variety grow nicely as informal hedges), barberry (*Berberis* spp.), spirea (*Spiraea* spp.), viburnum (*Viburnum* spp.), and forsythia (*Forsythia* spp.). As its branches weave together, a more established deciduous hedge can also provide privacy.

What are some trees or shrubs that grow well in **alkaline soil**?

Some woody ornamentals that grow in alkaline soil include the golden-rain tree (*Koelreuteria paniculata*), the American smoketree (*Cotinus obovatus*), Japanese cherry (including *Prunus* 'Tai-Haku' and *Prunus serrulata rosea*), lilac bushes (*Syringa* spp.), and mock orange shrubs (*Philadelphus* varieties).

What are some trees or shrubs that grow well in **acidic soil**?

Woody ornamentals that grow in acidic soil include most varieties of heaths and heathers (*Erica* and *Calluna* spp.), rhododendrons and azaleas (both *Rhododendron* spp.), and camellias (*Camellia* spp.). Also included in this group are magnolia (*Magnolia virginiana*), serviceberry or Juneberry (*Amelanchier arborea* or *grandiflora*), sourwood (*Oxydendrum arboreum*), mountain ash (*Sorbus* spp.), and Carolina silverbell (*Halesia carolina*).

What are some trees or shrubs that have **year-round interest**?

Barberries (*Berberis* spp.) have beautiful foliage that changes color in the fall as well as ornamental fruit year-round. Burning bush (*Euonymus alata*) has an interesting, corky shape in the winter and clear scarlet leaves in fall that give it its common name. Crape myrtle (*Lagerstroemia indica*) looks outstanding all year long with its beautiful flowers and fruit and stunning bark. Harry Lauder's walking stick (*Corylus avellana* 'Contorta') is a slow-grower that provides a distinctive silhouette in the winter with its spiraling branches. For its beautiful haze of purple leaves and interesting shape, the common smoke bush (*Cotinus coggygria*) is also a four-season winner.

> ## My garden budget is small.
> ## Are there any trees or shrubs that can be grown from cuttings?
>
> A number of woody ornamentals grow easily from cuttings. These include firethorn (*Pyracantha* spp.), forsythia (*Forsythia* spp.), cotoneaster (*Cotoneaster* spp.), dogwood (*Cornus* spp.), willow (*Salix* spp.), fothergilla (*Fothergilla* spp.), and wintercreeper (*Euonymus fortunei).*

Are there any trees that will stand up to the **punishing environment** between my street and sidewalk?

The area you describe has a number of factors that can make it difficult to grow trees in: exposure to wind and weather; exposure to salt (in cold weather areas); exposure to pollution from vehicles; limited amount of room for root system due to space considerations and generally compacted soil. In addition, these stresses make the trees much more vulnerable to insect infestations and disease. Trees such as the Bradford pear (*Pyrus calleryana* 'Bradford'), honey locust (*Gleditsia triacanthos* 'Inermis'), and green ash (*Fraxinus pennsylvanica*) can survive these stresses.

I have an **ugly view** of my neighbor's rusting junkheap of a car. Are there any shrubs that will eliminate this ugliness quickly?

Shrubs and small trees including amur maple (*Acer tataricum ginnala* 'Durand Dwarf'), bottlebrush buckeye (*Aesculus parviflora*), forsythia (*Forsythia* spp.), spreading cotoneaster (*Cotoneaster divaricatus*), and winter honeysuckle (*Lonicera fragrantissima*) grow quickly to screen less-than-desirable views. In warmer areas, try pineapple guava (*Feijoa sellowiana*) or yaupon (*Ilex vomitoria*).

What are some trees or shrubs with **plum-colored foliage**?

Burgundy or plum foliage can provide a distinctive accent in the sea of green that comprises many landscape plantings. The common smoke bush (*Cotinus coggygria*), Eastern redbud (*Cercis canadensis*), Japanese maple (*Acer palmatum atropurpureum*), barberry (*Berberis thunbergii atropurpurea*), purple-leafed plum (*Prunus cerasifera atropurpurea*), and purple beech (*Fagus sylvatica* f. *purpurea*) all have beautiful plum-colored foliage.

The Japanese maple (*Acer palmatum* 'Bloodgood') is a smaller maple that provides some shade, despite its size. (Steven Nikkila/Perennial Favorites)

What are some trees or shrubs with interesting **bark or branches**?

For the winter months, the stark beauty of trees with unusual bark or branches gives a landscape that needed "winter interest." River birch (*Betula nigra*) has lovely peeling pink bark, while the coils and twists of Harry Lauder's walking stick (*Corylus avellana* 'Contorta') provides comic relief to the barren and staid canopy trees of winter. Dogwood (*Cornus* spp.) and willow (*Salix* spp.) are colorful additions to a winter yard.

The magnolia (*Magnolia* spp.) is one of the most beautiful flowering trees and shrubs. It comes in many different cultivars which offer a great variety of colors and levels of adaptability. (Robert J. Huffman/Field Mark Publications)

What are some trees and shrubs with **variegated foliage**?

Trees and shrubs with variegated foliage can serve as focal points in mixed borders. *Weigela* 'Florida Variegata', variegated boxwood (*Buxus sempervirens* 'Aureo-variegata'), variegated box elder (*Acer negundo* 'Variegatum'), variegated holly (*Ilex aquifolium* 'Argentea Marginata'), and *Euonymous fortunei* 'Silver Queen' are a few of the woody ornamentals with variegated foliage.

What are some **white-flowering trees**?

The Japanese pagoda tree (*Sophora japonica*), Japanese lilac tree (*Syringa reticulata*), star magnolia (*Magnolia stellata*), serviceberry (*Amelanchier* spp.), sourwood (*Oxydendrum arboreum*), some crabapples (*Malus* spp.), Callery pear (*Pyrus challeryana*), and Carolina silverbell (*Halesia carolina*) all have lovely white flowers.

Which trees and shrubs have **decorative fruit or catkins**?

Holly (*Ilex* spp.) is typically the first shrub to be considered for its beautiful fruit. In addition to red, hollies also have white and black fruit. However, many other woody ornamentals also have beautiful fruit. *Pyracantha* spp. is another genus of evergreen shrub with beautiful, glossy leaves and red, orange, and yellow fruit. *Cotoneaster* spp. ranges from groundcover to shrub with lovely lovely red, orange, and yellow fruit as well. The snowberry (*Symphoricarpos albus*) bears, aptly enough, beautiful white to pink fruit in the autumn and winter. And although roses are usually considered for their flowers, their hips are a lovely sight in the fall and winter. Harry Lauder's walking stick (*Corylus avellana* 'Contorta') and other members of the Hazel family (*Cory-*

313

The Kentucky coffee tree (*Gymnocladus dioicus*) is a member of the legume family, with pea-like fruits and compound leaves. There is only one species in North America. (Robert J. Huffman/Field Mark Publications)

lus spp.) have beautiful yellow catkins. The Willow family (*Salix* spp.) is another attractive catkin-bearing family.

I live in an area where **water for landscaping** has been rationed. What are some trees and shrubs that will tolerate drought?

Gray birch (*Betula populifolia*), native hackberry (*Celtis occidentalis*), shadblow (*Amelanchier canadensis*), ash (*Fraxinus* spp.), amur maple (*Acer tataricum ginnala*), silver fir (*Abies concolor*), Kentucky coffee tree (*Gymnocladus dioica*), Rocky Mountain juniper (*Juniperus scopulorum*), pine (*Pinus* spp.), ginkgo (*Ginkgo biloba*), and the golden-rain tree (*Koelreuteria paniculata*) are some trees that tolerate drought. Shrubs include black chokeberry (*Aronia melanocarpa*), sumac (*Rhus* spp.), crape myrtle (*Lagerstroemia indica*), longacre potentilla (*Potentilla fruticosa*), common lilac (*Syringa vulgaris*), Oregon grape holly (*Mahonia aquifolium*), and yucca (*Yucca filamentosa*).

I'm interested in **growing native trees and shrubs**. Which grow well in moist soil?

Sourwood (*Oxydendrum arboreum*), white fringe tree (*Chionanthus virginicus*), summersweet (*Clethra alnifolia*), red-osier dogwood (*Cornus stolinifera*), winterberry

314

(*Ilex verticillata*) and inkberry (*Ilex glabra*), highbush blueberry (*Vaccinium corymbosum*), and swamp azalea (*Rhododendron viscosum*) are all American natives that thrive in moist soil.

I've just moved into a new house that has a full acre of property but no trees! Are there any trees that will provide me with instant privacy and shade?

There are a number of trees that grow quickly, but some of them such as silver maple (*Acer saccharinum*), tree of heaven (*Ailanthus altissima*), and weeping willow (*Salix babylonica*) have other less desirable characteristics that make them a poor choice for most homeowners. Better choices include the *Magnolia* genus, corktree (*Phellodendron amurense*), silverbell (*Halesia*), blue ash (*Fraxinus quadrangulata*), and American yellow-wood (*Cladrastis lutea*).

I planted a ginkgo tree this year and I love its beautifully shaped leaves that turn yellow in the fall. Unfortunately, a virus or something has attacked its fruit because they smell horrible. What can I do?

Ginkgo (*Ginkgo biloba*) trees are lovely but you need to choose a male (nonfruiting) tree for your landscape. Female ginkgo trees produce healthy but foul-smelling fruit that is quite messy as well. Next time, purchase your tree from a reputable grower who will work to ensure the tree you plant is a male one.

PLANTING

When is the best time of year to plant trees and shrubs?

It depends on the region you live in. In colder regions with early and late freezes, it is best to plant trees and shrubs between April and October. In warmer climates, ornamentals can be planted throughout the year. For all areas, however, if the site selected is exposed to heavy wind, the plant is marginally hardy, or the soil is too moist or too dry, then spring is the best time to plant.

I'd like to purchase some trees and shrubs for my backyard. How do I select healthy ones?

For any type of plant, be sure to examine the root system. Don't buy plants whose roots are growing out of their containers or that have black or discolored roots. Healthy orna-

Most trees and large shrubs are purchased from the nursery with their roots and soil balls covered in burlap and wrapped with rope or wire, thus called balled-and-burlaped. (Robert J. Huffman/Field Mark Publications)

mentals have firm white roots, good leaf color (beware of yellowing or curled leaves), and strong branches. While shape doesn't necessarily affect health, look for a specimen with a single, straight central leader branch and a symmetrical shape.

I'd like to **plant a tree** near my house to provide shade in the summer and keep it cool in the winter. How close to the house can I plant it?

A good rule of thumb to follow is to plant the tree at least half of its spread or width at maturity away from a building. Also, in order to be sure the tree is proportional to the house, be sure it won't get larger than twice the height of your home.

What is a **bareroot tree** and when should it be planted?

As its name would imply, a tree packaged for sale as bareroot is not potted nor does it have any soil around its roots. Instead, its roots are covered by peat moss or newspapers and then wrapped in plastic to preserve moisture. Because of this, they are highly perishable and need to be planted soon after they have been shipped. They are usually planted during the spring or fall when the plant is dormant. When purchasing these plants, examine the root system to be sure the plant has retained moisture around the roots and that bud break hasn't happened yet.

What is a **balled-and-burlapped tree** and when should it be planted?

A tree that has been balled-and-burlapped (B&B) has had its roots and soil ball covered in burlap and wrapped with rope or wire. Larger trees are usually shipped in this manner. These trees can be planted anytime during the growing season, although extra care should be taken during hot weather to protect the root hairs from exposure. When purchasing B&B trees, examine the root ball to be sure it is solid and that it doesn't wiggle at the trunk (indicating the root system may have been loosened from the plant).

What is a **container tree** and when should it be planted?

A container plant may have been started in a container or it may have been planted in a field and was potted up later. Container trees may be planted throughout the growing season.

The fruit of the American cranberry bush (*Viburnum trilobum* 'Marshall') is too acidic to be eaten fresh, but becomes more palatable when cooked. (Robert J. Huffman/Field Mark Publications)

What factors should I consider when deciding what **type of tree to plant** in my yard?

When choosing a tree or shrub, you must be sure that the environmental conditions of the site match the environmental requirements of the plant. Environmental factors include your region's hardiness zone, the conditions of the soil, the light available, and the wind and air circulation. Most ornamentals require well drained and evenly moist soil with a pH in the midrange of 5.5–7.0 and some light to grow. However, they vary in their specific light requirements. It is important to know both the ornamental's requirements and the light conditions in your landscape. An inappropriate amount of light can cause leaf scorch (too much light) or spindly growth (too little light), and it can affect the amount of flowering/fruiting and leaf color. While most plants require good air circulation to reduce the possibility of fungus, some ornamentals can suffer from desiccation or wind scorch if planted in an area that is too windy.

It is also important to consider the growth habit and physical traits of the tree. Physical traits include such characteristics as mature size, form or shape, color, texture, maintenance, and growth habits such as size and nature of an ornamental's root systems and overall speed of growth. Too many gardeners select plants based on their color, texture, and current size, only to find themselves pruning away to keep a shrub in check or hacking a tree down that has been planted too close to the house. Since woody ornamentals tend to be priced more expensively than other landscape plants and make an immediate impact on the landscape, most gardeners would do well to plan their purchases carefully.

I'd like to **plant a tree in the corner** of my yard but I think the area might be too wet. Can I still plant there?

Yes, but with some caution. Trees and shrubs that are planted in areas that are too wet can die quickly as a result of lack of oxygen to the roots. You could plant shallowly or on a berm (see instructions for planting a tree). You could also install a drainage system to carry away excess water. This would require placing an agricultural drain tile in the bottom of the hole. If the hole is less than six feet across, one tile should do it. If the hole is larger, you may need two lines of tile. The tile should lead away from the tree to a storm sewer or dry well (a hole filled with gravel where the water may drain). Your best bet is to select a tree that grows naturally in wet conditions, such as a river birch (*Betula nigra*).

How do I **plant my tree**?

You've begun, of course, by selecting the proper tree for the site. Next, dig a planting hole approximately two to three times the width of the tree's root ball and only as deep as the root ball. If you are unsure how deep to dig the planting hole, it is always better to dig the hole too shallow. Most of the strong, healthy roots are actually in the top 10 to 12 inches of the root ball. By planting a tree too deep, the roots can suffer from lack of oxygen or too much moisture, which kills the tree in the long run. If you have heavy clay soil, you can actually plant the tree or shrub with the top of the root ball slightly higher than the existing soil.

A crabapple tree (*Malus* spp.) in bloom produces beautiful white, pink, or red flowers. Some even produce fruit suitable for jelly or cider. (Robert J. Huffman/Field Mark Publications)

Remove any inorganic materials from around the root ball such as burlap, metal, and rope. If the root ball is contained in a wire basket, use cutters to loosen or remove the wire from the top eight to 10 inches. However, if the root ball begins to break apart while you are removing burlap or cutting off wire, then stop. With root-bound container ornamentals, cut and spread the roots slightly in order to prevent the roots from girdling the plant. For bareroot ornamentals, try to arrange the root system so that the roots are spread fairly evenly from the plant in its natural growing position.

Finally, don't add compost or any other soil amendments to the hole, just backfill with existing soil. If you have planted the tree in a site compatible to its growing requirements, the tree will thrive. In clay soil, adding compost or peat to the hole may encourage water to collect in the area. Fill the hole halfway up and water thoroughly to be sure any air pockets are eliminated. Then use the remaining backfill to fill the hole, water again, and tamp the soil slightly, making sure not to compact it. There is no need to prune the tree, except to remove dead, broken, or rubbing branches. Mulch the planting hole with approximately three inches of organic mulch, making sure that the mulch is several inches from the trunk. Staking is also unnecessary, unless the tree can't stand upright without support. Finally, don't forget to remove any tags or labels so that they won't girdle the trunk or limbs.

How do I **root-prune** a woody ornamental?

Root-pruning is the practice of digging a trench around a tree or shrub in order to concentrate its root growth in the soil below the top part of the plant. This makes it easier for the tree or shrub to be transplanted. Root-pruning should be done during the woody ornamental's dormancy period: after the leaves have fallen from a deciduous plant in the fall or before bud break in the spring. Otherwise, root-pruning can harm the plant.

In order to root-prune a tree or shrub, mark a circle around the plant at least as far as its drip line, and preferably slightly larger. Dig a trench between 10 and 20 inches deep, depending on the size of the tree. Fill the trench in with the soil that was removed. Then water thoroughly.

I've decided that a tree I planted last year needs to be **moved to a different location** in my yard. Can I just dig it up and move it?

Not if you want to give it the best chance of survival. In order to prepare trees for transplanting they need to be root-pruned at least six months or so before being dug up. This entails digging a narrow trench around the tree just outside its drip line (see previous question). Deciduous trees with trunks larger than one inch in diameter and all evergreens should be moved balled-and-burlapped. Smaller trees and shrubs less than three feet tall may be moved bareroot.

FERTILIZING AND CARE

I have often seen trees around office buildings and in parks that are **heavily mulched**. Is this the correct method for mulching?

No, many trees in public areas are mulched too heavily. This can reduce the amount of oxygen, water, and nutrients available to the tree roots. It also provides a place for rodents to hide while they nibble away at the bark at the base of a tree. When a mulch is applied so deep that it goes over the natural flare at the bottom of a tree, this can cause the rootstock to send up its own shoots. It can also cause girdling of the tree's roots.

Instead, mulch two to three inches deep, starting at six inches from the tree trunk and extending out to the tree's drip line. This will keep weeds down and moisture in, without any negative impact on the tree.

> ## My front yard would be perfect with a large maple tree growing in it. Is there any limit to the size of a tree that can be transplanted there?
>
> In general, the younger (and smaller) the tree, the better chance it has at surviving being transplanted. However, you can transplant trees that are quite large—close to full grown. This should only be done by experts in order to give the tree the best chance of survival, and even then there is no guarantee that the tree will survive the move. Large trees are more likely to suffer major shock from the move.

I have a dozen **tall trees** on my property that I love, except in the fall when their leaves fall. Do I really have to rake them all?

You need to consider a couple of factors. First, what types of trees are they? Maple and oak leaves tend to mat together when they get wet, suffocating everything beneath them. Second, what do you have planted underneath the trees? If the answer is grass, you really do need to rake them or the grass will die. Better yet, run your mower over them. The pulverized leaves are good for the lawn or can be used as a mulch in other areas. And consider converting the areas under the trees to groundcover or mulch. If the trees are planted in beds, you can leave the leaves to break down over the winter, digging them into the soil in the spring.

How often do I need to **water my newly planted tree**?

If your woody ornamental does not receive an inch of rainfall per week, it should be watered to meet this requirement. As with most plants, however, you must be careful not to overwater. Before watering, check the moisture in the root ball as well as the surrounding soil as these will differ. Using a soaker hose or a root feeder attachment (without fertilizer) on a slow trickle will allow the water to penetrate the roots of the tree.

How often do I need to **fertilize my tree**?

Newly planted trees should be fertilized carefully at planting time to ensure new roots are not burned by high nitrogen amounts. A small amount of slow-release fertilizer (no more than one pound of actual nitrogen per 1,000 square feet of planting—see Botany section) can be mixed with the backfill. More established trees have varying needs. Begin by looking at the plant to see if it is growing as vigorously as it should.

Next, check the coloration of the leaves. A common problem in trees is an abnormal yellowing of the leaves. Chlorosis, as it is called, is frequently caused by a lack of soluble iron or manganese in the soil.

In order to determine specific fertilizer needs for your tree, have the tree's soil tested by your local Extension Service office and have a foliar analysis done at the same time. With a foliar analysis, leaf samples from the entire tree are analyzed to determine nutrient deficiencies. Nutrient levels in the soil and the leaves may be different due to the impact of the soil pH level. Between the two, you should be able to determine your tree's needs. All plants require nitrogen for growth so you will need to use a fertilizer high in nitrogen. Phosphorous and potassium needs are more rare and would be indicated by the foliar and soil analysis. Most woodys respond to fertilizers in the 3:1:2 or 3:1:1 ratio.

What is **topdressing**?

Topdressing refers to the application of fertilizer to the soil surface around a plant. It is the least expensive and time-consuming method of fertilization. Fertilizer can be placed by hand (wearing gloves) or using a lawn spreader to ensure an even application. If a woody plant is growing in a lawn, apply fertilizer when the grass is dry to avoid burning the grass. Water the area thoroughly and rinse any excess into the soil to avoid excessive lawn growth.

What is the **drill-hole method** of fertilizing trees?

This method is most commonly used by commercial arborists. Holes are drilled eight to 12 inches deep in the soil around the tree in concentric circles two to three feet apart from one another beginning approximately three feet from the main stem and extending at least three feet outside the tree's drip line. Fertilizer is then distributed equally between the holes. This places granular fertilizer below grass roots and can aerate heavy or compacted soils.

I had a tall screen of arborvitae suffer from ice damage last winter. How can I protect them this year?

Arborvitae and similarly shaped evergreens commonly suffer from ice damage. Their frail branches can't bear the weight of the ice that collects as a result of their thick evergreen foliage and so snap off easily, leaving you with a bare trunk. Next winter, wrap your arborvitae in burlap, with the branches tucked up (as they have a tendency to do naturally). This will prevent water and ice from collecting in the crotches and enable your screen to survive another year.

How do you fertilize a tree with **water-soluble fertilizers**?

The liquid injection method of fertilization injects water-soluble fertilizers into the soil. While professionals use a high-pressure hydraulic sprayer, homeowners use a lance with a canister attached for fertilizer. When attached to a garden hose, water runs through the canister, dissolving the fertilizer and distributing it through the end of the lance. Follow the same instructions for holes as the drill-hole method. The water helps distribute the fertilizer more evenly and ensures the tree absorbs it. Without the fertilizer pellet, the lance can also be used with the garden hose to water the tree roots deeply.

What are the drawbacks of **applying fertilizer** to a tree's leaves?

Foliar application, or applying fertilizer to a tree's leaves, masks problems caused by iron, manganese, and zinc deficiencies but it can't provide all the necessary nutrients a plant needs. Effects of the application are only temporary (and expensive) and should only be used in emergency situations for valuable trees.

What are the drawbacks of **injecting fertilizer into a tree's trunk**?

Trunk implants and injections that place nutrients directly into a tree's xylem layer (beneath the bark) can mask problems caused by iron, manganese, and zinc deficiencies. Also, the act of boring a hole in a tree trunk is difficult, time consuming, and can cause decay, so this method should only be considered when others have failed.

I've seen many of my neighbors **wrapping their evergreens in burlap.** Is this necessary?

Wrapping evergreens in burlap protects their leaves from the drying effects of the wind. Another option is to use an antidessicant that is sprayed on the foliage. However, you're better off selecting a plant that is better suited to your climate. You can also stave off the drying effects of the wind on evergreens and deciduous plants if you water thoroughly until the ground freezes.

TRAINING AND PRUNING

Why are **ornamental plants pruned**?

Woody ornamentals are pruned for a number of reasons. Pruning can preserve the natural shape and size of a plant or can be used to limit it. It can also be used to train a plant such as a hedge or an espaliered tree. Pruning removes broken, diseased, dead, or undesirable limbs, which keeps the plant healthy and removes any danger to humans or buildings. Pruning removes older growth, rejuvenating elderly plants by spurring new growth. Proper pruning enables appropriate air circulation and light penetration to the center of a plant. Pruning can correct or direct the growth of trees by eliminating poor branch structures or weak crotches and removing suckers or water sprouts.

Do I need to **prune my trees and shrubs every year**?

This depends on the type of plant you have and at what point it is in its life cycle. Younger, fast-growing fruit trees may need more pruning to establish a shape that will lend itself to easy picking and reduce the incidence of bugs and disease. Many land-scape trees can be pruned every several years or when they begin to impact structures or trees around them. Hedges should not be pruned, except possibly at the sides, until they reach the desired height. Pruning should be done mainly for the health of the tree—to eliminate weak or tattered limbs, to remove water sprouts and suckers, to generate new growth, or to keep a particular disease such as fire blight in check.

We have a lovely old apple tree that just lost some major limbs in a wind storm. How should the **injured limbs be pruned**?

If only part of the branch has cracked off, remove the rest of the limb almost to the trunk of the tree, leaving a short collar to prevent insects and rot. There is no need to apply tar or concrete to the wound. The tree sap will act as a barrier to insects and rot. If the limb has been knocked down to the point of injuring the trunk, it's best to contact a qualified arborist. You may need to consider removing the tree.

> ## What is a tree sucker or water sprout?
>
> **A** tree sucker is a vigorous, upright branch that originates at the base of a tree. Water sprouts are similar growths that originate on the trunk or main branches of a tree. Both should generally be removed as they can interfere with the shape and proper growth of a tree. Sometimes water sprouts are left on to fill in an empty space on a tree, if they are at a proper height and crotch.

What is **stooling**?

Stooling is a kind of pruning technique commonly used on shrubs. In order to showcase their ornamental bark or leaves, all of the top growth of the shrub is removed to the stump or even to ground level to allow new growth to form at the base of the plant to replace that which has been removed. New growth tends to have better color and texture than older growth.

What is a **central leader**?

The central leader is the central trunk or axis of a tree. A straight, tall central leader is especially important for certain types of fruit trees in order to maintain their shape and promote air and light circulation in the center of a tree.

Should I **stake my tree** and, if so, how do I do it?

A tree needs to be staked when it cannot support itself, but staking should only be viewed as a short-term proposition. Newly planted trees generally don't need staking. However, if the tree is very large or is planted in a highly porous soil such as sand or in an area that receives a lot of wind, it may need extra support. In order to ensure minimum damage to the tree, use flexible stakes and soft material to attach the tree to the stakes. Use only one stake for a tree with a trunk diameter of less than two inches and two stakes placed on opposite sides of the tree for a trunk between two and four inches in diameter. Guy wires (wires inside protective hosing) are used to stake larger trees. These are placed around branch crotches (the angle where the branch meets the tree's trunk).

Stakes should be placed as low on the tree as possible. They should be placed in the ground approximately a foot away from the tree on the same side as the wind blows in order to provide proper support. Be sure to watch the tree carefully to ensure the stakes and attachment are not girdling the tree or overcompensating in terms of support. Most trees don't require staking for more than one season.

How do I **prune my woody ornamental**?

Before beginning to prune, consider what you are trying to accomplish and be sure it is within your ability and comfort zone to do so. Large-scale pruning of shade trees is something that is best left to professionals. For smaller trees and shrubs, keep the function and natural shape of the tree in mind when pruning. Forsythias (*Forsythia* spp.), for example, are often pruned to a round shape like evergreens but their natural form is a more elegant vaselike shape.

An example of how to stake a tree. (Robert J. Huffman/Field Mark Publications)

Start with clean, sharp tools including hand pruners, loppers for larger branches, and pole pruners to reach high branches. All cuts should be made upward to an outward-facing bud with the main goal being to open up the plant. If you thin out deciduous plants rather than cutting them back, you will avoid excessive growth at the top of the plant. Begin by removing dead, broken, diseased, and infested branches. Next, remove branches that cross each other or that are out of synch with the natural or desired shape of the plant. Prune branches that grow toward the crown or center of the plant in order to promote air and light circulation. Remove suckers and water shoots along with any old stubs to eliminate undesirable growth (suckers can grow from a plant's rootstock, resulting in a different shrub from the desired one).

Trees and shrubs have different growth habits and specific uses and therefore require different pruning. When pruning limbs from trees, be sure to retain only those with wide angles of attachment (called crotches) to the tree. These limbs are better able

> ## What is espalier?
>
> **E**spalier is the practice of training trees or shrubs to grow flat against a wall or trellis. Fruit trees are sometimes trained this way in order to maximize yield from a smaller orchard.

to withstand strong winds and storms. Be sure to leave room for lawn mowers and people underneath limbs. The position of a branch on the tree's trunk remains the same throughout the growth of the tree but it might dip closer to the ground as it widens.

Pruning should usually be done during the late winter or early spring, except in the case of spring-flowering woodys, pines, or trees that "bleed" or ooze sap heavily. Spring-flowering plants should be pruned after blooming in order not to disrupt their flowering (no harm done, just less of a show). When pine trees are pruned in order to encourage thicker growth, this should be done when their candles (new growth) are done growing but aren't quite firm. Trees that bleed can be pruned in late spring to early summer, after their first flush of growth. All trees and shrubs should be pruned in relatively dry weather, to limit the spread of disease.

What is the difference between **cutting back and thinning**?

Both refer to pruning of shrubs and trees, but with different purposes and results. When thinning an overgrown shrub, remove whole branches, which allows air and light to reach the center of the plant. Some new growth may occur as a result. Cutting back stems to side buds forces new growth, encouraging the plant to branch out. Cutting back hard means removing a great deal of the branch while shearing just occurs at the tips of the shrub.

How can I **force a forsythia branch into bloom**?

When the buds on a forsythia shrub begin to swell (in the Midwest this generally occurs in late March or early April), remove several branches by cutting them on a 45 degree angle. There is no need to crush the bottom of the branch. Place the branches in a container of warm water and place it in a sunny window. The branches should flower within the next few days. In general, the closer the shrub is to blooming when cut, the faster it blooms indoors. If you'd like to preserve the flowers as long as possible, keep the blooming branches in a cool room, away from direct sunlight. Other flowering shrubs or trees can be forced as well, including the popular pussy willow (*Salix discolor*), magnolias (*Magnolia* spp.), apple and crabapple trees (*Malus* spp.), and the *Prunus* genus, which includes plums and cherry trees.

How can I **create topiary** from my shrubs?

Before starting, be sure you understand and can execute the basics of pruning given previously. Topiary, or the practice of shearing plants into shapes or verdant likenesses of people and animals, requires a high degree of pruning skill to create elaborate shapes. Beginners can try their hand at shaping small globes of boxwood (*Buxus* spp.) or even a woody herb such as rosemary (*Rosmarinus officinalis*). Choose an inexpensive plant specimen so that your wallet won't feel the heat of your early attempts. Shoot for a basic shape like a globe or one that isn't too far from the natural shape of the plant. Keep your desired shape in mind and review the plant from all sides as you work. Prune in early spring (or according to the plant's needs) but feel free to remove extra growth up until fall. As you become more confident in your pruning you can attempt more complex shapes.

What is **pleaching**?

The technique known as pleaching encourages trees or treelike shrubs to form a thick screen or hedge by intertwining their branches. The result looks like a hedge on legs.

I planted a lovely red-stemmed dogwood several years ago but its **stem color seems to be fading** from year to year. What do I do?

The beautiful red stems of *Cornus alba* bring life to a winter landscape. The brightest stem color appears on new growth. In order to keep your dogwood lovely, it must be pruned regularly. You may choose to cut the shrub back hard every year in the early spring. The other option is to place the shrub on a three-year pruning cycle. Every year remove one-third of the stems to the ground, rotating every year. By leaving most of the shrub alone, you allow the dogwood to retain a more natural shape.

When should I **prune my French hydrangea bushes**?

French or bigleaf hydrangeas (*Hydrangea macrophylla*) flower on the previous year's wood. Therefore, in order to ensure you aren't removing buds for the following year, you should prune your hydrangeas immediately after flowering. If you've missed that opportunity, not to worry. Pruning for these beautiful shrubs should only be done every few years.

How do I **dry hydrangea blooms**?

The best hydrangea for drying is *Hydrangea macrophylla,* although any mopheaded hydrangea will do. Hydrangeas for drying should be cut at the end of the growing season. Otherwise, their petals will shrivel when drying. Try to cut them later in the day,

> ### What is coppicing?
>
> The practice of coppicing was traditionally used in managed forests in England to maximize the amount of wood that could be harvested. Rather than being pruned to a central leader or other shape, a tree was left alone to produce a cluster of small trunks which were then harvested every 20 years or so.

after the dew has dried on the plant. Place them in a vase without water and allow them to dry. That's it! There is no need to hang them upside down.

What is **pollarding**?

Pollarding is a method of pruning in which all of a tree's branches are cut off, leaving only a stub from which new growth emerges. This technique is used frequently in France for ornamental effect.

ROSES

I ordered several **rose bushes** from a reputable catalog but when they arrived they just looked like a bunch of sticks. Why?

Bareroot roses (*Rosa* spp.) have to be shipped in a dormant state since they aren't rooted in soil. Many plants, rose canes included, are shipped in their dormant state so that they aren't damaged and don't perish in transit. A plant at the height of its growth would require water, sunlight, and food—all of which are difficult to come by in a cardboard box. These roses should be planted as soon as possible.

I received several **rose bushes** as a housewarming gift. When can I plant them?

Bareroot roses (rose canes shipped in their dormant state) should be planted in the early spring in colder areas, early fall with milder winter areas, and in the winter in warm areas. They should be planted as soon as possible (within a week of receipt). If you can't plant them immediately, store the canes inside their packing materials in a cool but frost-free place and keep the roots moist. Roses planted in containers will establish best if planted in spring or fall, rather than the heat of summer. Potted roses should be soaked immediately and placed outside in a sunny area until you are ready to plant. If given your druthers, plant your rose bush on an overcast, misty day. Sun and wind can dry out the plant.

My rosebush says that it is **budded.** What does that mean?

This term refers to which root system your rose grows from. A budded rose joins a hardy rootstock (usually of a wild rose) to a more fragile hybrid tea or climber at a point called the bud union (swollen knob). Otherwise, a rose is grown on its own root system.

How do I **plant my rose bush**?

Start by soaking bareroot roses in water for several hours. The planting site should be located in an area that receives at least four hours (six is better) of sun per day, plenty of air circulation, and good drainage. If you live in a colder region, you should consider placing the rose bush in a sheltered area to protect it from cold winter winds. Dig a hole slightly larger than the root ball.

The planting depth of a budded rose is determined by your hardiness zone. If you live in the colder regions (zone 6 and colder), the bud union should be planted just below soil level to provide protection to the plant from freezing temperatures. If you live in warmer temperatures (zone 8 and warmer), the bud union should be planted just above soil level in order to more easily prune any undesirable suckers that spring from the wild rose rootstock. Gently tease the roots apart so that they have access to the soil. Some gardeners add a small amount of bonemeal when planting but it is not necessary. If you do so, mix the bonemeal in with the soil at the bottom of the hole and avoid chemical fertilizers that may burn the roots. Mix in compost with the backfill soil to bring the rose to its proper depth. Water the bush thoroughly and add more soil as it settles. If the weather is still below freezing, mound compost around the base of the bush to protect it.

How can I achieve the largest possible blooms on my **hybrid tea rose**?

In order to produce large blooms on hybrid teas such as *Rosa* 'Alexander', *R.* 'Baronne Edmond de Rothschild', and *R.* 'Peace', you should remove all buds except the terminal bud (the bud at the end of the growing tip of the stem) when the buds are very small. This practice, known as disbudding, ensures the cane's energy is directed toward producing one beautiful rose.

Hybrid tea roses have long pointed buds and large fragrant flowers that come in all shades and colors. They are ideal for cutting. (Robert J. Huffman/Field Mark Publications)

What is a **rose standard**?

A rose standard or rose tree is a cultivated rose that has been grafted on top of the tall, straight cane of a tougher rose. The result looks like a topiary. These types of roses require pruning of the top in order to retain a symmetrical shape.

When do I **prune my roses**?

A good rule of thumb is to prune when the forsythia in your area are in bloom. If you don't have a forsythia or don't know what they look like, examine the branches of your rose bush. When the buds are slightly swollen and reddish colored, you may begin pruning them.

How do I **prune my roses**?

The main goal of pruning is to promote a disease and mildew-free environment by allowing air to circulate freely in the center of the plant. A pruned plant also conforms to landscape standards of shape and size. While different types of roses require slightly different approaches, the basic steps to rose pruning are the same. Begin with the right tools. You will need thick gloves, preferably to your elbow. You'll also need bypass pruners (which will cut the canes cleanly instead of crushing them) as well as a pair of loppers for thicker wood. All cuts should be made at about a 45 degree angle just above an outward facing bud. This will promote air circulation in the center of the plant by ensuring new growth is directed away from the plant. For most roses, you will also remove at least one-third of the plant. Remember that most roses are underpruned, rather than overpruned.

The hybrid tea rose is one of the best varieties for cutting. (Robert J. Huffman/Field Mark Publications)

332

Start by pruning any dead or diseased wood that looks black, brown, or mottled. After pruning diseased wood, be sure to clean your pruners with a diluted bleach solution so that you avoid spreading the disease to other plants. Canes that cross each other should also be removed to eliminate injury caused by the limbs rubbing against one another. Any canes that have been damaged during the winter should be pruned just above the injury. Next, cut away rose hips and any blooms left from the previous year. Finally, remove any thin canes. Thicker canes produce the biggest blooms.

If you have a rose standard, be sure to prune the plant so that it remains symmetrical. On a hybrid tea rose, the largest blooms grow on new canes close to its base. So remove all canes except a few and cut these back to around a foot above the ground. Climbing roses should be tied to a trellis or fence with their canes bent downward in order to spur blooms all along the canes. Shrub roses should have all of their branches pruned by at least a third and be trimmed to retain their vase shape.

Are there any **drought-tolerant roses**?

All plants require some care but for a rose, the rugosa rose (*Rosa rugosa*) comes as close to low-maintenance as possible. It thrives in zones 2 through 10 and is drought tolerant.

Should **miniature roses** just be used as houseplants?

Actually, although they may be grown inside with extra care, miniature roses such as *Rosa* 'Black Jade', *R.* 'Meilucca', and *R.* 'Fire Princess' are best grown outdoors where they can receive enough sun and air circulation to keep them happy.

What are some plants that serve as attractive **companions for red roses**?

Weigela (*Weigela* spp.), butterfly bush (*Buddleia* spp.), English lavender (*Lavandula angustifolia*), iris (*Iris* spp.), catmint (*Nepeta* spp.), pinks (*Dianthus* spp.), and peony (*Paeonia* spp.) combine beautifully with red roses.

Are there any **roses that are native to the United States**?

Several roses are native to the United States, including Virginia rose (*Rosa virginiana*), which has rose-colored flowers and can grow up to six feet tall. Pasture rose (*Rosa carolina*) is a lower-growing shrub, while prairie rose (*Rosa setigera*) has arching, far-flung canes.

333

Thousands of varieties of roses have been produced from wild rose stock, including this example. (Robert J. Huffman/Field Mark Publications)

What do **strawberries and roses** have in common?

Both strawberries and roses are part of the *Rosaceae* family. Other members of this plant family include raspberries, blackberries, cherries, plums, apples, pears, peaches, and apricots. They are all highly favored by the Japanese beetle.

What is the difference between **old garden roses and modern roses**?

Old garden roses are those that were in existence before 1867 and all species of wild roses. Modern roses are roses that have been introduced since 1867.

What are a **rose's thorns** used for?

The thorns on a rose (and those of other plants) are actually branches that have modified over many generations to deter plant-eating animals. The thorns on a cactus are another good example of this modification.

Which roses are best grown for their **hips**?

The rugosa rose (*Rosa rugosa*) and dog rose (*Rosa canina*) produce excellent hips (the base of the flower left after the petals fall off). Rose hips are an excellent source of vitamin C and have a citrusy flavor of their own. They are often used to make tea. Hips are best harvested following a light frost.

I'd love to grow roses, but do I need to use a lot of chemicals to keep them looking their best?

No. In order to grow roses organically, you need to practice healthy gardening techniques. The ideal of a rose garden filled with nothing but roses can lead to disease and insect infestation, as is true of any monoculture. Instead, intersperse the roses with other types of plants such as catmint (*Nepeta* spp.), English lavender (*Lavandula angustifolia*), or lamb's ear (*Stachys byzantina*), as gray-leaved plants provide a wonderful foil for the dark green rose bushes. Plant the roses in a sunny location, unfettered by buildings or walls that can cut down on circulation and create a haven for disease. Keep the compost coming—roses like to be well fed to produce a lot of blooms. Water lavishly at the base of the plant, keeping water off the leaves. The exception is for insects: a strong squirt of the hose can take care of aphid infestations in a hurry. At the first sign of black spot, remove diseased foliage promptly. Finally, chose a rugosa (*Rosa rugosa*) or rugosa hybrid rose as they tend to be more disease resistant.

What is **hilling**?

Hilling or mounding roses is the practice of mounding dirt onto the crown of a rose bush in order to protect its bud union from freezing. Hilling is usually done after a hard frost, and only in cold areas. In fact, winter protection in warm areas can be harmful to your roses. But hilling is a relatively easy method to protect your tender roses in cold climates. Toss compost, topsoil, or wood chips onto the center of the bush, allowing the mulching material to form a cone approximately six to eight inches high. Remove the mulch in the spring.

Should roses be **pruned year-round**?

You should stop pruning your roses in late summer (August in northern areas). If you prune after this time (even when cutting roses for the table), you encourage new growth that won't be hardened off in time for winter. The result is a quick death for all those tender new shoots.

What do I need to do for my roses at the **end of the growing season**?

If you live in a cold climate and are growing tender roses, you may want to consider hilling them (see question above). In any climate, do rake up and get rid of the fallen leaves and plant debris. This reduces the chance of overwintering any disease spores or insects on your bushes. Don't prune, however, as you will encourage growth that will not have the chance to harden up before winter hits.

LAWNS, GROUNDCOVERS, AND ORNAMENTAL GRASSES

ESTABLISHING A LAWN

I needed to patch some bare spots in my lawn but the hardware store only had something called a cool-season grass mixture. What is a cool-season grass?

Cool-season grasses are winter hardy in regions north of zone 7. They remain evergreen for most of the year, but tend to become brown and parched during particularly hot weather. For this reason, they are not normally used in warm areas of the country. In order to properly maintain a cool-season lawn, it is important to mow the grass at a high setting and to use a mixture of different types of grasses when seeding it. Included among the different varieties of cool-season grasses are Kentucky bluegrass, fine-leafed fescues, and perennial ryegrass.

I just moved to the Southwest and was told that I'll need to plant warm-season grasses instead of the Kentucky bluegrass that I've always used. Is there anything I should know about warm-season grasses before I start work on my lawn?

As you probably guessed from the name, warm-season grasses are better able to handle hot climates than the ever-popular Kentucky bluegrass used in more northern climates. Warm-season grasses go brown and dormant in cool weather but are hardy enough to stand up to the heat in zones 7 and south. Warm-season grasses include zoysia, bermuda, St. Augustine, carpet grass, and bahia. They are more coarse in texture than cool-season grasses and are usually mowed short. Such grasses are also sometimes sold as an alternative grass in cooler regions of the country (especially grasses like zoysia) because they stand up to heavy foot traffic, but up north you are better off choosing a cool-season grass suited to your yard.

I live in the Midwest and have kids who love to play in the yard all day. It's great for them but is proving to be a little hard on my lawn. What are the most **durable types of grasses** to stand up to the hard play of my kids?

Not all grasses are created equal for maximum durability, so you do have a number of different types of grasses to choose from. New cultivars of tall fescue are hardy under heavy wear as well as drought. They also survive some shade and stay green throughout the year. Improved (as opposed to common or unimproved) perennial ryegrass also survives wear and tear. In warmer regions of the country, zoysia is a good choice for a high-use lawn.

I'm amazed at the way my lawn has started to creep into some of my garden beds. How do **lawn grasses reproduce** and spread so quickly?

Lawn grasses reproduce by setting seed, although sometimes lawn grasses do not produce viable seed (seed that will germinate) due to a variety of factors, such as sterile seed or less than ideal conditions. Lawn grasses also spread through new plants that grow from the crown of the grass plant. These are known as tillers. Some lawn grasses spread determinedly through underground creeping stems called rhizomes or aboveground creeping stems called stolons. This enables them to quickly fill in bare spots.

I'm planning on starting the lawn at my new house from sod as opposed to seed. But the lawn company I contracted with offered the option of starting with sprigs or plugs. What is the difference between **a sprig and a plug**?

Although it may sound confusing, the difference between a sprig and a plug is actually quite simple. A sprig is an individual bareroot grass plant while a plug is a tuft of sod. Warm-season grasses can be sold as sprigs and plugs in order to start lawns. Cool-season grasses are only available as seed or sod.

Some people have told me that the best way to start a lawn is using seed, while I know other folks who swear that sod is the best way to go. What are some of the advantages and disadvantages of **seeding a lawn**?

When it comes to deciding between seeding and sodding, there are a number of good reasons to start a lawn from seed. Seeding a lawn is cheaper than sodding it. You also have a larger selection of grass types to choose from so you can be sure to find grasses that are well suited to the particular conditions of your yard. If you take some care in selecting the grasses and in the initial planting and upkeep required when seeding a lawn, the results can look fabulous. A seeded lawn is also often less susceptible to

Sod is delivered rolled or stacked flat. It is best to lay sod as soon as possible, since it will dry out quickly. (Robert J. Huffman/Field Mark Publications)

problems like disease, insect infestation, and drought since it is allowed to establish a good, healthy root system.

Seeding a lawn, however, is much more labor intensive than sodding a lawn both in terms of initial planting and early maintenance on the newly seeded bed. Newly sown grass seed requires consistent and adequate moisture, constant vigilance against weeds, and the application of a fine mulch to protect the seed and seedlings from birds, erosion, and heat. Seed also takes longer to establish. In addition, in both cool and warm areas of the country, there is usually just a small window of time each year during which seeding can be done in order to take advantage of moist soil and cooler temperatures. As a result, seeding a lawn can often have poor results, especially in areas that receive a lot of use or are subject to erosion.

I just had my quarter-acre property seeded with grass. In order to achieve the best results—a lush, beautiful, weed-free lawn—how do I care for my **newly seeded lawn**?

The initial seeding of a lawn can be quite labor intensive. Proper maintenance in the early weeks is crucial to ensure that your efforts yield the desired effect. During the first several weeks after being seeded, a lawn should be kept evenly moist. Ideally, it should be lightly sprinkled a few times each day, but the initial application of a straw mulch should help to keep the seed moist until it germinates. Once the young seedlings are between one and two inches tall, half of the straw mulch used to keep the seed in place and moist should be removed to allow more light and air to reach the young seedlings.

After the lawn is two to three inches tall, it should be carefully mowed for the first time using a mower with a sharp blade. A dull blade can damage or even uproot the tender seedlings. The goal with the first mowing is to remove a little less than half of the grass blade. Just prior to this mowing, the lawn can be fertilized with a high nitrogen fertilizer applied at half-rate and watered-in well to prevent burning. Weed killers (even organic ones) should not be used until the lawn has been mowed several times. In the meantime, careful handpulling of broadleaf weeds will reduce competition for water and nutrients and discourage perennial weeds from becoming established.

We've just moved into our newly built house and would like to convert our muddy, construction-wreaked lot into a lush, green carpet as soon as possible. It's late fall and we'd like to get our lawn going immediately. What are the advantages and disadvantages of **sodding a lawn**?

Sod has many advantages over seed, in the right situation. For a barren lot like yours, sod provides instant gratification since it looks like a lawn immediately. Unlike seed, which needs warmer temperatures to germinate and establish, sod can be put down anytime during the year, as long as the soil beneath it can be worked. Sod can also be walked on almost immediately and tends to "take" better on slopes. However, sodding is much more expensive than seeding and is also backbreaking work, something you should keep in mind if you are considering doing it yourself. Finally, sod is not available in as wide a variety of grasses as seed, so if you have many different types of conditions on your property, seed is probably your best bet.

I've just had my lawn **newly sodded**. What do I need to do to ensure it becomes well established?

Initial care and maintenance of a newly sodded lawn is actually quite simple. A newly sodded lawn can be mowed as soon as it needs it, although you need to ensure you are removing no more than one-third of the height at a time. It should be watered daily in order to encourage the root system to become established. Once the sod has taken root, your lawn can be fertilized according to an established lawn maintenance schedule.

What kind of **lawn grass** is durable enough for my pets and kids to play on and still look good?

There are many durable species of grass available. Choosing the correct one for your yard depends on where you live. If you live in a southern region, zoysia grass is extremely durable and fairly easy to maintain with few problems. Zoysia tenuifolia also looks attractive enough with its fine texture. It is the least winter hardy of the zoysia species, however. In the North, all zoysia grass turns brown in the winter with some cultivars even dying in cold temperatures. In cooler areas, a mixture of different strains of Kentucky bluegrass, fine-leafed fescues, and improved perennial ryegrass results in a fairly durable lawn if your lot is sunny. With a shaded lot, a mixture of shade-tolerant cultivars is necessary.

I'm interested in reducing the amount of time I spend maintaining my lawn but would like it to look attractive. I've heard of something called an **ecolawn**. What kinds of grasses are planted in an ecolawn?

If you'd like to minimize the amount of time you spend caring for your grass or would just like a beautiful alternative to the usual grass mixtures, you may want to investigate the possibility of converting your lawn to an ecolawn. An ecolawn is planted with nonaggressive grasses and broadleaf flowering plants that tolerate being mowed regularly. Good nonaggressive grasses (so that they don't overtake the flowering plants) include Kentucky bluegrass, perennial ryegrass, and red and tall fescue. Plants such as common yarrow (*Achillea millefolium*), English daisy (*Bellis perennis*), strawberry clover (*Trifolium fragiferum*), and white clover (*Trifolium repens*) add color, texture, and life to an ecolawn.

In terms of upkeep, an established ecolawn requires little maintenance to keep it looking good. Get a mulching mower or allow the lawn to "keep its clips" (leave grass clippings on the lawn). This provides a regular source of nitrogen to the lawn, which in turn discourages weeds, pests, and disease. Watering is fairly simple. An ecolawn needs to receive only about one and a half inches of water each month during its peak growing period. Other than that, it is fairly happy with whatever rain falls. An ecolawn provides its owner with an enormous amount of enjoyment for the small amount of time invested in it.

LAWN CARE

I just had automatic lawn sprinklers installed but am unsure about when to program the system to run. What is the best time of day to **water my lawn**?

An automatic sprinkler system is a good investment if you can afford it since you can ensure your lawn is watered regularly, adequately, and efficiently. The best time of day to water a lawn is in the early morning. This gives the lawn enough moisture to make it through the heat of the day, while ensuring it is not damp during the cooler evening hours when it can succumb to disease. If this is impractical, the second best time of day to water a lawn is during the evening or nighttime hours. Although this does make the lawn (like any plant) more susceptible to disease and fungi, most home lawns do not fall prey to these problems. They occur with greater frequency on golf courses and in other commercial areas. Although you can water your lawn during the day, this can be somewhat wasteful as the water evaporates quickly due to the sun and wind.

I'd like to have a good-looking lawn this year but am puzzled by the variety of recommendations I've had on how often I should water it. What is the latest recommendation on how frequently I should **water my lawn**?

The latest recommendation from agricultural schools and Extension Service offices is to water lawns lightly and frequently (daily for a short period of time). In order to stay green, lawns require about an inch of water a week from human and heavenly sources. However, in deciding how frequently to water your lawn, consider water availability in your region (that precious water might prove useful elsewhere in your garden), how your lawn is used (lawns that receive heavy use usually need more watering), and how important it is to you to keep your lawn green (this year, it sounds like you're interested in keeping it green). If you spend a lot of time away from your home during the summer or are interested in reducing your water bill, you might consider letting your lawn go dormant—it will usually revive with rain— or using drought-resistant grasses.

I'm a new homeowner and have never had to care for a lawn before. My neighbor mows his lawn twice a week but he cuts it so low that you can see the soil underneath the turf. How often is it really necessary to **cut my lawn**?

Although your neighbor may be mowing frequently enough, it sounds like he is mowing his lawn too closely. A lawn should be mowed as often as it needs to be so that each time you cut it, you are not removing more than one-third of it. Removing more than one-third of the lawn at a time stresses it and can lead to problems with disease and weeds, besides giving the appearance of a bad haircut. Different kinds of grasses

343

> **I didn't have time to mow my lawn before it rained recently and then the rain came for three days straight and is still coming down. The lawn looks lush but it's so tall, I can't see outside my window. Can I mow my lawn as soon as the rain stops?**
>
> Although your lawn may really need it, it is really best to wait until the lawn has dried thoroughly before mowing it. If you mow your lawn immediately following a rain, you can have a couple of problems. Your lawn mower—even if its blade is sharp—has a tendency to chew up the grass when it is wet. In addition, those wet clippings quickly clog up the mower, slowing you down and possibly damaging the mower. Finally, just as with the rest of your garden, working around wet plants can encourage the spread of disease. So it's best to just wait a day or so before venturing out.

require different mowing heights. Cool-season grasses should be kept at around three inches high while warm-season grasses should be kept at around an inch high.

My old diehard bag mower finally gave out, so I went out and purchased a mulching mower. Unfortunately, in the time it took me to replace my lawnmower, the lawn grew several inches and the clippings the mower left behind after mowing were very thick. Do I need to rake them up?

The main idea behind a mulching mower is to eliminate the need to rake or bag clippings. In letting your lawn keep its clips, you're providing it with a free source of nitrogen (as opposed to expensive fertilizers) and you're reducing the amount of curbside waste you generate. You should consider mowing more frequently to decrease the amount of clippings you generate as well as to encourage a healthy lawn. However, when you are unable to mow more frequently and the cut grass is very thick, you should collect those clippings for your compost pile using a rake or whatever works for you. Heavy clippings can damage or kill the lawn.

I've never had to take care of a lawn before so the whole thing is new to me. I understand that I need to purchase a mower to cut the grass but what does it mean to edge a lawn?

Edging refers to the creation and maintenance of a fine edge between the sidewalk and the sod. Normally this is done using a tool with a rotating, sharp blade, although you

Typical lawn care includes mowing the lawn to an appropriate height. (Robert J. Huffman/Field Mark Publications)

can also use a spade if you have a very small edge to maintain. Edgers can be manual (quite backbreaking), electric, or gas-powered.

I just **edged my lawn** for the first time this spring and it was a lot of work! Is there an easier way to do it?

Unfortunately, no. There are gas- and electric-powered edgers that can make it easier, but usually that first edging of the season takes a bit of effort since your lawn continues to grow over the winter. If your lawn has not been edged in years, it can take even longer and is best attempted first using a spade to find the edge of the sidewalk or walkway. The best suggestion for maintaining a nicely edged lawn with the least amount of effort is to keep at it. Edging every couple of weeks should keep that lawn at bay.

Although my lawn is in pretty good shape overall, I'd like to eliminate some of the bare spots that have appeared and thicken up some of the thinner areas. When is the best time to **reseed my lawn**?

The best time to reseed your lawn depends on whether you have a cool-season lawn or a warm-season lawn, and when you have time to do it. Cool-season grasses grow best in cool weather, so it is best to plant these in late summer or early fall. Warm-season grasses become stressed in winter, so they are normally planted in the spring in order to have the summer to grow and thrive. These times are recommended in order to achieve the best results for your reseeding project. However, with careful monitoring for moisture levels and the use of a fine mulch to keep the seedbed cool and protected, you can reseed in early spring in cool-season areas.

I haven't had time to properly maintain my lawn over the past several years and it's really showing it. There are weeds and bare spots everywhere and the grass that does exist looks pretty sickly. How do I **renovate my lawn**?

To decide whether or not it is worthwhile to renovate your lawn, you need to take a close look at it. If your lawn has more than 50 percent good grass (or more grass than weeds), it is worth renovating. If your lawn has more weeds than grass (and it sounds like your lawn is in this category), it may be easiest over the long haul to start all over again. The best method for renovating a lawn is to overseed it. If you live in a region with cool-season grasses, renovation should take place in the fall, before the first frost. If you live in an area with warm-season grasses, renovate your lawn in the spring.

Actual renovation of a lawn is fairly simply but it can be troublesome if you have a lot of weeds. The first step in renovating a lawn is to mow it low—roughly half its normal height. This will allow the seed to make contact with the ground. Next, you need to remove as many weeds as possible from your lawn. If you have a small lawn, this should be fairly easy (if labor intensive) by handpulling and employing tools like an asparagus knife for weeds with taproots. If you have a larger area, you may wish to dig up large areas of weeds. Follow the directions in the question on patching a lawn (on page 348) to reseed the area. For a small lawn, follow up with a vigorous raking to loosen the thatch. For a larger lawn, you might consider renting an aerator to make the job speedy and thorough.

You're now ready to overseed. Seed the area at the suggested rate on the seed packaging. You can either use a drop spreader or spread the seed by hand. Cross the lawn twice, moving from side to side and up and down to ensure even coverage and adequate seed. Then topdress the lawn with a thin layer of compost (about a half-inch). Water well and continue to keep the area well watered until the grass comes up. If it is dry, you may be watering daily but it is important to keep the soil moist to achieve the best germination rate. Don't mow the lawn until the new grass is the usual mowing height.

I have a thatch problem but am unsure about what tool to purchase to get rid of it. What is the best method for **removing thatch** from my lawn?

There are a number of methods for removing thatch from the lawn, and they vary in their effectiveness. You may wish to purchase a dethatching rake or rent a dethatching machine, both of which have special tines to pull the thatch from the lawn. The rakes

> ## My lawn care service says I need a particular kind of expensive product to rid my lawn of thatch. What is thatch?
>
> Although thatch often gets a bad rap, a little bit of thatch is actually a good thing and a natural part of a healthy lawn. Thatch is dead organic material that forms between the soil and the grass of a lawn. It develops when organic material accumulates at a higher rate than it decomposes. Some varieties of grass produce more organic material (resulting in thatch) than others do. Too much fertilizer, overwatering, and soil compaction can also cause thatch to accumulate. But a thatch layer of less than an inch helps protect a lawn from extremes in temperature and heavy use. If thatch has accumulated past this point, the lawn retains less water and fertilizer and becomes stressed, making it an easy target for disease and insect invasions.

are pulled across the lawn at different angles, and they require a good amount of labor for large lawns. However, current research has shown that dethatching does not actually do much to reduce the amount of thatch. Core aeration is considered a better alternative.

I noticed my neighbor had little plugs of sod that had been uprooted and thrown all over his lawn. When I asked him about it, he said that he'd had his lawn aerated. What does that mean?

The process of core aeration removes plugs of soil from the turf. This causes the remaining grass roots to grow vigorously in order to replace the pulled turf, which in turn spurs plant growth. Core aeration also helps compacted turf by enabling water, nutrients, and air to reach existing plant roots. Another important benefit of core aeration is that the plugs, when broken up and distributed, provide a topdressing to the lawn that aids in decomposition of thatch as well as providing a source of nutrients. There are a variety of tools available for aerating your lawn, ranging from aerating machines to rototillers used with an aerating attachment.

Oh no! I had a problem with turf compaction and was told to try aerating my lawn. I just completed the job and it looks pretty bad. Did I do it wrong?

No, unfortunately your lawn just has to look bad at first in order to look better later. The process of pulling up cores or plugs of turf can cause the remaining turf to look a little rough. Consider overseeding your lawn and applying a light topdressing of com-

Sowing grass seed is only one part of patching a lawn. (Robert J. Huffman/Field Mark Publications)

post. Be sure to keep your lawn watered and it will look better than before in just a few weeks' time.

After all the time, money, and effort I've spent pampering it, I've discovered **brown spots** on my lawn. What should I do?

It can be aggravating to find spots marring a perfect sea of green grass when you have spent a lot of time on it. If you're a new dog owner or your lawn serves as a potty stop for neighborhood pooches, you'll find dark green patches where a dog has "watered" your lawn. These eventually turn brown. If you see the dog doing its business, immediately run water over the spot to dilute the ammonia that causes the burn. Otherwise, you might consider digging up the brown patches and reseeding them. Or you might consider turning your eye to other parts of your yard and letting the dogs have their day.

Is there a proper method for **patching a bare spot in my lawn**?

Patching bare spots is part of the regular maintenance of a lawn, since inevitably some bare patches will appear. Begin by removing any dead grass or perennial weeds in the spot. If the spot is low, add soil to meet the soil level surrounding it. If soil isn't needed, scratch at the surface of the spot with a rake to loosen the soil. Then broadcast seed of the same variety or varieties that are currently in the lawn fairly thickly. Rake the seed in, apply a light mulch such as straw, and water thoroughly. Keep the spot moist until the seedlings are established. You may also have success with a new dry seeding medium composed of mulch and seed that can be purchased at nurseries and garden centers.

What are some nonchemical means of **reducing lawn weeds**?

If you are establishing a new lawn, you can reduce the number of lawn weeds by making sure all weeds are removed (via smothering or handweeding) prior to installation of the new lawn. Make sure you select a grass that is recommended for your area and plant it at the proper time of the year. Cut the lawn to its recommended height and make sure it is regularly fertilized and watered to ensure the grass doesn't become stressed. A healthy lawn can beat out any weed competition.

I'm really not all that interested in lawn care but I do like to have a nice green lawn. This summer, however, I will be out of town for several months. What are the pros and cons of **letting a lawn go dormant**?

A dormant lawn turns brown, signaling that growth has slowed or stopped. In allowing your lawn to go dormant, you eliminate or reduce water and fertilizer usage as well as the cost and time associated with watering and fertilizing. However, for many people, a brown lawn isn't as aesthetically pleasing as a green one. A dormant lawn can also fall prey to insects, disease, and weeds.

What are some **organic methods of fertilizing** my lawn?

Many synthetic organic fertilizers such as ammonium nitrate, ammonium sulfate, and urea have a high potential for burning the lawn, so they need to be applied at a low rate and watered in well. Milorganite is a natural, organic, slow-release fertilizer that has far less potential for burning. Other options are processed manure and sifted compost that can be spread evenly over the lawn just prior to a rain. Using a mulching mower or leaving your clippings on the lawn can also provide extra nitrogen to the lawn.

My lawn care company is offering a special deal if I sign up to have my lawn fertilized every two weeks, starting in late summer. When should I **fertilize my lawn**?

It sounds as though your lawn care company is probably offering you more fertilizing than is necessary and certainly at the wrong time of year. If you live in a region where cool-season grasses are predominate, fertilize in the spring and again in fall to take advantage of two periods when your lawn will be undergoing growth spurts. In warm-season areas, fertilize just as the lawn "greens up" (late spring), then again several weeks later.

I have read a great deal about the benefits of a good leaf mulch for many plants. Why can't I just leave my **fall leaves** on the lawn to provide extra fertilizer over the winter?

While leaf mulch is certainly a good thing for most plants, including lawns, letting your leaves lie on the lawn over the winter will smother and kill the grass as the leaves become wet and matted down. Before the leaves become wet in the fall, run over them with your mower. The shredded leaves can be raked into the lawn, placed in the compost pile, or set under plants as a mulch.

Why should I leave **clover** growing in my lawn?

Up until the 1950s and the heyday of home chemical use, clover was considered a desirable thing in a lawn. Clover seed was actually sold by itself or mixed with grass seed for beautiful lawns. While clover does not stand up to heavy foot traffic, it mows well and feels good underfoot. And although lawn care companies will tell you differently, the presence of clover (*Melilotus, Trifolium* spp.) is actually a sign of a healthy lawn. Clover, like peas and other legumes, plays host to beneficial microorganisms that convert nitrogen from the air into a form that plants can use. So keeping clover in your lawn can help keep your Kentucky bluegrass looking good. From an aesthetic perspective, clover also adds a bit of interest to your yard with its fragrant pink or white flowers and beautiful leaves.

I have a small yard with a lot of sun and very few shade trees. Why do I have **moss in my lawn**?

Moss commonly grows in heavily shaded areas. But it also invades areas where the soil is not fertile or is acidic. It can grow if there is poor drainage in an area, limited air circulation, or compacted soil. To reduce the incidence of moss, be sure you are using a shade-tolerant species of grass and mowing high enough to discourage competition. You should also do a soil test to check the pH level and aerate the lawn if it has become compacted. Finally, if you are unable to grow grass well in the area, consider planting a shade-tolerant groundcover.

I'd like to spend time on the rest of my yard, instead of my lawn. How can I keep a **low-maintenance lawn**?

Begin by reducing the amount of lawn you have to begin with. Lawns just require more upkeep than other parts of the garden. Then eliminate lawn in hard-to-mow spaces

A garden such as this one, which replaces a traditional grass lawn, has many advantages, not the least of which is that it doesn't need mowing. (Robert J. Huffman/Field Mark Publications)

such as around trees and shrubs and on steep banks; use groundcovers or mulch rather than lawn. For other areas, eliminate as many difficult angles as possible by using broad curves around beds and employing the use of a mowing strip (bricks or other material laid side by side to create a strip for one wheel of the mower). Finally, learn to live with a few weeds and reduce watering in the summer or let the lawn go dormant.

GROUNDCOVERS

What is a **groundcover**?

A groundcover is loosely defined as any low-growing plant that spreads to cover the ground, looks attractive for at least a season, and keeps down the weeds. Any plant can be used as a groundcover, including low-growing shrubs, perennials, annuals, ornamental grasses, and the usual ivies.

Which is more expensive to maintain, **groundcover or lawn**?

Although groundcover can be more expensive to install initially, it does not require the same weekly upkeep as a lawn (mowing, edging, fertilizing, and watering).

What are some advantages to **substituting groundcovers for a grass lawn**?

Groundcovers are easier on the environment than lawns since less fertilizer and water are required to keep it looking good and no power tools are necessary to maintain it. Groundcovers also provide a yard with a distinctive look. For shady lawns, groundcovers are the perfect solution.

What are some **disadvantages of groundcover**?

The initial investment in groundcover can be quite expensive, especially if you have a large area to fill. Groundcovers are also not as durable as grass—if you have children, you will most likely need to have at least a small grassy area for them to play in.

How do I **plant groundcovers**?

Begin with a soil test to determine the pH level and ensure you have selected a groundcover that will thrive in the area. Remove any existing plants and loosen the soil to one to two feet, as with a perennial planting. Add any soil amendments and compost, then turn the soil to mix them in. Rake the area smooth and water well. Lay mulch down first, to reduce the labor required to mulch around so many small plants. Space plants according to their mature size and rate of growth, digging a hole large enough to accommodate the root system of the plant. Place the plant in the hole, letting the roots spread out, loosely fill with the dug topsoil, water well, and mulch. Using groundcovers in a large area can quickly become expensive. If you use a fast-growing groundcover, you can purchase smaller plants and space them far apart, with the plants filling in quickly. Remember, however, that you can always have too much of a good thing. A picture-perfect groundcover this year may be a lawn invader the next.

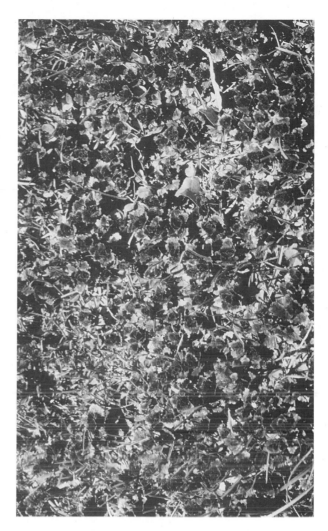

Creeping Charlie (*Lysimachia nummularia*), also called moneywort, spreads by trailing stems and can make a nice groundcover. It has a very aggressive growth habit. (Steven Nikkila/Perennial Favorites)

How do I **maintain my groundcover**?

Newly planted groundcovers should be kept moist until they are established—which can take up to a year with some plants. A light mulch can help the roots retain water. Weeding regularly ensures the groundcover is not competing for water and nutrients. Monitor for disease and insects and address problems promptly.

Which groundcovers are **evergreen**?

Evergreen groundcovers can provide a unifying theme to a yard when planted in the northern regions. Try evergreen ginger (*Asarum europaeum*), epimedium (*Epimedium* spp.), hosta (*Hosta* spp.), some lamium cultivars (*Lamium* spp.), *Astilbe chinensis*

GROUNDCOVER

Groundcovers, an alternative to traditional lawn grasses, are more valuable to wildlife. Groundcovers also require less maintenance than lawn space.

Groundcovers are excellent alternatives to lawns, especially in areas where grass is difficult to establish or maintain. (Robert J. Huffman/Field Mark Publications)

‘Pumila’, English ivy (*Hedera helix*), bearberry (*Arctostaphylos uva-ursi*), creeping juniper (*Juniperus horizontalis*), some cotoneaster (*Cotoneaster* spp.), perennial candytuft (*Iberis sempervirens*), St. John's wort (*Hypericum calycinum*), euonymous (*Euonymous fortunei*), periwinkle (*Vinca minor*), Allegheny foamflower (*Tiarella cordifolia*), and bergenia (*Bergenia cordifolia*).

Which groundcovers have **variegated leaves**?

Groundcovers with variegated leaves can add visual interest to a yard. Some variegated groundcovers include *Pachysandra terminalis* ‘Variegata’, *Pulmonaria saccharata*, *Ajuga reptans* ‘Variegata’, variegated Japanese Solomon's seal (*Polygonatum odoratum* ‘Variegatum’), round-leaved mint (*Mentha rotundifolia* ‘Variegata’), golden balm (*Melissa officinalis* ‘Aurea’), *Hosta crispula*, *Hosta fortunei* ‘Albopicta’, *Hosta undulata*, *Parthenocissus henryana*, periwinkle (*Vinca major* ‘Variegata’), English ivy (*Hedera helix* ‘Gold Heart’), and ribbon grass (*Phalaris arundinacea picta*).

Which groundcovers grow best in **shaded areas**?

Shaded areas are difficult to grow grass in. But groundcovers such as ajuga (*Ajuga reptans*), bergenia (*Bergenia cordifolia*), periwinkle (*Vinca minor*), bleeding heart (*Dicentra spectabilis*), English ivy (*Hedera helix*), lily-of-the-valley (*Convallaria majalis*), hosta (*Hosta* spp.), pachysandra (*Pachysandra terminalis*), wild ginger (*Asarum*), lungworts (*Pulmonaria*), and Chinese astilbe (*Astilbe chinesis* ‘Pumila’) all thrive in shaded areas, pleasantly replacing a straggling lawn.

Which groundcovers grow best in **sunny and dry areas**?

Groundcovers such as lamb's ear (*Stachys byzantina*), cranesbill (*Geranium dalmaticum*), Roman chamomile (*Chamaemelum nobile*), moss pink (*Phlox subulata*), pinks (*Dianthus* spp.), snow-in-summer (*Cerastium tomentosum*), catmint (*Nepeta* spp.), thyme (*Thymus vulgaris*), hens-n-chicks (*Sempervivum* spp.), daylily (*Hemerocallis* spp.), and showy sedum (*Sedum spectabile*) grow well in sunny, dry areas. Crown vetch (*Coronilla varia*) also thrives under these conditions, but can be quite invasive.

Which groundcovers grow best in **wet areas**?

If you have areas of your yard that are too wet for lawn, certain groundcovers may be a good alternative. Chinese astilbes (*Astilbe chinesis*), false goat's beard (*Astilbe taquetti* ‘Superba’), Japanese primrose (*Primula japonica*), daylily (*Hemerocallis* ‘Pink Damask’), cowberry (*Vaccinium vitis-idaea*), comfrey (*Symphytum grandiflorum*), *Pulmonaria* spp., and perennial forget-me-not (*Brunnera macrophylla*) all grow well in wet areas.

Astilbes (*Astilbe* spp.), native to Korea, Japan, and China, can be a lovely alternative to grass in shady areas with acidic soil. (Steven Nikkila/Perennial Favorites)

I have a **steep bank** that I don't want to mow. Are there any groundcovers that are suited to these conditions?

You need to find a groundcover that has a deep root system in order to stabilize the slope. Some groundcovers that take well to slopes include daylily (*Hemerocallis* spp.), a low-growing form of yarrow (*Achillea tomentosa*), and creeping juniper (*Juniperus horizontalis*).

I have large **open areas underneath my trees** where nothing will grow. Are there any groundcovers suited to these conditions?

Ajuga (*Ajuga reptans*) thrives in the dry shade under shallow-rooted trees like silver maples. *Gaultheria shallon* is more of a shrub and can become invasive, but it tolerates dry shade as well. Bethlehem sage (*Pulmonaria saccharata*), hosta (*Hosta* spp.), and pachysandra (*Pachysandra terminalis*) look right at home under trees.

I live in an area that receives less than 12 inches of rain a year. Are there any groundcovers that are **drought tolerant**?

Groundcovers can be good problem solvers in regions such as yours that receive little rain. Drought-tolerant groundcovers include woolly yarrow (*Achillea tomentosa*), pussytoes (*Antennaria dioica rosea*), wormwood (*Artemisia absinthium*), cape weed (*Arctotheca calendula*), rock cress (*Arabis procurens*), wall cress (*Arabis caucasica*), snow-on-the-mountain (*Euphorbia marginata*), blue fescue (*Festuca glauca*), perennial candytuft (*Iberis sempervirens*), several of the cotoneasters (*Cotoneaster* spp.), edelweiss (*Leontopodium alpinum*), creeping lilyturf (*Liriope spicata*), and creeping thyme (*Thymus serpyllum*).

Can **climbers** be used as groundcovers?

Yes, climbing plants are frequently used as groundcovers since they spread quickly and easily. You should choose a self-clinging climber that roots by means of adhesive disks or aerial roots for the best coverage. Climbers such as English ivy (*Hedera helix*), climbing hydrangea (*Hydrangea petiolaris*), and Virginia creeper (*Parthenocis-*

> ## How do I grow moss in a shady patch of my yard?
>
> The best method for growing moss is to begin with a sample from a moss patch. If you don't have any growing currently in your yard, ask permission from a neighbor or friend. Choose an area with soil that is slightly acidic and already moisture-retentive. To prepare the moss bed, clear the area of plant debris and rocks. Consider that the moss will show any dips or hills in the soil (this might be a design point) and edit the area as you see fit. Dampen the ground thoroughly and place the moss sample (or samples) on the new bed. Secure them to the ground using pins and add a small amount of peat moss to keep the moss moist and encourage contact with the ground. Keep the area damp. The moss should expand gradually to fill your bed (and further if you allow it).

sus quinquefolia) make excellent groundcovers. Twining or vining climbers such as *Clematis* spp. and perennial sweet pea (*Lathyrus latifolius*) are not as successful.

What are some groundcovers that can be grown in **warmer climates**?

While many groundcovers grown throughout the country can be raised in the warmer zones, a few of them are exclusive to the more temperate climates. The lovely baby's tears (*Soleirolia soleirolii*) is often used as a houseplant in cold areas, but in zones 9 and 10 it serves as a lovely groundcover. Weeping lantana (*Lantana montevidensis*) is a fast-growing rambler that is evergreen in zones 9 and 10. It also has beautiful pale pink and rose-colored flowers. Star jasmine (*Trachelospermum jasminoides*) is another wonderful choice for zones 9 and 10. This evergreen vine forms thick mats with beautiful fragrant white flowers.

What are some groundcovers with **colorful foliage**?

While many gardeners like to use evergreen groundcovers to unify their landscape, there are a number of groundcovers that can be used to add a punch of color to the yard. Hardy plumbago or leadwort (*Ceratostigma plumbaginoides*) has beautiful blue flowers. In the fall, its inconspicuous green leaves change to a gorgeous scarlet. *Ajuga reptans* 'Burgundy Glow' has blue flowers rising up in spikes. As befits its name, the rounded foliage is a deep wine color with a lovely glow to it. The leaves of lamb's ear (*Stachys byzantina*) are a soft blue-gray, made irresistible by their fuzziness. The deep green of *Cotoneaster horizontalis* changes to a burnt orange in the fall at the same time its branches are weighed down by zillions of red berries. Spotted deadnettle (*Lamium maculatum* 'Beacon Silver') has foliage that is practically silver with a thin edge of green. It also has bright pink flowers in the summer. Many of the heathers such as *Erica vulgaris* 'Robert Chapman' start the year a deep gold, then change to a mellow mixture of bronze and orange in the summer, and finish the year in a clear red or orange.

What are some groundcovers I can plant to **fill the gaps** left by crumbling brick on my patio?

Common thyme (*Thymus vulgaris*) is a good choice—it stands up to foot traffic, sends a wonderful fragrance up every time you step on them, and has gorgeous purple blooms in the late summer. In the fall, its deep green leaves change to a purple color with the first frost. The flowers of cranesbill geraniums such as *Geranium cinereum* bring beautiful blooms to patio cracks, although they're best placed where they'll receive little to no foot traffic. Creeping speedwell (*Veronica prostrata*) is another beautiful bloomer for crevices. Other choices include any of the low-growing sedums such as *Sedum spurium*, alpine poppy (*Papaver alpinum*), *Phlox amoena*, and sweet alyssum (*Lobularia maritima*).

Which groundcovers can I interplant with **spring bulbs**?

Groundcovers and bulbs are a natural combination. Groundcovers provide a perfect foil for the bright colors of spring bulbs and mask their dying foliage as spring changes to summer. Evergreen groundcovers such as periwinkle (*Vinca minor*), Japanese spurge (*Pachysandra terminalis*), ajuga (*Ajuga repans*), English ivy (*Hedera helix*), and bergenia (*Bergenia cordifolia*) serve to highlight the glorious colors of early- and late-blooming bulbs. In addition, plants such as perennial forget-me-not (*Brunnera macrophylla*) and violets (*Viola* spp.) combine well with bulbs and make lovely groundcovers in the right place.

Are there any **annual groundcovers**?

The term groundcover describes a plant's use as much as anything else, so groundcovers aren't limited to perennials. Plants such as annual forget-me-not (*Myosotis sylvatica*), annual candytuft (*Iberis umbellata*), sweet alyssum (*Lobularia maritima*), and moss rose (*Portulaca grandiflora*) can all be considered groundcovers.

ORNAMENTAL GRASSES

What are **cool-season ornamental grasses** and when should they be planted?

Cool-season ornamental grasses grow quickly in the cooler seasons of spring and fall. They bloom in early summer, go dormant and brown in the heat of the summer, then

Siberian bugloss (*Brunnera macrophylla*) can be used as a groundcover to be interplanted with bulbs. (Steven Nikkila/Perennial Favorites)

begin growing again in the fall. In regions of the country with mild winters, they may stay green through the winter. In the Midwest, they become dormant again. They should be planted during their growing seasons: early spring or fall. Blue oat grass (*Helictotrichon sempervirens*), blue fescue (*Festuca glauca*), prairie dropseed (*Sporobolus heterolepsis*), and giant feather grass (*Stipa gigantea*) are all cool-season grasses.

What are **warm-season ornamental grasses** and when should they be planted?

Warm-season ornamental grasses do their rapid growing in warm weather: spring and summer. Many of them change color in the fall, muting to a dormant brown or buff in the winter. They can be planted anytime the soil is warm. Warm-season grasses include the native big bluestem (*Andropogon gerardii*), fountain grass (*Pennisetum alopecuroides*), Japanese blood grass (*Imperata cylindrica*), wild oats (*Chasmanthium latifolium*), variegated purple moor grass (*Molinia caerulea* 'Variegata'), and maiden grass (*Miscanthus sinesis* 'Gracillimus').

What is a **sedge**?

A sedge is commonly considered a grass, but it is actually a member of a different plant family. Grasses are part of the Poaceae family, while sedges are part of the Cyperaceae family. Sedges differ from grasses in that they have achenes (one-seeded fruits similar to those of the sunflower) and solid stems. Sedges also appear more tufted, or all of a clump, than many varieties of grass.

When should my ornamental grasses be **divided**?

Like other perennials, ornamental grasses need to be divided occasionally to keep them healthy and looking their best. Once a stand of grass begins to crowd out its neighbors or leans over listlessly, it is time to divide it. Cool-season grasses are best divided in the early spring or fall. Warm-season grasses can be divided in the early spring also, before the plant is a foot tall. Divide them as you would any other clump-forming perennial: Use a spade or knife to cut the clump into smaller sections, loosen them with a spading fork, and replant.

I grew ornamental grasses for the first time last year and they were gorgeous, but this year they look sort of **droopy**. What can I do?

Prune them! Although their decorative seedheads should be left up for a lovely winter display, prune cool-season ornamental grasses back in early spring in order to make way for new growth. Warm-season grasses should be cut down to about six inches before they start growing again in the spring. In warmer climates, pruning grasses again in early summer (removing about two-thirds of the plant) also keeps plants more compact, making them less likely to flop over in midsummer.

How do I **prune** my ornamental grasses?

Start with gloves. Although they look harmless, the knifelike leaves on ornamental grasses are quite sharp. Using pruning shears, hold the shears at a 45 degree angle to the plant and begin cutting on the outside of the plant. Continue pruning slowly around the plant, ending after you work your way to the center of the clump.

What are some ornamental grasses that will grow in **acidic soil**?

Purple moor grass (*Molinia caerulea*) requires acidic soil. Most other ornamental grasses tolerate a wide variety of soils.

What are some ornamental grasses that prefer **alkaline soil**?

Blue oat grass (*Helictotrichon sempervirens*), feather grass (*Stipa calamagrostis*), big quaking grass (*Briza maxima*), and hair grass (*Koeleria vallesiana*) all prefer alkaline soils.

Are any ornamental grasses related to lawn grass?

As a matter of fact, the Poa genus includes Kentucky bluegrass (*Poa pratensis*) as well as alpine meadow grass (*P. alpina vivipara*), which is grown for its unusual panicles from which dangle tiny plantlets. Another Poa member, *P. chaixii,* is common in perennial borders.

How do **ornamental grasses reproduce**?

Almost all grasses reproduce by seeding themselves. This provides us with the beautiful sight of their feathery seedheads complementing their colors of russet and buff in the fall. Ornamental grasses also spread through rhizomes or underground stems. Some ornamental grasses expand the width of their clump and are known as clumping grasses. Others spread more quickly through runners and are known as spreading or running grasses. It is important to know how ornamental grasses reproduce as they can become invasive, especially in areas with mild winters.

What are some **clumping** ornamental grasses?

Clumping ornamental grasses are less invasive than running species. However, clumping grasses still require regular dividing to be kept in check. Some of the clumping ornamental grasses include purple moor grass (*Molinia caerulea*), giant feather grass (*Stipa gigantea*), Japanese blood grass (*Imperata cylindrica*), prairie dropseed (*Sporobolus heterolepsis*), tufted hair grass (*Deschampsia cespitosa*), blue fescue (*Festuca glauca* 'Elijah Blue'), and varieties of maiden grass (*Miscanthus sinesis*).

What are some **running** ornamental grasses?

Ornamental grasses that spread by runners need to be kept in check by regular dividing or through the use of a barrier set deep into the soil—six inches below their rootball. Some ornamental grasses that spread by runners include giant reed grass (*Arundo donax*), Japanese blood grass (*Imperata cylindrica* 'Rubra'), and canary grass (*Phalaris canariensis*).

I love the look of ornamental grasses but I have very **damp, moist soil**. Aren't grasses suited only to dry areas?

As a matter of fact, there are dozens of grasses that will thrive in the moist soil you have. They include Japanese blood grass (*Imperata cylindrica* 'Rubra'), heavenly bamboo (*Nandina domestica*), snowy woodrush (*Luzula nivea*), Bowles' golden grass (*Milium effusum*), zebra grass (*Miscanthus sinesis* 'Zebrinus'), purple moor grass (*Molina caerulea*), *Hakonechloa macra*, and maiden grass (*Miscanthus sinesis* 'Gracillimus'). In frost-free areas, look for giant reed grass (*Arundo donax* 'Variegata').

Are there any ornamental grasses that thrive in **shade**?

Wild oat (*Chasmanthium latifolium*) is a woodland plant that enjoys full shade. Japanese blood grass (*Imperata cylindrica* 'Rubra') enjoys a dappled shade, as does bottlebrush grass (*Hystrix patula*), sedges (*Carex* spp.), Bowles' golden grass (*Milium effusum*), *Hakonechloa macra*, feather reed grass (*Calamagrostis acutiflora*), and purple moor grass (*Molinia caerulea*). Fountain grass (*Pennisetum alopecuroides*), common quaking grass (*Briza media*), and many *Miscanthus sinesis* varieties also tolerate partial shade.

What are some ornamental grasses that **flower**?

A common sight are the pennisetums (*Pennisetum* spp.) with their arching flower stems followed by fluffy seedheads in the fall. Big quaking grass (*Briza maxima*) has lovely heart-shaped pendants that are also followed by seedheads in the fall. *Chasmanthium latifolium* has panicles of flowers resembling oats. These fade from pale green to a buff color in the fall. Fox-tail barley (*Hordeum jubatum*) bears long flower spikes. Other outstanding flowering ornamental grasses include *Stipa tenuissima*, Bowles' golden grass (*Milium effusum*), goldentop (*Lamarckia aurea*), plume grass (*Saccharum ravennae*), Pampas grass (*Cortaderia selloana*), and varieties of *Miscanthus sinesis*.

What are some kinds of **perennial ornamental grasses**?

Perennial ornamental grasses add beauty and permanence to your landscape with their four seasons of interest. Some outstanding perennial ornamental grasses include plume grass (*Saccharum ravennae*), big quaking grass (*Briza maxima*), common quaking grass (*Briza media*), maiden grass (*Miscanthus sinensis* 'Gracillimus'), zebra grass (*Miscanthus sinesis* 'Zebrinus'), fountain grass (*Pennisetum alopecuroides*), Japanese blood grass (*Imperata cylindrica* 'Rubra'), and blue fescue (*Festuca glauca*). Pampas grass (*Cortaderia selloana*) is perennial in zones 7 through 10. Feathertop (*Pennisetum villosum*) is a perennial grass in zones 9 and 10 but is often grown in other areas as an annual.

What are some kinds of **annual ornamental grasses**?

Many ornamental grasses are annual, so you can experiment with them in the landscape without spending a lot of money. Some annual grasses include hare's tail grass (*Lagurus ovatus*), little quaking grass (*Briza minor*), canary grass (*Phalaris canariensis*), and goldentop (*Lamarckia aurea*).

What are some ornamental grasses that **reseed** themselves?

Ornamental grasses that reseed themselves can be both a boon and a bane to the gardener. While they can spread nicely to cover bare areas, they can also invade parts of your garden that are doing well enough without them. To reduce the possibility of reseeding, you can remove their seedheads as they appear, but you will lose out on their decorative quality. Some annual grasses that spread from seed include hare's tail grass (*Lagarus ovatus*), big quaking grass (*Briza maxima*), and canary grass (*Phalaris canariensis*).

Are all ornamental grasses **natives**?

While the United States has a large number of native grasses, many ornamental grasses found at your local nursery are actually imports. Fountain grass (*Pennisetum* spp.) and *Miscanthus* species and cultivars are commonly used in "native" and "prairie-style" plantings, but they actually originated in more temperate areas than the United States. Fountain grass is found in parts of Asia and Australia, while *Miscanthus* originally grew in Africa and southeastern portions of Asia.

What are some **grasses** that are native to the United States?

The United States has a large and diverse population of native grasses. Grasses that thrive in sunny, dry areas include bluestem (*Andropogon* spp.), wild rye (*Elymus* spp.),

Indian grass (*Sorghastrum nutans*) is native to the United States. (Robert J. Huffman/Field Mark Publications)

purple love grass (*Eragrostis spectabilis*), Indian grass (*Sorghastrum nutans*), switch grass (*Panicum virgatum*), and the invasive ribbon grass (*Phalaris arundinacea picta*). Bowles' golden grass (*Milium effusum*) prefers moist shade.

How can ornamental grasses be used in a landscape **design**?

While ornamental grasses are certainly attractive, many gardeners are intimidated about using them in their yards. A frequent use of ornamental grasses, especially showy ones like Pampas grass (*Cortaderia selloana*), is as specimen plants or focal points. Try using a formal container with an ornamental grass—the change may surprise you! Ornamental grasses also weave well into a perennial border, especially one filled with late-blooming plants such as black-eyed Susan (*Rudbeckia hirta*), aster (*Aster* spp.), and sedum (*Sedum spectabile* 'Autumn Joy'). Drought-tolerant grasses are also the perfect plant for low-maintenance beds or xeriscapes. Feathery grasses can also provide a foil for more coarse-appearing plants such as canna (*Canna* spp.) or agave (*Agave* spp.). Smaller grasses, such as blue oat grass (*Helictotrichon sempervirens*), can be used as a groundcover or as edging.

HERBS

HERB PLANTING AND CARE

What is an **herb**?

The textbook definition of an herb is a flowering plant that lacks a woody stem. However, in the popular sense, the term herb refers to plants that have aromatic, medicinal, or culinary properties and so include some woody perennials.

What are some **perennial herbs**?

Beyond their appeal in returning to an herb garden year after year, perennial herbs are also frequently used in flower borders for their beautiful foliage and flowers. Perennial herbs include sage (*Salvia officinalis*), anise hyssop (*Agastache foeniculum*), hyssop (*Hyssopus officinalis*), chive (*Allium schoenoprasum*), wild leek (*Allium tricocccum*), yellow chamomile (*Anthemis tinctoria*), Roman chamomile (*Chamaemelum nobile*), costmary (*Chrysanthemum balsamita*), winter savory (*Satureja montana*), feverfew (*Chrysanthemum parthenium*), lovage (*Levisticum officinale*), salad burnet (*Poterium sanguisorba*), French tarragon (*Artemisia dracunculus*), tansy (*Tanacetum vulgare*), thyme (*Thymus* spp.), clove pink (*Dianthus caryophyllus*), sweet woodruff (*Galium odoratum*), lemon balm (*Melissa officinalis*), the mints (*Mentha* spp.), bee balm (*Monarda didyma*), sweet violet (*Viola odorata*), English lavender (*Lavandula angustifolia*), catnip (*Nepeta cataria*), sweet cicely (*Myrrhis odorata*), rue (*Ruta graveolens*), and common oregano (*Origanum vulgare*).

In warmer areas, herbs such as lemon verbena (*Aloysia triphylla*), lemongrass (*Cymbopogon citratus*), sweet fennel (*Foeniculum vulgare dulce*), sweet bay (*Laurus*   **365** *nobilis*), sweet marjoram (*Origanum majorana*), and rosemary (*Rosmarinus offici-nalis*) are also perennial.

What are some **annual and biennial herbs**?

Many annual and biennial herbs have culinary uses. Dill (*Anethum graveolens*), chervil (*Anthriscus cerefolium*), borage (*Borago officinalis*), shepherd's purse (*Capsel-la bursa-pastoris*), German chamomile (*Matricaria recutita*), anise (*Pimpinella anisum*), sweet basil (*Ocimum basilicum*), holy basil (*Ocimum canum*), and coriander (*Coriandrum sativum*) are among the annual herbs. Biennial herbs include angelica (*Angelica archangelica*), caraway (*Carum carvi*), sweet rocket (*Hesperis matronalis*), and parsley (*Petroselinum crispum*).

What **growing conditions** are required by herbs?

Although different herbs have different needs, in general most herbs thrive in a well-drained soil with a pH between 6.0 and 7.0 that receives full sun. Choose an area that receives good air circulation and you will have little trouble with pests and disease. Herbs also need to be in an area free from competition such as tree roots. Some herbs that are Mediterranean in origin thrive in poor, dry soil. These include rosemary (*Rosmarinus officinalis*), English lavender (*Lavandula angustifolia*), and other gray-leaved plants. Otherwise, soil of an average fertility will keep most herbs happy.

What do I need to do to prepare an **herb garden**?

Begin by selecting the design for your garden (see pages 382 and 383). Herbs are planted in a similar fashion to perennials. Loosening the soil to about a foot will allow moisture to penetrate the roots and keep the bed properly drained, which is a must for herbs. Add organic matter and turn it under. Remove any weeds, along with old tree roots. If you come across new tree roots, move your herb garden to another site. Herbs can also be planted with flowers and vegetables for their decorative and utilitarian qualities. Many herbs also do well in containers since they can be kept smaller and in peak flavor.

When can herbs be **planted**?

Like other plants, herbs may be hardy or half-hardy annual plants or perennial plants (see Annuals or Perennials chapter for more information). Hardy annual herbs can be either sown in the previous fall or in the early spring, as soon as the ground can be worked. Half-hardy annuals are always planted in the early spring and tender annuals can't be planted until after the last frost. Perennial herbs are usually planted whether from seed or plant, in the cooler weather of spring or fall in order to provide a gentle

Herb gardens are often formalized in design or have medicinal or culinary themes. (Robert J. Huffman/Field Mark Publications)

environment for the new plant or seedling to grow in. However, if you are planting your herbs in pots indoors, they can be started anytime.

How are herbs **started from cuttings**?

Herbs may be started from cuttings from perennial plants during their growth periods. Using a sharp knife or a set of pruners, remove a nonflowering shoot or woody stem around three to four inches long from the herb just below a set of leaves. Remove leaves from the bottom inch or so, and press the cutting into a peat pot with moist compost. Place it in a warm area. You can dab the end of the cutting in rooting hormone (available at nurseries and through mail order) before planting it in the compost, but it is not necessary. Once the herb has rooted, you may gently transfer it to another pot.

Which herbs may be started from **cuttings**?

Woody herbs such as rosemary (*Rosmarinus officinalis*), sweet bay (*Laurus nobilis*), hyssop (*Hyssopus officinalis*), and English lavender (*Lavandula angustifolia*) are best propagated from soft side-shoot cuttings, since these root more easily than those taken from the wood. Scented geraniums (*Pelargonium* spp.) are also easy to propagate from cuttings.

What is the proper method for **dividing** an herb plant?

Like other perennials, in most cases herb plant clumps can be easily divided. Carefully lift the plant to be divided out of the soil and remove excess soil from the root ball. If the roots are loose and fleshy, gently tease them apart to separate the plant into smaller sections, each with a good root system and top growth. If the plant is woody or fibrous-rooted, you can use two garden forks to pry the clump apart, or a spade or a garden knife to cut through the roots. Try to avoid new shoots or growth buds. Replant the new divisions immediately at the same depth in the soil as the original plant.

Which herbs may be **started from seeds**?

Annual herbs such as basil (*Ocimum basilicum*), anise (*Pimpinella anisum*), borage (*Borago officinalis*), German chamomile (*Matricaria recutita*), chervil (*Anthriscus cerefolium*), cilantro (*Coriandrum sativum*), cumin (*Cuminum cyminum*), dill (*Anethum graveolens*), pot marigold (*Calendula officinalis*), and summer savory (*Satureja hortensis*) are grown from seed. Some perennial herbs such as feverfew (*Chrysanthemum parthenium*), fennel (*Foeniculum vulgare*), hyssop (*Hyssopus officinalis*), lovage (*Levisticum officinale*), sage (*Salvia officinalis*), salad burnet (*Poterium sanguisorba*), valerian (*Valeriana officinalis*), and wormwood (*Artemisia absinthium*) may also be grown from seed, although they generally need more than one season before being harvested.

Which herbs are **self-seeders**?

If you plant herbs such as borage (*Borago officinalis*), caraway (*Carum carvi*), chervil (*Anthriscus cerefolium*), cilantro (*Coriandrum sativum*), dill (*Anethum graveolens*), fennel (*Foeniculum vulgare*), lemon basil (*Ocimum citriodorum*), Roman chamomile (*Chamaemelum nobile*), and wormwood (*Artemisia absinthium*), don't be surprised to see their young seedlings poking up around your garden. They're prolific self-seeders.

How should herbs be **watered**?

Herbs grown in containers may need to be watered daily, as pots (especially clay ones) tend to dry out quickly. Herbs grown outdoors should be watered frequently, daily during hot weather. Since most herbs appreciate well-drained soil, be sure their roots do not sit in water for any length of time.

How should herbs be **fertilized**?

Many perennial herbs such as rosemary (*Rosmarinus officinalis*), English lavender (*Lavandula angustifolia*), and sage (*Salvia officinalis*) prefer a poor soil to grow in. Fertilize these plants at the beginning of the growing season (topdressing with compost or a sprinkling of bonemeal, watered in well) and no more than monthly after that. Annual herbs such as sweet basil (*Ocimum basilicum*) respond well to fertilizing, but select a liquid fertilizer such as fish emulsion or compost tea at half strength and use it every two to three waterings. Your best bet is to keep adding organic matter such as compost to the soil regularly.

Do herbs require **pruning**?

Yes. Pruning woody herbs such as English lavender (*Lavandula angustifolia*) and rosemary (*Rosmarinus officinalis*) allows them to retain a neat and compact shape in the landscape. All basil (*Ocimum basilicum*), sage (*Salvia officinalis*), and scented geraniums (*Pelargonium* spp.) have a tendency to become leggy or spindly without pruning. Harvesting itself is, of course, a form of pruning. All herbs are stimulated into new growth by pruning, so shape them at least every month or so if they are just ornamental herbs.

Which herbs benefit most from **pruning**?

Herbs with woody stems usually benefit most from pruning. Herbs like French tarragon (*Artemisia dracunculus*), English lavender (*Lavandula angustifolia*), thyme (*Thymus vulgaris*), winter savory (*Satureja montana*), and rue (*Ruta graveolens*) respond with compact, bushy growth if they are pruned. Remove their growing tips to encourage this bushiness. Prune woody herbs early in the spring, just as new growth begins to emerge.

369

How and when should I prune English lavender?

English lavender (*Lavandula angustifolia*) looks best when it has a full, rounded shape. It should be pruned every year with its first flush of growth in the early spring. If it has been a while since you pruned your lavender, cut back every second or third stem to the base and trim the remaining stems by one-third, shaping the entire plant into a rounded shape as you go. Your lavender should respond with a flourish of new growth and blooms.

Although rosemary (*Rosmarinus officinalis*) is a woody herb, it only needs to have any dead stems pruned out in the spring and minor shaping of any straggly growth. If you have old rosemary plants that have become overgrown, cut them back by half in late spring. They will respond with a generous flush of new growth. Another woody herb, sage (*Salvia officinalis*), should be pruned after flowering.

Why aren't my **sage plants** flowering?

Actually, not all sage plants (*Salvia* spp.) bloom. A variegated variety of sage, *Salvia officinalis* 'Tricolor', is one of the nonblooming sages. If your sage is not variegated, it could be because you pruned your sage heavily in the spring, when it sets its flower buds (see previous question). Without pruning, garden sage will set forth a deep violet-blue flower in the summer, a color that is set off nicely by its blue-green leaves.

Why is my **basil** wilting in the sun? I thought herbs needed full sun to thrive.

There could be a number of reasons why your basil (*Ocimum basilicum*) is droopy. If you are growing it in a pot that is too small, the basil could be potbound with not enough room for its roots to receive nutrients and water. Turn the container over and check to see if roots are poking through the drainage hole. If so, it's time to change pots. Or your plant may be in need of water. Stick your finger into the container or soil around the plant and feel the moisture level a few inches down. If it's dry, you need to water.

Finally, you may live in a region or state such as southern California or parts of the South and West in which full sun (six or more hours of light per day) is too much for the variety of basil you're growing. Some sweet basils can be heat intolerant. Try sheltering it with a larger plant, providing it with a few hours of morning sun but shielding it from the midday sun.

Do herbs need to be **mulched**?

In areas with cold winters, herbs such as English lavender (*Lavandula angustifolia*), rue (*Ruta graveolens*), and sage (*Salvia officinalis*) are said to benefit from a mulching of evergreen boughs over that season. However many gardeners confess that they leave these herbs uncovered in their yards and they manage just fine. Thyme (*Thymus vulgaris*) dies out if covered in leaves or other wet mulch over the winter. During the growing season, all herbs with the exception of those native to hot and dry areas, such as rosemary (*Rosmarinus officinalis*), sage, and common oregano (*Origanum vulgare*), will benefit from a light mulch to retain moisture at their roots.

When should herbs be **harvested**?

Herbs used fresh can be harvested anytime, although the flavor of some herbs change once they've set flower. Herbs used for drying should be harvested before the herbs set flower, on a day that is dry rather than rainy. Flowers for drying should be picked in the morning, just as the flowers have opened. Seedheads should be picked when the seeds have become ripe and brown.

How can herbs be **frozen for use later**?

Herbs should be picked fresh at the peak of their season. The leaves can then be rinsed and gently shaken to remove most of the water and stored whole in freezer bags. Another option is to place a leaf, flower, or finely chopped herb in each section of an ice cube tray. Fill the tray with water, and freeze overnight. You can leave the cubes in the tray if you'll be using them in the next several days or remove them and place them in a freezer bag for later use.

How do I **dry herbs**?

You can dry herbs either by hanging them or laying them flat. To hang herbs, pick them fresh and clean as above. Place them in small bunches and fasten their stems together with string and hang in a cool, dry space. Check often and compost any bunches that develop mildew immediately. Herbs and flower petals can also be dried by being laid flat on window screens in a cool, dry space. Gently move them around every few days to discourage moisture.

How can I keep **mint** from taking over my garden?

Species of *Mentha* spread rampantly by runners and can take over a garden in no time without some preventative measures. If you are already overwhelmed by spearmint (*M. spicata*) or peppermint (*M. piperita*), dig up as much of the plant as possible, making certain to follow and dig up as many runners as you can. Place all plant material (leaves, roots, etc.) into the trash, as opposed to the compost pile. Keep an eye out for the mint's reappearance and be persistent in its removal. If you are contemplating a purchase or "gift" of mint, plant it in a container. Although it is quite vigorous, the plant does tend to peter out after several years so you may want to divide and replant it.

I live in zone 4. How can I keep my **basil plants going through winter**?

The best way to keep your basil (*Ocimum basilicum*) plants going is to take cuttings of them and root them. Throughout the summer, keep your basil picked in order to prevent it from flowering. This will keep the herb from going to seed. In the late summer, take cuttings from your healthiest nonflowering plants. Each cutting should be about three to four inches in length from the tip of the stem. Strip away the leaves on the bottom half of each cutting. Place the cuttings in a short jar, glass, or cup of clean water, keeping the leaves above water, putting only a few cuttings in each container to keep them from crowding each other. Place them in a window, out of direct sunlight, and be sure to change the water daily. After a week or so, fine roots will appear from the bottom half of the stem and you can pot up your cuttings in small three-inch pots. They now need a sunny window or a good fluorescent light. As the plant becomes larger, you can transplant it. Again, keep it picked to prevent it from flowering and going to seed.

I'd like to grow **catnip** to dry for my cats and to make tea, but my cats keep nibbling it to nothing before I get the chance. Any suggestions?

Catnip (*Nepeta cataria*) has a heavenly scent that cats go mad for. Unfortunately, they haven't the self-control to think about imbibing later. Or more likely, they do have the self-control, but they're just being contrary. In any case, try placing plastic forks and knives into the soil, forming a circle around your catnip plant. While the plasticware won't hurt the kitties (or the gardener), the herb's "plastic armor" should prevent them from nibbling the mint to nothing.

I'd like to grow **lemongrass** to use in Asian recipes but I've only seen it sold fresh in markets. Can it be grown from cuttings?

Lemongrass (*Cymbopogon citratus*) is an herb that has traditionally been used in Asian cooking for centuries, but Westerners are only just beginning to enjoy it. Growing this newly popular and tender perennial herb from cuttings is easy. Purchase a small bunch of these stalks (available at gourmet and Asian grocery stores). Trim off the lower one-third of the stalks, removing their outer sheaths if they are beginning to brown. Place in a glass of water with the ends of the stalks just barely covered. Once the roots emerge, transplant directly into the ground outdoors or into containers. Choose your location carefully as lemongrass eventually grows up to four feet high. Since lemongrass is only hardy in zones 9 and 10, you will most likely need to prune them down in the fall and overwinter in a sunny location indoors.

HISTORICAL, CULINARY, AND HEALING PROPERTIES OF HERBS

What are some **fragrant herbs**?

Herbs and plants known for their aromatic qualities include bee balm (*Monarda didyma*), chamomile (*Chamaemelum nobile*), sweet marigold (*Tagetes lucida*), English lavender (*Lavandula angustifolia*), fennel (*Foeniculum vulgare*), mint (*Mentha* spp.), rosemary (*Rosmarinus officinalis*), roses (*Rosa* spp.), scented geraniums (*Pelargonium* spp.), lemon balm (*Melissa officinalis*), lemon verbena (*Aloysia triphylla*), sweet woodruff (*Galium odoratum*), artemisias (*Artemisia* spp.), patchouli (*Pogostemon cablin*), sweet marjoram (*Origanum majorana*), sweet violet (*Viola odorata*), and sweet cicely (*Myrrhis odorata*).

Which herbs are **frost tolerant**?

Frost-hardy herbs include angelica (*Angelica archangelica*), anise (*Pimpinella anisum*), borage (*Borago officinalis*), catnip (*Nepeta cataria*), chive (*Allium schoen-*

prasum), fennel (*Foeniculum vulgare*), horseradish (*Armoracia rusticana*), English lavender (*Lavandula angustifolia*), lemon balm (*Melissa officinalis*), mint (*Mentha* spp.), wormwood (*Artemisia absinthium*), sage (*Salvia* spp.), parsley (*Petroselinum crispum*), yarrow (*Achillea millefolium*), thyme (*Thymus vulgaris*), sorrel (*Rumex acetosa*), rue (*Ruta graveolens*), and rosemary (*Rosmarinus officinalis*).

Which **parts of herbs** are useful?

The parts of an herb that are useful vary from herb to herb. Most herbs are used exclusively for their leaves. Other plants like coriander (*Coriandrum sativum*), fennel (*Foeniculum vulgare*), and dill (*Anethum graveolens*) have both flavorful leaves and seeds that each add a unique flavor to dishes. Both the flowers and leaves of chive (*Allium schoenoprasum*) add a mild onion flavor to dishes. The flowers are usually used only in salads. Angelica (*Angelica archangelica*) is grown mostly for its stems. Horseradish (*Armoracia rusticana*) is grown exclusively for its roots. Branches, leaves, and flowers of English lavender (*Lavandula angustifolia*) may be used to scent a drawer of linen or sweaters.

What are *fines herbes*?

Fines herbes is an herb mixture used by the French to flavor everything from omelettes to soups. The ingredients in *fines herbes* are chervil (*Anthriscus cerefolium*), chive (*Allium schoenoprasum*), French tarragon (*Artemisia dracunculus*), and parsley (*Petroselinum crispum*).

Are there any **sages** that are grown for their decorative foliage?

The *Salvia* genus is comprised of nearly a thousand species, most with lovely foliage. Within the species of common sage (*Salvia officinalis*), varieties such as 'Aurea' (known as golden sage), 'Variegata' (yellow-variegated gray-green leaves), 'Purpurascens' (purple-leaf sage) and its variegated form, and the well-known 'Tricolor' (white-variegated leaves edged in purple) provide beautiful ornamentation to an herb garden or perennial border.

What are some herbs with **purple or dark red foliage**?

Since herbs are frequently grown for their decorative qualities in both the garden and on the table, it can be helpful to know the colors of their foliage. Purple- and scarlet-leafed herbs range in color from a deep claret to grape. Perilla (*Perilla frutescens*) has a leaf color that is somewhere between red and purple. The leaves of 'Tricolor' sage (*Salvia officinalis* 'Tricolor') are green, pink, and purple. There are a number of different varieties of purple basil (*Ocimum basilicum aurauascens*) including 'Dark Opal',

Chives (*Allium schoenoprasum*) in bloom can make a nice border for a garden or accent a rock garden. (Robert I Huffman/Field Mark Publications)

'Purple Ruffles', 'Osmin', and 'Red Rubin'. Bronze fennel (*Foeniculum vulgare*) has a burgundy cast to its feathery foliage.

What are some herbs with **gray foliage**?

Gray-leaved herbs are frequently native to Mediterranean countries and provide a refreshing oasis for the eye in a sea of green herbs. Rosemary (*Rosmarinus officinalis*), mullein (*Verbascum thapsus*), cotton lavender (*Santolina chamaecyparissus*), English lavender (*Lavandula angustifolia*), southernwood (*Artemisia abrotanum*), wormwood (*Artemisia absinthium*), garden sage (*Salvia officinalis*), German chamomile (*Matricaria recutita*), and catnip (*Nepeta cataria*) are all herbs with gray foliage.

What are some herbs with **variegated foliage**?

There are several herb varieties that appear with variegated foliage. As with most variegations, these may have arisen originally as a genetic mutation or virus but were bred to appear consistently. Sage (*Salvia officinalis*) has a few variegated forms including golden sage or 'Icterina', 'Variegata' (yellow-variegated gray-green leaves), and 'Purpurascens Variegata' (variegated purple-leaf sage). Other variegated herbs include variegated thyme (*Thymus vulgaris* 'Variegatum'), pineapple mint (*Mentha suave-*

375

olens 'Variegata'), and variegated oregano (*Origanum vulgare* 'Variegatum'). There is also a very rare gold-variegated rosemary (*Rosmarinus officinalis*).

What is the **easiest herb** to grow?

This is a matter of opinion, but for the money, sweet basil (*Ocimum basilicum*) is one of the easiest herbs to grow from seed. The most important tip to remember when growing basil (and most other herbs) is that it sulks in cool weather. So don't transplant it outdoors until all danger of frost has passed. In areas warmer than zone 7, you can direct seed your basil in the garden once this happens. North of zone 7, you may start your plants indoors about a month and a half before all danger of frost has passed. Use a light soil mix and press seeds gently into the moistened soil. Wrap the container in plastic wrap and keep in a warm place until the seeds have germinated. Basil needs a lot of light and should be allowed to dry out between waterings. Transplant the seedlings in small groupings to reduce shock and make sure they are hardened off properly before setting them out. If you have a late cold spell, keep the plants indoors rather than risk stunting them.

What is **potpourri**?

Potpourri is a mixture of the scented portions of plants (herbs and flowers). They can be made either moist or dry. Moist potpourris keep their scent longer but are an unattractive brown color, so they are usually kept in a covered container. Many moist potpourris can also be gently heated to persuade the scent to fill the room. Dry potpourris are more attractive and usually feature rose buds or petals or other dried flowers. Since they are left uncovered, they tend to lose their scent more quickly.

Which herbs are used in **potpourri**?

Potpourri has as many recipes as there are makers of it. Common herbs found in potpourri include rose (*Rosa* spp.) petals or whole flowers, clove pink (*Dianthus caryophyl-*

What is a *bouquet garni*?

A *bouquet garni* or "garnished bouquet" is a mixture of herbs that is wrapped and tied in cheesecloth or other porous material and placed in a dish as it is being prepared. The *bouquet garni* is then removed before the meal is served. This adds a wonderfully strong essence and flavoring to a recipe. Bay leaf (*Laurus nobilis*) is the most common ingredient in a *bouquet garni*.

lus) English lavender (*Lavandula angustifolia*), larkspur (*Delphinium consolida*), sweet bay (*Laurus nobilis*), and lemon verbena (*Aloysia triphylla*). Spices used in potpourri include cinnamon bark (*Cinnamomum*), allspice (*Pimenta dioica*), nutmeg (*Myristica fragrans*), and clove (*Eugenia caryophyllus*).

How do I make a **sachet**?

Sachets may be used to scent drawers, closets, and pillows—virtually anything can benefit from the gentle fragrance of a sachet. Sachets are very easy to make. Use a small square of attractive cloth. It is not necessary to sew the edges unless a more finished look is desired. Place a small amount of dried plant materials such as rose (*Rosa* spp.) buds or petals, clove pink (*Dianthus caryophyllus*), German chamomile (*Matricaria recutita*), English lavender (*Lavandula angustifolia*—an important ingredient in a good sachet), and lemon verbena (*Aloysia triphylla*) into the center of the cloth and apply a drop or two of essential oil. Close the cloth around the herbs and flowers and twist the remaining cloth at the top. Tie securely with a ribbon. Now place it in your linen closet or drawer.

Which herbs can be trained into **topiary**?

It is possible to create a topiary from plants other than conventional shrubs. Rosemary (*Rosmarinus officinalis*), sweet bay (*Laurus nobilis*), English lavender (*Lavandula angustifolia*), scented geranium (*Pelargonium* spp.), lemon verbena (*Aloysia triphylla*), and other herbs that have woody stems can all be trained into topiary.

Which herbs may be used to **make tea**?

Herbs such as German chamomile (*Matricaria recutita*), hyssop (*Hyssopus officinalis*), and lemon balm (*Melissa officinalis*) are traditionally used for tea. Bee balm (*Monarda didyma*) is also known as wild bergamot, since its flavor is similar to that of the bergamot orange, which is used to give Earl Grey tea its distinctive flavor. Other

377

herbs used for tea include the mints (*Mentha* spp.), tansy (*Tanacetum vulgare*), sage (*Salvia officinalis*), rosehips (*Rosa* spp.), lemongrass (*Cymbopogon citratus*), scented geranium (*Pelargonium* spp.), borage (*Borago officinalis*), lemon verbena (*Aloysia triphylla*), valerian (*Valeriana officinalis*), elder (*Sambucus nigra*), rosemary (*Rosmarinus officinalis*), and thyme (*Thymus vulgaris*).

Which herbs can be used to create **low hedges**?

English lavender (*Lavandula angustifolia*) is a favorite hedging plant for herb gardens and perennial borders due to its rounded shape and fragrant gray foliage. The artemisias such as southernwood and wormwood (*Artemisia abrotanum* and *A. absinthium*) are used less frequently but are also very attractive as hedges. The blue-green foliage of rue (*Ruta graveolens*) makes for an unusual hedge but it can cause a skin irritation with some people. Lavender cotton (*Santolina chamaecyparissus*) is commonly used in herb and knot gardens as well.

What proportion of **dried herbs** equals a proportion of fresh herbs?

Dried herbs are much more potent than fresh ones. Twice as many fresh herbs are needed to equal a single measurement of dried herbs.

What are some **edible flowers** and how are they consumed?

Nasturtium (*Tropaeolum majus*), daylily (*Hemerocallis* spp.), and violet (*Viola* spp.) —the whole flower or their petals—can be eaten in salads. Nasturtium has a slightly sharp, peppery taste while violets are sweeter. The young leaves of the daylily can also be chopped finely and put in salads or eaten fried. Pot marigolds (*Calendula officinalis*), not the usual garden variety marigold, can be used to flavor and color dishes, similar to saffron. Chive flowers (*Allium schoenoprasum*) can be used in the same

Oregano (*Origanum vulgare*) is a perennial herb native to Greece and the island of Cyprus. Its flavor is associated with Mediterranean cuisine. (Robert J. Huffman/Field Mark Publications)

manner as garlic (*Allium sativum*) because their mature blooms have a pungent flavor. Rose petals (*Rosa* spp.) are used to make jellies and syrups.

Which home-grown herbs are used in **Mediterranean cuisine**?

Thyme (*Thymus vulgaris*), common oregano (*Origanum vulgare*), sweet marjoram (*Origanum majorana*), rosemary (*Rosmarinus officinalis*), sage (*Salvia officinalis*), and winter savory (*Satureja montana*) are all used in Mediterranean cuisine. These plants thrive in poor, dry soil and do not care to be mulched.

Which home-grown herbs are used in **Asian cuisine**?

Basil (*Ocimum basilicum*), fennel seed (*Foeniculum vulgare*), coriander seed and cilantro (*Coriandrum sativum*), and garlic (*Allium sativum*) can all be grown in most backyards and used to flavor Asian cuisine.

Which herbs are members of the **onion family**?

Garlic (*Allium sativum*) and chive (*Allium schoenoprasum*) are both members of the *Allium* genus, whose plants are known as much for their beautiful blooms as their pungent qualities. Other family members include wild leek (*Allium tricoccum*) and Chinese chive (*A. tuberosum*).

Which herbs (besides mint) are members of the **mint family (Labiatae)**?

Hyssop (*Hyssopus* spp.), lemon balm (*Melissa officinalis*), bee balm (*Monarda didyma*), catnip (*Nepeta cataria*), rosemary (*Rosemarinus officinalis*), sage (*Salvia* spp.), savory (*Satureja* spp.), thyme (*Thymus* spp.), germander (*Teucrium chamaedrys*), and lamb's ear (*Stachys byzantina*) all belong to the mint family.

Which herbs can be **grown inside**?

Although most herbs can be brought inside, some of them tolerate it better than others. These include scented geraniums (*Pelargonium* spp.), rosemary (*Rosmarinus officinalis*), sage (*Salvia* spp.), sweet bay (*Laurus nobilis*), chive (*Allium schoenoprasum*), and cilantro (*Coriandrum sativum*).

What are some herbs that tolerate **shady conditions**?

Herbs that tolerate shady sites include wintergreen (*Gaultheria procumbens*), cilantro (*Coriandrum sativum*), parsley (*Petroselinum crispum*), Roman chamomile (*Cham-*

aemelum nobile), dill (*Anethum graveolens*), sweet woodruff (*Galium odoratum*), oregano (*Origanum vulgare*), thyme (*Thymus vulgaris*), sage (*Salvia officinalis*), bee balm (*Monarda didyma*), borage (*Borago officinalis*), German chamomile (*Matricaria recutita*), violet (*Viola odorata*), and mints (*Mentha*). Both violets and mints can be invasive, even in shaded areas, so you might consider growing them in pots.

What is **lady's mantle**?

Lady's mantle or *Alchemilla vulgaris* is a dainty perennial with scalloped and pleated green leaves that are tipped in silver. It flowers in summer, with fragile acid-yellow blossoms. Lady's mantle received its common name for the shape of its leaves, which are similar to a woman's cloak. Lady's mantle grows best in a moist soil receiving light shade in zones 3 through 8. Some of the *Alchemilla* species were traditionally used to stop bleeding and as an astringent. In the garden, it functions as a groundcover or an edging plant—best grown in groups.

Are there any herbs that thrive in **acid soils**?

Some herbs actually prefer slightly acidic soils. These include sweet woodruff (*Galium odoratum*), tansy (*Tanacetum vulgare*), angelica (*Angelica archangelica*), dill (*Anethum graveolens*), basil (*Ocimum basilicum*), lovage (*Levisticum officinale*), chervil (*Anthriscus cerefolium*), and mint (*Mentha* spp.).

My herb garden has a **stepping stone path** through it. Are there any herbs that I can grow to creep up between the stones?

Any of the creeping thymes (*Thymus* spp.) work wonderfully in paths as they will thrive in little soil and lots of sun. Although regular stomping on them will crush

Rosemary (*Rosmarinus officinalis*) and lavender (*Lavandula angustifolia*) are both herbs that grow well in an indoor garden if given plenty of moisture (regular watering and misting). Many other culinary and cosmetic herbs can be grown on a sunny windowsill. (Robert J. Huffman/Field Mark Publications)

them, thyme is fairly durable and provides a wonderful scent when stepped on. In mid- to late summer, their blooms provide additional color to the garden.

Which herbs can be used as **groundcovers**?

Creeping or low-growing herbs make excellent groundcovers since they cover an area nicely and often provide the additional bonus of a pleasant scent when walked on or brushed against. Some herbs commonly used as groundcovers include sweet woodruff (*Galium odoratum*), thyme (*Thymus vulgaris*), a shrubby form of yarrow (*Achillea ageratifolia*), violet (*Viola odorata*), bouncing Bet (*Saponaria officinalis*—but it can be invasive), creeping savory (*Saturega repanda*), creeping comfrey (*Symphytum grandiflorum*), and coltsfoot (*Tussilago farfara*—also invasive).

What are some **traditional herb garden designs**?

A formal herb garden is usually square or circle with a focal point (such as a birdbath or urn) at its center. Brick or gravel paths are usually edged with low-growing herbs such as German chamomile (*Matricaria recutita*), thyme (*Thymus vulgaris*), and lamb's ear (*Stachys byzantina*), which radiate from the center, breaking the square or circle into pie wedges, each planted with a different herb. Herbs can also be planted in a border with the tallest herbs, such as dill (*Anethum graveolens*), planted at the back, medium-height herbs such as basil (*Ocimum basilicum*) in the middle, and low-growing herbs like thyme (*Thymus vulgaris*) at the front. Herbs also thrive in containers—strawberry pots with each pocket planted with a different herb (tall growers at the top, trailing plants at the sides).

Which herbs are traditionally used in **knot gardens**?

Herbs in knot gardens are pruned or sheared regularly. Woody herbs that grow close to the ground such as English lavender (*Lavandula angustifolia*), lavender cotton (*Santolina chamaecyparissus*), rosemary (*Rosmarinus officinalus*), germander (*Teucrium chamaedrys*), and hyssop (*Hyssopus officinalis*) are often used in knot gardens.

Where does the herb **lavender** get its name?

The aromatic herb lavender (*Lavandula* spp.) has been used to add fragrance to soaps and perfumes since the days of the Romans. The name comes from the Latin word *lavare*, which means "to wash." While the Romans had bathhouses, using actual soap and water became *passé* following the fall of the Roman Empire. Lavender was used instead in perfumes, which were placed on the body to mask any unfortunate scents.

Is **pepper** an herb?

Pepper is actually considered a spice. Black and white peppers, the most commonly used peppers, are really the same plant—*Piper nigrum*. *Piper nigrum* is an evergreen woody perennial climber that grows in tropical areas such as India and Sri Lanka. In other temperate areas, it can be grown in a greenhouse and may even bear fruit. The spice comes from the fruit that is harvested at different points of ripeness for different uses. Fruit used for black pepper is harvested when the fruit is mature but still green. Fruit used for white pepper is picked when it is very ripe and red or yellow in color. The outer skin is removed, revealing the white center.

What is the difference between **catmint, catnip, and catgrass**?

Catnip (*Nepeta cataria*) is a species within the catmint (*Nepeta*) genus. Catnip is also used to make a tea that is said to be a soothing therapy for a cold. While *Nepeta cataria* is definitely appealing to cats, most species of *Nepeta* are used in the garden for their beautiful blue flowers. "Catgrass," usually sold in combination packets with catnip, is actually nothing more than common lawn grass, which many cats do enjoy nibbling at now and again.

What is it about **catnip** that makes it so irresistible to cats?

The beautiful fuzzy gray-green leaves of catnip (*Nepeta cataria*) release an oil when they are crushed or brushed against. It is this oil that cats are attracted to, although humans appear to be immune. The oil persists in the plant, even after the leaves are dried. So you can preserve catnip leaves at the end of the summer for your feline friend's winter stash.

What are some herbs that are used to **flavor drinks**?

Costmary (*Chrysanthemum balsamita*) was once known as alecost since it was used to give beers a balsamic flavor. Sweet woodruff (*Galium odoratum*) is used with German sparkling wine to make May wine. Rootbeer was once made from herbs, barks, and roots, including wintergreen (*Gaultheria procumbens*) and sarsaparilla. The leaves of bee balm, or bergamot (*Monarda didyma*), are used not only in tea but to flavor wine. Cilantro (*Coriandrum sativum*) is sometimes used to flavor liqueurs. Many members of the mint or *Mentha* species are often used to flavor drinks. Favorites include spearmint (*Mentha spicata*), applemint (*M. rotundifolia*), and peppermint (*M. piperita*). Other herbs used to flavor drinks include hyssop (*Hyssopus officinalis*).

What is a **simple**?

A *simple* is an herb that is believed to have medicinal value. Simples have been gathered from the wild for healing purposes since medieval times. Herbal healing has seen a rapid increase in popularity over the past decade as individuals seek alternative therapies. Garlic (*Allium sativum*) is an example of a plant or bulb that is currently much in demand for its reputed ability to boost a person's immune system.

Which herbs were traditionally used to **cure the common cold**?

Horehound (*Marrubium vulgare*), marsh mallow (*Althaea officinalis*), ephedra (*Ephedra* spp.), violet (*Viola* spp.), thyme (*Thymus vulgaris*), and verbascum (*Verbascum* spp.) were all used in various remedies to cure the common cold. Some are still used in cold preparations today.

What are some traditional medicinal uses of **anise**?

Anise (*Pimpinella anisum*) has been planted by gardeners as far back as ancient Egypt, Greece, and Rome for both its culinary and medicinal qualities. It has been traditionally used by European herbalists to treat flatulence, indigestion, and stomachache. It is also has a mild expectorant quality and so is used to treat congestion, cough, and cold symptoms and often flavors cough syrups and lozenges. Anise has a sweet flavor reminiscent of licorice, so it is commonly given to children and adults alike.

What are some historical culinary uses for **violets**?

Violets (*Viola* spp.), long a sweet sign of spring, are no longer commonly used in cooking (although they are sometimes used to garnish dishes and salads). Since the lovely scent of violets disappears when they are dried, they were often preserved to retain their fragrance. Vinegar, oil, and sugar were excellent mediums in which to preserve them, so cooks made violet syrup, oil of violets, and violet vinegar.

What are some reputed medicinal qualities of **basil**?

Basil (*Ocimum basilicum*) is so beloved for its myriad culinary uses that its reputed qualities as a healing herb are sometimes overlooked. This mild, yet flavorful herb has been used to reduce headaches and nausea. It is reputed to be beneficial for both a mother and her nursing infant, increasing the mother's milk and expelling gas in the baby. It has also been used both as an antiseptic and as a stimulant.

What are some historical uses for **wormwood?**

Wormwood, one of the artemisias, is used to make absinthe, a green liqueur. It is also used as a flavoring in other liqueurs, vermouths, and bitters. Wormwood, as its name implies, was reputed to be useful for its ability to rid the body of worms. This may be due to its bitter flavor. It was also traditionally used to treat indigestion and anorexia.

How has **bay** been used over the centuries?

Bay leaf (*Laurus nobilis*) was a sacred herb in Greek mythology and was woven into wreaths and crowns to honor athletes, heroes, and artists. In Europe, bay has been used to treat flatulence. More recently, native species of bay such as California bay laurel were used by Native Americans to relieve symptoms of rheumatism and to treat stomach ailments and headaches.

What are some reputed healing qualities of **borage**?

Borage (*Borago officinalis*), with its lovely blue flowers, is often a featured element in herb gardens. Traditionally, borage was thought to lift both body and emotion. It was used to treat depression and to bolster confidence. It was used by herbalists to make a tea to reduce fevers, calm souls, and to revive patients on the mend. It is currently being researched for its positive effects on eczema and other skin ailments, as well as for pre-menstrual symptoms.

What are some historical medicinal uses for **yarrow**?

Yarrow (*Achillea millefolium*) was used fresh, as well as dried and crushed, to treat a myriad of disorders. It was believed to promote perspiration, useful for ridding the body of fevers and colds. It was also known as soldier's woundwort for its styptic quality and was applied directly to wounds to stop bleeding. The root of the yarrow has been used as an anesthetic or to reduce the effects of toothaches. Yarrow tea is reputed to improve the condition of rashes and hemorrhoids.

How has **wild ginger** been used over the centuries?

The roots of *Asarum canadense,* or wild ginger, were used both fresh and dried. Native Americans used the herb to relieve stomach cramps, fever, colds, and heart palpitations. It was also a frequent antidote for snake bites and a preventative against digestive ailments. Species of ginger native to Europe and China were used in similar fashion in those countries.

What are some historical names for **horehound**?

Horehound (*Marrubium vulgare*) has been called bull's blood, eye of the star, and seed of Horus. It has had medicinal and culinary uses since ancient Egypt and until recently was available in British pharmacopoeias. Its hairy leaves and flowering tops have

> ## What are some reputed medical benefits of fennel?
>
> Fennel (*Foeniculum vulgare*) has a myriad of medicinal uses as noted in the *British Herbal Pharmacopoeia*. A number of them relate to its influence on the digestive tract. Fennel is said to stimulate the appetite, while also having diuretic properties. Chinese herbalists prescribe fennel to help promote breast milk production and reduce gas in infants. Its cleansing and anti-inflammatory properties make it useful as a mouthwash and to wash the eye. The part of the plant most frequently used for healing is the seeds.

traditionally been used to treat bronchitis, expel worms, encourage perspiration, soothe itchy skin, and promote menstruation. Related to the mint family, horehound has naturalized freely throughout the United States and Europe.

Is **horseradish** used for anything other than as a condiment?

While the roots of horseradish (*Armoracia rusticana*) add a wonderful bite to sandwiches and of course a finishing touch to roast beef, they are also valued for their reported medicinal benefits. Horseradish has been used throughout the ages as an appetite stimulant as well as a diuretic. Freshly grated horseradish clears the sinuses instantly and so is used in a poultice to treat congestion. This same property alleviates muscular aches and pains as well. It was traditionally used to expel worms and, as horseradish contains vitamin C, to prevent scurvy.

Does **lavender** have any value as a healing herb?

Lavender (*Lavandula* spp.) has historically been used to treat depression—perhaps because its wonderfully scented leaves and blossoms are reminiscent of spring and new beginnings—and is employed by modern aromatherapists for this reason. Lavender has been said to keep stinging insects away and can be hung in dried bunches or rubbed directly on the skin for this effect. It has also been used in a poultice to treat congestion. When ingested in a tea, lavender is believed to calm the stomach and stimulate the appetite. Steam generated from a lavender-infused water is said to relieve colds and flu. Finally, lavender is sometimes taken as a preventative.

How has **garlic** historically been used?

Garlic (*Allium sativum*) has been used as a healing herb since the earliest civilizations, as illustrated by hieroglyphics produced during the building of the pyramids. It has been used around the world as a preventative against the effects of infectious diseases such as the plague and as a general antibiotic. Chinese and European herbalists used garlic to treat respiratory illnesses and high blood pressure. Modern scientists are currently investigating the bulb's impact on blood pressure. For these qualities as well its essential use as an ingredient in many dishes, garlic is often refered to as "the stinking rose."

What are some beneficial properties of **peppermint**?

Peppermint (*Mentha piperita*) is not considered a culinary herb but reportedly has many medicinal benefits. Peppermint tea is used by the Chinese as a refreshing drink in hot weather. Peppermint contains menthol, which is used as an antiseptic in mouthwashes, and to clean cuts. Its sharp flavor has a stimulating effect. But peppermint's most frequent use is to treat digestive disorders. Peppermint relieves indigestion and flatuence, as well as morning sickness. It is frequently added to gum, candy, toothpaste, soap, and medicine.

What are some beneficial properties of **spearmint**?

Spearmint (*Mentha spicata*), like its close cousin peppermint, is widely used for its digestive benefits. However, since spearmint has a "warmer" flavor, it is milder and taken more frequently by children and the elderly, or to treat general stomachache. Spearmint is often taken for minor cases of heartburn, nausea, indigestion, flu, and motion sickness. It also appears in gum, candy, toothpaste, soap, and medicine.

What are some culinary and medicinal uses for **hyssop**?

The fresh leaves of hyssop (*Hyssopus officinalis*) have a bitter taste and can be used in small quantities to add zip to vegetables and salads. It can also be dried for use in tea. The tea is reputed to relieve symptoms of nervousness or hysteria. When combined with horehound (*Marrubium vulgare*), hyssop is used to treat coughs. In a poultice, hyssop has traditionally been used to treat muscle aches and rheumatism.

Does **mustard** have any medicinal value?

Mustard (*Brassica juncea* and *B. nigra*) is a cousin of cabbage, kohlrabi, and broccoli. The leaves and blossoms of all of these plants are used for culinary purposes. Mustard also supposedly has medicinal value. A ground mixture of the seeds is used to treat digestion or improve the appetite. However, since it is such an acidic herb, it should be used with care. More frequently, mustard is used as a poultice or plaster to relieve congestion.

What are some traditional uses of mullein?

The stems of mullein (*Verbascum thapsus*), which stands five feet tall, were once dipped in suet and used as medieval candles. Hence, it is sometimes known as "the candlewick plant" or "torches." Perhaps because of its illuminating qualities, mullein was considered in India to protect against evil spirits. Almost all parts of the plant have reputed medicinal value, with the exception of the seeds, which are toxic. An infusion of dried flowers, with the plant material removed, has been used to treat respiratory infections. Mullein oil is said to cure ear aches and any irritation of the mucous membranes. The roots, as well as the leaves and flowers, are believed to have a sedentary effect.

What are some traditional uses of **sage**?

Sage or *Salvia officinalis* is most commonly considered a culinary herb, used to flavor a Thanksgiving turkey and stuffing, as well as other white meats and sausages. Sage is reported to have value as a healing herb. It has frequently been used as an antiseptic in natural mouthwashes and gargles and to treat cuts and abrasions. Sage is considered by some to be a stimulant and a preventative, keeping the digestive tract, nervous system, and sexual organs healthy. Like many other herbs, sage has also been used to treat digestive problems such as flatuence. Legend has it that drinking sage tea in the spring promotes a long life.

What is **hypericum** used for?

Hypericum calycinum is one of the woundworts—St. John's wort. As such, it has been used by homeopaths and herbalists to treat wounds and bruising. St. John's wort is sometimes known to be combined with other herbs such as pot marigold (*Calendula officinalis*) and witch hazel (*Hamamelis* spp.) to improve its effect. It has also been used as an antidepressant.

What is **chamomile tea** taken for?

Chamomile tea, made from the leaves and flowers of either Roman chamomile (*Chamaemelum nobile*) or German chamomile (*Matricaria recutita*), has been used traditionally to calm nerves and improve digestion. Chamomile flowers can also be added to the bath for this purpose. Chamomile tea is also sometimes used as a hair rinse to add highlights to blond or light brown hair.

How was **chicory** traditionally used?

Fresh chicory (*Cichorium intybus*) leaves were harvested by Native Americans to be steeped in water and drunk like coffee. Some Europeans also drank a kind of chicory drink, and the French still add chicory directly to their coffee to temper coffee's acidity. This complements the use of chicory by herbalists to aid in digestion. It was once used to treat jaundice as well as skin irritations and swellings.

What is **echinacea** made from?

Echinacea is actually a perennial plant, better known as the purple coneflower (*Echinacea purpurea*). It was traditionally used by the Lakota to guard against infection. More recently, echinacea is being researched for its ability to boost the body's immune system and protect humans from viruses. As a result, it has begun appearing in drugstores and health food stores as an herbal supplement.

Does **parsley** have any value other than as a limp garnish?

The ubiquitous sprig of parsley lying spent next to the daily special makes for a sad culinary experience. Parsley (*Petroselinum crispum*) is actually a wonderfully flavorful herb when eaten fresh or frozen (it has little to no taste when dried). It is a rich source of vitamin C and combines well with garlic to add a fresh taste to vegetable and meat dishes. As a healing herb, parsley is considered to be a diuretic and is reputed to relieve menstrual cramps.

What is **salad burnet** used for?

Salad burnet (*Poterium sanguisorba*) is a little-known culinary herb. Its leaves resemble parsley somewhat. They taste and smell, however, of cucumber. Salad burnet is usually added to salads or to flavor light alcoholic beverages. It is best eaten fresh.

What are some herbs used for their **flowers**?

While blossoms and buds are ornamental features in many plants (besides their important role in pollination), herb flowers have many culinary and medicinal uses. The petals and whole flowers of roses (*Rosa* spp.), German and Roman chamomile (*Matricaria recutita* and *Chamaemelum nobile*), elder (*Sambucus nigra*), purple coneflower (*Echinacea purpurea*), pot marigold (*Calendula officinalis*), mullein (*Verbascum thapsus*), chive (*Allium schoenoprasum*), and violet (*Viola* spp.) have a variety of herbal uses.

Does **valerian** have any value as a medicinal herb?

Valerian (*Valeriana officinalis*) is sometimes used in potpourri and is also known to be attractive to cats. In addition to these uses, valerian is traditionally used in herbal remedies for its tranquilizing effects. Herbalists sometimes prescribe valerian for tension or excitability and for the relief of cramps.

Dill (*Anethum graveolens*) is cultivated for its leaves and seeds, which are used for pickling and preparing other foods. (Robert J. Huffman/Field Mark Publications)

How are **dandelions** used by herbalists?

Despite a bad reputation given them by lawn care companies, dandelions (*Taraxacum officinale*) are a very versatile plant. Its botanical name translates loosely as "the official remedy." Dandelion flowers, leaves, and roots are all used by herbalists and cooks. Young dandelion greens add a refreshingly bitter bite to salads and are a good source

While bouncing Bet (*Saponaria officinalis*) is commonly considered a weed for its invasive properties, it also has some value as an herbal treatment. It has been used to soothe bruises and as a shampoo. Bouncing Bet is traditionally known as a gentle soap for delicate and antique fabrics. It should not be ingested.

of vitamin A and calcium. The root is supposedly a diuretic, which aids in the cleansing of the liver. In Europe, it is used by herbalists as a treatment for diabetes.

How was **dill** traditionally used?

Native to the Mediterranean, dill (*Anethum graveolens*) has been used as a flavoring for breads, salads, meats, and soups by many cultures. It is believed to have been used by the ancient Egyptians to promote digestion. Modern herbalists continue to use dill in this tradition and promote its ability to increase maternal milk production as well.

Resources

Books

A–Z of Evergreen Trees & Shrubs. New York: Reader's Digest, 1998.

The American Horticultural Society A–Z Encyclopedia of Garden Plants. New York: DK Publishing, 1997.

Ashmun, Barbara Blossom. *200 Tips for Growing Beautiful Perennials*. Chicago: Chicago Review Press, 1998.

Ashmun, Barbara Blossom. *200 Tips for Growing Beautiful Roses*. Chicago: Chicago Review Press, 1998.

Austin, Sandra. *Color in Garden Design*. Newtown, CT: Taunton, 1998.

Baker, Jerry. *The Impatient Gardener*. New York: Ballantine, 1998.

Baker, Jerry. *The Impatient Gardener's Lawn Book*. New York: Ballantine, 1998.

Ball, Jeff and Liz Ball. *Rodale's Landscape Problem Solver*. Emmaus, PA: Rodale Press, 1989.

Ball, Jeff and Liz Ball. *Yardening*. New York: Macmillan Publishing Co., 1991.

Bartholomew, Mel. *Square Foot Gardening*. Emmaus, PA: Rodale Press, 1981.

Barton, Barbara. *Gardening by Mail*, 4th ed. Boston: Houghton Mifflin, 1994.

Benjamin, Joan, ed. *Great Garden Shortcuts*. Emmaus, PA: Rodale Press, 1996.

Bennett, Jennifer and Turid Forsyth. *The Annual Garden*. Somerville, MA: Firefly, 1998.

The Big Book of Flower Gardening: A Guide to Growing Beautiful Annuals, Perennials, Bulbs & Roses. Alexandria, VA: Time-Life Books, 1997.

The Big Book of Garden Design: Simple Steps to Creating Beautiful Gardens. Alexandria, VA: Time-Life Books, 1998.

Bird, Richard. *Beds and Border*. New York: Stewart, Tabori & Chang, 1998.

Bisgrove, Richard. *The Gardens of Gertrude Jekyll*. Little, Brown and Co., 1992.

Boufford, Bob. *The Gardener's Computer Companion*. San Francisco: No Starch Press, 1998.

Bradley, Steven. *Keeping the Garden in Bloom: Watering, Dead-Heading, and Other Summer Tasks*. New York: Stewart, Tabori & Chang, 1998.

Brennan, Georgeanne and Kathryn Kleinman. *Backyard Bouquets: Growing Great Flowers for Simple Arrangements*. San Francisco: Chronicle Books, 1998.

Breskend, Jean Spiro. *Backyard Design: Making the Most of the Space Around Your Home*. New York: Bulfinch Press, 1991.

Brookes, John. *John Brookes' Natural Landscapes*. New York: DK Publishing, 1998.

Brookes, John, ed. *RD Home Handbooks: Garden Planning*. Pleasantville, NY: Reader's Digest, 1992.

Brooklyn Botanic Garden handbooks.

Brown, Deni. *Garden Herbs*. New York: DK Publishing, 1998.

Campbell, Stu. *Let It Rot! The Gardener's Guide to Composting*. Pownal, VT: Storey Publications, 1990.

Caring for Your Plants. New York: Reader's Digest, 1998.

Cathey, H. Marc. *Heat-Zone Gardening: How to Choose Plants That Thrive in Your Region's Warmest Weather*. Alexandria, VA: Time-Life Books, 1998.

Christopher, Tom and Marty Asher. *The 20-Minute Gardener*. New York: Random House, 1997.

Clarke, Ethne. *Gardening with Foliage Plants: Leaf, Bark, and Berry*. New York: Abbeville Press, 1997.

Clausen, Ruth R. and Nicolas H. Ekstrom. *Perennials for American Gardens*. New York: Random House, 1989.

Colby, Deirdre. *City Gardening: Planting, Maintaining, and Designing the Urban Garden*. New York: Simon and Schuster, 1987.

Cooke, Ian. *The Pathfinder's Guide to Tender Perennials*. Portland, OR: Timber Press, 1998.

Coombes, Allen J. *Dictionary of Plant Names*. Portland, OR: Timber Press, 1994.

Coombes, Allen J. and Kim Tripp. *The Complete Book of Shrubs*. New York: Reader's Digest, 1998.

Cooney, Norma. *The Kitchen Garden: Fresh Ideas for Luscious Vegetables, Herbs, Flowers and Fruit*. New York: Friedman/Fairfax, 1998.

Coughlin, Roberta M. *The Gardener's Companion: A Book of Lists and Lore*. New York: Harper Perennial, 1991.

Courtauld, George. *An Axe, a Spade and Ten Acres*. London: Secker & Warburg, 1983.

Cox, Jeff. *Jeff Cox's 100 Greatest Garden Ideas: Tips, Techniques, and Projects for a Bountiful Garden and a Beautiful Backyard*. Emmaus, PA: Rodale Press, 1998.

Cox, Jeff. *Perennial All-Stars: The 150 Best Perennials for Great-Looking, Trouble-Free Gardens*. Emmaus, PA: Rodale Press, 1998.

Crandall, Chuck and Barbara Crandall. *Courtyards and Patios: Designing and Landscaping Elegant Outdoor Spaces*. New York: Friedman/Fairfax, 1998.

Crockett, James Underwood. *Annuals*. New York: Time-Life Books, 1971.

Cullen, Mark, and Lorraine Johnson. *The Urban/Suburban Composter: The Complete Guide to Backyard, Balcony, and Apartment Composting*. New York: St. Martin's Press, 1992.

Cunningham, Sally Jean. *Great Garden Companions: A Companion-Planting System for a Beautiful, Chemical-Free Vegetable Garden*. Emmaus, PA: Rodale Press, 1998.

Damrosch, Barbara. *The Garden Primer*. New York: Workman Publishing, 1988.

Dannenmaier, Molly. *A Child's Garden: Enchanting Outdoor Spaces for Children and Parents*. New York: Simon & Schuster, 1998.

Davis, Brian. *The Plant Selector*. New York: Sterling, 1998.

Dirr, Michael A. *Dirr's Hardy Trees & Shrubs: An Illustrated Encyclopedia*. Portland, OR: Timber Press, 1997.

Dirr, Michael A. *Manual of Woody Landscape Plants*. Champaign, IL: Stripes Publishing Company, 1977.

DiSabato-Aust, Tracy. *The Well-Tended Perennial Garden: Planting and Pruning Techniques*. Portland, OR: Timber Press, 1998.

Ellefson, Connie, Tom Stephens, and Doug Welsh. *Xeriscape Gardening: Water Conservation for the American Landscape*. New York: Macmillan, 1992.

Elliott, Charles. *The Transplanted Gardener*. New York: Lyons & Burford, 1995.

Ellis, Barbara and Fern Marshall Bradley. *The Organic Gardener's Handbook of Natural Insects and Disease Control*. Emmaus, PA: Rodale Press, 1992.

The Encyclopedia of Organic Gardening. Emmaus, PA: Rodale Press, 1978.

Environmentally Friendly Gardening: Easy Composting. San Ramon, CA: Ortho Books, 1992.

The Family Handyman Landscape Projects: Planning, Planting & Building for a More Beautiful Yard and Garden. New York: Reader's Digest, 1998.

Fell, Derek. *Derek Fell's Handy Garden Guides*. New York: Friedman/Fairfax.

Fell, Derek. *The Encyclopedia of Flowers*. New York: Michael Friedman Publishing Group, 1994.

Fell, Derek and Carolyn Heath. *550 Perennial Garden Ideas*. New York: Simon & Schuster, 1994.

Ferguson, Nicola. *Right Plant, Right Place: The Indispensable Guide to the Successful Garden*. New York: Fireside Books, 1992.

Field, Ann and Gretchen Scoble. *The Meaning of Flowers*. San Francisco: Chronicle Books, 1998.

Fish, Margery. *We Made a Garden*. United Kingdom: W. H. & L. Collinridge Ltd., 1956.

Flowerdew, Bob. *Good Companions: A Guide to Gardening with Plants That Help Each Other*. New York: Summit Books, 1991.

Frieze, Charlotte M. *The Zone Garden Series*. New York: Fireside Books, 1997.

Garden Design. New York: Meigher Communications.

A Garden for All Seasons. London/New York: Reader's Digest, 1991.

Gardens Illustrated. London: John Brown Publishing.

Greenoak, Francesca. *Water Features for Small Gardens*. North Pomfret, VT: Trafalgar Square Publishing, 1996.

Greenwood, Pippa. *Basic Gardening: 101 Essential Tips*. New York: DK Publishing, 1998.

Greenwood, Pippa. *The New Gardener: The Practical Guide to Gardening Basics*. New York: DK Publishing, 1995.

Grey, Mara. *The Lazy Gardener*. New York: Macmillan, 1998.

Hadfield, Miles. *Pioneers in Gardening*. First published 1955. London: Bloomsbury Publishing, 1996.

Hamilton, Geoff, ed. *RD Home Handbooks: Organic Gardening*. Pleasantville, NY: Reader's Digest, 1991.

Harmonious Technologies. *Backyard Composting: Your Complete Guide to Recycling Yard Clippings*. Ojai, CA: Harmonious Press, 1992.

Harper, Pamela J. *Designing with Perennials*. New York: Macmillan, 1991.

Heilenman, Diane. *Gardening in the Lower Midwest: A Practical Guide for the New Zones 5 and 6*. Indiana University Press, 1994.

Heriteau, Jacqueline. *American Horticultural Society Flower Finder*. New York: Simon & Schuster, 1992.

Hill, Lewis. *Pruning Made Easy: A Gardener's Guide to When and How to Prune Everything, from Flowers to Trees*. Pownal, VT: Storey Books, 1998.

Hillier, Malcolm. *Container Gardening Through the Year*. New York: DK Publishing, 1998.

Holmes, Roger and Rita Buchanan. *Home Landscaping: Mid-Atlantic Region*. Upper Saddle River, NJ: Creative Homeowner Press, 1998.

Holmes, Roger and Rita Buchanan. *Home Landscaping: Northeast Region*. Upper Saddle River, NJ: Creative Homeowner Press, 1998.

Holmes, Roger and Rita Buchanan. *Home Landscaping: Southeast Region*. Upper Saddle River, NJ: Creative Homeowner Press, 1998.

Hynes, Erin. *Rodale's Weekend Gardener: Create a Low-Maintenance Landscape to Enjoy Year-Round*. Emmaus, PA: Rodale Press, 1998.

Jackson, Richard and Carolyn Hutchinson. *How to Win at Gardening: A Practical A-to-Z Guide to a Better Garden*. New York: Reader's Digest, 1998.

Jaworski, Henry. *Summer Bulbs*. Shelburne, VT: Chapters, 1998.

Jay, Roni. *Gardens of the Spirit: Create Your Own Sacred Space*. New York: Sterling, 1998.

Johnson, Hugh. *Principles of Gardening*. New York: Simon & Schuster, 1996.

Joyce, David and John Elsey. *The Perfect Plant for Every Site, Habitat, and Garden Style*. New York: Stewart, Tabori & Chang, 1998.

King, Michael and Piet Oudolf. *Gardening with Grasses*. Portland, OR: Timber Press, 1998.

Kolls, Rebecca. *Rebecca's Garden: Four Seasons to Grow On*. New York: Avon Books, 1998.

Kourik, Robert and Deborah Jones. *The Lavender Garden: Beautiful Varieties to Grow and Gather*. San Francisco: Chronicle Books, 1998.

Lacy, Allen. *The Gardener's Eye and Other Essays*. New York: Atlantic Monthly Press, 1992.

Lima, Patrick. *The Art of Perennial Gardening*. Somerville, MA: Firefly, 1998.

Loewer, Peter. *Step-by-Step Wildflowers & Native Plants*. Des Moines, IA: Meredith Corp., 1995.

Longley, Susanna. *The Weekend Gardener*. New York: Reader's Digest, 1998

Lovejoy, Ann. *Gardening from Scratch: How to Turn Your Empty Lot into a Living Garden*. New York: Macmillan, 1998.

MacCaskey, Michael and National Gardening Association Editors. *Gardening for Dummies*. Foster City, CA: IDG Books, 1996.

Marken, Bill and National Gardening Association Editors. *Annuals for Dummies*. Foster City, CA: IDG Books, 1998.

Marken, Bill and National Gardening Association Editors. *Container Gardening for Dummies*. Foster City, CA: IDG Books, 1998.

Marshall, Fern, ed. *Rodale's All-New Encyclopedia of Organic Gardening*. Emmaus, PA: Rodale Press, 1992.

Martin, Deborah L., and Grace Gershuny, eds. *The Rodale Book of Composting: Easy Methods for Every Gardener*. Emmaus, PA: Rodale Press, 1992.

McGourty, Fred and Pam Harper. *Perennials: How to Select, Grow and Enjoy*. Los Angeles: Price Stern Sloan, 1985.

Mitchell, Henry. *Henry Mitchell on Gardening*. Boston: Houghton Mifflin, 1998.

Murray, Elizabeth. *Monet's Passion: Ideas, Inspiration and Insights from the Painter's Gardens*. San Francisco, CA: Pomegranate Art Books, 1989.

Noordhuis, Klaas T. and David Tomlinson, ed. *The Garden Plants Encyclopedia*. Somerville, MA: Firefly, 1998.

O'Connor, Jane and Emma Sweeney. *The Complete Idiot's Guide to Gardening*. New York: Alpha Books, 1996.

Ogden, Shepherd. *Step by Step Organic Vegetable Gardening*. HarperCollins, 1992.

Organic Gardening. Emmaus, PA: Rodale Press.

Pick the Right Plant: A Sun & Shade Guide to Successful Plant Selection. Alexandria, VA: Time-Life Books, 1998.

Plants & Gardens News (newsletter). Brooklyn, NY: Brooklyn Botanic Garden.

Proctor, Rob. *Country Flowers: Wild Classics for the Contemporary Garden*. New York: Running Heads, 1991.

Raworth, Jenny and Val Bradley. *The Complete Guide to Indoor Gardening*. New York: Abbeville, 1998.

Reddell, Rayford Clayton. *All-America Roses*. San Francisco: Chronicle Books, 1998.

Richardson, Beth. *Gardening with Children*. Newtown, CT: Taunton, 1998.

Riley Smith, Mary. *The Front Garden: New Approaches to Landscape Design*. Houghton Mifflin, 1991.

Roach, Margaret. *A Way to Garden: A Hands-On Primer for Every Season*. New York: Clarkson Potter, 1998.

Rutledge, Cooper. *Backyard Battle Plan: The Ultimate Guide to Controlling Wildlife Damage in Your Garden*. New York: Penguin, 1998.

Schneck, Marcus. *Creating a Butterfly Garden*. New York: Fireside Books, 1994.

Schultz, Warren. *The Chemical-Free Lawn: The Newest Varieties and Techniques to Grow Lush, Hardy Grass*. Emmaus, PA: Rodale Press, 1989.

Schultz, Warren and Carol Spier. *Garden Details: Accents, Ornaments, and Finishing Touches for Your Garden*. New York: Friedman/Fairfax, 1998.

Seidenberg, Charlotte. *The Wildlife Garden: Planning Backyard Habitats*. Jackson, MS: University Press of Mississippi, 1995.

Seton, Susannah. *Simple Pleasures of the Garden: Stories, Recipes & Crafts from the Abundant Earth*. Emeryville, CA: Conari Press, 1998.

Small Gardens. London: Ward Lock Ltd., 1990.

Smith, Charles W. G. *The Big Book of Gardening Secrets*. Pownal, VT: Storey Books, 1998.

Smittle, Delilah, ed. *Rodale's Complete Garden Problem Solver: Instant Answers to the Most Common Gardening Questions*. Emmaus, PA: Rodale Press, 1998.

Squire, David. *The Concise Gardening Encyclopedia: The Complete Guide to Planning, Creating, and Maintaining Your Garden*. Philadelphia, PA: Courage Books, 1997.

Stell, Elizabeth P. *Secrets to Great Soil: A Grower's Guide to Composting, Mulching, and Creating Healthy, Fertile Soil for Your Garden and Lawn*. Pownal, VT: Storey Books, 1998.

Stuckey, Maggie. *Gardening from the Ground Up: Rock-Bottom Basics for Absolute Beginners*. New York: St. Martin's Press, 1998.

Sunset Garden Pests & Diseases. Menlo Park, CA: Sunset Publishing Corp, 1993.

Swain, Roger B. *The Practical Gardener: Mastering the Elements of Good Growing*. New York: Henry Holt and Company, 1989.

Tatroe, Marcia and National Gardening Association Editors. *Perennials for Dummies*. Foster City, CA: IDG Books, 1997.

Taylor, Patricia A. *Easy Care Perennials*. Fireside Books, 1989.

Taylor, Patricia A. *Easy Care Shade Flowers*. Fireside Books, 1993.

Taylor, Patrick. *Making Gardens: An Essential Guide to Planning and Planting*. Portland, OR: Timber Press, 1998.

Taylor's Guide to Annuals. Boston: Houghton Mifflin, 1986.

Taylor's Master Guide to Gardening. Boston, New York: Houghton Mifflin, 1994.

Taylor's Pocket Guide to Herbs and Edible Flowers. Houghton Mifflin, 1990.

Thomas, Ian. *The Culpeper Guides: How to Grow Herbs*. Exeter, Devon, England: Webb & Bower, 1988.

Turner, Carole B. *Seed Sowing and Saving: Step-by-Step Techniques for Collecting and Growing More Than 100 Vegetables, Flowers, and Herbs*. Pownal, VT: Storey Books, 1998.

Uber, William C. *Water Gardening Basics*. Upland, CA: Dragonflyer Press, 1988.

Walheim, Lance and National Gardening Association Editors. *Roses for Dummies*. Foster City, CA: IDG Books, 1997.

Weiss, Gaea and Shandor Weiss. *Growing & Using the Healing Herbs*. Emmaus, PA: Rodale Press, 1985.

Wells, Diana. *One Hundred Flowers and How They Got Their Names*. Chapel Hill, NC: Algonquin Books, 1997.

White, Hazel. *Paths and Walkways: Simple Projects, Contemporary Designs*. San Francisco: Chronicle Books, 1998.

White, Hazel. *Water Gardens: Simple Projects, Contemporary Designs*. San Francisco: Chronicle Books, 1998.

Williams, Bunny and Nancy Drew. *On Garden Style*. New York: Simon & Schuster, 1998.

Williams, Carol. *Bringing a Garden to Life*. New York: Bantam, 1998.

Williams, Robin. *Reader's Digest Garden Design: How to Be Your Own Landscape Architect*. Pleasantville, NY: Reader's Digest, 1995.

Wyman, Donald. *Wyman's Gardening Encyclopedia*. Macmillan Publishing Co., 1971.

Yepsen, Roger. *1,001 Old-Time Garden Tips: Timeless Bits of Wisdom on How to Grow Everything Organically, from the Good Old Days When Everyone Did*. Emmaus, PA: Rodale Press, 1998.

Yepsen, Roger B., Jr. *The Encyclopedia of Natural Insect and Disease Control*. New York: Rodale Press, 1984.

Your Organic Garden with Jeff Cox. Emmaus, PA: Rodale Press, 1994.

Magazines

American Homestyle and Gardening
New York Times Co.
110 Fifth Ave.
New York, NY 10017 USA

Phone: (212)878-8700
Fax: (212)463-1269

Atlanta Homes and Lifestyles
Wiesner Inc.
1100 Johnson Ferry Rd. NE, Ste. 595
Atlanta, GA 30342 USA
Phone: (404)252-6670
Fax: (404)252-6673
E-mail: althomes@aol.com

Build and Green
Build and Green
2922 W. 6th Ave., Studio D
Vancouver, BC, Canada V6K 1X3
Phone: (604)730-1940
Fax: (604)730-7860

Canadian Gardening
Camar Publications Ltd.
130 Spy Ct.
Markham, ON, Canada L3R 5H6
Phone: (905)475-8440
Fax: (905)475-9246

Carolina Gardener
P.O. Box 4504
Greensboro, NC 27404 USA

Country Home
Meredith Corp
1716 Locust St.
Des Moines, IA 50309-3023 USA
Phone: (515)284-2015
Fax: (515)284-2552
E-mail: countryh@asm.mdp.com

Fine Gardening
The Taunton Press, Inc.
63 S. Main St.
P.O. Box 5506
Newtown, CT 06470-5506 USA
Phone: (203)426-8171
Fax: (203)270-6751
Toll-free: 800-283-7252

Fleurs, Plantes et Jardins
Editions Versicolores Inc.
1320 Blvd. St. Joseph
St.-Joseph, PQ, Canada G2K 1G2

Phone: (418)628-8690
Fax: (418)628-0524

Flower & Garden
KC Publishing, Inc.
700 W. 47th St., Ste. 310
Kansas City, MO 64112 USA
Phone: (816)531-5730
Fax: (816)531-3873

Green World
Green World
12 Dudley St.
Randolph, VT 05060-1202 USA
E mail: gx297@cleveland.freenet.edu

The Herb Quarterly
Long Mountain Press, Inc.
P.O. Box 689
San Anselmo, CA 94979-0689 USA
Phone: (415)455-9540
Fax: (415)455-9541
Toll-free: 800-371-4372

Horticulture
98 N. Washington St.
Boston, MA 02114 USA
Phone: (617)742-5600
Fax: (617)367-6364
E-mail: hortmag@aol.com

House Beautiful
Hearst Corporation
1700 Broadway
New York, NY 10019 USA
Toll-free: 800-289-8696

Journal of Therapeutic Horticulture
American Horticultural Therapy Association
362A Christopher Ave.
Gaithersburg, MD 20879-1280 USA
Phone: (301)948-3010
Fax: (301)869-2397

Kitchen Garden
The Taunton Press, Inc.
63 S. Main St.
P.O. Box 5506
Newtown, CT 06470-5506 USA
Phone: (203)426-8171

Fax: (203)426-3434
Toll-free: 800-888-8286

Martha Stewart at Home
Time Inc.
Time-Life Bldg., Rockefeller Center
1271 Avenue of the Americas
New York, NY 10020-1300 USA
Phone: (212)522-1212
Fax: (212)765-2699

Minnesota Horticulturist
Minnesota State Horticultural Society
1755 Prior Ave. N.
Falcon Heights, MN 55113 USA
Phone: (612)643-3601
Fax: (612)643-3638
Toll-free: 800-676-6747

The National Gardener
102 S. Elm Ave.
St. Louis, MO 63119 USA
Phone: (314)968-1664

National Gardening
National Gardening Association
180 Flynn Ave.
Burlington, VT 05401 USA
Phone: (802)863-1308
Fax: (802)863-5969
URL: http://www.garden.org
Toll-free: 800-538-7476

Organic Gardening
Rodale Press, Inc.
33 E. Minor St.
Emmaus, PA 18098 USA

General Gardening Websites

Adventures in Gardening: http://www.gardenguy.com

American Association of Botanical Gardens and Arboreta: http://www.mobot.org/AABGA

American Community Gardening Association: http://communitygarden.org

American Horticultural Society: http://www.ahs.org

Better Homes and Gardens: http://www.bhglive.com/gardening/index.html

Calendar of Gardening Events: http://www.gardencalendar.com

The Compost Resource Page: http://www.oldgrowth.org/compost

Digital Seed: http://www.digitalseed.com

The Garden Catalog List: http://www.cog.brown.edu/gardening/cat.html

Garden.com by Garden Escape: http://www.garden.com

The Garden Gate: http://www.prairienet.org/ag/garden/homepage.html

GardenNet: http://gardennet.com

Garden Pages: http://www.gardenpages.com

Garden Planet: http://www.worldleader.com/garden/index.htm

Garden Solutions: http://www.gardensolutions.com/cgi-bin/WebObjects/GardenSolutions

The Garden Spider's Web: http://www.gardenweb.com/spdrsweb

Garden Town: http://www.gardentown.com/index.html

Garden Web: http://www.gardenweb.com

Garden Web Ring: http://www.webring.com

Gardening.com: http://www.gardening.com

Herb Finder: http://www.woodny.com/garden/herbfinder.html

HGTV (Home & Garden Television): http://www.hgtv.com

HomeArts: Bloom!: http://homearts.com/depts/garden/00gardcl.htm

Horticulture Online: http://www.hortmag.com

Lawn Institute: http://www.lawninstitute.com

Master Composter: http://www.mastercomposter.com

Mr. Grow: http://www.mrgrow.com

Natural Gardening Online Catalog: http://www.naturalgardening.com

Nuseryman.com: http://www.nurseryman.com

Pacific Northwest Gardening: http://www.nwgardening.com

Plant Adviser: http://www.plantadviser.com

Plant World: http://www.plantworld.com

Southern Gardening: http://www.southerngardening.com

Sunset: http://www.sunsetmag.com

Traditional Gardening: http://traditionalgardening.com

The Trellis: http://wormsway.com/trellis.html

USDA Home Gardening: http://www.usda.gov/news/garden.htm

Virtual Gardener: http://www.pathfinder.com/vg

WebGarden: http://www.hcs.ohio-state.edu/hcs/WebGarden.html

Weekend Gardener: http://www.chestnut-sw.com/weekend.html

Botanical Garden Websites

Arnold Arboretum: http://www.arboretum.harvard.edu

Atlanta Botanical Garden: http://www.atlgarden.com

Australian National Botanic Garden: http://osprey.erin.gov.au/index.html

Birmingham Botanical Gardens: http://www.bbgardens.org

Boerner Botanical Gardens: http://uwm.edu/Dept/Biology/Boerner/index.html

Botanica: The Wichita Gardens: http://www.botanica.org

Brooklyn Botanic Garden: http://www.bbg.org

Chicago Botanic Garden: http://www.chicago-botanic.org

Desert Botanical Garden:
    http://cissus.mobot.org/AABGA/Members.page/desrt.bot.grdn.html

Descanso Gardens: http://www.descanso.com

Fioli Historical House & Gardens: http://www.fioli.org

Franklin Park Conservatory & Botanical Garden: http://www.fpconservatory.com

Huntington Botanical Garden: http://www.huntington.org/BotanicalDiv/HEHBotanical
    Home.html

Huntsville-Madison County Botanical Garden: http://www.hsvbg.org

Idaho Botanical Garden: http://www.avocet.net/ibg

Jerusalem Botanical Garden: http://www6.huji.ac.il/~botanic

Kew Gardens: http://www.rbgkew.org.uk/index.html

The Lady Bird Johnson Wildflower Center: http://www.wildflower.org

Longwood Gardens: http://www.longwoodgardens.org

Missouri Botanical Garden: http://www.mobot.org

Mitchell Park Horticultural Conservatory: http://www.uwm.edu/Dept/Biology/domes

The Morton Arboretums: http://www.mortonarb.org

Mynelle Gardens: http://www.Instar.com/mynelle

Myriad Botanical Gardens: http://www.okccvb.org/myrgard/myrgard.html

Nani Mau Gardens: http://www.nanimau.com

The National Arboretum: http://www.ars-grin.gov/ars/Beltsville/na/index.html

National Garden (U.S. Botanical Garden): http://www.nationalgarden.org

New York Botanical Garden: http://www.nybg.org

The Niagra Parks Botanical Gardens: http://www.npbg.org

Olbrich Botanical Gardens: http://www.ci.madison.wi.us/olbrich/olbrich.html

Paronella Park: http://www.gspeak.com.au/paronella

QuadCity Botanical Gardens: http://www.qcbotanicalgardens.org

Quail Botanical Gardens: http://members.aol.com/quailbg/quail.html

Royal Botanical Garden Edinburgh: http://www.rbge.org.uk

Royal Botanical Gardens: http://www.rbg.ca

San Antonio Botanical Garden: http://www.sabot.org

Skylands: The New Jersey State Botanical Garden: http://www.njskylandsgarden.org

Sonnenberg Gardens: http://www.sonnenberg.org

The South Carolina Botanical Garden: http://agweb.clemson.edu/hort/scbg/intro.html

The State Botanical Garden of Georgia: http://uga.edu/~botgarden

Strybing Arboretum & Botanical Gardens: http://www.mobot.org/AABGA/member.pages/strybing

Sydney Royal Botanic Garden: http://www.rbgsyd.gov.au

University of Delaware Botanic Gardens: http://bluehen.ags.udel.edu/udgarden.html

Associations

African Violet Society of America (AVSA)
2375 North
Beaumont, TX 77702 USA
(409) 839-4725, (409) 839-8484
Toll-Free: 800-770-AVSA
Fax: (409) 839-4329
E-mail: avsa@avsa.org
URL: http://www.avsa.org

The Alpine Garden Society
AGS Centre
Avon Bank
Pershore
Worcestershire WR10 3JP
United Kingdom
(UK) 01386 554790
Fax: (UK) 01386 554801
URL: http://www.alpinegardensoc.demon.co.uk/index.html#AGS

American Begonia Society (ABS)
157 Monument Rd.
Rio Dell, CA 95562-1617 USA
(707) 764-5407
Fax: (707) 764-5407

American Community Gardening Association (ACGA)
100 N. 20th St., 5th. Fl.
Philadelphia, PA 19103-1495 USA
(215) 988-8785

Fax: (215) 988-8810
E-mail: sallymcc@libertynet.org
URL: http://www.ag.arizona.edu/bradleyl/acga/main-frm.htm

American Daffodil Society (ADS)
1686 Grey Fox Trails
Milford, OH 45150 USA
(513) 248-9137
Fax: (513) 248-0898
E-mail: daffmlg@aol.com
URL: http://www.mc.edu/~adswww

American Dahlia Society (ADS)
c/o S. McQuithy Boyer
16816 CR 10
Bristol, IN 46507 USA
(219) 848-4888
E-mail: manorsam@aol.com
URL: http://www.dahlia.com/guide/index.html

American Fuchsia Society (AFS)
San Francisco County Fair Bldg.
9th Ave. & Lincoln Way
San Francisco, CA 94122 USA
(408) 257-0752
E-mail: sydnor@ix.netcom.com
URL: http://members.aol.com/amfuchsia/fuchs.as

American Gloxinia and Gesneriad Society (AGGS)
c/o Jessie Crisafulli
290 Federal St.
Belchertown, MA 01007 USA
(413) 323-6661
URL: http://aggs.org

American Hibiscus Society (AHS)
P.O. Drawer 321540
Cocoa Beach, FL 32932-1540 USA
(407) 783-2576
Fax: (407) 783-2576

American Horticultural Society (AHS)
7931 E. Boulevard Dr.
Alexandria, VA 22308 USA
(703) 768-5700
Toll-Free: 800-777-7931
Fax: (703) 768-8700
E-mail: gardenahs@aol.com
URL: http://www.ahs.org

American Hosta Society (AHS)
9448 Mayfield Rd.
Chesterland, OH 44026 USA

American Iris Society (AIS)
8426 Vinevalley Dr.
Sun Valley, CA 91352 USA
(818) 767-5512
Fax: (818) 767-8513

American Ivy Society (AIS)
P.O. Box 2123
Naples, FL 34106-2123 USA
(937) 862-4700, (941) 261-0388
Fax: (941) 261-8984
E-mail: 103630.3722@compuserve.com
URL: http://www.ivy.org

American Peony Society (APS)
250 Interlachen Rd.
Hopkins, MN 55343 USA
(612) 938-4706

American Primrose Society (APS)
41801 SW Burgarsky Rd.
Gaston, OR 97119-9407 USA
(503) 985-9596
URL: http://www.eskimo.com/~mcalpin/aps.html

American Rhododendron Society (ARS)
11 Pinecrest Dr.
Fortuna, CA 95540 USA
(707) 725-3043
URL: http://www.rhododendron.org/start.cfm

American Rose Society (ARS)
P.O. Box 30000
Shreveport, LA 71130-0030 USA
(318) 938-5402
Fax: (318) 938-5405
E-mail: ars@ars-hq.org
URL: http://www.ars.org

Azalea Society of America (ASA)
c/o Mrs. William Lorenz
P.O. Box 34536
West Bethesda, MD 20827-0536 USA
(703) 323-0114

Bonsai Clubs International (BCI)
P.O. Box 1176

Brookfield, WI 53008-1176 USA
(414) 860-8807
Fax: (414) 641-0757
E-mail: bonsairmt@aol.com
URL: http://www.bonsai-bci.com

Bromeliad Society (BSI)
c/o Carolyn Schoenau
P.O. Box 12981
Gainesville, FL 32604-0981 USA
(352) 372-6589
Fax: (352) 372-8823
E-mail: bsi@nervm.nerdc.ufl.edu

Cactus and Succulent Society of America (CSSA)
c/o Seymour Linden
1535 Reeves St.
Los Angeles, CA 90035 USA
(310) 556-1923
Fax: (310) 286-9629
E-mail: u4bia@aol.com
URL: http://www.cactus-mall.com/cssa

Cymbidium Society of America (CSA)
c/o Paula Butler
P.O. Box 2244
Orange, CA 92669 USA
(714) 532-4719
Fax: (714) 532-3611

Dynamics International Gardening Association (DIGA)
Drawer 1165
Asheboro, NC 27204-1165 USA

Epiphyllum Society of America (ESA)
P.O. Box 1395
Monrovia, CA 91017 USA
(310) 670-8148

Garden Club of America (GCA)
598 Madison Ave.
New York, NY 10022 USA
(212) 753-8287
Fax: (212) 753-0134

Garden Writers Association of America (GWAA)
c/o Robert C. LaGasse
10210 Leatherleaf Ct.
Manassas, VA 22111 USA
(703) 257-1032

Fax: (703) 257-0213
URL: http://www.hygexpo.com/gwaa

Gardeners of America (GOA)
5560 Merle Hay Rd.
P.O. Box 241
Johnston, IA 50131-0241 USA
(515) 278-0295
Fax: (515) 278-6245

Gardenia Society of America (GSA)
P.O. Box 879
Atwater, CA 95301 USA
(209) 358-2231

Heritage Rose Foundation
1512 Gorman St.
Raleigh, NC 27606-2919 USA
(919) 834-2591
E-mail: rosefoun@aol.com

Heritage Roses Group (HRG)
R.D. 1, Box 299
Clinton Corners, NY 12514 USA
(914) 266-3562

Hobby Greenhouse Association (HGA)
8 Glen Ter.
Bedford, MA 01730-2048 USA
(617) 275-0377
Fax: (617) 275-5693
E-mail: jhale@world.std.com
URL: http://www.hortsoft.com/hga.html

Indoor Gardening Society of America (IGSA)
944 S. Munroe Rd.
Tallmadge, OH 44278-3363 USA
(212) 666-5522

International Geranium Society (IGS)
P.O. Box 92734
Pasadena, CA 91109-2734 USA
(619) 727-0309
Fax: (818) 908-8867

International Lilac Society (ILS)
9500 Sperry Rd.
Kirtland, OH 44094 USA
(216) 946-4400
Fax: (216) 256-1655

International Oleander Society (IOS)
P.O. Box 3431
Galveston, TX 77552-0431 USA
(409) 762-9334

International Water Lily Society (IWLS)
1401 Johnson Ferry Rd.
Ste. 328 G, No. 12
Marietta, GA 30062 USA
(770) 977-3564

Los Angeles International Fern Society (LAIFS)
P.O. Box 90943
Pasadena, CA 91109 USA
(818) 441-3148, (310) 803-6887

Median Iris Society (MIS)
682 Huntley Heights Dr.
Ballwin, MO 63021 USA

National Council of State Garden Clubs (NCSGC)
4401 Magnolia Ave.
St. Louis, MO 63110-3492 USA
(314) 776-7574
Fax: (314) 776-5108

National Fuchsia Society (NFS)
c/o Rietkerk's
11507 E. 187th St.
Artesia, CA 90701 USA

National Gardening Association (NGA)
180 Flynn Ave.
Burlington, VT 05401 USA
(802) 863-1308
Fax: (802) 863-5962

North American Fruit Explorers (NAFEX)
1716 Apples Rd.
Chapin, IL 62628 USA
(217) 245-7589
URL: http://www.nafex.org

North American Gladiolus Council (NAGC)
c/o Eugene Demer
2624 Spurgin Rd.
Missoula, MT 59801 USA
(406) 728-7871

North American Heather Society (NAHS)
c/o Karla Lortz
E. 502 Haskel Hill Rd.

Shelton, WA 98584 USA
(360) 427-5318
Fax: (360) 427-5318
E-mail: heaths@gte.net
URL: http://www.humbold1.com/heathers

North American Lily Society (NALS)
P.O. Box 272
Owatonna, MN 55060 USA
(507) 451-2170
E-mail: nats@ll.net
URL: http://www.lilies.org

North American Rock Garden Society (NARGS)
c/o Jacques Mommens
P.O. Box 67
Millwood, NY 10546 USA
(914) 762-2948
E-mail: mommens@ibm.net
URL: http://www.nargs.org

Pacific Orchid Society of Hawaii (POS)
c/o Doug B. Schafer
1778 Hoolana St.
Pearl City, HI 96782 USA
(808) 455-7541

Plumeria Society of America (PSA)
P.O. Box 22791
Houston, TX 77227-2791 USA
(713) 780-8326

Reblooming Iris Society (RIS)
4 Marland Ave.
Towsonton, MD 21286 USA
(410) 337-9118

Rose Hybridizers Association (RHA)
21 S. Wheaton Rd.
Horseheads, NY 14845-1077 USA
(607) 562-8592
E-mail: lpeterso@stny.lrun.com

Seed Savers Exchange (SSE)
3076 N. Winn Rd.
Decorah, IA 52101 USA
(319) 382-5990
Fax: (319) 382-5872

Society for Japanese Irises (SJI)
9823 E. Michigan Ave.

Galesburg, MI 49053 USA
(616) 665-7500

Society for Louisiana Irises (SLI)
Box 40175
University of Southwestern Louisiana
Lafayette, LA 70504 USA
(318) 856-5859

Society for Pacific Coast Native Irises (SPCNI)
4333 Oak Hill Rd.
Oakland, CA 94605 USA
(510) 638-0658

Society for Siberian Irises (SSI)
c/o Ruth Wilder
802 Camellia Dr.
Anderson, SC 29625 USA
(803) 224-6966

Species Iris Group of North America (SIGNA)
c/o Richard Kiyomoto
486 Skiff St.
North Haven, CT 06473 USA
(203) 789-7238

Catalogs

Appalachian Gardens
  Box 82
  Waynesboro, PA 17268-0082
  (717) 762-4312
  Fax: (717) 762-7532

Autumn Glade Botanicals
  46857 W. Ann Arbor Trail
  Plymouth, MI 48170
  Fax: (313) 459-2604

Bently Seeds, Inc.
  16 Railroad Avenue
  Cambridge, NY 12816
  (518) 677-2603
  Fax: (518) 677-5676

Berlin Seeds / Raker's Greenhouse and Nursery
  5371 County Road 77
  Millersburg, OH 44654
  (216) 893-2811

Bluestone Perennials
7211 Middle Ridge Rd.
Madison, OH 44057
(216) 428-7535
Fax: (216) 428-7198

Bovees Nursery
1737 S.W. Coronado
Portland, OR 97219
(503) 244-9341

Brittingham Plant Farms
P.O. Box 2538
Salisbury, MD 21802
(410) 749-5153
Fax: (800) 749-5148

The Bulb Crate
2560 Deerfield Rd.
Riverwoods, IL 60015
(708) 317-1414

W. Atlee Burpee & Co.
300 Park Ave.
Warminster, PA 18991-0001
(800) 888-1447

Carroll Gardens
P.O. Box 310
4444 E. Main St.
Westminster, MD 21158
(800) 638-6334

The Cook's Garden
P.O. Box 535
Londonderry, VT 05148
(802) 824-3400
Fax: (802) 824-3027

DeGiorgi Seed Company
6011 "N" St.
Omaha, NE 68117-1634
(402) 731-3901
Fax: (402) 731-8475

Earl May Seed Company
208 N. Elm St.
Shanandoah, IA 51603-0099
(712) 246-1020

Farmer Seed & Nursery
P.O. Box 129

818 NW 4th St.
Fairbault, MN 55021
(507) 334-1623

Forest Farm
990 Tetherow Rd.
Williams, OR 97554-9599
(503) 846-6963

Gallina Canyon Ranch
P.O. Box 706
Abiquiu, NM 87510
(505) 685-4888
Fax: (505) 685-4888

Gardener's Eden
P.O. Box 7307
San Francisco, CA 94120-7307
(800) 822-9600

Gardener's Supply Company
128 Intervale Rd.
Burlington, VT 05401-2850
(802) 660-4600
Fax: (802) 660-4600

Gardens Alive!
5100 Schenley Pl.
Lawrenceburg, IN 47025
(812) 537-8650
Fax: (812) 537-8660

The Gourmet Gardener
8650 College Blvd., Suite 2051N
Overland Park, KS 66210-1806
(913) 345-0490

Greer Gardens
1280 Goodpasture Rd.
Eugene, OR 97401-1794
(503) 686-8266
Fax: (503) 686-8266

Gurney's Seed & Nursery Co.
110 Capital St.
Yankton, SD 57079
(605) 665-1671

Henry Field's Heritage Gardens
1 Meadow Ridge Rd.
Shenandoah, IA 51601-0700
(605) 665-5188

Iris City Gardens
502 Brighton Place
Nashville, TN 37205-2556
(615) 386-3778

Jackson & Perkins
1 Rose Lane
Medford, OR 97501-0701
(800) 292-GROW

Johnny's Select Seeds
Foss Hill Road
Albion, ME 04910-9731
(207) 437-4301
Fax: (207) 437-2165

Judy's Perennials
1206 Maple Ave.
Downers Grove, IL 60615
(708) 969-6514

J. W. Jung Seed Co.
335 S. High Street
Rondolf, WI 53956

Klehm Nursery
Route 5, Box 197
Penny Rd.
South Barrington, IL 60010-9555
(800) 553-3715

The Landis Valley Museum
2451 Kissel Hill Rd.
Lancaster, PA 17601
(717) 569-0401

Langenbach Fine Tool Co.
P.O. Box 453
Blairstown, NJ 07825
(800) 362-1991
Fax: (201) 383-0844

Laurie's Landscape
2959 Hobson Rd.
Downers Grove, IL 60517
(708) 969-1270

Le Jardin du Gourmet
P.O. Box 75
St. Johnsbury Center, VT 05863-0075
(800) 659-1446
Fax: (802) 748-9592

Lee Gardens
Box 5
Tremont, IL 61568
(309) 925-5262

A.M. Leonard
P.O. Box 816
6665 Spiker Rd.
Piqua, OH 45356-0816
(800) 543-8955, (513) 773-2696

Liberty Seed Company
P.O. Box 806
New Philadelphia, OH 44663
(800) 541-6022
Fax: (216) 364-6415

Mellinger's
2310 W. South Range Rd.
North Lima, OH 44452-9731
(216) 549-9861

Milaeger's Gardens
4838 Douglas Ave.
Racine, WI 53402-2498
(414) 639-2371

The Natural Garden
38 W443 Highway 64
St. Charles, IL 60174
(708) 584-0150

The Natural Gardening Company
217 San Anselmo Ave.
San Anselmo, CA 94960
(415) 456-5060
Fax: (415) 721-0642

Nich Gardens
1111 Dawson Rd.
Chapel Hill, NC 27516
(919) 967-0078

Nichols Garden Nursery
1190 North Pacific Highway
Albany, OR 97321-4580
(503) 928-9280
Fax: (503) 967-8406

Nor'East Miniature Roses, Inc.
P.O. Box 307
Rowley, MA 019696

(508) 948-7964
Fax: (508) 948-5487

Park Seed Company
P.O. Box 46
Highway 254 North
Cokesbury Road
Greennwood, SC 29647-0001
(803) 223-7333

Pinetree Garden Seeds
Box 300
New Glouchester, ME 04260
(207) 926-3400
Fax: (207) 926-3886

The Propagators Private Stock
8805 Kemman Rd.
Hebron, IL 60034

Riverhead Perennials
5 Riverhead Lane
East Lyme, CT 06333
(203) 437-7828

Roslyn Nursery
211 Burrs Lane
Dix Hills, NY 11746
(516) 643-9347

Seeds of Change
P.O. Box 15700
Santa Fe, NM 87506-5700
(505) 438-8080
Fax: (505) 438-7052

Seed Savers Exchange
3076 North Winn Rd.
Decorah, IA 52101

Sequoia Nursery
2519 E. Noble Ave.
Visalia, CA 93292
(209) 732-0190
Fax: (209) 732-0192

Sheffield's Seed Company, Inc.
273 Auburn Road, Rte. 34
Locke, NY 13092
(315) 497-1058

Shephard's Garden Seeds
30 Irene St.

Torrington, CT 06790-6627
(203) 482-3638
Fax: (203) 482-0532

R.H. Shumways
P.O. Box 1
Graniteville, SC 29829-0001
(803) 663-9771

Silver Creek Supply, Inc.
R.D. #1, Box 70
Port Trevorton, PA 17864
(717) 374-8010

Smith & Hawken
117 E. Strawberry Dr.
Mill Valley, CA 94941
(800) 776-3336

Southern Perennials and Herbs
98 Bridges Rd.
Tylertown, MS 39667
Fax: (601) 684-3729
E-Mail: sph@neosoft.com

Spring Hill Nurseries
6523 N. Galena Road
P.O. Box 1758
Peoria, IL 61651-9968

Springvale Farm Nursery, Inc.
Moxier Hollow Rd.
Hamburg, IL 62054
(618) 232-1108

Stark Bros. Nurseries and Orchards Co.
P.O. Box 10
Louisiana, MO 63353-0010

Sunrise Enterprises
P.O. Box 330058
West Hartford, CT 06133-0058
(203) 666-8071
Fax: (203) 665-8156

Surry Gardens
P.O. Box 145
Surry, ME 04684
(207) 667-4493

Thompson & Morgan
P.O. Box 1308
Jackson, NJ 08527

(800) 363-2225
Fax: (908) 363-9356

Totally Tomatoes
P.O. Box 1626
Augusta, GA 30903-1626
(803) 663-0016
Fax: (803) 663-9772

Trees on the Move
P.O. Box 462
Cranbury, NJ 08512
(609) 395-1366

Tripple Brook Farm
37 Middle Road
Southhampton, MA 01073
(413) 527-4626

TyTy Plantations
P.O. Box 159
TyTy, GA 31759
(912) 382-0400

Vermont Bean Seed Co.
Garden Lane
Fair Haven, VT 05743
(802) 273-3400
Fax: (803) 663-9772

Wayside Gardens
1 Garden Lane
Hodges, SC 29695-0001
(800) 845-1124

Weiss Brothers Nursery
11690 Colifax Highway
Grass Valley, CA 95945
(916) 272-7657

White Flower Farm
P.O. Box 50
Litchfield, CT 06759-0050
(800) 503-9624
Fax: (860) 496-1418

White Oak Nursery
6145 Oak Court
Peoria, IL 61614
(309) 693-1354

Wildseed Farms
1101 Campo Rosa Rd.

P.O. Box 308
Eagle Lake, TX 77434
(800) 848-0078
Fax: (409) 234-7407

Willhite Seed Incorporated
P.O. Box 23
Poolville, TX 76487
(800) 828-1840
Fax: (817) 599-5843

Winterthur Museum and Gardens
Winterthur, DE 19735
(800) 767-0500

Wood Prairie Farm
RFD 1, Box 64
Bridgewater, ME 04735-9989
(800) 829-9765
Fax: (800) 829-6494

Worms Way Indoor/Outdoor Garden Supply
4620 South State Road
Bloomington, IN 47401
(812) 876-6446

Wrenwood of Berkeley Springs
Route 4, Box 361
Berkeley Springs, WV 25411
(304) 258-3071

Index

Italicized page numbers indicate photographs.

421

423

425

427

428

433

441

KNOW IT ALL?
NOW YOU CAN!

The Handy Bug Answer Book™

NEW *The Handy Bug Answer Book* offers easily understood answers to
approximately 1,200 common and uncommon bug- and insect-related questions.
Do flies have eyes? How much blood can a mosquito drink? How much toxin do
bees carry in their stingers? Written in an engaging style that appeals to readers of
all ages, *The Handy Bug Answer Book* explores different types of bugs and their
ecosystems, and explains why bugs are beneficial to life on Earth.

The Handy Bug Answer Book is divided into topical chapters with subtopic sections
and includes a master index and 130 color and black-and-white photos.

Dr. Gilbert Waldbauer • 1998 • Paperback • 310 pp.
ISBN 1-57859-049-3

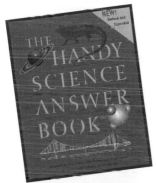

The Handy Science Answer Book; 2nd Edition

Can any bird fly upside down? Is white gold really gold? This best-selling book
covers hundreds of new sci-tech topics from the inner workings of the human body
to outer space and from math and computers to planes, trains and automobiles.
Handy Science provides nearly 1,400 answers compiled from the ready-reference
files of the Science and Technology Department of the Carnegie Library of Pittsburgh.
Includes more than 100 illustrations.

1997 • paperback • 598 pp.
ISBN 0-7876-1013-5

The Handy Weather Answer Book®

What is the difference between sleet and freezing rain? Do mobile homes attract tornadoes? You'll find clear-cut answers to 1,000 frequently asked questions in *The
Handy Weather Answer Book*. A cornucopia of weather facts, *Handy Weather* covers
such confounding and pertinent topics as tornadoes and hurricanes, thunder and
lightning, and droughts and flash floods, plus fascinating weather-related phenomena
such as El Niño, La Niña and the greenhouse effect. Includes 75 photos plus tables.

Walter A. Lyons, Ph.D. • 1996 • paperback • 430 pp.
ISBN 0-7876-1034-8